BUNNY

BUNNY

The Real Story of Playboy

RUSSELL MILLER

Holt, Rinehart and Winston

New York

TO RENATE

Copyright © 1984 by Russell Miller
All rights reserved, including the right to reproduce this
book or portions thereof in any form.
First published in the United States in 1985 by
Holt, Rinehart and Winston, 383 Madison Avenue,
New York, New York 10017.
Published simultaneously in Canada by Holt, Rinehart and
Winston of Canada, Limited.

Library of Congress Cataloging in Publication Data
Miller, Russell.
Bunny, the real story of Playboy.
Originally published: London : M. Joseph, 1984.
Includes index.
1. Playboy (Chicago, Ill.) 2. Playboy Enterprises.
3. Hefner, Hugh M., 1926–   . I. Title.
PN4900.P5M5   1985   051   84-28967

ISBN: 0-03-063748-1

First American Edition

Designed by Lucy Albanese
Printed in the United States of America
3   5   7   9   10   8   6   4   2

ISBN 0-03-063748-1

Contents

Contents

Acknowledgments

The author and publishers would like to thank the following for permission to reproduce their photographs in this volume: John H. McGonigal (picture 3), Benny Dunn (7), Popperphoto (8 and 34), the BBC Hulton Picture Library (9, 10, 24, 26 and 27), Syndication International (12 and 13), *Playboy* (14 and 15), Brenard Press Ltd. (16), United Press International (17, 28, 29, 30, 31, 33 and 35), Camera Press (18, 20 and 21), Rex Features Ltd. (19), Keystone (25), and Robin Laurence (32).

Every effort has been made to attribute illustrations correctly. We apologize for any omissions or inadequacies; they are unintentional, and will be remedied in future editions.

The extract from *The Presidential Papers* by Norman Mailer, copyright © 1963 by Norman Mailer, is reproduced by permission of the author and his agents, Scott Meredith Literary Agency Inc., 845 Third Avenue, New York.

Preface

Hugh Hefner will not like this book because it largely re-flects how other people see him, rather than how he sees himself.

Hef views himself as a reformer and thinker, a man who, through the power of his unique magazine, liberated the world from the shackles of puritanism and reintroduced *fun* into our lives. He has no reason to doubt this view, since for most of his adult life he has been surrounded by sycophants and shielded from the outside world. If a sliver of incertitude was ever to cross his mind, he need only look for reassurance to the bound volumes of his magazine, which unblushingly sing his praises and tirelessly chron-icle his tedious parties.

He believes his influence and philosophy have made him many enemies and it is to these enemies he ascribes the considerable misfortunes of Playboy Enterprises, Inc. Behind every setback suffered by the company, its chairman can see a right-wing cabal dedicated to his destruction. "If you don't understand that," he told me once, quite seriously, "you don't understand the thing we have been struggling with, the greater social issues. . . ."

Outside Hef's circle, the perspective is somewhat different. It is of a man in late middle age who refuses to grow up, who lives in a house full of toys, who devotes much of his energy to playing kids' games, who falls in and out of love like a teenager, who enjoys pajama parties and is cross when his gravy is lumpy.

When I began researching this book in the United States, I received zero cooperation from Playboy. No one at Playboy would speak to me. No one returned my calls. No one replied to my letters. But eventually word got through to Hefner that I had been talking to Victor Lownes, his former friend, in London, and one evening, during a violent thunderstorm, he telephoned me at the house where I was staying in Rhode Island.

For more than an hour, he ranted about the terrible injustice that had been done to Playboy in London by the loss of its gaming licenses, hinting darkly at political conspiracies. Twice the call was cut off by bolts of lightning, twice he came back on the line to continue the tirade. At the end of this wild and rambling monologue, Hefner agreed to cooperate and promised to let me talk to any of his executives. All he wanted, he said, was for me to be "straight."

"How shall I set it up?" I asked him. "Through Rich Nelson?"

"Who's he?" said Hef.

"He's your director of public relations, Mr. Hefner."

I had been trying to talk to Rich Nelson every day for a month, but he was always in a meeting and always too busy to return my calls. Next morning I telephoned again and told his secretary that I had been speaking to Hefner and that Nelson had thirty minutes to ring me back. Five minutes later, he was on the line: "Hi, Russ, good to talk to you."

Hefner gave me hours of his time at Playboy Mansion West and was always friendly, charming, and courteous, if at times inclined to meander. This was his answer when I asked him why he had agreed to pay off corrupt public officials in New York in the early sixties:

"Well, you're in the area of, of, you know, the moral issues involved in extortion. As far as we were concerned, it was a shakedown. You get yourself into a curious kind of area when you are talking about kidnappings and shakedowns and paying off terrorists. 'Nother words, there are situations where it's more complicated. For me, the moral issue is not so clear. 'Nother words, er, no one should ever pay a kidnapper, and I realize now we're talking life compared to, er, or ever do business with a terrorist, or, 'nother words, if you always did that you know you would have much less of that to deal with. So in the abstract, that's the right position. But there is a difference between living your life day by day on a pragmatic level, even a moral level pragmatically, and making those individual decisions in terms of, er, you know, at the time and what may be, what you may believe in in a more abstract sense. Very obviously, I wish we had never done it."

People say that Hefner's daughter, Christie, inherited many of her father's characteristics. Verbosity is not one of them. At a reception at the Playboy Mansion in Chicago, I suggested to her that she was perhaps a little young to be running the company. She fixed me with her brown eyes and rapped out an answer with barely a pause for breath: "Being young is an advantage and let me explain why this is so. First of all, it needs to be understood I don't intend to do this by myself, I want to build a good management team. Being Christie Hefner and being twenty-nine years old, my stake is in the long-term future of the company and my vision is for the long-term health of the company. I think that is critically important for a company that wants to be on the cutting edge of ideas about society and the way society works. There are an awful lot of companies being run by middle-aged men and not run very well, so there is certainly not any magic number at which one becomes competent. I understand what I know and I understand what I don't know. I am willing and anxious to bring together a team of people—both insiders and outsiders—who will work with me bringing to bear experience and expertise that will complement my own."

Many of the people who helped me put together this fascinating story will be found in the narrative. They are a disparate bunch. Hefner's arch rival, Bob Guccione, received me in his astonishing rococo palace on the east side of New York and revealed his continuing plans to topple *Playboy*. Linda Lovelace sat in her pin-neat little house on Long Island, with her daughter on her lap, and recalled unhappy times at the Playboy Mansion. Jodie McRae, Hefner's black valet, fell off a barstool in Chicago laughing about his adventures with Playboy. Victor Lownes invited me for a weekend at Stocks, his English country house, and offered me

$10,000 if I could beat his Pacman score. In the Hustler Mansion, just the other side of Sunset Boulevard from the Playboy Mansion, renegade publisher Larry Flynt did not want to talk about Hefner—he wanted to talk about his bid to become the first pornographer president of the United States.

To all the people, in Chicago, Los Angeles, New York, Washington, New Jersey, London, and Paris, who gave so freely of their time to reminisce, go my heartfelt thanks. I am particularly indebted to Lord Allen and Michael Hogan, chairman and secretary respectively of the British Gaming Board; to James Flanagan and his colleagues at the Division of Gaming Enforcement at Trenton, New Jersey; to the ever helpful and courteous assistants at the Library of Congress in Washington; to my friend Philip Norman; to Peter Jackson, editor of *The Sunday Times Magazine*; to Michael Sissons of A. D. Peters & Co.; and to Jennie Davies of Michael Joseph Ltd.

Finally I want to thank my children for allowing me to devote time to the book that they might reasonably have expected to be theirs. And to my wife, Renate, goes my loving gratitude for, well, she knows.

Russell Miller
Buckinghamshire,
England
1984

Foreplay

Summer 1983. State Street, "that great street," is a dirty, desolate, and depressing street for most of its length. It runs straight and potholed from the Chicago city line, up through the black ghettos of the South Side, an aching wasteland of derelict factories pitted with broken windows, instant slum apartment blocks, vandalized playgrounds encased in chain-link fencing, and vacant lots where weeds sprout gamely from the rubble and from the rusting hulks of abandoned automobiles. Those shops that remain open are protected by barricades of steel mesh. One or two men occupy every doorway, staring sullenly onto the street, heedless of the taunting cluster of skyscrapers to the north.

After State Street passes under the El, the elevated iron railroad girdling the core of the city and known as the Loop, it becomes an unprepossessing precinct of fading department stores, cinemas, shoe chains, and fast food outlets. A forlorn attempt to revive the street's flagging fortunes failed: tourists are advised to avoid the area at night. Across the Chicago River, State Street briefly boasts the famous scalloped, cylindrical towers of Marina City, before immediately plunging once again into a dreary landscape of parkings lots, no-hope business ventures, and fleapit hotels with zigzag iron fire escapes clinging to their grimy brick façades.

Only three blocks to the east is Michigan Avenue, a chic, tree-lined shopping boulevard of such prestige that the natives of Chicago immodestly describe it as the "Magnificent Mile." But here on State Street, the commerce is largely confined to moneylenders, dealers in second-hand clothes, liquor stores, and diners of strictly limited culinary ambition, like "Mr. J's Dawg and Burger."

Just north of Frenchy's Bookstore, which offers an all-night 25-cent peep show as well as Doc Johnson's marital aids, State Street makes a slight bend to the west, the first kink in its length for sixteen miles, and undergoes a miraculous transformation. It becomes a *parkway*. There is a little triangular piazza with a splashing fountain and a sign requesting passersby not to feed the pigeons. The sidewalks are dappled by the shade of copper beech trees. There are apartment buildings with colored canopies and uniformed doormen who salute the regular joggers in their designer sweat suits. There are little boutiques with French and Italian names. The restaurants have menus outside in shining brass frames.

On the left-hand side of North State Street Parkway there still may be found fine examples of the townhouses built at the end of the nineteenth century for the cream of Chicago society and for the industrialists who reaped fortunes from the railroads hauling cattle, hogs, and sheep into Union stockyards for slaughter and packing.

One such house, between Schiller and Goethe Streets, is a regal brick and stone edifice with a mansard roof and a façade of lavish beaux arts detail. Behind its shuttered windows there is a wondrous pleasure palace where one man lived out his own fantasies and, by proxy, those of millions of other men around the world. Inside, the bars are stocked, the glasses polished. There is a Frank Sinatra record on the stereo turntable in the ballroom. The water in the heated swimming pool glistens silkily and through the lisping waterfall there may be glimpsed the soft romantic lights of the Woo Grotto. In the Games Room, a psychedelic array of pinball machines click and throb anxiously. Ten neat pins wait under the automatic pin-spotter for the roll of a ball in the bowling alley. Everything is ready for a party, except there are *no people*.

The Playboy Mansion is deserted, a great ghostly monument to outrageous hedonism.

Mr. Hugh Marston Hefner, chairman of Playboy Enterprises, Inc., for whose delight this indoor playground was created, became disenchanted with traveling some few years ago when a temporary financial difficulty obliged him to part with his private airliner—a black-painted DC-9 equipped with a dance floor, an elliptical bed, and a sunken Roman bath. He used it regularly to commute between his Mansion in Chicago and his Mansion in Los Angeles. Cruelly deprived of this facility and unable to face the rigors of scheduled air travel, he decided henceforth to stay in one place and plumped for Los Angeles. However, lest he should return, the Chicago Mansion is maintained in a state of constant readiness.

Thus it is that a closed-circuit television camera still scrutinizes anyone who rings the bell at 1340 North State Parkway, and credentials are checked by a maintenance man in blue overalls before the massive iron-grille door swings open on silent hinges to reveal an empty reception lobby with a bronze abstract entitled *Modern Woman.* An oak staircase rippled with red carpet leads up to a plain white door set in an oak-paneled wall. Screwed to the door there is a small brass plaque engraved in copperplate with the legend SI NON OSCILLAS, NOLI TINTINNARE. Latin scholars will immediately recognize the ancient adage: "If you don't swing, don't ring."

Behind this door is a wide passageway hung with paintings by Jackson Pollock, Franz Kline, and Willem de Kooning, luminaries of the abstract expressionist movement that enjoyed such a vogue when Mr. Hefner was in residence. On the left-hand side at the end of the passageway is a gallery flanked by four oak pillars overlooking the main room of the house, an enormous, echoing, baronial hall of a room with windowless oak-paneled walls and a lofty beamed ceiling inlaid with carved frescoes. Sixty feet long and thirty feet wide, the proportions are so ludicrous that at first sight the grand piano in the corner looks like a miniature. Who would believe that a room of such *majesty* could be found in a private house in Chicago?

Here, Hefner held his famous Friday night parties in the sixties. Today there is no music, no chatter, no laughter to be heard in the Mansion, in fact no sound at all except the faint hiss of the air conditioning. But the room where most of the guests congregated is still furnished just as it was then, when it was invariably described as "the ultimate bachelor pad." Suits of medieval armor stand mutely on each side of the broad steps leading down from the gallery and, never mind the oak paneling, the walls are adorned with more contemporary paintings: a large black and white Kline on the left-hand wall, Larry Rivers on the right, and Picasso's *Nude Reclining* over the marble fireplace in the distance at the opposite end of the room.

A door to the left of the fireplace leads directly into the kitchen, which is fitted out in gleaming stainless steel, exactly like the kitchen of a large hotel. Once there was a cordon bleu chef on duty here around the clock, ready to prepare the fried chicken that Mr. Hefner might order at any time. Now, the working surfaces are clear and wiped clean, the pots and pans hang undisturbed in racks above the cold ovens.

Mr. Hefner's private quarters, located in the heart of the Mansion, are virtually sealed off from the rest of the house. A pair of floor-to-ceiling French doors gives access to this sanctum, which is muffled throughout by astonishingly thick white carpet. On the left is a comfortable white-painted study hung with original cartoons and Playboy memorabilia. To the right is a small sitting room, across which, carefully nurtured legend has it, countless Bunnies have beaten a path, since it leads to the master bedroom and, gulp, the *bed*.

Still standing in the center of the room and pristinely unoccupied is the fabled round bed upon which Mr. Hefner spent so much of his time. A television camera, mounted on a tripod sunk into the carpet, is pointed ostentatiously at its center. Eight and a half feet in diameter, the bed has an internal motor that will allow it to rotate, rather crankily these days, 360 degrees in either direction or vibrate while it is at a standstill. Despite heroic efforts, Mr. Hefner was never really able to satisfactorily explain why anyone should want a *rotating* bed. He used to burble about it "creating four different environments" by facing him in different directions at the press of a button, but it was hard to understand why he could not simply turn his head and achieve the same basic effect. Such was worldwide media interest in the bed, that a journalist once asked seriously where one bought sheets for an eight-and-a-half-foot-diameter round bed. "I haven't the vaguest idea," Hefner replied.

On the other side of the bedroom, which has the same gloomy oak-paneled walls and beamed ceiling as the "baronial hall," is a door to Mr. Hefner's exotic bathroom. As intemperance is the all-too-obvious hallmark of the Playboy Mansion, it comes as no surprise to find in Mr. Hefner's bathroom a marble Roman bath, a jacuzzi able to accommodate a dozen people in neighborly comfort, psychedelic lighting, and a velvet-covered water bed with mirrors fixed to the ceiling above and the walls behind. Mr. Hefner was able to stay in touch with his pleasure palace and the world even while attending to bodily functions: a television and telephone console are set into the wall of the bathroom.

A brass and oak spiral staircase connects Mr. Hefner's private quarters with an executive office suite on the floor above. Here there is a conference room with a huge circular table and microphones concealed in the chandelier. Neat piles of paper are stacked alongside the electric typewriters on the desks once used by the secretaries. Everything is ready for work to begin, except, surprisingly, the telephone directories, which are years out of date. The front page headline on a copy of the *Chicago Sun-Times* left on one of the desks shrieks NIXON—I WON'T RESIGN.

The remainder of the Mansion is largely occupied by guest suites, all identified by the color of the decor. As a rule of thumb, the guest suites tend to become less luxurious in proportion to their distance from Hefner's quarters, but none of them approaches the spartan conditions of the Bunny dormitories on the third and fourth floors. In stark contrast to the push-button extravagance below, the furnishings of the dormitories abruptly take on the aspect of a rather parsimonious girls' boarding school—thin cord carpet, bunk beds, wooden lockers, and communal washrooms. The rent per girl was $50 a month. The pigeonholes for the Bunnies' mail are all forlornly empty; on the wall nearby are telltale holes where their pay phone, long since removed, was mounted.

Up here, no doubt, atop this candy castle, the Bunnies sat on their bunk beds studying their Bunny Manuals: "Always remember your proudest possession is your Bunny tail. You must make sure it is white and fluffy."

Although Hefner did not step inside the place for years, he steadfastly refused to consider suggestions that it should be sold. But today Playboy can no longer afford such profligacy, and the fabled Chicago Mansion is at last for sale, a symptom of Playboy's hard times. The prince of pleasure is unlikely to suffer too much from its loss, however, since he claims to have found paradise in the security of his Los Angeles fun palace.

It is hot and sultry, this afternoon in Los Angeles. Deep in the basin, the beleaguered city's traditional smog hangs heavy in a poisonous gray-brown mantle hugging the downtown skyscrapers and the sweating ghettos and the interlaced freeways streaming with automobiles. But up in Holmby Hills, a pocket of privilege ten miles between Bel Air and Beverly Hills, the air is clear and sweet and fit for the resident millionaires to breathe. Just a block to the south of where Sunset Boulevard snakes through Holmby Hills stands Playboy Mansion West, a gray stone house with mullioned windows and crenellated walls, built in the style of a Victorian Gothic English vicarage and surrounded by five acres of exotic, semitropical gardens.

In this little bit of heaven, black rabbits with shining pelts scamper through the flowering shrubs, peacocks and flamingos pick superciliously across lawns trimmed to resemble green velvet, tinkling girlish laughter may be discerned from somewhere behind the house, squirrel monkeys chatter madly in a hidden copse, and brightly colored birds flit through the stand of towering redwood trees that screens the Mansion from the outside world and the cruising limousines on Sunset Boulevard. It would surely be a veritable Garden of Eden were it not, perhaps, for the piped music wafting unexpectedly from fake rocks wired with stereo speakers and spread around the property, and the satellite receiving dish rising out of the lemon grove. This great saucer, tilted toward the heavens, enables a spectrum of television programs to be beamed down to the Mansion from the blackness of space.

Mr. Hefner hardly ever steps foot outside the grounds, and he would never be discovered strolling through the gardens at this time, for it is only three o'clock in the afternoon and he rarely rises before four. Upstairs in the Mansion, thick drapes are pulled across the windows of the master bedroom to shut out the sun.

Under the black silk coverlet on the huge four-poster bed, Mr. Hefner slumbers in the company of Miss November 1981, a busty blonde from Saskatoon who is currently the object of his ardor. In the headboard of the bed, which naturally sinks out of sight at the press of a button, Mr. Hefner keeps a collection of kinky little trinkets like dildoes, vibrators, chains, and studded leather harnesses, as well as the economy-size bottles of Johnson's Baby Oil with which he likes to massage his partner. On top of the headboard are four white Magic Wand vibrators by General Electric, all plugged in and ready to go. Three low-light video cameras are attached to the bed's carved oak frame and linked to twin six-foot television projection screens and four twenty-five-inch monitors. All six screens can show different pictures simultaneously. As a romantic finishing touch, the bed has its own psychedelic lighting, capable of drenching the occupants in an ever-changing pattern of swirling colors.

None of these facilities is presently in use, of course, for the prince and his current princess are sleeping. But elsewhere on the property there is much activity, since a full-time staff of more than ninety people is required to run the Mansion in a manner pleasing to the Chairman of Playboy Enterprises, Inc.

In the kitchens, a butler prepares the tray that will be whisked up to Mr. Hefner the moment he demands breakfast. Everything must be laid out *just so*, even to the placing of the personalized matchbooks, which must be propped in an ashtray in such a fashion that the side bearing the name Hugh M. Hefner faces upward. If the other side, featuring the Playboy Bunny logo, faces upward, Mr. Hefner will *notice* and undoubtedly raise the matter with Mary O'Connor, the Executive Assistant to the Office of Chairman, who will point out the mistake to the house supervisor, who will rebuke the shift leader for that day, who will bawl out the butler concerned.

"Hef's the easiest man in the world to please," says Mary O'Connor, "providing everything is done just the way he wants it. I'll give you an example. He likes his gravy prepared in a particular way. It's not a difficult way, but it's a certain way. And he wants it like that *all the time*. Now, you'll get a new cook in and he'll decide he knows a better way of doing it and he thinks Hef'll love it. Wrong. He won't. Hef'll want to know why I've put a man on shift without properly training him how to make the gravy."

Cooking for Mr. Hefner is not the most rewarding of culinary experiences as he eats virtually nothing but fried chicken, pot roast, and sandwiches. A book is kept in the kitchen containing the standard procedure for preparing everything he eats, starting with how to build a ham sandwich—one slice of ham, one leaf of lettuce, two slices of *fresh* Wonder Bread straight from the package. But it is the gravy that causes most problems. Mary O'Connor usually sticks her finger in it before it goes up to Hefner to ensure it is not too thick or greasy. If she is worried about it, she'll invite a second opinion from another chef or an experienced butler. "Sometimes I'll get a whole crew into the kitchen," she says, "and ask them what they think. If I am not sure a dish is right, I'll eat it first and then get the cook to do it again."

Mary is a tall, briskly efficient, gray-haired woman in her middle years who describes herself as a "kinda fast-lane person" as a result of her interest in motor racing. She has worked for Hefner since 1969, and thus sees nothing odd about convening solemn conferences in the kitchen to discuss the texture and flavor of Mr. Hefner's gravy. She started as manager of the Chicago Mansion in the days when it was the tradition of the house that guests could order anything they wanted—*anything*—and get it. "It caused a lot of headaches," she recalls. "You'd get guests who wanted a certain type of chocolate chip cookies, or lemon pie without sugar in it, or certain flavors of yogurt. They could be very demanding. Here, it's much easier because we don't do that any longer. If we don't have what a guest wants, we don't have it."

Shortly before four o'clock, Hefner's special buzzer (different in tone from those used by guests or visitors) sounds in the kitchen and there is some initial jostling among the duty butlers to avoid answering it. Hefner is held in great awe by junior staff, none of whom is allowed to speak to him unless Hefner first speaks to them. "Yessir," says the butler obliged to pick up the phone. "Standard breakfast," says the voice at the other end of the line. "Rightaway sir," says the butler, and already the chef is cracking eggs into a frying pan.

Now that Hefner's appearance is imminent, the butlers in their black trousers and white shirts and black waistcoats fan out through the house, checking each room, replenishing huge bowls of sweets and peeled nuts, stacking packs of Hefner's tobacco—Mixture No. 79—in predestined places, sharpening the pencils that must be set alongside the piles of white memo pads with "Playboy Mansion West" printed in gold on each page, reverentially straightening copies of *Playboy* magazine, filling the refrigerators in every room with the Pepsi-Cola that Hefner drinks straight from the bottle during every waking hour.

There are four principal rooms on the ground floor of the Los Angeles Mansion, not counting the entrance hall with its lofty beamed ceiling, white marble floor and ornate bronze chandelier, sweeping staircase, and first-floor galleries of intricately carved oak. (A visitor once asked one of Hefner's resident girlfriends if the chandelier was copper or brass. "Whichever is better," she replied after only a moment's hesitation.)

To the left of the entrance hall, or the Great Hall as it is inevitably known, is a large and comfortable living room furnished with walnut and mahogany bound in brass, soft leather chesterfield sofas, and a dark brown carpet. By one leaded window stands the custom-made Monopoly table, with special slots for the money, which is printed with a Lincoln-style picture of Hefner on one side and engravings of the two Playboy mansions on the other. The dice are stamped with the HMH monogram and instead of conventional pieces, Hefner and his friends play with three-inch high silver figurine replicas of themselves. Hefner plays Monopoly every Tuesday, Thursday, and Saturday evening, usually with the same four men. They like to have girls around during the game to watch or shake the dice or move the pieces; girls are rarely allowed to play. A running score of how many games each player has won is maintained through the year and at the end of the year the top scorer is presented with a little trophy engraved with his name.

The library, leading off the living room, boasts very few books with the exception of the Encyclopaedia Britannica and bound volumes of *Playboy* magazine. Framed pictures of Hefner on the front cover of different magazines dominate one wall and over the door is a framed needlepoint worked by Miss Barbi Benton, one of Mr. Hefner's long-departed lovers. It reads: "Be it ever so humble, there is no place like home."

On the other side of the Great Hall is the Mediterranean Room which has a green tiled floor, a sculptured fountain, and lustrous indoor plants, and a Regency dining room, featuring a woven rug of blue heraldic design, blue velvet drapes, pictures by Dali, de Kooning, and Pollock and a long, polished table set with twelve chairs upholstered in blue velvet.

Upstairs, Hefner's private quarters occupy most of the space, although one complete room is allocated to the 350 bound volumes of his scrapbook. A trained archivist, Amy Miller, is employed to keep it up to date. Such is the abundance of material that she is still struggling to get past 1977. Hefner has a Johnsonian concern for his place in history and has carefully preserved everything he has written or drawn, along with everything that has been written about him, no matter how derogatory. His election by *Hustler* magazine as "Asshole of the Month" is pasted into its chronological slot and features a caricature of Mr. Hefner emerging from an unidentified anus.

The scrapbook begins in March 1943, when he was a senior in high school drawing a cartoon strip for the school magazine. It now occupies floor-to-ceiling filing cabinets fitted around three walls of the room where Amy Miller works. All the cuttings and pictures are pasted onto special paper guaranteed not to deteriorate for at least three hundred years and the room is protected by three fire alarms and an automatic sprinkler system. Mary O'Connor is convinced these archives will eventually end up in the Smithsonian.

While Mr. Hefner is enjoying his breakfast, Miss Miller is preparing to pack up for the day, being one of the few members of the Mansion staff to work conventional hours. Just down the corridor from her office, the Video Department is manned seven days a week from eleven o'clock in the morning right through the night until four o'clock in the morning next day. Four technicians are employed here to tape television programs for Mr. Hefner and edit out the commercials. Every week, Mr. Hefner marks the *TV Guide* with the programs he wants recorded, usually movies, favorite series like "Macmillan and Wife," or regular shows like "Saturday Night Live." This becomes the bible for the video department, which delivers the tapes to Hefner daily. He stacks them in piles all over the floor of his bedroom.

Mr. Hefner now possesses a private collection of video tapes so extensive that he can never hope to see them all, even if he was to spend the rest of his life watching television. No one questions the need or the point of the video department's toils, since no one questions Mr. Hefner about anything.

At five o'clock, Mr. Hefner emerges from the master bedroom in blue silk pajamas, a velvet bathrobe, and maroon velvet slippers with the HMH monogram worked in gold on each toe. He is shorter than he appears in photographs, slight of frame, and etiolate in complexion, with gray-tinged hair combed rather too carefully across the top of his head. Shadowed by a gum-chewing bodyguard, he strolls downstairs for the first round of business meetings in the library. This is a time convenient to virtually no one but Mr. Hefner; indeed, the Chairman of Playboy Enterprises, Inc., is normally preparing for bed about the time staff at his headquarters in Chicago are arriving for work.

This afternoon's meeting is the monthly editorial get-together at which *Playboy* editors keep their publisher in touch with the progress of the magazine and plans for forthcoming issues. Although Hefner no longer edits the magazine line by line as he did in the early days, he invariably selects the cartoons, the cover picture, and the Playmate. This last duty is conducted with all the sensitive finesse of a vet examining a cow. The size, shape, and color of a girl's nipples can be the subject of considerable laconic discussion and every part of her displayed anatomy is scrutinized and commented upon in a fashion more appropriate to discussing a slab of meat than a human being. If Hefner rejects a particular picture, his decision is considered to be the last word on the subject; few editors would dare ask *why* he did not like it. Dwight Hooker, a former *Playboy* staff photographer, claims the record for rejections: Hefner once turned down five hundred of Hooker's pictures of a particular Playmate before he was satisfied.

Around six o'clock, Mary O'Connor hands over her duties to the night secretary, Joni Mattis. One of the original Bunnies in the first Playboy Club in Chicago and the Playmate in November 1960, Miss Mattis wields formidable power because she handles the List—the document that decrees each day who shall be admitted into Mr. Hefner's private Shangri-la.

It is not easy to get into Playboy Mansion West. The grounds are surrounded by a high perimeter fence wired with sensors able to detect suspicious sounds or movements along its entire length. Closed-circuit television monitors every car approaching the Mansion's substantial iron gates, which are always kept closed. If a car stops at the gates, a disembodied voice emanating from a boulder on the left-hand side of the drive will demand the names of the occupants. If the names appear on a copy of the List held in the security control room, a guard will press the button that opens the gates. If the names are absent, the gates remain closed. It is said, not entirely facetiously, that the Queen of England, Frank Sinatra, and the President of the United States might perhaps stand a chance of gaining access to Playboy Mansion West without their names appearing on the List, but no one else.

The List assumes its greatest importance on Fridays and Sundays, which are party nights at the Mansion, and Miss Mattis must ensure that there are sufficient pretty girls on the List to far outweigh the number of men, as this is an axiomatic feature of all Playboy parties. The preferred ratio is twice as many girls as men. Some of Hefner's cronies assist Miss Mattis by cruising the UCLA campus, which is conveniently close by, looking for suitable girls to invite. None of them objects to this little chore, as there are few surer ways of incurring Mr. Hefner's pleasure than to arrange for a bevy of young big-breasted blondes to be brought to a Mansion party.

Hefner inspires fierce loyalty among the people close to him and Miss Mattis takes her duties *very* seriously. She always carefully inquires what girls look like before adding their names to the List, but sometimes she gets badly let down and a girl not quite up to standard slips through the net. Miss Mattis is furious if this happens, since it reflects on her efficiency. If the unthinkable occurs and an ugly girl, a real *dog*, somehow gets through the gate, Miss Mattis tries to get her off the property before Hefner catches sight of her. If this unfortunate creature has been brought by another girl, Miss Mattis will punish that girl by striking her name from the List or putting her "on pass," Mansionspeak for probation. If a man is responsible, Miss Mattis has to watch her step as the men on the List are all friends of Hefner's; a quiet word of reproach might have to suffice.

Girls are forbidden to bring boyfriends into the Mansion, except with a special dispensation, rarely given, from Hefner himself. Should a girl arrive with a man at the gates, he will be turned away. If she refuses to go in without him, they will both be turned away. "Hefner doesn't want any good-looking young guys around the place," a butler explains churlishly. The butlers, some of whom are both young and good-looking, are not allowed to fraternize with girls invited to Mansion parties, on pain of dismissal.

Long before Hefner has finished his meeting, guests are arriving for tonight's party, it being a Friday. In the security control room, a guard with a .45 revolver casually stuck in his belt sits in front of a bank of television monitors, picking his teeth with a broken matchstick and ticking names on the List as concealed cameras follow the progress of limousines climbing the Mansion's steep drive.

Fifteen hefty security men are on the payroll, including Mr. Hefner's personal bodyguards. All of them are armed and most were formerly employed by the Los Angeles police department. On duty, they maintain contact with each other by two-way radios. There is rarely any trouble at the Mansion, which is perhaps just as well since the guards receive regular training in unarmed combat, assault techniques, the use of gas grenades, and, somewhat unnecessarily, self-defense.

Early guests tend to congregate around the open-air bar on a stone-flagged terrace at the back of the house, between the swimming pool and the bath house. The pool is artfully contrived to look as if it is carved from natural rock and appears to connect, under a stone bridge, with a pond full of silvery carp. Swimsuits are provided for anyone who wants them, although girls are earnestly encouraged not to be too modest and nudity, *Playboy* magazine reported, "is one aspect of the pleasantly persuasive sensuality that pervades this special place." Swimmers venturing through the waterfall splashing down from a rocky outcrop find themselves in a large, softly lit grotto hung with ferns and tropical flowers. This scented lagoon, fitted with numerous jacuzzis, is usually the scene of considerable action later in the evening.

Weekly parties at the Mansion follow an invariable routine.

On Friday nights the buffet is at eight o'clock and a movie is shown at nine. On Sundays the buffet is at six and the movie is at eight. Hefner never eats with his guests at the buffet. This evening, as usual, he makes an appearance a few minutes before the movie is due to begin and threads through the crowd with Miss November 1981 on his arm, smiling broadly and announcing left and right: "It's movie time! It's movie time!"

While the buffet is being served, the butlers prepare the living room for the screening. The layout is always the same. A couch for Mr. Hefner and his lady occupies the central position in the front row of seats. At his fingertips is a control box with which he can adjust focus and sound and rewind the film to see certain scenes again. On the table by his side, in a fixed and predetermined layout, are an ashtray, matches, pipe, six pencils and six pads, a dish of freshly cooked and hand-popped popcorn coated in butter with a little extra butter on the side, a bottle of Pepsi, two clean napkins, and a little salt cellar. Popcorn is also served to any other guests who want it, but it's not hand-popped like Hefner's. When everyone is seated, Hefner waves his hand and the movie begins.

After the movie, the host determinedly leads the way to the Games House, a stone and slate building in a clump of trees across the lawn in front of the Mansion. Here, Hef and his friends fall upon the pinball machines and the Space Invaders and the football game and the pool table and endless other amusements with little whoops of delight. In the Mansion's staff quarters an electronics engineer stands by ready to rush across should, heaven forbid, any machine malfunction.

Hefner spends many happy hours of every day in the Games House and has become so adept at some of the electronic machines that he has had them rewired to make them more difficult. A special kid glove is kept on the Pacman machine, his favorite, so that he does not get calluses on his hand from wrestling with its single joystick control. The names of the highest scorers in each game are recorded in white plastic letters and figures on a black plaque fixed to the wall alongside each machine. Hef appears regularly in the top slot and his 1,689,020 on the Playboy pinball machine is reckoned to be unbeatable. If he is playing alone in the Games House and notches up a particularly high score, he will, in the interests of fair play, summon a security guard to witness it before ordering it to be recorded on the wall.

For those guests not drawn to the noisy rough and tumble of the Games House, the romantic setting of the Woo Grotto exercises a powerful attraction. The warm, scented waters, the changing colors of the underwater lights, the soft piped music, the caress of the jacuzzi, what more could lovers want except, perhaps, a little privacy? But in the wonderful world of Playboy, this last commodity is considered unnecessary, almost prudish. As Larry Dietz, a former articles editor at *Playboy*, says: "An invitation to the grotto is a euphemism for let's go fuck."

Hefner likes to describe the Mansion as his magic kingdom and in a sense this is appropriate since reality is certainly suspended once its iron gates have closed behind you. Months pass without Hefner ever stepping foot outside the grounds. He claims there is no necessity for him to leave, since he is able to import everything he needs. He never goes out to visit friends, expecting them to come to him. He has no interest in travel or taking vacations. "There is no place in the world I would rather take a vacation than right here," he says. "People accuse me of being out of touch. That's ridiculous. I have a very clear picture of what's going on out there, I can assure you. What I have tried to do, 's'matter of fact, is take a lot of time-wasting out of my life, so I can spend *more* time staying in touch. I don't need to go out to do that. Most of one's real understanding of what is going on comes from the media, not waiting for a bus or going shopping."

Pampered and cocooned in his citadel of sensualism, his every wish granted, the prince of pleasure will be perfectly content to stay in his "magic kingdom" for the rest of his life.

Let not the real world intrude on his bliss. The real world is on the other side of the fence and Hugh M. Hefner wants no part of it.

1

How about Playboy?

Chicago, 1952, late one summer night. On the Near North Side, lights are flicking out in the expensive apartments overlooking the silently heaving black silk of Lake Michigan. A young man is dawdling along Lake Shore Drive in the shadows, stopping every now and again to stare up at a lighted window, craning his neck to see inside. He often walks here alone at night, dreaming of some day when he will be a part of this privileged world, when it will be *his* shadow moving about up there, *his* sports car parked in the darkened garage. He imagines himself in a luxurious bachelor penthouse, with the hi-fi and lights low, mixing a couple of cocktails, loosening his black tie, and casually turning to face the beautiful, smiling girl he will surely seduce before dawn.

That this is fantasy may be deduced from his appearance alone. He wears a zoot suit with wide shoulders and lapels, but it is cheap, crumpled, and poorly tailored, drooping unhappily on his skinny frame. A crew cut bristles above his gaunt features and jug-handle ears. On his feet, he has a pair of scuffed loafers and white socks, which he considers to be the height of fashion. Hugh Hefner is twenty-six years old, broke, frustrated and miserable.

16

Walking the streets at night allows him to escape, if only for a while, the humdrum, bourgeois existence in which he feels increasingly trapped. He has failed several times to earn a living as a cartoonist, which is what he really wants to do, so he is working as a sales promotion manager for a seedy magazine publisher. He is married and already beginning to resent it; his wife is pregnant. Sometimes he wonders what went wrong; school was so quickly followed by college, army, work, marriage, and now, a family. Whatever happened to *living*?

Prominent among the good things he felt he was missing was sex. Hefner thought a lot about sex, read a lot about it, and pored over the pictures in magazines like *Wink, Flirt, Cutie, Giggles*, and *Eyeful*, which he was able to obtain under the counter from a bookshop he knew in Dearborn Street.

Such purchases needed to be made discreetly in the early fifties since the fear and suspicion generated by Senator Joe McCarthy's witch hunt for Communists, queers, and "egg-sucking phony liberals" tended to bracket any kind of loose living with subversion and conspiracy. It was not an atmosphere that encouraged magazine publishers to take risks, and nudes were largely confined to naturist publications—some genuine, some spurious—with titles like *Sunshine and Health* and *Modern Sunbathing*, or photography magazines, which were able to publish nude studies as "art photography." In one genre, the model posed in some sylvan glade, on tiptoe, frequently carrying a beach ball; in the other, she was usually draped with a curtain in a manner fondly believed to be reminiscent of Greek classical sculpture. Neither form was particularly exciting, but Hefner bought them all.

Conventional men's magazines rarely strayed into the dangerous area of sex. Mostly they subsisted on a diet of hairy-chested prose ("One-Man Marine Army Who Conquered Bloody Batu") and hollow-chested advertising ("Amazing Invention Quickly Helps to Give You a *Strong Manly Voice*"). Women rarely made an appearance in the editorial columns, except perhaps to be rescued from a giant octopus or grizzly bear. Hefner was bored by these endless tales of the great outdoors. His idea of a good men's magazine, he liked to say to anyone who would listen, would be one that directed its attention toward the great *indoors*.

Glenn Hefner was born in a sod hut with a dirt floor in Holdredge, Nebraska. Raised in a devout Methodist family, he followed the dictum of Horatio Alger, studied hard, worked his way through college and graduated from Nebraska Wesleyan University in 1918. Three years later, he married his high-school sweetheart, Grace Swanson, the daughter of a farmer, and they moved to Chicago, where Glenn found a job as an accountant with the Advance Aluminium Casting Corporation. Their first son, Hugh, was born on April 9, 1926; a second son, Keith, arrived in January 1929.

When Hugh was four years old, the Hefners moved to a detached two-story brick house on New England Avenue, in a middle-class suburb on the west side of Chicago, where the urban sprawl of the city was slowly encroaching on the prairie. Glenn Hefner worked hard and was a good provider but saw little of his sons, since he left for work early every morning and did not return until late, six days a week. He never complained about the long hours and counted himself fortunate to keep a job right through the years of the Great Depression, when many of his friends found themselves on welfare.

The boys' upbringing largely devolved on Grace, a small, slim woman with curly brown hair and a firm belief in Puritan principles. There was no drinking or smoking in the Hefner household, bad language of any kind was not tolerated, and although there was no Methodist chapel nearby, Sundays were devoted to observance of the Lord's day: Hugh and Keith were not allowed out to play, the Bakelite radio was firmly switched off, and if they became restless indoors they were sent "out back" to draw at a workbench or model with clay. Neither of the boys found these restrictions particularly unusual or irksome; every other day they were out with the neighborhood guys, roaming the prairieland where meadowlarks still soared and snakes slithered through the coarse grass.

At Sayre Grammar School, a yellow brick building on its own grassy block just down the alley from his home, Hugh proved himself to be a quick learner, but somewhat shy and withdrawn. He spent a great deal of time daydreaming and drove his teachers to distraction with his habit of doodling in class. "He has me at my wits end," his fourth-grade teacher, Della Dawson, wrote to his mother. "For the past week I've had to speak to him two or three times, every time he has a study period. He doesn't do his arithmetic, geography, or spelling unless I stand right at his elbow. He *constantly* draws. I've tried persuasion, scoldings, and appeal to his love for his mother—all to no avail."

Mrs. Hefner was not pleased by the letter and lectured Hugh on the need to pay attention at school. He was contrite and composed an explanatory rhyme entitled "Why I Waist Time," which he presented to his mother:

> *I think I get to dreaming,*
> *Of something I might do,*
> *And I forget my studies,*
> *And what I'm supposed to do.*

In the sixth grade, Hugh launched a classroom newspaper, which he called "The Pepper," as he was the only boy in the class who could type—he taught himself on an old Royal when he was nine—his name appeared on the masthead as "H. Hefner, Editor and Tiper." For two years he painstakingly pasted every issue into a scrapbook and chronicled the paper's history. A laboriously typed account described an early crisis: "Ray Troike started another paper. Kenneth Kitzing said that his brother could get their paper run off on a mimeograph which would make theirs better than ours. Then Ray said that for every news story brought in he would pay two cents. This started all our men moving over to their paper. Soon there was no one left but Warren, Gordon, Jack, James, and I. Then James quit leaving four of us. Then we signed a pledge not to quit till we were absolutely finished. Then at recess two days later Warren came running in shouting 'Ray's paper fell through.' Yes, his paper couldn't keep up so they stopped before they had even put out a paper and so they joined up with us."

The issue of May 27, 1938, ran into censorship problems. "In the second column at the bottom," Hugh noted, "there was a story that the teachers didn't want published, so we blocked it out with sticky paper." The next edition—a four-page Vacation Issue published on June 10, 1938—marked a technological breakthrough. "One day James Brophy said as we were making the paper, 'I'll bet if I make a mark on this stencil with my fingernail it will show up like a line on the paper.' And sure enough it did. So we got a special pencil and made headlines and pictures."

Outside of school, young Hugh became increasingly involved in a world of his own making. The aimless doodling had developed into a passion for drawing cartoons and constructing elaborate stories with wild, fantastic characters. Between the ages of twelve and fourteen he drew more than seventy different cartoon strips, colored each frame and bound them into neat volumes. One of the first characters he created was Cranet, a red-haired, pug-nosed adventurer who flew from Earth to Mars, freed the enslaved Martians from their cruel ruler, was himself crowned emperor of the planet, and cropped up in later volumes on other escapades around the solar system. In addition to cartoons, Hugh also wrote some forty-five short stories and "novelettes," mostly science fiction, horror stories, or tales of the supernatural. Many were included in his "Shudder Magazine," which was passed around to members of the "Shudder Club," recruited at five cents annual membership. His output was prodigious; he would spend hours sitting on the workbench in the backyard, filling loose-leaf sheets of lined paper with frenetic scribblings and illustrations of the weird creatures inhabiting his imagination.

From comics and magazines he progressed to movies, and with the help of his best friend, Jim Brophy, he produced and starred in a film called *Return from the Dead*. He wheedled the loan of a 16mm camera from his next door neighbor by offering to keep his front path clear of snow all through the coming winter. Hef—only his parents called him Hugh—was a scientist who had created a Frankenstein-type monster, played by the obliging Brophy. A girl from down the street was the scientist's wife. In the dramatic final scene, the scientist staggers from his house into the street, collapses, and dies with blood pouring from his mouth. A melted Hershey bar made a realistic substitute for blood on black-and-white film.

When he was sixteen, he began a major work, a "Comic Autobiography," which was to run to seven weighty volumes simply to cover the period from his birth to graduation from high school. Written in the form of a satirical illustrated diary, it largely recorded the adventures of two friends—Goo Heffer (Hef) and Jim Mopey (Broph). The first volume, "School Daze," was dated

March 15, 1943, when Goo and Mope were students at Steinmetz High School, always referred to in the diary as "Stinkmuch."

Steinmetz School, an imposing brick and stone building overlooking its own football field and running track, was ten minutes' walk from Hefner's home. As a student he was well liked, but better known for his extracurricular activities than for his academic ability. He was president of the Student Council, was active in the drama and literary societies, contributed cartoons to the *Steinmetz Star*, and was elected official cartoonist for the school yearbook. He graduated in January 1944, forty-fifth in a class of 212, was voted Class Humorist, One of the Best Orators, One of the Most Artistic, One of the Most Likely to Succeed, One of the Most Popular, and One of the Best Dancers.

Volume seven of the "Comic Autobiography," "Goo Heffer Graduates," included an illuminating self-portrait of the author: "Goo's a lanky, Sinatra-like guy with a love for loud flannel shirts and cords in the way of garb and jive for music. He looks and acts a lot like a high school kid you'd see in a movie. A very original fellow, he has his own style of jiving and slang expressions. His interests go to cartooning, acting, writing songs, horror stories and comic strips with Mope, crooning and collecting jive records. Likes Dot Noback, but is fickle when it comes to women and knows it."

Later he noted: "Mope's tastes in women are surprisingly like my own. I've fallen for two of his old girlfriends and he dates two of my old flames."

Seventeen-year-old Hefner was not as worldly-wise about women as he portrayed himself. He was shy with the opposite sex, developed a stutter when talking to a girl, and suffered agonies of embarrassment when attempting to put his arm around her. Sex was never openly discussed in the Hefner home, although Grace made an honest attempt to explain the facts of life to her sons with the help of a book on child development loaned to her by a "trained friend." When a neighborhood kid also got a peek at the book, poor Grace earned a rebuke from the boy's mother. "You should keep that book away from my son," she said angrily. "God should have arranged things better. I wish children could be born without sex."

When Hefner graduated in 1944, the world was still at war. In the comfortable environs of a Chicago suburb, war meant growing victory gardens, giving blood to the Red Cross, collecting scrap metal for the government, and salvaging waste paper. The real war, where young men met horrible deaths on unknown coral islands in the Pacific, was a long way away.

Rather than wait for the inevitable draft, Hefner volunteered for the U.S. Army, more in a spirit of getting it over with than out of any patriotic fervor. Two weeks before he was due to report, he met Mildred Williams at a party. Millie was the daughter of a Chicago streetcar motorman and also a student at Steinmetz High, a fact that Hefner found difficult to believe—he could not understand how he had failed to notice her. He thought that Millie was *the* most wonderful girl he had ever met in his life and before he left for basic training at Camp Hood, Texas, he extracted a promise from her that she would write to him.

Like thousands of other young men, Hefner was bored with and resentful of his time in the army. Worse, his sheltered Methodist upbringing ill-prepared him for life in the barracks, and he found the language and behavior of the military profoundly shocking. For a boy who had only just turned eighteen, who had never touched a drink in his life, never smoked, never swore, and was a virgin, the infantry came as an exceedingly nasty surprise. He was appalled by the casual way G.I.s talked about getting the "clap" and their desire to relate the lurid details of their sexual encounters. "I've just had my first taste of wine," he wrote home to his parents, "but don't worry, it was just Episcopal Holy Communion."

After basic training, Hefner was given a job as a clerk because he could type. Three times he was told he would be going overseas, but his papers never came through. He whiled away the days drawing cartoons for camp newspapers, filling the gaps in his "Comic Autobiography," and writing long and affectionate letters to Millie. Hitler was defeated in Europe, the A-bomb was dropped on Japan, and World War II ended before Private Hefner was able to lay down his typewriter. He was discharged in March 1946 and returned thankfully to civilian life, to Chicago, and to Millie.

He kicked his heels for a few months and then enrolled through the G.I. Bill at the University of Illinois. It was no coincidence that Millie was already a student there. He had vague ideas of making a career in journalism, but chose to major in psychology and double up on courses in creative writing, art, and sociology, hoping to complete the four-year curriculum in about half the usual time.

Hefner was happy at the university. Although he lived in a fraternity house, he was able to spend a lot of time with Millie. They would walk through the campus hand-in-hand after classes, listen to records together, play noisy games of bridge with other couples, and go to dances most weekends. Hefner sang with a little rhythm combo that played at campus dances; he tried to imitate the style of Frankie Laine. Sometimes he was able to borrow a car to take Millie to a drive-in movie; on the backseat they would pet furiously and behind misted windows Millie would plead with Hef to be patient and to wait.

Almost inevitably, Hefner became managing editor of a campus magazine, *The Shaft*, and contributed frequent articles and cartoons to the university newspaper, *The Daily Illini*. He followed the college football team as an ardent supporter and after Illinois won the 1947 Rose Bowl, beating UCLA 41–14, he recorded the event in his "Comic Autobiography," adding exuberantly: "Who cares if Communism is moving across Europe and Palestine is caught in the throes of civil war?"

In 1948, the first Kinsey Report was published. Hefner read every word and wrote an enthusiastic review for *The Shaft*, attacking the hypocrisy of public attitudes toward sex. Kinsey's findings, indicating that 86 percent of American men experienced sexual intercourse before marriage, 70 percent had intercourse with prostitutes, and 40 percent indulged in extramarital intercourse, revealed an extraordinary discrepancy between private behavior and public attitudes that Hefner thought was truly shocking.

It was the Kinsey Report that aroused his interest in sex as a subject of legitimate study, rather than the source of considerable frustration in his courtship of Millie. He began avidly reading medical journals, nudist magazines, marriage guidance handbooks, books on sex law, and any work with a vaguely erotic or pornographic content. That summer, in a motel room in Dansville, Illinois, Millie finally acquiesced to his urgent pleadings to "go the whole way." They became officially engaged in December and made plans to marry in June 1949.

Millie had graduated from the University of Illinois before Hefner and took a teaching job some distance away while Hefner continued his studies. Since neither of them owned a car, they were not able to see as much of one another as previously, but Hefner was content to devote himself to his books in preparation for his own graduation in February.

Shortly before he was due to take his finals, there was a dramatic crisis in their relationship. During a cold weekend when they were both in Chicago, Hefner borrowed his father's car and took Millie to see Loretta Young in a movie called *The Accused*. During a climactic scene in which Loretta Young is prompted by her conscience to confess to killing a man who tried to rape her, Millie began sobbing uncontrollably and asked Hefner to take her home. Sitting outside in the car, she became hysterical and finally blurted out that she had been having an affair with another teacher in the school where she was working.

Hefner was dumbfounded that she could have done such a thing: he began to cry. Millie whispered tearfully that she would understand if he no longer wished to marry her, but he would not hear of it. They sat talking for a long time. He finally made her promise to end the affair immediately and assured her that he would not let it come between them.

During February and March, Hefner applied to every magazine and newspaper in Chicago for a job, without any success. He tried selling two cartoon strips—"Gene Fantus, Psycho-Investigator" and "Freddie Frat," an accident-prone preppie—to national syndicates, but none of them was interested. He landed a commission writing a movie review column for a short-lived "what's-on" weekly magazine called *Dale Harrison's Chicago*, but he did not get paid, had to buy his own tickets, and in any case the magazine folded after a couple of issues. Thoroughly dispirited and increasingly desperate, he took a job in the personnel department of the Chicago Carton Company, consoling himself with the thought that his employer was at least peripherally involved with printing, even if it was only on cardboard boxes.

On June 15, Millie and Hef were married at the Saint John

Bosco Rectory in Chicago, close to where they had both grown up. By then Hefner was very firmly an agnostic, but he agreed to be married by a Catholic priest to please Millie and her family. It was a modest wedding, reflecting the conservative, middle-class tastes of both families. Millie wore a white dress and looked, everyone agreed, radiant. Hefner grinned a lot. After the ceremony, Hefner drove Millie off in his father's car for a brief honeymoon at Styza's Birchwood Lodge in Hazelhurst, Wisconsin.

A week later, back in Chicago, they moved in with Hefner's parents, since there was no question of their finding enough money for a place of their own. It was an arrangement that soon caused problems for the young couple, problems that were exacerbated by Hefner's importunate decision to throw away his $45-a-week job with the carton company. He hated the place and was bored by the work; when he discovered that the hiring policy excluded Jews, Negroes, or anyone with a long, foreign-sounding name, he used this as justification to Millie for leaving.

They were able to get by on her salary as a teacher, while Hefner stayed at home drawing more and more cartoons. His efforts at selling them were no more successful than previously. For a few weeks he became enthused by the idea of launching a picture magazine devoted to Chicago and put together a dummy issue titled *Chi*, but his hopes crumbled when the difficulties of raising finance quickly proved insuperable. Millie, increasingly tetchy at her husband's apparent disinclination to find a regular job, suggested he return to college to study for a master's degree, which might perhaps enable him to find a job he liked. Hefner agreed.

In February 1950, he enrolled in graduate school at Northwestern University and bought himself an old car—a 1941 Chevy Club coupé—to travel back and forth to the campus at Evanston. He planned to study sociology, but stuck at it less than six months. In a term paper on "Sex Behavior and the U.S. Law," he called for a complete overhaul of the penal code relating to sex laws, arguing that if the existing laws were enforced "virtually everybody would be in prison." (Oral sex, even between husband and wife, was still illegal in many states.) His professor gave him an A for research, but marked it down to B+ as he disapproved of Hefner's conclusions.

Hefner decided there was no future for him in academic life and left Northwestern in June, after only one semester. Back looking for work again, he began checking the Help Wanted ads in the *Chicago Tribune* and applied for a job as an advertising copywriter for Carson, Pirie, Scott, a popular department store in Chicago's Loop. He was offered a try-out at $40 a week and took it.

With his ego bolstered by the thought that he could now consider himself a professional writer, Hefner enjoyed the work at Carson, Pirie, Scott. He had his own desk in a small cubicle, he could rattle out reams of breathless promotional prose on a typewriter with ease, and he found the company congenial. Most of his colleagues were young, bright college graduates; among them was Leroy Neiman, then a free-lance men's fashion illustrator. Hefner saved enough to buy Millie a television set to try to ease the continuing problems of starting married life in his parents' home.

After work each day, Hefner immersed himself in another hopeful publishing venture. Entirely undaunted by his inability to sell either individual cartoons or cartoon strips, he began devising a *book* of cartoons satirizing Chicago. Working in their upstairs bedroom, he roughed out hundreds of cartoons and made a final selection with the help of Millie, his brother Keith, and Leroy Neiman, whose work he much admired. He called the book *That Toddlin' Town* and added a subtitle, *A Rowdy Burlesque of Chicago Manners and Morals.*

The publishers he approached all turned him down, but this time Hefner would not be defeated. By scrimping and saving and borrowing money from friends and family, he scraped together nearly $1,000 and found a printer. The money stretched to producing 5,000 paperback copies of a reasonable quality.

Dedicated to "a wife named Millie, my soul mate and sole support," *That Toddlin' Town* was inevitably an amateurish production. The cartoons were crudely drawn and not particularly subtle (one man to another, passing a girl with her skirt blown up around her waist revealing her garters: "I've really been looking forward to this chance to see the Windy City"). Nevertheless, Hefner was pleased with the book and promoted it with unflagging energy. During his lunch hour and on weekends, he visited every bookshop in Chicago, buttonholed the manager, and persuaded him to take a few copies for sale at $1.00 each. He sent review copies to every radio and television station and every newspaper in the area. He got himself interviewed on the "Ernie Simon Show" on television, persuaded Werner's bookshop on South Michigan Avenue to put on a little window display of some of the original artwork, and advertised the book for sale by mail order from his home. The *Chicago Tribune* carried a brief review, calling it "an irreverent satire . . . with a collection of drawings that look like the kind *Esquire* might judge too racy for their readers." Little by little, the piles of unsold books stacked at Hefner's home began, miraculously, to diminish.

While all this was going on, Hefner left Carson, Pirie, Scott for a job as a copywriter with the Leo P. Bott advertising agency, but promoting and selling *That Toddlin' Town* occupied so much of his attention that he was fired after five weeks. By luck he heard that *Esquire*, then based in Chicago, was looking for a promotional copywriter: he applied for the job and got it, at $60 a week, starting immediately. He was thrilled.

Esquire was Hefner's favorite magazine. He considered it to be the arbiter of taste and style, the very last word in male sophistication. He had bought it for years whenever he could afford it, read it with admiration, laughed at the cartoons, and spent many happy hours studying the lustrous girls drawn by Alberto Vargas and George Petty. While he was still at school, he decorated his bedroom walls with Petty and Vargas girls from *Esquire*, a relaxation of Mrs. Hefner's austere household standards that she justified to her husband by saying she did not want to discourage Hugh's artistic inclinations.

The titillating girlie drawings in *Esquire* made it the most daring men's magazine in America during the forties; the U.S. Post Office, for long the self-imposed guardian of public morality, had several times declared *Esquire* to be obscene and therefore unfit to be carried in the mail. But by the time Hefner joined *Esquire*, the magazine was trying to disentangle itself from its prurient image and the editors were embarked on what had become known as the "rescue of *Esquire* from bawditry." Hefner was deeply disappointed, since in his view the magazine was not nearly bawdy enough. He settled down to writing direct-mail shots for the subscription department and soon realized he was stuck in just another nine-to-five job. He had imagined that at a place like *Esquire* he would be working with suave men-about-town and girls approximating the delicious inventions of George Petty. Instead, it was an office like any other office.

When, late in 1951, *Esquire* decided to move to New York, Hefner chose not to follow. (Later, it would become *Playboy* magazine legend that he asked for a $5.00 raise, was refused, and quit on the spot. It was a good public relations gimmick, heavily milked, with frequent variations on the theme that *Esquire* could have saved itself competition from *Playboy* for a measly $5.00 a week. As it is recalled at *Esquire*, Hefner did not want to move to New York and simply passed up a $5.00 a week cost-of-living raise.)

The truth was that Hefner was comfortable in Chicago and those fast-living sophisticates in the East held considerable terrors for a boy born and brought up in the heartland of the Midwest. He had sold almost all the copies of *That Toddlin' Town* and, although he had made very little money, he considered himself to be a published author, a man seen to be going places. Had he not appeared on *television*? "The thing I really want is here in the Windy City," he confided in the continuing saga of the "Comic Autobiography."

In May 1952, Millie and Hefner at last moved out of his parents' house and into a home of their own. Millie had discovered she was pregnant, news Hefner greeted with mixed feelings, since he was already beginning to feel that he had never been able to enjoy any real independence. They found a five-room apartment at 6052 South Harper Avenue, in the Hyde Park area of Chicago, not far from the lake. The interior was dirty and run-down, but it had "potential" and was in a reasonable neighborhood, close to the university.

Both of them set to, cleaning and decorating with first-home enthusiasm. Hefner borrowed $1,000 from his father to buy furniture: they chose the latest contemporary designs, agreeing that it would be better to have a few good pieces than a roomful of cheap junk. Hefner's original cartoons figured prominently in the interior scheme and the place was completed with considerable wit and style; full-color comic strips were used as wallpaper in the baby's bedroom, and in the living room Hefner framed their chest X-rays and hung them on one wall labeled "Millie" and "Hef." When they had finished, Hefner persuaded the *Chicago Daily News* to feature the apartment in a two-page spread under the headline HOW A CARTOONIST LIVES.

Sightings of visitors from outer space in "flying saucers" caused a flurry of excitement in America around this time and prompted Hefner to try his luck with another cartoon strip based on the adventures of little green men in flying saucers, but his attempts to peddle it around the Chicago newspapers met with the same unenthusiastic response as his previous efforts.

After leaving *Esquire*, Hefner found a job paying $80 a week as promotion manager of the Publishers' Development Corporation, a small magazine group whose impressive title somewhat belied its operations. P.D.C. was based in a brownstone house on Dearborn Parkway and, along with *Shooting Goods Retailer*, included in its eclectic stable *Modern Man*, *Art Photography*, *Modern Sunbathing*, and *Sunbathing Review*—all of them successful "girlie" magazines relying either on naturism or art to justify their nude pin-ups.

In truth, many of P.D.C.'s pin-ups looked more like strippers well past their prime than naturists, but the introduction of a beach ball into the picture could work wonders. Some of the "naturists" in the sunbathing magazines were also photographed indoors, which was rather puzzling, but the Publishers' Development Corporation managed to stay out of trouble.

Hefner had no qualms about promoting such magazines and looked on the job as useful experience, for he was still clinging to the hope that one day he would be able to launch a magazine of his own. "He used to talk a lot about becoming a publisher himself," said Vince Tajiri, who also worked at P.D.C., "but I don't think anyone took much notice. I thought he was very immature for his age. He was totally unsophisticated, but he had this obsession with sex. When he had nothing else to do he would draw pornographic cartoons of Blondie and Dagwood."

While he was working for the Publishers' Development Corporation, Hefner made another attempt to resurrect the idea of a picture magazine about Chicago, somewhat in the style of *The New Yorker*. A couple of staffers he had met at *Esquire*, who had also decided to stay in Chicago, expressed interest in the project.

They put together a new dummy, retitled *Pulse*, and had another go at raising sufficient finance. They failed miserably, by tens of thousands of dollars. Hefner was forced to face the depressing fact that they had come nowhere near to getting the magazine launched and it was during this time that he began slipping out in the middle of the night and taking long, contemplative walks along the lake shore, looking up at apartments where the rich lived and wondering miserably if he would ever get a chance to taste the good life.

On the day after the presidential elections, Millie gave birth to a baby girl, whom they christened Christie Ann. Hefner was naturally delighted, but the novelty of fatherhood soon wore thin and he returned to brooding about a magazine of his own. He hung around newsstands, flicking through one magazine after another. In bookshops in the Loop he found back issues of *Life*, *Look*, and *Esquire*, including the notorious March 1937 issue of *Look*, which printed stills from a Czechoslovakian movie, *Ecstasy*, showing actress Hedy Lamarr swimming nude with one nipple clearly exposed. It caused a sensation at the time and resulted in the film either being banned or censored almost everywhere it was shown.

He also studied, with a professional interest, as many illicit girlie magazines as he could afford to buy. In publications like *Wink* and *Cutie* the girls were blowsy broads with smeared make-up, worldly eyes, and the look of having been around. They posed on rumpled beds in seedy motel rooms, wearing lingerie that looked as if it could do with a wash and scuffed stiletto heels. Hefner decided it would not be difficult to produce something better.

In December 1952, he switched jobs once again and became circulation director of a magazine called *Children's Activities*. The editorial content was rather far removed from his own areas of interest but the job, at $120 a week, provided him with more valuable experience. He was hired to mount a direct-mail subscription campaign, which he put together from scratch, and from which he learned a great deal about distributing a national magazine.

By the beginning of 1953, Hefner was convinced that he would never be happy until he had a magazine of his own. He briefly considered cashing in on the 3-D craze by producing a magazine of pin-ups shot in 3-D, providing with each copy a pair of cardboard spectacles with one green lens and one red. Expense ruled out this adventure at a very early stage and so he began jotting down ideas for a new men's magazine that would combine elements of those already available—the editorial quality of *Life* and *Esquire*, the explicit pictures of *Modern Sunbathing*, and the earthy sensuality of *Wink* and *Flirt*.

"I'd like," he noted in volume fifty-two of the "Comic Autobiography," "to produce an entertainment magazine for the city-bred guy—breezy, sophisticated. The girlie features would guarantee the initial sale, but the magazine would have quality too."

Hefner began discussing his ideas with a friend, Eldon Sellers, whom he had met years before, at a dance at Steinmetz High School. Sellers was working as a salesman. Five years older than Hefner, he was already separated from his wife and would go down to Millie and Hef's place at 6052 South Harper most evenings to play Ping-Pong and talk hopefully about the magazine they were going to produce. They kept a tally of how many games each of them won and by the time a title for the magazine emerged— they agreed on *Stag Party*—the score was 373 games to 371.

Stag Party was to be a magazine for the bright, young, urban male who was interested in girls, fun, and good living, a "contemporary equivalent," Hefner would explain, "of wine, women and song although not necessarily in that order."

He began working on rough layouts before he had any idea where or how he could find the funds. He had no money at all of his own and he still owed his parents several hundred dollars. But this time he was determined that nothing would stand in his way. In June, he called at the Lake Shore National Bank and asked for a household loan. Since he had a steady job—he was still working at *Children's Activities*—his application was put forward for consideration, but his employment record was deemed too erratic to risk too large an advance. The bank offered him $200. He took it. He went straight down the street to a loan company and hocked the furniture he had bought with the money borrowed from his parents. This time he was able to raise $400.

A few days later, Hefner stumbled across a much-needed stroke of luck. He was sitting at breakfast with Millie, flicking through the pages of a trade publication called *Advertising Age*, when a news story about the famous Marilyn Monroe calendar caught his eye. It mentioned, in passing, that the calendar had been printed by the John Baumgarth Company in Melrose Park, Chicago. Hefner hastily finished his breakfast, pecked Millie on her proffered cheek, hurried out, jumped into his Chevy, which now had a hanging front fender, and headed for Melrose Park.

Marilyn Monroe posed in the nude for a calendar in 1949, when she was just another hopeful, out-of-work actress hanging around Hollywood. Photographer Tom Kelley persuaded her to agree to the session at a time when she badly needed the money. He paid her $50. There were three pictures, shot with "nothing on but the radio" she would later recall, and a number of semi-nude poses.

Kelley sold the complete set of pictures for $500 to the John Baumgarth Company, which specialized in producing calendars of all kinds. Baumgarth, well stocked with pin-ups, did not bother to make use of the pictures until Marilyn had been noticed in her first important role in *The Asphalt Jungle*. By the time she was a star, the Marilyn Monroe calendar was as famous as she was, although it was only ever distributed as a giveaway promotion by garages, haulage contractors, engineering companies, and the like. The pictures were considered far too erotic to be sent through the U.S. mail, so Baumgarth produced a special version, with a black negligé overprint, for any companies wanting to distribute the calendar by post. No magazine had dared print the pictures, with the exception of a minuscule two-color reproduction that had been featured in *Life* magazine's cover story on Marilyn in April 1952.

Because of the risk of prosecution for obscenity, John Baumgarth believed that there was probably no other use to which the pictures could be put and was surprised, therefore, when Hefner showed up at his office, without an appointment, on the morning of June 13, 1953, and asked if he could buy the rights to publish the Monroe nude pictures in a magazine he was planning to launch.

Baumgarth showed him all three pictures. One shot had never been used and, in Hefner's opinion, it was the sexiest of the three. Marilyn was shown lying on a backdrop of red velvet, her lips sensuously parted, peeking out straight at the camera from behind an upraised arm. Not only was there no mistaking that she had nothing on but the radio, but her raised nipples, deliciously pink, were clearly in view. Baumgarth agreed to take $500 for magazine rights and offered to throw in the color separations, which would save Hefner considerable processing costs. Hefner was delighted with the deal.

With the rights in his pocket to publish a truly sensational pin-up in the first issue of *Stag Party*, Hefner felt that at last he was making progress. At least, he thought, his magazine could not fail to be noticed. Back at 6052 South Harper, he sat down at the kitchen table and composed a letter to drum up support from the bigger newsstand wholesalers in the United States, some of whom he knew personally from his days at the Publishers' Development Corporation. It was an important letter and Hefner put everything he had into it, agonizing over each line until he was satisfied. He began typing . . .

Dear Friend:

We haven't even printed our letterhead yet, but I wanted you to be one of the very first to hear the news. STAG PARTY— a brand new magazine for men—will be out this Fall and it will be one of the best sellers you've ever handled.

It's being put together by a group of people from ES-QUIRE who stayed here in Chicago when that magazine moved east—so you can imagine how good it's going to be. And it will include male-pleasing figure studies, making it a sure hit from the very start.

But here's the really BIG news! The first issue of STAG PARTY will include the famous calendar picture of Marilyn Monroe—in *full color*! In fact—every issue of STAG PARTY will have a beautiful, full-page, male-pleasing nude study—in full natural color!

Now you know what I mean when I say this is going to be one of the best sellers you've ever handled.

STAG PARTY will sell for 50¢ and you'll receive your copies at a profitable 38¢. It will be supplied to you on a *fully returnable* basis and, of course, we will pay all shipping costs.

Fill out the postage-paid AIR MAIL reply card enclosed and get it back to me as quickly as possible. With four color

printing on the inside pages, we've got to confirm our distribution quantities right away.

It will be nice doing business with you again—especially
with a title as good as this one.

Cordially,
Hugh M. Hefner
General Manager

Hefner calculated, correctly, that the confident tone of his letter
would gloss over the real state of his preparedness. He certainly
felt no need to name the "group of people from ESQUIRE" (since
it was a group of one, Hugh M. Hefner, briefly employed in the
promotion department), neither did he point out that *Stag Party*,
at that time, comprised no more than a pile of rough layouts and
scribbled ideas, and the rights to publish a couple of pin-up pictures.

Amazingly, only two of the twenty-five newsstand wholesalers
Hefner approached said they wanted to see the first issue before
placing an order. The remainder came up with smallish orders—
3,000 from Philadelphia, 2,000 from Newark, New Jersey, 1,000
from Norfolk, Virginia, 8,000 from New York. Hefner meanwhile had invested his last $100 in printed stationery headed Na-
tionwide News Company—an entirely fictitious title that he thought
sounded good—to circulate to the 800 independent newsstand
operators. Hefner reckoned he would need advance orders for
20,000 copies before he could go ahead.

With his own meager capital quickly exhausted, his friend
Eldon Sellers suggested forming a corporation and selling stock
as a way of raising finance. In July, H.M.H. Publishing Company
was incorporated under the laws of the State of Illinois, the in-
corporators being Hugh M. Hefner, Mildred Hefner, and Eldon
Sellers. A former U.S. Air Force pilot and first violinist with the
Indianapolis Symphony Orchestra, Sellers was more than just a
friend to Hefner during the hectic days preceding the launch of
the magazine. He was sounding board, sidekick, and financial
adviser.

Although he was still involved in a full-time job (as indeed
was Hefner), Sellers was instrumental in helping to get the magazine out. He borrowed $2,000 from a girlfriend to buy stock

himself and persuaded many other people to invest small amounts. He made a deal with an engraver to complete all the plates for the first issue in return for stock. He accompanied Hefner on a round of potential printers to help him make the best possible deal. The Rochelle Printing Company, about seventy-five miles outside Chicago, eventually got the contract after agreeing to print the black-and-white section of the magazine and deferring half the cost—$1,250—for ninety days.

Grace and Glenn Hefner, only vaguely aware of the kind of magazine their son was intending to produce, invested $1,000 in stock; Hefner's brother Keith scraped together $500, which he paid in installments; a neighbor in South Harper chipped in his life savings—$500. It was not long before sales of stock had raised close to $10,000, largely due to the salesmanship of Eldon Sellers. "Hef was not much of a salesman," said Sellers. "I had once done some door-to-door selling of vacuum cleaners and did pretty well. When he was in college I told him he ought to try it. He did and ended up having to buy the demonstrator himself. Later, when I used to bring people to see him about starting the magazine, he would do a great job telling them about his ideas, explaining the magazine. But that would be the end of it. He would never *ask* for anything."

On top of holding down his job at *Children's Activities*, negotiating with printers, encouraging newsstand operators to place orders, and prodding investors to buy stock, Hefner was also frantically trying to put together the editorial content of the first issue. He had a very clear idea of what he wanted, but very little money to pay contributors. He approached Random House to buy a John O'Hara short story entitled *Days* and was told the fee would be $1,000—completely out of his reach. *The New Yorker* haughtily turned down his request to reprint a James Thurber story, on the grounds that only magazines of "established reputation" were considered suitable vehicles for *New Yorker* material. Ernest Hemingway's publisher similarly rejected Hefner because his magazine had not "demonstrated its character."

Hefner was grimly resolved, if it became necessary, to write and illustrate the entire issue himself, but he struck a rich vein when he looked at what material was available in the public domain—published before 1903 and therefore out of copyright. He found a Sherlock Holmes story by Sir Arthur Conan Doyle and another piece by Ambrose Bierce.

Long after Millie had gone to bed each night, Hefner worked at a card table in the living room with crumpled, rejected layouts littering the floor all around him. Although he had a strong sense of design, he had no formal training in the graphic arts and he could not get the *look* of the magazine right. He wanted slick, sophisticated, up-to-the-minute graphics that would proclaim the magazine's quality, and he simply could not achieve what he wanted on his own. A friend from *Esquire* days eventually recommended he go to see a young designer by the name of Art Paul, who had recently set up his own studio in the Loop, on Van Buren.

The moment Hefner walked into Paul's studio, he was struck by the artwork hanging on the walls and declared himself impressed. Paul, then twenty-eight years old and a graduate of the Illinois Institute of Design, was far from impressed with Hefner, who had not shaved for three or four days and was wearing an old coat frayed at the collar and cuffs. He was also suffering from a stiff neck, which somehow made him look even less like a man going places in the publishing business.

As Hefner began to talk about his magazine with all his usual passion, Paul revised his first impression. He liked Hefner's obvious dedication and enthusiasm, he liked what he had to say about the visual and editorial concept he was hoping to achieve. Hefner showed him a rough of the cover along with some tentative layouts—all his own work. Paul thought they were awful and offered the opinion that it looked too much like a movie magazine. "Yes, yes," Hefner said, "you're right." After they had talked for some time, Hefner asked Paul if he would take on overall design and art direction of *Stag Party*. Paul refused, saying he already had too much work and could not spare the time. Privately, he believed it was extremely unlikely that *Stag Party* would ever get to a second issue. However, pressed by Hefner, he agreed to draw an illustration to go with a short story scheduled for the launch issue.

When Hefner left Art Paul's studio that afternoon, he had decided that Paul was the only man he wanted to be art director of his magazine. They met again, frequently, over the next couple of weeks and after a great deal of persuasion, Paul eventually agreed to design the first issue, on the condition that Hefner did all the leg work—collecting illustrations from various contributors, finding the right photographs, organizing the prints, delivering manuscripts. Paul also agreed, reluctantly, to take payment in stock. "I was very, very hesitant because I did not have much of my own resources and I was not very confident the magazine would have a future. In the end, I decided to take a gamble." (It paid off handsomely—Paul became a dollar millionaire.)

On September 11, 1953, Hefner resigned from *Children's Activities*, explaining to the general manager, Clifford Schabile, that he was off to start his own magazine. When Schabile raised an inquiring eyebrow, Hefner hastily reassured him that what he had in mind was unlikely to be competing with *Children's Activities*. "If you fail," Schabile warned, after listening to Hefner's plans, "you won't even have a shoestring left."

By this time the content of the magazine was pretty well decided. In addition to the short stories by Arthur Conan Doyle and Ambrose Bierce, there was a Boccaccio story on adultery, an article on football with photographs supplied free by the University of Illinois, a page of party jokes, a black-and-white spread of pictures showing nude sunbathing in California, an article on the Dorsey brothers, then at the height of their popularity, an article on modern desk design with pictures supplied free by a desk manufacturer, a stilted photo feature showing couples undressing while playing a "strip quiz," and a page of advertisements called "The Men's Shop," offering items for the sophisticated man, such as a fur-covered ice bucket. Marilyn Monroe, in full color, occupied the center of the magazine's forty-eight pages.

Tipped off by Hefner, the journal *American Cartoonist* published a story about plans for the launch of *Stag Party*, describing its format and pointing out that it represented a new outlet for cartoonists. A few days later, Hefner received a letter of complaint from a New York attorney representing the publishers of *Stag* magazine. *Stag* was a field-and-stream magazine owned by a publisher who felt that confusion would result from a competing magazine called *Stag Party* and requested, through his lawyer, that Hefner desist.

Even so late in the day, it was not an unwelcome letter since Hefner was becoming increasingly disenchanted with the title, while Art Paul had never liked it from the start and had said so.

That weekend, Hefner, Millie, Eldon Sellers, and a group of friends sat around at 6052 South Harper putting forward suggestions for a new title. *Gent, Gentry, Gentleman, Pan,* and *Satyr* were all in the running at one stage until Eldon Sellers suddenly said: "How about *Playboy*?" Hefner liked it immediately. It had a Scott Fitzgerald flavor, he said, and conjured up just the image he wanted to project.

That evening, Hefner phoned Art Paul and asked him to design a new symbol for the magazine. He had wanted something like the little "Esky" figure that cavorted through the pages of *Esquire* and Paul had originally been toying with a stag design. For the new title, Hefner suggested a rabbit in a tuxedo as being "cute, frisky, and sexy" and thus embodying the personality of the magazine. It took Paul about half-an-hour to design the famous Playboy bunny. "There was," he said, "simply no more time to spend on it."

At home, Millie tried, uncomplainingly, to look after the baby and maintain a semblance of domestic order as the apartment degenerated into a kind of madhouse, with paper and photographs scattered everywhere, excitable young men rushing in and out, the telephone ringing incessantly. She had long before given up hope of interesting Hefner in anything but the magazine. With deadlines already closing in, he was struggling with an all-important editorial that would introduce readers to the magazine and explain its philosophy. After many hours at the typewriter, he finally produced a masterly piece that intuitively touched base with his generation:

> If you're a man between 18 and 80, PLAYBOY is meant for you. If you like entertainment served up with humor, sophistication and spice, PLAYBOY will become a very special favorite.
>
> We want to make it very clear from the start, we aren't a "family magazine." If you're somebody's sister, wife or mother-in-law and picked us up by mistake, please pass us along to the man in your life and get back to the *Ladies Home Companion*.
>
> Within the pages of PLAYBOY you will find articles, fiction, picture stories, cartoons, humor and special features culled

from many sources, past and present, to form a pleasure-primer styled to the masculine taste. Most of today's "magazines for men" spend all their time out-of-doors—thrashing through thorny thickets or splashing about in fast-flowing streams. We'll be out there too, occasionally, but we don't mind telling you in advance—we plan spending most of our time inside.

We like our apartment. We enjoy mixing up cocktails and an *hors d'oeuvre* or two, putting a little mood music on the phonograph and inviting in a female for a quiet discussion on Picasso, Nietzsche, jazz, sex.

We believe, too, that we are filling a publishing need only slightly less important than the one just taken care of by the Kinsey Report. The magazines now being produced for the city-bred male (there are 2—count 'em—2) have, of late, placed so much emphasis on fashion, travel and "how-to-do-it" features on everything from avoiding a hernia to building your own steam bath, that entertainment has been all but pushed from their pages. PLAYBOY will emphasize entertainment. Affairs of state will be out of our province. We don't expect to solve any world problems or prove any great moral truths. If we are able to give the American male a few extra laughs and a little diversion from the anxieties of the Atomic Age, we'll feel we've justified our existence.

In early October, Hefner and Paul began spending more and more time in Rochelle, at the works of the Rochelle Printing Company. If an illustration was not right, Paul would do another one on the spot. Hefner rewrote text to make it fit, wrote the captions page by page and headlines to fit new page layouts. Sometimes they worked right through the night.

When the presses at last began to roll, Hefner, Paul, and Eldon Sellers all waited in a coffee shop across the street from the works for the first copy to be available. Hefner was exhausted and nervously aware of the importance of the moment. If *Playboy* flopped, he was finished. He tried not to think about how many years it would take him to pay back all he owed, particularly as he had rashly promised many friends who had bought stock that he would make sure they got their money back if the venture failed.

At the very last minute, Hefner made a significant alteration to the cover. His confidence, which had sustained him through the preceding months of hectic preparations, suddenly failed and he asked for the date to be taken off the cover. Maybe there won't be a second issue, he said to Art Paul in justification. If it doesn't sell in the first month we'll just have to leave it on the newsstands until it does.

2

Wow! Miss October Was Really the Most!

The print order for the first issue of *Playboy* magazine was 70,250 copies and by November 1953, it could be found on the racks of those newsstands in the bigger cities that dared to peddle such risqué publications. Marilyn Monroe, fully clothed, waved invitingly from the cover, which gave little away except that the magazine offered "Entertainment for Men," cost 50¢ and included, for the first time in any magazine, the famous Marilyn Monroe nude in full color.

In Chicago, Hefner found himself hanging around the newsstands in the Loop almost every day, both fearful and fascinated by the existence of his magazine. While affecting to flick through the pages of some other publication, he scanned the customers out of the corner of his eye, *willing* them to pick up *Playboy*. Whenever someone bought a copy, usually after a furtive peek inside at Miss Monroe, the "Sweetheart of the Month," Hefner felt his skin prickle with excitement. Sometimes, when the newsstand owner was not looking, he would surreptitiously move the *Playboy* stack to a more prominent display position, closer to *Esquire* and *The New Yorker* and further from the unwanted companionship of *Modern Man* or *Sunbathing*.

After a week, it seemed to Hefner that there were noticeably fewer copies of *Playboy* available on some of the newsstands he visited in Chicago, and the arrival of such a brash new magazine had not gone unnoticed. *Time* described *Playboy* as "slick and sassy," the *Saturday Review* said it made "old issues of *Esquire*, even in its most uninhibited days, look like Trade bulletins from the W.C.T.U.," and *Newsweek* reported that *Esquire* men were "probably peering uneasily over their shoulders" since "a rival, younger by a generation, bolder by several inches of neckline, was fighting its way into the old gentlemen's hunting grounds."

Just two weeks after the magazine was first put on sale, the distributor telephoned Hefner to say that *Playboy* was selling well everywhere. "It's the hottest title we've ever handled," he said and urged Hefner to press ahead with a second issue. Hefner needed no persuasion; he was waiting only to make sure he was not bankrupt.

The second issue of *Playboy* magazine confidently carried a date—January 1954—on its cover and the name of Hugh M. Hefner on its masthead as editor and publisher. Neither Hefner nor Art Paul had wanted to put their names on the first issue, in case it flopped. Hefner had calculated that he needed to sell 30,000 copies of the first issue to break even. When the returns came in, total sales amounted to 53,991. The young publisher celebrated his success by buying a new, red Studebaker convertible with whitewall tires to replace the Chevy, which had finally broken down and been condemned to the scrapyard.

Pecking at his typewriter late one night, surrounded by the incredible chaos that was now a permanent feature of the living room in his South Harper apartment, Hefner struggled to express his feelings in the intimacy of his scrapbook. "What do you say when a dream comes true? What words do you use? How can a guy possibly express a thing like this? I own a magazine—a magazine of my very own—or, more precisely, I am president of, and hold a majority of the stock in, a corporation that owns a magazine. It is all very, very unreal. The dream has come true too quickly to be fully appreciated."

Hefner put together three issues of the magazine in the apartment, working either in the kitchen (the printer complained about butter stains on the copy) or on a small folding card table set up in the living room. Millie did her best to put up with the piles of paper everywhere and tried not to nag him about waking the baby when his typewriter rattled through the night, but there were inevitable tensions. Hefner was trying to do too many things at once. His friend Eldon Sellers recalls playing bridge with him in the evenings while he was eating a meal and editing copy at the same time. "He'd get mad at Millie, throwing his cards across the room," said Sellers, "for very little things."

In January, Hefner rented an office—a small apartment on the top floor of a gray-painted townhouse at 11 East Superior Street, next door to the Salvation Army headquarters and directly opposite the Holy Name Cathedral. The proximity of a questionable magazine was not the worst indignity visited upon the cathedral: its yellowstone façade was still pockmarked from the machine gun bullets that had killed gangster Hymie Weiss, boss of the O'Banion mob, back in the thirties. Al Capone had set up machine-gun nests across the street to deal with the luckless Hymie after a disagreement.

Apart from Hefner, the staff comprised Art Paul, whom he had finally persuaded to join full-time, Eldon Sellers, who acted as general manager, and Ray Russell, a writer Hefner hired from the obscurity of Walgreen Drug Store's house organ. Hefner's father, an accountant, set up bookkeeping procedures and looked after the accounts part-time.

Everyone did a bit of everything, except Art Paul, who gruffly refused Hefner's request to empty the wastepaper baskets on his way out of the office one evening, and similarly refused to help carry the office copies of the magazine the printer dumped on the doorstep every month. Hefner and Russell had to hump the heavy bundles up three flights of stairs, and every time they did it Russell wished he had had the guts, like Paul, to tell Hefner he hadn't been hired as a manual laborer.

Russell took over many of the in-house writing chores, knocking out headlines, captions, fillers, and jokes as well as contributing both fiction and nonfiction features. Hefner determinedly pursued big-name writers for the major features and was delighted when he found an Erskine Caldwell story he could afford for the February 1954 issue. He followed up with pieces by Somerset Maugham, Thorne Smith, and Robert Ruark. When the money ran out, both he and Russell sifted through material available in the public domain. Young, enthusiastic, and largely inexperienced, they worked from issue to issue, learning from each other, from their mistakes, and from the pressing requirement to produce a new issue each month. They discussed endlessly, heatedly, and earnestly every aspect of the magazine, sometimes chewing over ideas and arguing far into the night. Once a month, the three of them drove out to Rochelle in Hefner's Studebaker to close the next issue, usually working right through the night, correcting proofs, cutting over-matter, and writing new copy to fit holes.

Hefner, who thought nothing of working thirty-six hours without a break, bought a bed for his office and soon took to staying overnight, sometimes with a nurse from nearby St. Francis Hospital to keep him company. At first, he diligently returned to the marital home on weekends, but neither Millie nor marriage interested him as much as his magazine and his weekend visits became less and less frequent. He made sure Millie and the baby, Christie, wanted for nothing and immersed himself in *Playboy*, living more or less full time in the office.

With the publication of the first anniversary issue, *Playboy* magazine could boast a circulation of 175,000 copies. The staff of seven celebrated with sandwiches and coffee in a booth at Charmet's Coffee Shop, not far from the office on the corner of Michigan and Chicago avenues. "I knew we were in business to stay," said Hefner, "so I picked up the check."

No one, *no one*, anticipated the phenomenal and immediate success of *Playboy* magazine; indeed, many people wondered how long Hefner would be able to stay out of jail. Even if he was not arrested for peddling obscene material, it was assumed it was only a matter of time before public outrage forced him to close down. But neither eventuality occurred. Instead, the line on the circulation graph went on climbing as if it would never peak. By the beginning of 1956, the circulation was 500,000; by 1959, it had hit 1,000,000 and overtaken *Esquire*.

It was as if America had been waiting for *Playboy* and, in a way, it had. A few years earlier, during the McCarthy era, the magazine could never have survived in the prevailing climate of intolerance, suspicion, and fear. The Senator from Wisconsin would doubtless have branded *Playboy* an enemy of America, quite as dangerous to the health of the nation as the "Commies." But by the mid-fifties, McCarthy had disappeared from the scene, exposed as a tyrant and a drunk, his downfall hastened by the televising of Senate hearings that revealed him to be no more than a repulsive bully.

In the wake of the witch hunts, when any kind of nonconformism was equated with disloyalty, there was a positive desire to embrace new ideas and loosen the nation's corsets. The Korean war had ended with an armistice signed at Panmunjon and Eisenhower, in the White House, was still immensely popular. Suddenly the fifties took on a distinctly up-beat and carefree aspect. Students stuffed telephone booths in celebration and hung their naked backsides out of automobiles—a craze known as "mooning."

Art became modern. Abstract expressionists like Jackson Pollock, Franz Kline, and Willem de Kooning covered canvases with wild splashes of color, mystifying shapes, and great globs of paint, breaking free from the straitjacket of representational work. Writers, too, sensed freedom: in 1954, a Russian émigré by the name of Vladimir Nabokov was correcting the final galley proofs of his novel *Lolita*, the unforgettable story of a seedy professor's seduction of a wayward adolescent. The fact that *Lolita* could even be *considered* for publication in the United States was profound evidence of new liberalism.

With the economy booming, consumers and teenagers made a forceful appearance on the American scene, spending as never before in supermarkets, department stores, and the first shopping malls. Products that an earlier generation would have considered unattainable luxuries—automobiles, trailers, holidays, stereo sets, swimming pools, and a limitless range of electric appliances— became the expected perquisites of the "American dream." Fashions could afford to change with astonishing rapidity, even for men, who stepped out in *pink* shirts.

Television, almost unknown at the end of World War II, could now be found in 29 million homes. The United States, with only 6 percent of the world's population, possessed 60 percent of all the automobiles in the world, 58 percent of all the telephones and 45 percent of all the radios. These Bakelite citadels in miniature, once focal points for the family to gather to listen to President Roosevelt's "fireside chats," were now tuned to stations broadcasting popular music mawkishly preoccupied with falling in and out of love: "Cry," "Little Things Mean a Lot," "Mister Sandman": "Send me a dream, make her complexion like peaches and cream . . ."

Sex was not yet making an appearance in popular lyrics, but it was certainly on everyone's mind. To a generation brought up to believe that sex was furtive and dirty, the Kinsey reports were a revelation. If *Sexual Behavior in the Human Male*, published in 1948, was a shocker, the report on female sexual behavior that followed five years later was a sensation, revealing to America a remarkable truth: nice girls *did*. And on the vinyl-upholstered backseats of two-tone automobiles with soaring tail fins and glistening chrome, more and more young men were discovering, to their surprise and delight, that Kinsey was right.

Playboy was welcomed as a guidebook to this new "good life." *Playboy* told its readers what to wear, what wine to drink with what meals, what records to listen to, what movies to see. Its authoritative tone soothed their anxieties that they might inadvertently wear the wrong necktie or mix a cocktail incorrectly. In particular, *Playboy* espoused sex as a healthy and enjoyable recreational activity, free from guilt.

All of this was for Hefner's benefit. He made no secret of the fact that he produced the magazine for himself: it unashamedly pandered to his fantasies. He wanted to be a suave, sophisticated man-about-town, sexually liberated, irresistible to women, and a masterful lover. Thus it was to this fantasy figure that *Playboy* magazine made its pitch. It was an unbeatable formula.

To read *Playboy* was to join an imaginary smart set of guys who lived in penthouses, drove sports cars, and were worldly-wise about wine and women. For 50¢ a month, a struggling insurance salesman with a nagging wife and mounting debts could enter the wonderful world of *Playboy*, where cuff links mattered. "Let your cuff link collection reflect the fresh seasonal spirit with semiprecious gems in cool colors—particularly onyx, jade, blue jasper and topaz. Silver and gold, always in good taste, will glisten no less sumptuously this year. Avoid coronation-size jewelry—it tends to be vulgar."

Playboy on Christmas parties: "Generally a room that can

accommodate 50 people comfortably at a pre-dinner cocktail party will have a capacity of about 25 for dining, drinking and dancing . . ."

Playboy on weekends: "Of all the delightfully romantic social occasions invented by man, none has the glamorous excitement of the weekend house-party in the country . . ."

Playboy on travel: "One of the most satisfying ways to get away from it all is on a private yacht . . ."

Hefner would allow nothing to puncture the myth that *Playboy* readers had it made. Even the advertisements had to reflect the image of the *Playboy* reader as man-about-town. The magazine never accepted advertising for hair restorers, trusses, slimming aids, self-improvement courses, acne cures, athlete's foot powder, and the like, lest an impression be created, heaven forbid, that *Playboy* readers ever needed such products. No sir, in the wonderful world of *Playboy*, men had hair on their chests as well as their heads. They were the kind of men who were always offered the best table in a restaurant, who never had to hurl themselves in front of a waiter to be served. They were legendary Lotharios, could uncouple any known bra with one hand while expertly mixing a martini with the other. They never had their faces slapped.

That, at least, was the fantasy *Playboy* would package, ever more expertly, over the years. Pivotal to the package was the Playmate.

Before *Playboy*, few American men had ever seen a girl's breasts exposed in a color photograph, except in the pages of *National Geographic*, which was able to publish pictures of primitive tribes untroubled by clothes in the safe knowledge that it could never be accused of sexual exploitation. No self-respecting American male was going to feel a stirring in his loins at the sight of a naked Aborigine woman with sagging breasts and a bone through her nose, standing in a jungle clearing and grinning at the camera with sharpened teeth. But the Playmate, ah, there was a girl to dream about: she was white, young, blonde, wholesome, American, and always available, right there in the center of the magazine.

Hundreds of letters attested to the Playmate's popularity every month: "*Wow!* Miss October was really the most. She can be my

Playmate of the Month, every month, every year, every eon. How about an encore? *Wow!*"

"I thought I'd been around and seen them all, but your buxom Betty Blue really does . . . I mean she's . . . ah, you know what I mean."

The Playmate of the Month rendered American men speechless with admiration, envy, and awe. In crew cuts and crew-neck sweaters, they would browse at newsstands and, with studied casualness, pick up *Playboy*, turn to the center pages as if by accident, and . . . *jeepers creepers!* The blood rushed to the cheeks, the pulse quickened. Folding the magazine and hastily handing over their 50¢, they limped away with their Playmate, one hand thrust into a trouser pocket.

Playmates were to become as much a part of America in the innocent fifties as drive-in movies, hoola hoops, and Davy Crockett hats. Blonde, big-breasted, and red-lipped, artfully draped in chiffon and white fur, they could be found pinned up in college rooms across the nation, in factories, offices, and filling stations. Traveling salesmen carried Playmates in their sample bags for company in lonely motel rooms. The ships of the U.S. Navy sailed with Playmates covertly stuck behind locker doors. When Eisenhower sent paratroopers to Little Rock, Arkansas, to assist the enrollment of nine black students in school, carefully folded Playmates provided off-duty solace for the young soldiers under the sheets in bed or in the privacy of a lavatory, where the doors could be locked without suspicion.

No one knew better than Hefner the importance of the Playmate. His editors would sometimes agitate to be rid of this thorn in the vulnerable side of their integrity as serious journalists, but he would never hear of it. Without the Playmate, the magazine would die. Hefner recognized that fact, faced up to it and devoted an inordinate amount of time to her ritualistic selection. "If a guy digs a broad," he explained, "you'd expect him to dig photos of broads. And if he doesn't dig broads, he's got a problem."

The Playmate made her debut in the second issue of *Playboy* magazine (Marilyn Monroe was "Sweetheart of the Month"), and for several months she was selected from a job lot of color plates Hefner bought from the John Baumgarth Company at the time he acquired the Marilyn Monroe pictures. Thus early Playmates tended to be indistinguishable from run-of-the-mill calendar cheesecake, a fact that did nothing to diminish the ardor of the readers, who struggled in their letters to find superlatives of sufficient potency to describe their admiration. The radio gang of the U.S.S. *Power*, for example, wrote to say it had voted Miss November, "the girl we would most like to swab down with."

"This pulchritudinous Playmate of the Month is becoming," the magazine trumpeted in December 1954, "the new American Love Goddess and her admirable proportions have been credited with an assist in the early demise of Christian Dior's Flat Look."

When the stock of Baumgarth calendar nudes was exhausted, *Playboy* began employing professional models to pose for the centerfold. There was no risk, in those guileless days, of exposing too much of the model's charms since Eastman-Kodak simply refused to process any frames they considered to be indecent. Nipples were just about acceptable, providing they were not too blatantly displayed, but there was never, ever, a hint of pubic hair.

As late as 1959, when *Playboy* published pictures of completely nude strippers shot with a hidden camera in a Chicago honkytonk, the FBI raided the magazine, confiscated the negatives and contact sheets, and threatened prosecution. Fortunately, Vince Tajiri, the photo editor, had taken the precaution of having G-strings painted on the original negatives and a duplicate film made. The dubious FBI agents were finally convinced that it was not pubic hair that could be seen in the magazine, but little triangular G-strings.

Hefner wanted what he described as a "seduction-is-imminent" look to the first Playmates to pose for the magazine and wanted himself cast in the role of seducer. It was achieved with a conspicuous lack of subtlety. Miss April 1955 could be seen lounging on a charcoal-gray sofa in a pair of checked matador pants and nothing else, with Hefner's pipe lying prominently in an ashtray nearby. The same pipe made another appearance, artistically positioned on the floor, with Miss August, who was perched on a high stool in one of Hefner's shirts, casually unbuttoned.

Miss November stood in the bath with a yellow towel wrapped loosely around her. Hefner's tie was hung over the bathroom mirror and his razor, shaving mug, and brush, *still soapy*, stood on the wash basin. No reader could miss the implication.

The embryonic cult of the publisher as Playmate-seducer was not entirely wishful, since Hefner frequently made love to Miss July on the bed in his office on the top floor of 11 East Superior Street. Miss July was identified in the magazine as "Janet Pilgrim," perhaps a necessary pseudonym as her real name was Charlene Drain. A twenty-year-old blonde with large breasts ("well endowed" was the most commonly applied euphemism at that time), Miss Drain worked in the magazine's subscription department on the second floor, in which position she had attracted the publisher's formidable attention. He took her out to dinner in his new bronze Cadillac convertible and they began dating regularly on those evenings when Hefner could bear to be parted from the real love of his life—the proofs, schedules, layouts, manuscripts, artwork, illustrations, and other impedimenta of his magazine in production.

Charlene soon succumbed to the editor's advances, but no mention of their relationship appeared in *Playboy*. Instead, the magazine chose to promote a ludicrously improbable story to explain how Janet Pilgrim found her way into the center pages. It was said that she needed a new Addressograph machine to handle the increasing volume of subscriptions and when she raised the matter with Hef, he responded, with a chuckle, that he would buy her one if she would pose as a Playmate. Well, one thing led to another and whatever the truth, she could be found in the July issue sitting at a dressing-table with an off-the-shoulder negligé just covering her nipples. In the background is the shadowy figure of a man in evening clothes: Hefner.

"We suppose it's natural to think of the pulchritudinous Playmates," the story noted, "as existing in a world apart. Actually, potential Playmates are all around you: the new secretary at your office, the doe-eyed beauty who sat opposite you at lunch yesterday, the girl who sells you shirts and ties at your favorite store. We found Miss July in our own circulation department . . ."

Janet Pilgrim marked a turning point in the history of the American pin-up: she was the first nice girl to take off her clothes for the camera. To pose in the nude was still widely considered to be disgraceful, disgusting even. When, the previous year at the Cannes Film Festival, starlet Simone Silva obliged a jostling posse of photographers by removing her halter top, the event made headlines around the world, not least because it happened *in front of Robert Mitchum!* This last point was considered particularly shocking, but then it was still a time when wives were often reluctant to expose their bodies to their husbands and nudity was the preserve of the naturist, the artist's model, and the stripper, all of whom were viewed with equal suspicion.

Pilgrim—did not her very name epitomize virtue?—changed all that. It was clear she was a nice girl because she had never posed in the nude before and she worked in an *office*. Why, there was even a picture of her in a demure dress "discussing the magazine's rising circulation with publisher Hugh M. Hefner," also soberly attired in a dark suit and check tie, his hair neatly combed.

Playboy was inundated with ecstatic letters about Miss Pilgrim and Hefner realized he had stumbled across a formula that struck a deeply responsive chord with his readers. The "seduction-is-imminent" genre was swiftly abandoned and replaced by the brilliant concept of the Playmate as "girl next door," a girl with a reputation as unblemished as her body, a girl who would never dream of posing in the nude except just this once, just for *Playboy*.

To further foster the myth, *Playboy* began constructing fanciful little picture stories describing how and where the girl was discovered. She was photographed in her natural habitat—shopping, riding, strumming a guitar, or whipping up a pancake. The "editorial we" was universally—and clumsily—employed to involve the reader in the thrill of the chase. Of Miss November 1955, the magazine recorded:

> We were looking over hi-fi components when we saw her. We wanted to walk up and talk, but thought better of it. After some chit-chat with a salesman, she wandered out and across the street to a soda fountain and we, naturally enough, followed. She noticed us there, which isn't too surprising since we sat on a stool right next to her and kept asking her to pass napkins, straws and such. She asked about the Leica M-3 hanging from our shoulder. What kind of camera was it, she wanted to know, and were we a photographer. Well of course we were a photographer . . .

All this was nonsense. Miss November, a United Airlines stewardess, was a current girlfriend of a *Playboy* staffer.

The cute, fresh-faced, snub-nosed, blonde, all-American cheer-leader Playmate was the greatest imaginable turn-on for Americans accustomed to anonymous pin-ups with knowing eyes and come-hither expressions, threatening broads who looked as if, off camera, they smoked and swore and chewed gum. None of the imitators *Playboy* spawned in its wake ever understood the importance of the "girl next door"—they thought they could challenge *Playboy*'s supremacy by publishing raunchier pictures of sexier girls. It was a mistake. The kind of men who read *Playboy* definitely did not want to look at pictures of girls who were *sexy*, who knew it all, who made wisecracks like "Are you in?" or "Have you finished?" That was too much like real life: too intimidating.

The attraction of the Playmate was the absence of threat. Playmates were nice clean girls; there was nothing to be feared from seducing them. Afterward they would no doubt admit, with shining eyes, that it was wonderful.

Miss Pilgrim made two further appearances in *Playboy*, an indication not so much of her popularity as of an initial shortage of suitable "girls next door" willing to remove their clothes. Models and actresses filled in—Jayne Mansfield was an early Playmate—but Hefner was always unhappy using girls whose pictures might appear in other magazines. His recurrent nightmare was that a girl who had been seen only seminude in *Playboy* might be found totally nude in some "cheap, tawdry girlie magazine."

Eventually, a "finder's fee" of $250 was offered to anyone submitting photographs of a girl chosen as a Playmate. A condition of payment was that she had never previously posed in the nude for any other publication. In fact, once word got about that nice girls posed for *Playboy* without being banished from decent society, plenty of other nice girls stepped forward and unbuttoned their blouses. It was not long before so many girls wanted to be a Playmate that photographer Dwight Hooker complained about being trampled underfoot in the rush. "You have to fight them off with a baseball bat," he snarled.

Miss Pilgrim, meanwhile, briefly became something of a celebrity, making personal appearances at fraternity dances and business conventions in a tight black sweater embroidered with the

Bunny logo, a white cheerleader's skirt, and black high-heeled shoes. Anyone who bought a lifetime subscription to the magazine for $150 was rewarded with a personal phone call from Janet Pilgrim, who congratulated him on his wisdom and good taste. Her affair with Hefner was as brief as her renown: he was soon directing his attention toward another Playmate, eighteen-year-old Joyce Nizzari, a beautiful dark-eyed model from Florida. Janet Pilgrim left Chicago in 1958 and moved to Texas, where she married a rather more conventional businessman and settled down to raise children.

The success of her personal appearances prompted Playboy to set up a neat little sideline in hiring out Playmates at $50 a day ("The presence of a Playmate guarantees a smash event"). The girls were required to sign a contract agreeing to keep their physical appearance and personal conduct "beyond reproach." Playboy's celebrated concern for the status of women may be perceived in Clause Five of the contract: "In the event that the Playmate permits neglectful changes in her physical appearance such as excessive loss or addition of weight, or any other physical change that detracts from her attractiveness, so that her promotional value is impaired, *Playboy* magazine reserves the right to terminate this contract."

As the circulation of *Playboy* edged toward that of *Esquire*—in January 1957, *Playboy* sold 687,593 copies compared to *Esquire's* 778,190—Hefner liked to take little digs at his former employer. He posed for a spread of photographic cartoons, one of which showed him sitting at a desk saying: "I'm truly sorry, Mr. Smart [then publisher of *Esquire*], but at present our staff is at full capacity. Leave your name with the office boy and I'll call if something comes up."

Esquire responded to the competition offered by *Playboy* and its host of second-rate imitators—*Dude, Gent, Cavalier,* and the like—by getting rid of its own centerfold. The famous air-brushed pin-ups drawn by George Petty and Alberto Vargas for *Esquire* had been given greater prominence during World War II so that the magazine could qualify for a bigger paper allocation by claiming it boosted G.I. morale and contributed to the war effort.

Founding editor Arnold Gingrich, who had recruited Ernest Hemingway, Dashiell Hammett, and many other great names as contributors to *Esquire*, believed that the magazine sacrificed its original tone and sophistication when it looked for a broader audience. He certainly did not want to compete in the skin-book market and decided to distance *Esquire* from that market by throwing out the girls and relying on the magazine's literary quality to maintain its circulation. By 1959, *Playboy* had overtaken *Esquire*.

Clay Felker, then newly hired as an editor, explained laconically: "*Playboy* out-titted us."

3

What Does It Feel Like, Being a Living Legend?

Only one member of the staff of *Playboy* magazine in the fifties could legitimately claim to be a playboy and it was not Hefner. It was the magazine's promotion director, Victor A. Lownes III. Tall, handsome, debonair, independently wealthy, and a conspicuous philanderer, Lownes actually lived the good life espoused by *Playboy*. He loved parties, girls, and sex and was never happier than when enjoying all three simultaneously. He was the personification of *Playboy*'s mythical reader and he was later to occupy in the organization a position of importance second only to that of Hefner.

Two years younger than Hefner, Lownes grew up in Florida in a large house with servants, a cook, and a seventeen-year-old nursemaid to look after his kid brother, Tom. It was the nursemaid, Essie Klopfer by name, who introduced young Victor to sex by describing to him the anatomical details of her tussles with men in situations of romantic ardor. Victor, going on ten, exhibited a precocious interest that would never wane.

When he was twelve, his father, a building contractor, attempted to warn the boy of the dangers of smoking by offering him a cigar and insisting he smoke it to the end, presumably in the hope that he would be sick. Victor smoked it right through and asked for another. Not long afterward, fooling around with a .22 rifle prior to a schoolboy hunting expedition in the Everglades, Lownes shot and killed a friend of his own age. It was a tragic accident: the other boy was on Victor's bicycle, Victor pointed the borrowed rifle at him, not knowing it was loaded, and said: "If you don't get off this minute you're a dead man." He squeezed the trigger and there was an explosion.

After this incident, Mr. and Mrs. Lownes decided their son would benefit from being sent away from home and they enrolled him as a cadet at the New Mexico Military Institute, where an unforgiving code of discipline was rigidly applied. Victor endured it, greatly sustained by the kindred spirit he had discovered in his roommate—Nicky Hilton, son of the hotel tycoon. Nicky would return from weekends spent at the El Paso Hilton, not too far distant, with a chinking bagful of miniature bottles of tequila.

In 1944, Victor engineered a premature departure from the military academy by enrolling at the University of Chicago, which he discovered would accept students before they had finished high school. At the university jazz club, he met Judy Downs, the campus beauty, president of her sorority, and the daughter of a wealthy cattle rancher from Arkansas. They married in the university chapel on her twentieth birthday in September 1946. Victor was eighteen years old. Judy's parents gave him a new De Soto automobile as a wedding present and paid for a house to be built for them in the prestigious suburb of Evanston, on the lake shore just north of Chicago.

After completing his B.A., Victor signed on for a master's degree at the School of Business, but became increasingly weary of academic life and never bothered to take the finals. In his spare time, he took on occasional promotional work, more for fun than for money; at one point he was the classified advertising manager for *Dog World* magazine. His first full-time job was with the Silent Watchman Corporation, which manufactured industrial time locks. "I was promoted to manager of the branch office within a few months," he liked to say, "due solely to hard work, conscientiousness, and the fact that my grandfather owned the company."

By the early fifties, Lownes felt himself trapped by marriage and green-lawn suburbia. He had everything a man could want—

a beautiful, loving wife, two fine children, a magnificent home, and a good job. The problem was, he was bored beyond belief. He hated the tennis club, the endless round of cocktail parties and barbecues, the small talk, and the smug respectability of the middle-class American dream. Extramarital sex, he ruefully reflected, represented his only prospect of excitement. One day in 1953, he simply walked out and never returned.

Victor went to look for the kind of life Hugh Hefner would fantasize about in the magazine he was at that moment preparing for publication. After staying in a small hotel for a couple of months, he found a perfect bachelor pad on North Wells Street— an old coach house largely comprising one enormous room, ideal for parties. The bedroom was a curtained recess in one wall. "It was an ideal arrangement," Victor noted. "Many of the girls I was consoling myself with seemed to think so, too."

Gatherings at North Wells Street were noisy, crowded, and frequent, since Victor was anxious to make up for the fun he had missed, or thought he had missed, while he was a married man. In the spring of 1954, he threw a special party for comedian Jonathan Winters, then appearing at the Empire Room in the Palmer House Hotel in Chicago. Victor was dating one of the girls in the show, Mary Ann La Joie, and invited the entire cast along with his usual crowd of friends, one of whom asked if he could bring along the guy running that new magazine, *Playboy.*

Lownes's first impression of Hefner was that he looked like a college student. Victor had been wearing Brooks Brothers since he was sixteen years old and he was somewhat taken aback to find the publisher of an *avant garde* men's magazine wearing white socks. His assumption, uncharacteristically charitable, was that Hefner probably led such a wild social life that he did not have time to be fashion conscious. Only later did he discover that Hefner *liked* white socks and believed they were good for his feet.

Despite the white socks, the two men took to each other immediately. Victor recognized in Hefner a man with interests very close to his own and he was impressed to observe Hefner making advances to Mary Ann La Joie's roommate Shirley, even though he had brought a date along to the party. Later in the evening, they fell to talking and Victor, who was an amusing storyteller, recounted how he had organized a sell-out concert at the Blue

Angel nightclub in Chicago for Mabel Mercer, a singer he much admired. Hefner liked his enthusiasm and suggested he should write a piece about her for *Playboy*.

Thereafter, Hef and Victor could often be seen in each other's company at parties or at neighborhood bars, wherever the action was. For a while they double-dated Mary Ann La Joie and her roommate, but, as Victor so charmingly pointed out: "We would always have number-one girlfriends who would publicly be seen to be our property. Then there would be a few spares in the background."

They liked to hang out at the East Inn, a basement joint on East Superior Street, where they sometimes picked up girls. Impromptu parties frequently materialized from evenings at the East Inn: a gang of them would head over to Vic's place, bottles clanking in their pockets, and play strip poker or charades or an encounter game called "Buzz" played to the beat of Hefner's bongo drums. Dawn would usually find three or four couples still smooching to Ella Fitzgerald, and Victor entwined with a young lady behind the curtain drawn discreetly across his alcove bedroom.

When he had nothing better to do, Victor loitered around the *Playboy* offices, waiting for Hefner to finish work so they could go out to play. Being Victor, he liked to know what was going on, liked to be involved, and he was soon putting forward ideas for promoting the magazine. As a university student, he had worked for a while as campus representative for Chesterfield cigarettes and he suggested recruiting campus reps for *Playboy*, offering free subscriptions instead of commissions. Hefner thought it was a terrific idea, particularly since the volume of mail pouring into *Playboy* attested to the magazine's popularity on campuses across America. ("The whole gang thinks your colored sections are really *gone*—mad *and* cool.") An advertisement in the magazine at the beginning of the school year prompted hundreds of replies and *Playboy* representatives could soon be found on more than three hundred campuses.

In November 1955, Hefner asked his friend to join the magazine full time as its promotion director. Victor became the walking, talking personification of the Playboy image, promoting the magazine on the advertising luncheon circuit, dreaming up wild and wonderful stunts, traveling everywhere with pretty girls at his side. His natural flair for promotion perfectly complemented Hefner's editorial talent. Hefner, who was uncomfortable with strangers and did not like to leave his office during the day, was much influenced by his promotion director. It was noted that soon after Victor's arrival Hef abandoned his white socks, zoot suits, and penny loafers in favor of an Ivy League look more in keeping with a successful young publisher. Wherever Victor sat "became head of the table," and it was said that when Victor started talking, Hefner "saw everything in technicolor." Certainly Victor was the more flamboyant and extrovert of the two, but he never challenged Hefner's authority, and whereas his demeanor was commonly domineering and arrogant, he would often appear subservient in Hefner's presence.

Lownes's first important contribution to the magazine was to open the advertising floodgates. To begin with, *Playboy* had not been considered a suitable marketplace by major advertising agencies and their clients; there was real concern that products would be irreparably tainted by appearing in such a publication. As Hefner adamantly refused to accept the kind of advertising that was available—of the "Doctor Marvel's Patent Hair Restorer" variety—the first editions of *Playboy* survived on the cover price alone. Lownes got out and about among the agencies and soon broke down resistance, first bringing in the menswear market. Response to the first full-page advertisements ($650 for black and white, $1,075 for four-color) was so phenomenal that other advertisers came in a rush. "I had a closet full of ten-foot poles," said Lownes, "from advertisers who said they would never touch *Playboy* with a ten-foot pole."

To further improve the magazine's reputation with advertisers and readers alike, Hefner wrote a subscription pitch in the April 1956 issue that attempted to put to rest the notion that playboys were faintly disreputable.

What is a playboy? Is he simply a wastrel, a ne'er-do-well, a fashionable bum? Far from it. He can be a sharp-minded young business executive, a worker in the arts, a university professor, an architect or an engineer. He can be many things, provided he possesses a certain point of view. He must see life not as a vale of tears, but as a happy time, he must take joy in his work, without regarding it as the end of all living; he must be an alert man, an aware man, a man of taste, a man sensitive to pleasure, a man who—without acquiring the stigma of voluptuary or dilettante—can live life to the hilt. This is the sort of man we mean when we use the word playboy. Does the description fit you? If so, we imagine you will agree that *Playboy* belongs in your life. And we suggest you enter your subscription at the first opportunity.

Hefner's anxiety to create the right image for *Playboy* certainly influenced his choice when he wanted to appoint an editorial director to take over the day-to-day running of the magazine: he chose Auguste Comte Spectorsky, an East Coast sophisticate, former editor of *Park East*, and author of three books, among them *The Exurbanites*, a best-selling study of changing social patterns in the early fifties. Spectorsky, born in Paris and named after the nineteenth-century French positivist philosopher who added the word "sociology" to the language, was just the man to bring a touch of class and New York urbanity to *Playboy*.

Enshrined in corporate legend is a story of how Hefner telephoned Spectorsky in New York, where he was working as a senior editor for WNBC-TV, and conducted the following conversation:

"My name is Hugh Hefner. Have you ever heard of me?"

"No."

"Have you ever heard of *Playboy* magazine?"

"No."

"Well, may I ask you another question? Are you irrevocably wedded to television?"

"I'm not irrevocably wedded to anything."

"Good. I'll be in New York tomorrow to see you."

It is just possible that Spectorsky had never heard of Hefner, but unlikely that he had never heard of *Playboy*. He was, after all, savvy to what was going on in the publishing world and by then, the year was 1956, everyone in publishing had registered the arrival of *Playboy*. However the contact was made, he certainly thought long and hard about Hefner's offer of a job, not so much because it was with *Playboy* magazine but because it would mean leaving

New York and moving to Chicago. To someone like Spectorsky, there was nothing in the Midwest but prairie. A starting salary of $750 a week, stock options, and a large expense account, plus a job for the lady he was intending to make his fourth wife, helped him to overcome his reservations.

Spectorsky made an inauspicious start in his new job by telling Hefner that the first thing he had to do was change the name of the magazine. You will never get top writers to work for a magazine with a name like *Playboy*, he said. He suggested *Smart Set* would be more appropriate. Hefner was appalled, but not wishing to alienate his new executive, he sidestepped the idea, mumbling something about "evolution not revolution." Spectorsky never mentioned it again.

It was likely that Spectorsky wanted to change the title for reasons of his own: he was the kind of man who would have been happier working for a magazine called *Smart Set* than one called *Playboy*. Certainly no one believed that top writers were deterred by the title: all they wanted was money, as Spectorsky knew. By paying more than any other magazine—he began offering fees of up to $2,000 for a short story that would fetch no more than $400 in *Esquire*—Spectorsky rapidly upgraded the fiction in *Playboy*, bringing in names like Vladimir Nabokov, James Baldwin, John Steinbeck, Kenneth Tynan, and Nelson Algren, and investing the magazine with the class and sophistication Hefner so earnestly desired. For a Ray Bradbury story about a man obsessed with Picasso, published in 1957, the magazine used Picasso as an illustrator, jauntily describing him in the contents as "Mr. Double-P himself" and neglecting to obtain his permission. In conjunction with the Bradbury opus, readers were advised, "You'll find some piquant Picassos."

Alliteration was the bane of *Playboy*'s editorial style. While Spectorsky was struggling to establish the magazine's literary reputation, regular contributors were capable of producing the most dire prose. Thomas Mario, the food and drink editor, was acknowledged master of alliteration guaranteed to make the least sensitive reader cringe. Writing on the subject of clams, he was moved to describe that "mischievous mollusc's piquant personality." Then there was a "bracing batch of tinkly, tasty, frosty coolers, cunningly concocted for the exclusive dogday delight of

Playboy readers and their fetching friends." And a "paean of praise to a luscious lily" introduced a piece about *onions*.

Mr. Mario had been the headwaiter at a men's club on Long Island and was appointed an editor after contributing a feature in 1954 entitled "An Oyster Stew for a Quartette of Playboys." If the alarm bells rang about the "quartette," they were ignored. Apart from alliteration, Mr. Mario's other talent was the use of the ponderous pun, employed with an awful inevitability. "Of all feasts," he wrote, "a casserole is the most moveable."

The fashion editor, Blake Rutherford, was slightly more restrained, although he was perfectly capable of bemoaning the "gruesome garbage" worn to the beach by so many otherwise "right-thinking guys." For the beach it had to be India Madras swim trunks with a fly front, and *never* those terrible "balloon-bottomed boxer shorts."

"Blake Rutherford" was Jack Kessie, a graduate of Drake University in Des Moines who had contributed a free-lance piece in January 1955 and was hired as an associate editor at $100 a week, partly because Hefner liked the way he looked. He had a kind of casual elegance that Hefner thought exemplified the *Playboy* style.

There was nothing casual about Blake Rutherford's advice, which was directed exclusively at the mythical man-about-town reader and could be positively dictatorial in tone. In a feature on evening clothes under the headline "The Return to Black," he lectured sternly: "Now we said black, not midnight blue, not maroon, not burnt ochre. Just black. Black looks and feels right, so leave your rainbow-hued jackets to the funny-type entertainers on TV."

For yachting, Mr. Rutherford recommended light slacks tough enough to offer protection from sun and spray, marine-blue sweat-shirts, and zip-up jackets. And for cocktails in the yacht club later "you'll want to change—well, naturally—into a navy-blue blazer with brass buttons and white or gray slacks." The more adventurous yachtsmen could sport "regatta-stripe" slacks without risking Blake Rutherford's disapproval.

Blake Rutherford naturally assumed his readers owned yachts, didn't everyone? Sitting out there in middle America, the readers of *Playboy* loved it.

In 1956, Hefner won his first important battle against a powerful guardian of public morality—the U.S. Post Office. Most magazines in the United States were allowed to mail subscription copies at second-class postage rates. Hefner applied for the mailing privilege as early as October of 1954, confident that *Playboy* fulfilled the requirements of the U.S. Postal Act: namely, that it was published regularly, had a paid-up subscription list, and contained more editorial than advertising pages. He reckoned without the intervention of Arthur Summerfield, President Eisenhower's Postmaster General.

Summerfield was a man of unyielding moral convictions who had frequently declared his determination to keep "obscene material" out of the U.S. mail. He viewed the proliferation of magazines like *Playboy* with the greatest possible distaste.

The Post Office normally took between four and six weeks to issue a second-class permit. Hefner heard nothing for six months. Every time he inquired about the progress of his application, he was fobbed off with an assurance that it was being processed, but there was some kind of delay "in Washington." Meanwhile, hundreds of new subscriptions were pouring in every day, more than the magazine's small staff could handle. At times it appeared that *Playboy*'s success would overwhelm the business and in March 1955, the pressures became so great that Hefner was forced to skip an issue. An editorial in the April edition apologized and promised readers an extra issue toward the end of the year.

Summerfield acted swiftly. An adjudication from the U.S. Post Office was issued within days of the April edition appearing on the streets. *Playboy*'s application was refused, since second-class mailing privileges could only be granted to magazines published "regularly." Having missed an issue, *Playboy* demonstrably could not meet that criterion.

Hefner knew precisely what was going on. He had also become aware of other problems with Postmaster General Summerfield's minions. In some parts of the country, particularly the Bible Belt in the South, the magazine was not getting through to subscribers, presumably because local postmasters were deciding on their own initiative it was not fit to be delivered. And in Chicago, incoming mail addressed to *Playboy* at East Superior Street was deliberately delayed, sometimes for weeks. Hefner was hardly surprised: in a predominantly Irish Catholic city like Chicago, which had recently elected Richard Daley as mayor, he did not expect his magazine to be too popular.

He kept quiet for the time being, tried another application and waited three months for a reply. This time, the application was refused because of the magazine's "editorial content." Details of the objection were not at first stated, but since publications like *Modern Sunbathing* had enjoyed second-class mailing privileges for years while publishing nude pictures much more explicit than those that appeared in *Playboy*, Hefner assumed the problem did not lie with the Playmate. This assumption was confirmed when Post Office officials blithely put forward their proposals for the changes that would be required for the editorial content to be "approved." Essentially, *Playboy* was to stop advocating the heinous and sinful notion that sex was a recreational activity to be enjoyed.

Hefner was indignant. "We don't think Postmaster General Summerfield has any business editing magazines," he declared. "We think he should stick to delivering mail." With this, *Playboy* went to court, objecting not only to the refusal of its application for a second-class permit but also to the unjustified interference with its mail. In November 1955, the magazine won on all counts. A judge instructed the Post Office to grant temporary second-class privileges to *Playboy* and ordered the magazine's incoming and outgoing mail to be delivered without delay. Six months later, the temporary permit was confirmed and the magazine was refunded $100,000 as compensation for the delay. "Henceforth," Hefner crowed, "*Playboy* will be edited in Chicago, not Washington."

It was a good moment to win such a victory and be thus thinly legitimized, for it must have seemed to much of America that the very fabric of society was under attack. The newspapers were full of stories about young people ripping movie seats from their mountings during the movie *Blackboard Jungle*, which featured a song called *Rock Around the Clock* by Bill Haley and His Comets. And a former truck driver from Tupelo, Mississippi, with long sideburns, a greased duck-tail hairstyle, and a defiantly curled upper lip promised unimaginable horrors to come. To many

Americans, Elvis Presley was an abomination. One churchman described him as a "whirling dervish of sex." No one had ever seen a singer bump and grind on stage as if, as if . . . well, a district attorney summed up the feelings of many perturbed parents by describing his act as "obscenely suggestive." His swiveling hips were clear evidence to decent folk that the sexual revolution, whatever *that* was, had gone too far.

Following hard on the anarchic thump of rock music came the Beat movement, launched by Jack Kerouac's odyssey, *On the Road.* The beatniks, with their beards and sandals and dirty feet, mystified middle America as much by their rejection of the consumer society as by their appearance. What could be more bewildering than to discover a generation of young people who not only experimented with drugs, but cared nothing for material possessions, were devoid of ambition, and casual about sex? Beatniks (did not their very name have a suspicious Commie ring?) threatened to turn society upside down by searching for "kicks" rather than the better-job, bigger-car materialism of the American dream.

Compared to these unwashed freaks, *Playboy*'s go-getter, button-down, man-in-a-Hathaway-shirt-with-eyepatch snob appeal was positively welcome. Well, at least it was normal *and American.*

It might have seemed to Hefner, by 1957, that he could do no wrong. Flushed by the success of *Playboy* and his victory over the Post Office, he pressed ahead with plans to launch a second magazine, *Trump.* It was to be a slick, full-color, humor magazine, something like a more sophisticated *Mad*, and he hired Harvey Kurtzman, one of the founders of *Mad*, as editor.

Trump appeared on the newsstands in January 1957, and immediately ran into trouble when the distributor, American News Company, went bust. A second issue could not be published until March, by which time *Trump* had run up debts of $95,000.

The timing could not have been worse. Playboy was in the process of an expensive move into new offices at 232 East Ohio Street, having long since outgrown the townhouse on East Superior. Advertising and sales figures suddenly dipped as the result of a brief recession and the American National Bank and Trust Company of Chicago, concerned that Playboy was overextended, refused to renew the company's lines of credit.

Hefner had no alternative but to strangle *Trump*, virtually at birth. To absorb the losses he stopped drawing a salary for a while, asked his senior executives to take a pay cut, and put up 25 percent of the company's stock as collateral for a short-term loan of a quarter of a million dollars.

When the crisis passed, Hefner hired an accountant friend, Bob Preuss, as business manager. Preuss had shared a room with Hefner at the University of Illinois and inevitably they had become friends, although they were very different characters. After graduation, Preuss set up as a certified public accountant, married, and settled down with his family. Quiet and softly spoken, he found Playboy in a state of some chaos when he arrived as business manager:

There was no financial planning because there was not enough money for that. The big decision was which bills do I pay today? The problem was that the company was growing like mad and was always short of cash because you had to pay for more magazines before you had collected from the previous one.

It was hectic and fun in those days. Everyone was young, ambitious and overworked. Meetings with Hefner would sometimes go on all night, but no one ever complained. The atmosphere was very informal and friendly and you were aware that it was an exciting place to work.

Playboy's new offices on East Ohio Street were in a squat red brick building with four floors, between Michigan Avenue and the lake. It was an unprepossessing headquarters, chiefly re-markable for an elevator of such sluggishness that Victor Lownes could frequently be found kicking it in a rage. Hefner had a pleas-ant apartment, which also served as his office, on the top floor, furnished in typical *Playboy* style: the living room featured an "electronic entertainment wall" straight from the pages of the magazine.

Around this time, *Playboy* began assiduously promoting an image of its editor unrecognizable to his colleagues. "We'd like you to meet Editor-Publisher Hugh M. Hefner," the June 1957 issue declared, "the man responsible for the pulse, the personality and the very existence of this magazine. The lean, restless young fellow who presides over *Playboy* is something of a phenomenon in the publishing world. . . ."

In the accompanying photograph, the lean young man, crew-cut Mr. Cool in a dark suit, button-down shirt, and striped tie, could be seen standing at the bottom of the stairs in the lobby at 232 East Ohio, one hand on the banister, the other casually shoved into a trouser pocket. A smiling blonde, waiting at the elevator, looks admiringly in his direction.

". . . His dress is conservative and casual. He always wears loafers. There is an electronic entertainment wall in his office. Brubeck, Kenton or Sinatra is usually on the turntable when Hefner is working. He likes jazz, foreign films, Ivy League clothes, gin and tonic and pretty girls—the same sort of thing *Playboy* readers like—and his approach to life is as fresh, sophisticated and yet admittedly sentimental as is the magazine."

If this was Hefner, who was that gaunt, unshaven guy with tousled hair, padding about the office in crumpled pajamas, swilling Pepsis, and working all night? "Walking about in pajamas and no shoes," said picture editor Will Hopkins, "he always reminded me of a guy who'd just had an appendectomy."

One advantage of the new office building was that it had a side entrance and back stairs, so that girls could slip in and out of Hefner's quarters more or less unobserved. Legions of young ladies, quivering with anticipation, trod those well-worn stairs. There were secretaries and receptionists from the magazine, dancers from the Chez Paree nightclub around the corner, girls he met at parties with Victor Lownes, girls introduced by photographers, and, of course, many Playmates.

When tiny stars appeared on the front cover of the magazine, a rumor took hold that they indicated Hefner's rating of the Playmate's performance as a lover. They *actually* indicated the regional edition, but who, at Playboy, would want to deny a useful rumor?

Obsessively concerned with chronicling his own career, Hefner secretly started a logbook in which he recorded the details of every girl to whom he had made love—date, name, place, position, and so forth. Under the general comments column, he would make little notations like "Good at BJ's," meaning blow jobs. (Years later, when a secretary in the Playboy Mansion discovered where Hefner kept the blue-bound book, then somewhat dog-eared, it provided the staff with hours of covert amusement.)

By this time, Hefner no longer maintained any pretense that his marriage was extant. He could not conceal the fact that his first love was his magazine and from 1954 onward he had made only rare visits home to Millie. A second child, David, was born in August 1955, and for a while Hefner made an attempt to make the marriage work. He bought a luxury apartment for them on North Sheridan Road, overlooking the lake, but he could no more stay at home and be a good husband than he could stop himself lusting after every new Playmate. Within a matter of months, he was back in his apartment at the office.

"My life with Millie has been a rocky one for more than three years," he noted in his scrapbook in the summer of 1957, "and we've been partially separated for much of that time. This month we made it official. The reasons for the failure of our marriage are multiple and it is hard to place the blame, but in the end, she has suffered the most from it, for I have the magazine to keep me going."

They divorced, amicably, in April 1959. Hefner was glad to be free. With the *Trump* crisis far behind him and *Playboy* magazine making bundles of money (sales in 1958 produced $4,200,000), he was ready for conquests of a more demanding nature than the next Playmate. In August, Playboy promoted a brilliantly successful jazz festival at the Chicago Stadium, attracting capacity crowds for each of five performances, featuring artists like Louis Armstrong, Duke Ellington, Count Basie, Dizzie Gillespie, Ella Fitzgerald, and Peggy Lee.

The event nearly did not happen. Playboy was at first given permission by city officials to stage the festival at Soldier Field, a huge arena on the lake shore close to the city center. It was a cozy arrangement: the jazz festival would form part of the Festival of Americas, which was being sponsored that summer by the city of Chicago. Victor Lownes, who was running the show, began signing bands to appear and had committed more than $100,000 of Playboy's money when the dumbfounding news came through that permission to use Soldier Field had been summarily withdrawn.

Neither Hefner nor Lownes believed the city's lame explanation that the crowds might damage the cinder track, and their skepticism was entirely justified. Roman Catholic church leaders did not want a magazine like *Playboy* associated with the Festival of Americas. The Very Reverend Monsignor John M. Kelly, editor of the Catholic *New World*, quietly contacted park officials, Mayor Daley, and members of the festival organizing committee and drew their attention to the magazine's reputation. None of these worthies needed much persuading that Playboy was not a suitable sponsor for an event in the festival.

Hefner, bitterly suspicious of the truth, resolved that the Playboy Jazz Festival *would* take place, inside or outside the Festival of Americas, with or without the help of the city bureaucracy. Lownes was sent to scout for alternative venues: he was turned down by the owners of the Stockyards Arena, but secured the Chicago Stadium, which was smaller and more expensive than Soldier Field but still acceptable.

Extensively advertised as "the biggest jazz Festival in the world" (Victor was not given to modesty), it was held over a long weekend, attracted more than 60,000 fans, and was adjudged, by Victor at least, to be "an enormous triumph." Playboy lost $40,000, but gained a great deal of publicity, most of it favorable. Hefner donated the first day's takings to the Urban League, a gesture he fervently hoped was not lost on his enemies.

Just two months later, Hefner made his debut as a television celebrity on a Chicago station, WBKB. Wearing a tuxedo and gripping a pipe with white knuckles, he gamely faced the camera and intoned: "Good evening. I'm Hugh Hefner. Welcome to the party." Then he stuck the tobaccoless pipe in his mouth, sucked furiously, and smiled, as if he was having a wonderful time.

"Playboy's Penthouse" (a title that would cause some anguish in the years to come) was the brainchild of two independent television producers in Chicago, who approached Hefner with the idea of presenting the Playboy lifestyle on television. They had it all worked out: the setting would be a bachelor pad, "the kind of paradise high above a city every guy is looking for," and the show would be a swinging party, with lots of pretty girls and show business celebrities casually dropping by to entertain. The names of Louis Jourdan or Mort Sahl were mentioned for the role of host, who would act as if the party was taking place in his own penthouse.

Hefner liked the idea a lot, with one small exception. If it was going to be presented as a Playboy party, then clearly only one man could be considered to play host—himself. He stubbornly refused to listen to the argument that the role needed a professional actor with television experience. No, if there was going to be a show, it was going to be Hefner's show.

During rehearsals, Hefner was so awkward and nervous that someone suggested he hold a pipe so he would have something to do with his hands. Later it was agreed he should put tobacco in it to reduce the strange wheezing noise it made when he sucked on it. Later still, in the interests of television verisimilitude, Hefner actually *lit* the pipe—and became an addicted pipe-smoker.

The first show went on the air, in black and white, on October 24, 1959. Hefner had some impressive guests to welcome to the party, among them Ella Fitzgerald and Nat King Cole, but he also invited Spectorsky along for moral support. It was a mistake. Spectorsky had worked in television in New York and was a witty and sophisticated *bon vivant*. He shamelessly upstaged Hefner, whose nervousness was all too apparent. By the end of the show, it was Spectorsky who was remembered as Mr. Playboy, whereas Hefner, according to one unkind crack, "looked like a guy who had borrowed his uncle's apartment for the weekend."

Spectorsky was not invited to appear on the show again, although his absence did not help much: Hefner's performance remained resolutely wooden throughout the series. "Playboy's Penthouse" ran for twenty-six weeks, but was never taken up by a network, although it was syndicated to a few individual television stations around America. None of the stations in the South would consider it, because of Hefner's insistence on socializing with black entertainers.

Toward the end of 1959, an enterprising realtor contacted Bob Preuss at Playboy to inquire if Mr. Hefner might be interested in purchasing a rather unique property that was shortly to come on the market. It was nicely timed. Hefner had been planning to build the ultimate Playboy townhouse on a narrow site between fashionable brownstones in Bellevue Place, on the Near North Side, but he had just been told that the design—a striking multi-level structure around an indoor swimming pool—would be prohibitively expensive to build, even for Playboy.

Preuss, the dutiful lieutenant, agreed to look at what the realtor had to offer, 1340 North State Street Parkway, and came back with his eyeballs swiveling. Lownes went to have a look and rushed back to Hefner to tell him he *had* to see it. Hefner went and decided instantly he wanted it. "I had no idea," he said, "that a house of that scale and grandeur existed in Chicago."

The purchase price was $370,000. Playboy paid cash and immediately invested a further $400,000 on vital improvements necessary to make the house worthy of the name that Hefner had already chosen: the Playboy Mansion. Most of the money went into converting the six-car garage into a swimming pool. Hefner could not swim, but this did not appear to matter. (More than $3 million would eventually be spent on improvements to the Mansion, not counting the $550,000 it cost to buy the house next door in 1970.)

The Playboy Mansion was the house of Hefner's dreams, yet there were times when he could hardly believe his dreams were coming true. Shortly after taking up residence at 1340 North State Street Parkway, he made a note in his scrapbook in the breathless, gee-whiz, student idiom that he still employed, even though he was by then in his mid-thirties. "It's difficult to bring into perspective and fully appreciate, but we are truly becoming, in our own time, a legend. And what does it feel like, being a living legend? Well, it feels just great!"

There was, perhaps, one element missing in the Playboy Mansion when Hefner moved in. There were no girls. It was a deficiency that would very soon be made good, for the Bunny was about to be invented.

4

"Always Remember, Your Proudest Possession Is Your Bunny Tail"

Most nights, the lights burned late on the top floor at 232 East Ohio Street; sometimes it was one o'clock in the morning before Hefner reluctantly dictated his last memo and acceded to Lownes's urgent pleadings that they should hit town. There was plenty of time in the wheezing elevator to discuss where to go, but it was not unusual for them to be still undecided when Hefner started the engine of his new silver Mercedes 300SL, which he parked in a garage across the street and which he had bought to replace the bronze Cadillac—considering its rakish streamlining to be more in keeping with the Playboy image.

Chicago in the early hours of the morning did not offer limitless entertainment for a couple of swingers. Many of the neighborhood bars had the look of a lonely Hopper cityscape, with an all-night drunk clinging blearily to a stool at one end of the bar, and a bored bartender polishing glasses at the other. The clip-joints on Rush Street, the "glitter gulch" where B-girls entertained roistering businessmen visiting the city for conventions, were jumping until around four, but they held no attraction for the likes of Victor A. Lownes III and his friend, Hef. Normally they would end up in an all-too-familiar spot—either the East Inn, the Chez Paree, the Black Orchid, or the Cloisters—and bemoan the fact that there was not a better place to be. Once in a while they would talk idly about starting a club of their own, the kind of place where they could hang out with their friends in an atmosphere that was relaxed, intimate, and sophisticated. Yes, relaxed and sophisticated, that was very much how they saw themselves.

Perhaps nothing would have come of the idea had not *Playboy* published a story, in 1959, about the new "Gaslight" key clubs, which featured buxom cocktail waitresses laced into saucy costumes said to be inspired by the gay nineties. More than three thousand readers wrote in to ask how they could join a Gaslight club. Lownes was astonished by the response and suggested to Hefner that they should think of doing something similar themselves. If there were three thousand *Playboy* readers interested in joining a Gaslight club, how many thousands would join a Playboy club? The magazine could be used to promote the club and the club could be used to promote the magazine. Beautiful!

"Show business was in my blood," said Lownes, recalling this historic moment. "I could see the Club in my mind, even as I said it: gorgeous girls, eye-pleasing ambiance. Everything suggested to me that the Playboy Club idea could be a winner." Hefner agreed. Victor, of course, knew just the guy to help get them started—his friend Arnie Morton, who managed a club called Walton Walk where Victor occasionally dined. Arnie was the son of a well-known Chicago restaurateur and grew up in the food and entertainment business; his father, Morton C. Morton, was famous as the inventor of the "Mortoni" cocktail, a lethal mixture of gin, vermouth, and a peeled Bermuda onion. By happy chance, Arnie was looking for a new opportunity when Victor sounded him out on the idea of a Playboy club and he volunteered his services in return for a percentage. A deal was struck under which 50 percent of the stock in a new company, Playboy Clubs, International, was held by H.M.H. Publishing, and Hefner, Morton, and Lownes split the remainder.

As it was a Playboy venture, all three partners were sensible of the first decision to be made: the club would have glamorous waitresses, certainly, but what should they *wear?* Hefner was strongly in favor of short, frilly nighties and calling the girls Playmates, bolstering an illusion that they had stepped from the magazine's center pages; Lownes and Morton were not convinced. Also present at this epoch-making discussion was a girlfriend of Lownes, a beautiful Latvian refugee by the name of Ilse Taurins. It was she who shyly suggested dressing the waitresses like the Playboy rabbit logo. Hefner said he had already considered that idea, but there was a fundamental problem—the Playboy logo was, very definitely, a *male* rabbit. It seemed like an impasse, but Ilse said her mother was a seamstress and she could probably persuade her to run up a prototype *female* rabbit costume, if the men were interested. They were.

A few days later, Ilse could be found standing in the center of the ballroom at the Playboy Mansion wearing a kind of satin corset with a fluffy ball pinned to her backside and a curious pair of ears attached to her head, while Hefner, Lownes, and Morton circled around examining her from all angles. Victor was frankly disappointed: "It was a letdown. It looked more like a bathing costume with ears than an attractive garment for a cocktail waitress. I thought Hefner would throw it out." But Hefner thought it had possibilities—he particularly liked the tail. How would it be, he wondered aloud, if the girl did not have long enough legs to show the outfit off to advantage. He asked Ilse to yank up the sides of the costume to expose her upper thighs. Ilse obliged and all three men agreed the effect was dramatic. Then Hefner suggested the addition of collar and cuffs, to further dispel the bathing suit image, and a little dickie bow to match the one on the Playboy logo. By the end of the day, the Bunny had been born.

On January 4, 1960, an advertisement appeared in the *Chicago Tribune* offering "great opportunities for the thirty most beautiful girls in Chicagoland" to earn in excess of $250 a week in a new key club catering to Chicago's most prominent executives and sportsmen. "To serve our exclusive clientele and decorate the club, we are looking for thirty single girls between 18 and 25. Experience is not necessary. Just be beautiful, charming and refined." Applicants were invited to the Playboy Building at 232 East Ohio between noon and five-thirty P.M. on the following Saturday.

More than four hundred girls turned up and paraded in bathing suits through the magazine's photographic studio, displaying their charms against a blue paper backdrop. "Most of them were awful," said Lownes, who prided himself on having very high standards. But thirty girls were eventually selected and Morton took over their training.

Lownes found premises for the club through Arthur Wirtz, owner of the Chicago Stadium. Wirtz, a canny Chicago property developer, had been impressed by Playboy's ability to fill the stadium for the jazz festival (no one had ever done it before in midsummer) and when he heard Playboy was planning to open a club, he offered Lownes the Colony Club, a property he owned on East Walton Street. Wirtz suggested a price of $100,000, but Lownes quickly discovered the Colony had failed under four successive managements and was unenthusiastic until Wirtz made a new offer: Playboy could have the building at a very low rent, plus a percentage of the profits, if any. Lownes thought it was a terrific deal, since it minimized Playboy's risk; later he would discover that Playboy paid more in rent during the first two years than it would have cost to buy the building.

Battalions of builders and decorators with ladders and pots of paint moved into 116 East Walton Street to transform the Colony into the Playboy Club and bring into being the lifestyle promoted by *Playboy* magazine. Each of four floors was designed as a "room" in a mythical and fabulous bachelor pad—there was a Playroom, a Penthouse, a Library, and a Living Room. Teak and leather furniture, wood-paneled walls and rich, autumnal shades prevailed in the decor. *Playboy* magazine was in evidence everywhere— from framed original cartoons in the "cartoon corner" of the Living Room, to huge, back-lit pictures of Playmates in the Playmate Bar.

Morton, to whom both Lownes and Hefner deferred on practical matters, suggested that the club should serve the kind of simple meal—like a steak and a salad—that a playboy might feel able to prepare for a girl without his masculinity being threatened. They would offer a strictly limited selection of entrées—no soups or hors d'oeuvres or fancy desserts—and standardize all the prices. Everything, a drink, a steak, a pack of cigarettes (with an obligatory Playboy lighter), would cost $1.50.

The price of a "key" to the club was fixed at $50 for residents of Chicago and $25 for out-of-towners. First advertisements produced a gratifying response and *Playboy* magazine allocated considerable space to inform its readers that they would soon be doubly blessed—with a magazine and a *club* of their own. What could be cozier?

When the Playboy Club opened its doors for the first time on February 29, 1960, there was a line outside that straggled right around the block, heedless of the bitter cold and Chicago's famous wind blowing off Lake Michigan. Inside, every room was noisy and crowded and the "thirty most beautiful girls in Chicagoland," who had been hired to "decorate" the club, were actually hefting trays of drinks and discovering the fearsome reality of being a Bunny. Hefner and Lownes and a group of friends showed up around midnight and stayed until the club closed at 4:00 A.M.

It was a wonderfully successful opening night, only marred by one small crisis. Shortly after Victor arrived he noticed that the Bunny who was serving him with a drink had *taken her ears off.* When he asked why, she told him the ears were killing her, and a lot of the other girls too. They were impossible to wear, she said. Victor looked around and realized, with mounting fury, that a number of the Bunnies were earless. Storming into the kitchen, he bellowed orders to the "room directors" that all the Bunnies must wear their ears at all times. Such mutinous behavior would never be allowed again.

There were lines outside the Playboy Club for weeks afterward. A reporter from New York compared the crowds with those that daily assembled outside Radio City Music Hall. "I can't believe it," said comedian Red Skelton after an evening jostling with the hordes inside the club. "All those guys paying for a key that gives them the privilege of buying drinks at a buck fifty a throw and gawking at some half-dressed broads."

The Bunny, it was evident, was a potent attraction, even though it was made widely known that she was unavailable for anything but the serving of cocktails. While the magazine endlessly advised its readers to get out and enjoy sex, it rigorously excluded Bunnies from the fun and games. A Bunny could not date a customer, nor could she reveal her telephone number, on pain of ignominious dismissal from the hutch. Keyholders could *look* all they liked, but touch? *Never!* Just like the Playmate, the Bunny was adored because she offered the thrill of sex without the threat of having to do anything about it.

Playboy made its "look-but-don't-touch" policy clear from the outset, as much to protect the company as to protect the girls. Hefner recognized that the faintest whiff of scandal would be valuable ammunition for his enemies and insisted on unbending standards of propriety; indeed, the protection of the Bunny's virtue was to become something of an obsession. Her working life was circumscribed by an elaborate code of ethics as stern and specific as that of a nun in a silent order. To test her fealty, private detectives were hired to try to tempt her into the commission of some misdemeanor, of which there was an astonishing variety, painstakingly chronicled in the Bunny Manual. Through all these trials she was expected to be fresh and pretty and to charm keyholders while politely removing their hands. Debbie Harry, lead singer of the rock group Blondie, worked as a Bunny for a while and said the most arduous requirement was to "keep smiling while infuriated wives stubbed out cigarettes on your thighs."

Nevertheless, those citizens with an inclination to be disgusted preferred to assume that the Playboy Club was nothing but a front for a whorehouse, that unimaginable debauchery took place behind its doors, and that those Bunny creatures, with their bosoms bulging from the tops of their disgraceful costumes, were no better than common prostitutes.

Such blue-nosed bigotry was perhaps to be expected in the year that Miss Sarah Gibson Blanding, president of Vassar College, declared in ringing tones that premarital sex was "offensive and vulgar behavior." Contraceptives were still banned by law in Connecticut. The most popular song of the year was the guileless "Itsy Bitsy Teeny Weenie Yellow Polka Dot Bikini." There was no hint of the modern apocalypse to come in the age of Aquarius, which would render the Bunny as titillating as a plastic doll.

That she became so affectionately regarded, with her risible floppy ears and tufty tail, was due in large measure to Hefner's younger brother, Keith, the Director of Bunny Training. It was Keith who refined the concept of the Bunny and somehow transformed a waitress into an enduring sex symbol of the sixties.

Keith Hefner was having something of a lean time as an actor when his brother offered him a job in 1961 as a room director in the Chicago club. Two years younger than Hugh, he had studied method acting under Lee Strasberg at the Actors' Studio in New York, but the apogee of his career to that date was the role of Johnny Jellybeans on a children's television show in Baltimore. He had little in common with his brother except a passion for girls: working closely with Bunnies suited him perfectly. In no time at all he was promoted from room director to Director of Bunny Recruitment and then, a few months later, to Director of Bunny Training.

To Keith, the nightclub business was show business and the Bunnies were the stars. He rewrote recruiting advertisements to attract the kind of girls he wanted: "ACTRESSES—MODELS—DANCERS—BE A PLAYBOY CLUB BUNNY. Here is a chance to earn $200–$300 a week in show business while waiting for the big break. . . ." Successful applicants at the "casting session" were given a leaflet entitled "What Is a Bunny?" aimed at calming any fears they might have had that they were taking a job as a waitress:

A Bunny—like the *Playboy* Playmate—is the girl next door. She is the American romanticized myth . . . beautiful, desirable, and a nice, funloving person. A Bunny is not a broad or a "hippy." She may be sexy, but it's a fresh healthy sex—not cheap or lewd. The Playboy Club is more like show business than the saloon business, and the Bunnies are the stars. We have managers for directors, bartenders for stage managers, and porters and busboys for stagehands. You—the stars—are what bring the people into the Club. You are what gives the Club its glamor and, therefore, we want to make sure that it stays legitimate glamor. We stress that Bunnies should not get too familiar with customers for just that reason. Men are very excited about being in the company of Elizabeth Taylor, but they know they can't paw or proposition her. The moment that they felt they could become familiar with her, she would not have the aura of glamor that now surrounds her. The same must be true of our Bunnies . . .

This little homily, written by Keith, did not so much gloss over duties like humping trays, as simply ignore them. It concluded, with characteristic restraint: "We'll do everything in our power to help make you—the Bunny—the most envied girl in America, working in the most exciting and glamorous setting in the world."

During training, Keith liked to stress to the girls that going out onto the floor of the club was like stepping onto a stage. "Just like the star of a Broadway show," he would say, "you have got to leave your worries and anxieties behind when you go out there. You've got to sell your personality to the audience, make them have a good time." Drawing on his training in the "method" school of acting, he advised new Bunnies to take a moment to think of something funny or happy that had happened in their lives before going out, so that they would be naturally smiling and vivacious when they stepped onto the floor. "When I walk through a room at the club," Keith warned, "I want to see four girls *bubbling* and two *pleasant*."

Bunnies had much to learn under Keith's diligent tutelage. They needed to be able to master the Bunny Dip, a curious technique of serving drinks invented by the resourceful Keith to prevent customers enjoying an uninterrupted view down a Bunny's décolletage: "A Bunny does not reach awkwardly across a table, she holds her tray away from a patron and gives graceful, stylized service by arching the back as much as possible, then bending the knees to whatever degree is necessary and raising the left heel." They had to be able to recognize 125 drinks and 29 garnishes ("Sidecar. Rim glass with lime and frost with sugar . . ."). Keith also taught them such niceties as how to light a patron's cigarette "without obstructing his view of the lady at his table."

All of this, and much more, was spelled out in the famous Bunny Manual, a forty-four-page booklet of sober instructions that defied parody. That the young ladies to whom it was addressed did not roll on the floor clutching their sides was a tribute to the success of Keith's indoctrination. "Always remember," said the Manual, "your proudest possession is your Bunny Tail. You must make sure it is white and fluffy." The wardrobe mistress had a supply of clean cottontails to replace those becoming worn or dirty.

The Manual laid down precisely what Bunnies were required to arrange on their trays before approaching a customer. "A service tray will be additionally supplied with (a) a clean bar cloth or sponge (b) a pen (c) a tip tray (d) a small flashlight (e) a fueled and flinted Playboy Lighter (f) the proper number of blank table checks (g) cocktail napkins (h) clean ashtrays (i) Playboy matches and (j) tax chart." Having assembled this formidable collection of paraphernalia, she was then to welcome the keyholder with the approved words. "*Never*," section 521 of the Manual chided, "express your request for a keyholder's order in a crude and trite phrase such as 'What'll you have?' "

Bunnies were not allowed to chew gum on duty or drink anything (not even water), except during Bunny Breaks. Bunnies were not allowed to sit down, but were required to "perch" in an approved fashion, although never too close to where a patron was seated. While perched, but *never* while standing, one Bunny at a time was allowed to smoke, providing she took a puff and then set the cigarette in an ashtray. Needless to say, Bunnies were not allowed to reveal their last names or their addresses or even the time when they finished work. Furthermore, boyfriends or husbands meeting Bunnies after work were requested to wait at least two blocks from the club (this to prevent any keyholder getting the idea that Bunnies were ever touched by male hands).

Section 523 of the Manual dealt briskly with a potentially embarrassing exception to the no-dating rule. Clearly neither Hefner nor Lownes wanted to find themselves barred from dating their own Bunnies, neither did they want the exclusion to cover close friends or celebrities or important journalists. A system was devised under which certain privileged people were given what were called No.1 Keys, which not only absolved them from having to pay for anything in the club (their bills were "absorbed"), but also enabled them to entertain Bunnies, who were not normally allowed into the club when off duty. As Section 523 briefly explained: "Employees may enter and enjoy the facilities of the Club as bona-fide guests of No.1 Keyholders."

Elsewhere, the Manual adopts a rather different attitude: "Any Bunny who arranges to meet or be met by a Keyholder, guest or employee of the Club, either on or off the Club premises, will be immediately dismissed."

Retribution awaited Bunnies who strayed from the edicts of the Manual. Every violation was awarded a number of demerits, as laid down in Section 520: a dirty cottontail would cost five demerits; chewing gum, ten demerits for the first offense, twenty for the second; messy hair, bad nails, bad make-up, five demerits each; addressing the room director by his first name, five demerits; lateness returning to duty after a break, one demerit per minute; profane language, ten demerits—the list was long and comprehensive. Any Bunny notching up one hundred demerits sealed her own fate; she was terminated.

Demerits could, of course, be wiped out by merits, which were awarded to particularly good Bunnies in accordance with the scale in the Manual. A commendation for good service, for example, was worth five merits and winning the Bunny of the Week Award (by topping the drinks average) was rewarded by twenty-five merits. Cash bonuses could also be earned with merits; otherwise Bunnies were dependent on tips, which they customarily tucked into the tops of their costumes, known in Bunnyspeak as the "vault."

Policing the merit/demerit allocation, which any British public schoolboy would instantly recognize, was the enigmatic figure of the Bunny Mother, who was presented to new Bunnies as a friend, adviser, and counselor, but whose actual function more closely resembled that of a drill sergeant.

She was supported by the endeavors of Willmark Service System, Inc., a private detective agency hired to send undercover agents into the Playboy Club, posing as keyholders, to check on the behavior of the Bunnies. They were almost always recognized by their shifty expressions and the fact that they never ordered more than two drinks—apparently the limit of their expense account.

A long memorandum from Hefner to the Willmark company made his expectations clear: "Our licenses are laid on the line any time any of our employees in any way engages, aids, or abets traffic in prostitution. . . . Use your most attractive and personable male representatives to proposition the Bunnies and even offer as high as $200 'right now' for a promise of meeting you outside the Club later. Ask a barman or any other male employee if any of the girls are available, on a cash basis for a 'friendly evening.' Tell him you will pay the girls well or will pay him for the girls. . . ."

Willmark agents were also asked to check on the general appearance of the Bunnies, looking for malefactions like runs in their stockings, heels less than three inches high, underwear poking out of the costume, crooked ears or tails not in good order. "When the show is on," the memorandum continued, "check to see if the Bunnies are reacting to the performers. When a comic is on, they are supposed to laugh."

By 1961, the Chicago Playboy Club had 106,000 keyholders and in its first year it sold more food and drink than any other restaurant or club in town. Its success astounded observers of the Chicago nightclub scene, who were unable to understand why the Mafia tolerated such competition.

In the early sixties, the Syndicate still controlled Chicago nightlife, just as it had since Prohibition days. "The criminal element," an FBI report noted, "is in complete control of many establishments serving liquor to patrons and all of the cabarets featuring strip-tease entertainment in the main Chicago night-life areas." The effect of this control, the report added, was to make it virtually impossible for an honest businessman to remain in the "tavern business". He faced a choice of either closing down or "cooperating" with the Syndicate by paying a "tax" to remain open (usually around $500 a month) and purchasing all supplies and services from Syndicate firms.

The Playboy Club at 116 East Walton Street was very much

Reprinted from February 7, 1962 Issue

on Syndicate turf, yet appeared to be immune from the attention of the mob. No one could understand it. There were rumors that a black wreath with white lilies had been delivered to the club on the opening night as a warning, and that a brick had been hurled through the window: both were untrue.

The truth was curiously prosaic. Soon after it became clear that the Playboy Club was going to be a success, a prominent mobster with a daunting reputation as an extortionist and hitman approached Hefner at a party and said he was interested in "investing" in Playboy. Hefner knew who he was and nervously suggested that they should talk in the office, rather than at the party. Next day, Hef discussed the incident with Victor and Arnie and they agreed that the best strategy to fend off such "investors" would be to emphasize the considerable opposition Playboy already faced from conservatives at City Hall and the Mayor's office. When the man arrived for his appointment at 232 East Ohio, Hefner could barely conceal his nerves, but he managed to listen politely while his visitor outlined his interest in purchasing franchises for more Playboy Clubs. "I don't know what business you're in, John," Hefner said at last, swallowing hard, "but I feel that you have your enemies and we have ours and I really don't think it would be a good idea for them to join forces against us." He went on to elaborate Playboy's problems with officialdom. It appeared to be a persuasive argument: to Hefner's great relief, the meeting ended soon afterward on friendly terms and Playboy received no further "offers."

However, the Playboy Club could not entirely disassociate itself from the Chicago underworld, since the Syndicate ran many of the services the Club required, as well as controlling the teamster locals who delivered supplies and hauled garbage. The valet-parking and hat-checking concession at the Club was awarded to a firm with links to organized crime, as was the garbage collection contract, which went to the West Suburban Scavenger Service, owned by Willie "Potatoes" Daddano. Lownes was indignant whenever Playboy was accused of patronizing organized crime. "If the mob runs the only laundry service in town," he said, "what are we supposed to do? Let our members sit at tables covered with filthy linen?"

Potentially even more embarrassing to the Playboy Club was its instant popularity with leading Syndicate figures like Sam Giancana, Eddie "Big Head" Vogel, Joseph Di Varco, Gus Zapas, and the Buccieri brothers, some of whom were seen squiring off-duty Bunnies about town, a privilege everyone knew was denied ordinary mortals. When a columnist in the *Chicago Tribune* remarked that the Playboy Club showed every sign of becoming a Mafioso hangout, Lownes turned his formidable ingenuity to the problem and came up with a neat idea. He had a notice board made up for display in the entrance of the club to list the names of all the members "At the Playboy Club Tonight," hoping that known crooks would be reluctant to advertise their presence. Sadly, it did not work: errant husbands who had told their wives they were working late were equally unwilling to advertise their presence and members were hastily assured they could instruct the Door Bunny not to post their names, if they so wished.

These were but teething problems. In every way that mattered, the Chicago Club was a success and plans were hastily drawn up to open Playboy Clubs in other cities across the United States. Lownes was anxious to move quickly to prevent possible competitors from stealing "our best ideas," perhaps forgetting for a moment that some of Playboy's best ideas were actually stolen from the Gaslight clubs. Before the end of 1960, franchises were sold to open Playboy Clubs in New Orleans and Miami, and negotiations were in progress for clubs in Phoenix, Arizona, and St. Louis.

Meanwhile, Lownes flew to New York to seek a suitably prestigious site in Manhattan, mercifully unaware of the flak ahead. Playboy's determination to open a club in New York would plunge Hefner into a web of intrigue that would still be causing him serious problems more than twenty years later.

Not long after the Chicago club opened, Arnie Morton was approached by an individual called Ralph Berger, a flashy little man in his mid-fifties with gray hair slicked back over the top of his head and a taste for sharp suits. Morton knew Berger slightly— he ran a real estate and public relations firm in Chicago and had a reputation as a small-time fixer. (What was less well known was that he had been indicted in 1935, along with several members of Al Capone's gang, on a charge of attempting to dispose of $37,000 worth of bonds stolen from a mail truck.)

Berger told Morton he had heard that Playboy was planning to open a club in New York and he thought he might be able to help as he had very good contacts with the licensing authorities in New York State. The company might have "serious problems" getting a liquor license, he said, as Martin Epstein, Commissioner of the New York State Liquor Authority, held the view that key clubs were illegal in New York. Playboy was already going over this ground with the city of Chicago, which had challenged the legality of key clubs and demanded that the Playboy Club be opened to everyone. The company had complied while the issue was being determined in the courts. Morton said he was sure they would win the case, as they would in New York, if they had to go to court. Maybe it need not come to that, Berger replied, as Epstein was a good friend of his. Indeed, the very next week he was entertaining him in Chicago; perhaps Morton would like him to put in a good word on Playboy's behalf? Without much enthusiasm, Morton suggested that Berger and Epstein should visit the Playboy Club as guests of the company, so that Epstein could see the operation.

Two weeks later, Berger again turned up to see Morton. He said that Commissioner Epstein had not had time to visit the Playboy Club while he was in Chicago, but he was very upset that Playboy had begun sending out mailings to prospective members in the New York area. Shifting nervously from foot to foot, Berger relayed a startling message; if Playboy wanted a liquor license in New York, Commissioner Epstein would want a fee of $50,000. Morton was too surprised to be angry. He laughed and asked why they should pay for a license to which they were legally entitled. You don't understand, Berger warned him. Another club had paid $60,000 to get a liquor license and was still having problems because it had not "gone through the proper channels."

No one laughed when Morton reported the conversation to Hefner, Lownes, and Preuss at a meeting in the Mansion that evening. None of them had any doubt that Berger was being used as a middle man for a shakedown, but none of them considered going to the police. "We didn't like it," said Lownes, "but we thought maybe that was the way things were done in the big city. We were complete innocents." After some discussion, it was agreed that Morton should check Berger's claims and if what he said was true and $50,000 would guarantee Playboy a liquor license, they should pay up.

On August 15, 1960, Morton and Berger flew to New York for a meeting with Epstein at the SLA offices in Manhattan. It turned out to be little more than a handshake in the lobby—Epstein apologized and said he had another urgent appointment—but it was significant because it was clear, even from that brief encounter, that Berger and Epstein were friends. Morton reported to Hefner that he thought Berger would be able to "deliver" the commissioner. A week later, Playboy began the first major wave of membership mailings in New York, confident its liquor license was assured.

In November, Lownes found ideal premises for the club—a six-story building, formerly used as an art gallery and offices, near the Sherry Netherland Hotel on 59th Street, east of Fifth Avenue. Renovation work began immediately and advertising was booked to enroll "charter keyholders" of the soon-to-be-opened New York Playboy Club. Meanwhile, the company's liquor license application appeared to be stymied by the original objection about charging for admission keys, even though Playboy had by now won its case in Chicago.

Shortly after the New Year's holiday, Hefner and Lownes boarded a flight for New York to see Epstein and sort out the problems. When they arrived at the SLA offices, they were surprised to see a man wearing a top hat, tail coat, and spats walking up and down outside carrying a placard reading: "The State Liquor Authority Is Crooked and Corrupt." "By the time we came out," said Lownes, "I felt like joining him."

Epstein, then seventy-three years old, made no bones about his demands: he wanted $50,000 in cash if Playboy wanted a liquor license, but there was still the difficulty of the admission keys. Pacing back and forth in front of a window, the old man kept muttering: "Keys aren't allowed here. Keys aren't allowed here." Lownes repeatedly asked him to show them the statute saying key clubs were illegal; Epstein refused. Finally the commissioner called the meeting to a close and abruptly dismissed his visitors. "I had the feeling," Hefner said, "that we hadn't performed properly or said the right things."

A few days later, Berger telephoned Morton and told him that Epstein was very angry and wanted nothing more to do with Playboy, or those "boy scouts," Hefner and Lownes. Morton asked him to try and "keep the door open."

For several months, nothing was heard from New York about the fate of Playboy's application for a liquor license. Then, in late April, the odious Berger again made contact with Morton. The $50,000 deal with Epstein was still on, he said, but Playboy would also have to make a deal with Epstein's "political boss"—L. Judson Morhouse. Morton was flabbergasted. L. Judson Morhouse, a well-known attorney, was not only chairman of the New York Republican State Committee, he was also a close friend of Governor Nelson A. Rockefeller. Morton immediately reported this new development to Hefner and it was decided that Morton should seek a meeting with Morhouse in New York to identify the nature of the "deal" he would require.

Mr. Morhouse, a pillar of the WASP establishment, was charming when Morton arrived at his office overlooking the Hudson River in New York on May 2, 1961. He said he would have no difficulty in assisting Playboy to obtain a liquor license: he would either intercede with Commissioner Epstein or replace him, as he was overdue for retirement, or he could even secure a legislative amendment of the state's liquor laws. Morton was impressed. There was, however, the small matter of a fee. Morton waited, wondering what was coming. For his services, Morhouse said, he would want $100,000 to be paid in installments over a five-year period, an option to purchase $100,000 worth of Playboy stock if the company went public, and a concession to operate a string of gift shops within Playboy Clubs. All of this, he made clear with a smile, was naturally quite separate and supplemental to whatever "arrangements" had been made with Commissioner Epstein. Morton was dumbstruck, mumbled something about needing to consult his colleagues, and returned to Chicago to break the news to Hefner that a friend of the Governor of New York intended to blackmail Playboy.

For all the eyebrows that might be raised over Hefner's private life, he was in many ways a profoundly moral man, faithful to his Nebraska Methodist roots. He was loyal to his friends, concerned about injustice, caring for the underdog. Above all, he was incapable of dishonesty and he was genuinely appalled by the news from New York. But for the first time in his life, he was unsure how to respond to a proposal he recognized stank of corruption.

Lownes, Morton, and Preuss gathered for a hastily convened meeting at the Mansion. There was some discussion about blowing the whistle and going to Frank Hogan, the New York District

Attorney, with the whole story, but they had no confidence they would get a fair hearing and no confidence in their status. *Playboy* was still widely considered to be nothing more than a dirty magazine. How would a dirty magazine fare making accusations against a friend of Governor Rockefeller? Who would be believed? They fretted further about how high the corruption extended. If a close friend of the governor was prepared to attempt such blatant extortion, who could tell *who* might be involved?

Even if they were able to expose Epstein and Morhouse, what then? Hefner knew from experience, they all did, that they could expect little sympathy from bureaucrats or politicians, many of whom might read *Playboy* in private, but described it in public as an immoral and licentious publication. If they antagonized those officials with the power to grant or refuse Playboy's license application, pedantic interpretation of the small print could deny Playboy a license for years. As Victor said, they could "take the soap out of the washroom and close us down for lack of proper washing facilities." Apart from the millions of dollars already invested in the New York Playboy Club, more than 60,000 people had already paid $25 in advance for a key and, not unnaturally, they were beginning to agitate for the club to be opened.

The outcome of the meeting was perhaps predictable: all four men agreed to keep quiet. Lownes and Morton were dispatched to New York with instructions to try and make a better deal with Morhouse. He was to be told Playboy was willing to pay $100,000 in return for a guarantee of a liquor license, but there were "problems" with the stock option and gift shop demands. Negotiations with Morhouse continued for several weeks. At the end of June he was invited to Chicago to "tie up the details," and at this meeting he was finally persuaded his stock option and gift shop proposals were unworkable because of public disclosure requirements. Morhouse was naturally anxious to avoid anything appearing on the public record that could link him with the Playboy Clubs and asked for his $100,000 "fee" to be paid through H.M.H. Publishing Company.

Through the second half of 1961, Playboy made agreed payments to Morhouse and Commissioner Epstein, as well as handing over smaller sums to Ralph Berger, who had been promised $5,000 for his "services." Early in December, Playboy's application for a liquor license was approved and the New York Playboy Club opened for business.

Unknown to everyone concerned, the New York County District Attorney's Office was conducting an investigation into corruption at the State Liquor Authority and was privy to most of the Playboy deal, having tapped Berger's telephone.

The investigation was kept secret until November 1962, when Commissioner Epstein, by then a sick man, was called to testify before a grand jury. Governor Rockefeller issued a statement urging all liquor licensees to cooperate with the inquiry, promising that anyone who did so would suffer no reprisals affecting the conduct of their business. Hefner and his pals chose to keep their heads down.

On December 12, the books and records of the New York Playboy Club were subpoenaed by the District Attorney. Morton telephoned Morhouse to warn him that the books reflected payments he had received from Playboy and Morhouse made a desperate bid to save himself by writing a letter to Playboy, dated December 20, attempting to establish himself as a consultant to the company. It was too late. With the net closing in, Playboy dispatched an emissary to the District Attorney's office to work out an immunity deal in return for their cooperation. Belatedly, the four heroes from Chicago agreed to tell all they knew.

Ralph Berger, described as the "go-between," was the first to be indicted, on a charge of conspiring with Arnold Morton and other "unindicted co-conspirators" to bribe Commissioner Epstein. Defense counsel Joseph E. Brille, cross-examining Morton in the witness box, suggested that Playboy officials were so "desperate" to obtain a liquor license that they resorted to bribery. "I didn't think I was bribing a public official," Morton retorted indignantly. "I felt I was being blackmailed."

Berger was sentenced to a year in prison, a conviction affirmed by the Appeals Court but ultimately overturned by the United States Supreme Court in a famous decision that restricted the use of evidence obtained by "electronic eavesdropping"—the tap on Berger's telephone. Commissioner Epstein was adjudged to be too ill to stand trial, but Morhouse, his political career in ruins, was indicted and found guilty, to the intense embarrassment of

". . . Your Proudest Possession Is Your Bunny Tail"

WEATHER
Cloudy, rain
or drizzle,
55-60.
Tomorrow:
Partly cloudy,
near 70.

Sunrise 5 M A M.
Sunset 6 11 P M.
Sunrise Tomorrow
5 39 A M

New York Post

© 1963 New York Post Corporation
Reentered as 2nd class matter Nov. 23, 1949, at the Post Office of New York under Act of March 3, 1879

LATE CITY

Over the
Counter Stocks
Scratches

Vol. 162
No. 43   NEW YORK, MONDAY, APRIL 1, 1963   10 Cents

MORHOUSE GOT 18G FROM 'PLAYBOY'

By PAUL HOFFMAN

Former State GOP Chairman L. Judson Morhouse received $18,000 to represent Playboy Enterprises without, according to his attorney, doing a thing for it.

Morhouse, who refused to waive immunity before the grand jury in DA Hogan's probe of the State Liquor Authority, got "retainers" of $10,000 as attorney and $8,000 as public-relations counsel.

He declined today to discuss the dealings, but his attorney, Sol Gelb, insisted Morhouse was hired to represent Playboy magazine—not its offshoot, the Playboy Club, whose license dealings were a target of the DA's investigation.

"Playboy consulted him. They had plans. Then this whole thing (the SLA investigation) came up and they didn't get around to it," Gelb said. "They just thought he would serve the business well as a lawyer."

Gelb said Morhouse did not return the "retainers."

A few hours before his grand jury appearance Jan. 9, Morhouse resigned as vice chairman of the State Thruway Authority and as director of the Lake George Park Commission, thus avoiding automatic dismissal under state law. He had resigned as GOP chairman a few weeks earlier.

The grand jury resumes deliberations today. Last Friday the jury's term was extended to June 28. It was originally empaneled last December and has heard about 100 witnesses on charges of graft and corruption in the SLA.

Morhouse was mentioned this week in Life magazine as one of several Republican lawyers active in dealings with the SLA. The Life article named among the lawyers Hyman D. Siegel, former law associate of State Attorney General Lefkowitz.

his colleagues in the Republican Party in the State of New York. Rockefeller later commuted his prison sentence on the grounds of Morhouse's ill health.

While all this was going on, the New York Playboy Club ran into further problems when the City License Commissioner, Bernard J. O'Connell, denied the club a cabaret license. "It would appear clear," he ruled, "that the applicant's main appeal to its prospective customers is the lure of its scantily clad waitresses. The impression is created by the club's publicity releases, truly or falsely, that they are available to twist with club members at private parties." Such audacious activity, he decreed, was definitely not "in the public interest." The club appealed, producing the Bunny Manual as evidence of virtue and causing considerable hilarity

91

among those unfamiliar with its bizarre contents. The club eventually won but was unable to present live entertainment, other than musicians, for the duration of the appeal.

Playboy put the boldest possible face on the whole tawdry business of the liquor license. During the appeal against the denial of a cabaret license, the District Attorney's office had sent a letter to the Commissioner of Licenses acknowledging the assistance of Playboy officials in obtaining the indictment and conviction of Berger and Morhouse and requesting that no adverse action be taken with respect to Playboy's pending cabaret license application. Much was made of this letter and it was soon being loosely interpreted as an official "vote of thanks" to Hefner and his colleagues for their "courage in coming forward to fight extortion," as Lownes would later describe it. But no matter how Playboy's public relations men dressed the events, it was clear that Hefner had blundered in his handling of the affair. What was the excuse for not immediately going to the police the moment a bribe was first mentioned? There was none.

Away from New York, Playboy Clubs fared rather better, opening in Los Angeles, San Francisco, Detroit, Baltimore, St. Louis, Pittsburgh, Boston, and Dallas with barely a hiccup. In Baltimore, indignant housewives mounted a picket and temporarily stopped a Playboy Club from opening, a protest that puzzled local men since not far from the club was the notorious "Block," where strip-tease queens like Candy Barr and Blaze Starr performed nightly and no one peered too closely into the darkened booths around the stage. As a reporter for the *Baltimore Sun* noted: "How could Baltimore possibly be corrupted by a few dozen carefully screened young ladies who stayed tightly encased in their corsets and weren't even allowed to sit down with a customer?"

Bunnies were soon regarded around the nation as blameless creatures of spotless virtue, although there was a glimpse of a darker side to the story in Chicago, when a Bunny named Constance Petrie was found dead from an overdose. The man with whom she was living apparently told the police that she came home drunk at five-thirty in the morning and so he slapped her. Five hours later she was found dead in bed with four empty pill bottles at her side. Further inquiries revealed that Bunny Connie, who was twenty-six years old, had been sacked two days earlier by the Playboy Club for refusing to take a lie-detector test after someone had accused her of prostitution and smoking marijuana.

An unapologetic Victor Lownes readily confirmed to the *Chicago Sun-Times* that Bunnies were indeed "offered" lie-detector tests. "We try to protect ourselves and the girls if we hear any bad rumors about them. She had a delightful personality. Very sweet. She wasn't the prettiest Bunny in the place, but she had such a nice personality that sort of made up for it. When she refused to take a lie test, that was no indication that she was guilty of anything. But it was an indication that we could not afford to keep her in our employ."

Another Bunny who appeared on the "P.M. East" television show and confessed that she did not really like being considered an accessory to a man was promptly fired for her temerity. Prejudice of another kind was encountered when Playboy moved into the South: local laws banned blacks from entering the Playboy Club in New Orleans, and in Miami white keyholders frequently walked out if blacks entered the club.

Toward the end of 1961 (the year the "Freedom Riders" tried to force integration in the South and were brutally attacked by whites in Alabama), Lownes sent a memo to Ray Baribeau, manager of the Miami club: "It is not necessary for you to report to me on the reactions or lack of reactions among customers at the club when Negroes are present, as there is no question but that we are going to adhere to our policy of complete integration—no matter what stupidity is manifested by some of our members."

In New Orleans, the company chose to comply with the law rather than close down the club and blacks were excluded until the Civil Rights Act was passed in 1964. Yet despite striving to do right, Playboy was often criticized for condoning segregation in New Orleans. In vain did the company point out to its critics that a black girl was among the first Bunnies hired in Chicago, perhaps because Lownes liked to refer to her as the "chocolate Bunny."

Playboy's swinging image also took a bit of a knock when there were reports that the clientele of the Chicago club comprised mainly conventioneers, out-of-town salesmen, and middle-aged roisterers who shouted banalities at each other during the entertainment and wolf whistled at the Bunnies. But who cared? The Chicago club was said to be the most profitable bar, per square foot, *in the world*. And a new line in the gift shop, a Bunny tail mounted on a walnut plaque engraved CAUGHT LIVE AT THE BUNNY CLUB, was selling like crazy at $15 apiece.

The fame of the Bunnies even spread behind the Iron Curtain, to Moscow, where *Literaturnaya Gazeta*, the official organ of the Soviet Writers' Union, reported that Hefner used his magazine "purely to publicize his nightclubs, where nearly naked waitresses with little bunny ears as the main piece of attire titillate the dying emotions of sedate patrons." By the summer of 1963, Hefner was able to announce to the world the important information that Playboy was employing 24½ tons of Bunnies with a collective chest measurement of 15,516 inches.

Where was Victor A. Lownes III at this moment of triumph? Nowhere to be seen. He had, according to his own account, decided to quit. This was news to Preuss and Morton, both of whom thought they had sacked him.

Victor had become unbearable. In his position as Vice President of Playboy Clubs, International, in charge of promotion and entertainment, he was occasionally brilliant and frequently maddening. "Victor was a terrific, lovable guy," says Preuss. "He was also a son-of-a-bitch. No one could handle him." His management style was that of a madman, screaming and ranting at underlings, pacing up and down in his office like a caged animal, and giving way to terrible tantrums. Once, in a rage, he pulled the telephone clean out of the wall.

His ability to find new talent for cabaret in Playboy Clubs was undeniable. Comedian Dick Gregory was working in a car wash when Lownes hired him for the Playboy Club and gave him his first break in show business. He also signed an unknown singer called Barbra Streisand, although she never actually appeared at a Playboy Club—by the time she was due to work for the club, she was already too famous to bother with nightclub acts. Victor liked to say, because he loved to shock, that he made a point of never seeing an act before booking it. He relied on *Variety* and trusted agents for the initial booking: audience-reaction reports decided whether or not an act was rehired.

While no one could deny Victor's gifts, neither could they ignore the fact that for much of the time he was "a pain in the ass." On the one hand, he was bright, amusing, gracious; on the other, he was a tyrant who instilled terror in those unfortunates who were obliged to work for him. He could barely conceal his contempt for the keyholders who patiently lined up to get into a Playboy Club: to him, they were shmucks. He called the lines "shmuck strainers" because they filtered out the kinds of people he wanted to see in the clubs—those who, like himself, would never dream of standing for hours in line.

On five separate occasions, Preuss was ordered to get rid of Victor. Each time, Hefner changed his mind because he could not bear to upset his friend. Victor's final downfall came when he entered into a power struggle with the man he somehow perceived to be his deadliest rival: Hefner's brother, Keith.

Keith clearly considered that he knew more about show business than Victor and liked to criticize the acts Victor hired for Playboy Clubs. Nothing could be more calculated to enrage Victor and he, in turn, never missed an opportunity to take Keith to task. Their antagonism dated back to an incident at the Chicago club, when Keith was still a lowly room director. Victor had had flashing lights installed to indicate to arriving keyholders which rooms had most space available. One night Victor came into the club and discovered that one room was packed and another was empty. Keith had forgotten to switch on the appropriate signs in the lobby; Victor bawled him out on the spot.

"I think Victor was jealous of Keith," said Lee Gottlieb, who worked for Victor at the time. "He thought that Keith, as a blood relative, stood between him and Hefner. He would ask people what Keith was doing yesterday or the day before, and it was clear he was amassing evidence to take to Hefner to discredit Keith.

"But there were already moves afoot to get Victor to take a leave of absence; there was talk of sending him around the world. He was getting on everyone's nerves. Working for him was a terrible experience—a lot of people thought he was crazy. One night I heard that there was a board meeting at which Victor was going to present his case for getting rid of Keith.

"Next morning, Victor telephoned me at the office and asked me to meet him at his coach house on Walton Street. It was a typical Victor scene when I got there. He was in his bathing trunks and there were two or three young women lying out in the yard. A black maid poured drinks and Victor said suddenly, 'I'm retiring—leaving the company. I've told Hef that I want you to take over promotion of the clubs.' "

Hefner, who hated any kind of personal confrontation, had instructed Preuss and Morton to fire his old friend. But to sweeten the blow he retained Victor as a consultant, and suggested he should go to New York as president of the New York Playboy Club, where at least he would be out of the way.

Hardly had Victor settled in New York before a beautiful blonde set out to shatter the myth of the Bunny that Victor had done so much to create.

Among the hundreds of girls who answered the advertisements for Bunnies at the New York Playboy Club was a former dancer and beauty queen who said her name was Marie Ochs. She was lying. Her name was Gloria Steinem; she was a Phi Beta Kappa, magna cum laude graduate of Smith College, and she was on one of her first assignments as a journalist: *Show* magazine had commissioned her to write an exposé of the Bunny.

At her interview, Steinem was handed a glossy brochure entitled "Be a Playboy Club Bunny," illustrated with color photographs of Bunnies going about their glamorous business. There was a Bunny serving film star Tony Curtis with a cocktail; a group picture of smiling Bunnies with Hef on "Playboy's nationally syndicated television show"; Bunnies handing out *Playboy* magazine at a veterans' hospital ("just one of the many worthwhile community projects in which Bunnies participate"); a meeting with the Bunny Mother offering "friendly, personal counseling"; and a bikini-clad Bunny lounging on the deck of a yacht flying the Bunny flag. "When you become a Bunny," the brochure promised, "your world will be fun-filled, pleasant and always exciting."

After four weeks working as a Bunny, Steinem found a very different world, inhabited by exploited, overworked, and exhausted waitresses with swollen feet. Her report, published in the summer of 1963, was devastating. It painted a strangely Orwellian picture of dispirited, no-hope girls tottering around in agonizingly

uncomfortable costumes so that they could be lurched at and prop-
ositioned and pinched by the men it was their duty to serve. At
the same time, they were fed a constant diet of propaganda telling
them what glamorous lives they were leading: "The Playboy Club
world is filled with good entertainment, beautiful girls, fun-loving
playboys . . . it's always on the go, like a continuous house party.
Cheerful Bunnies feel as though they are among the invited
guests. . . ."

It was not a party to which Steinem would have wanted an
invitation. She reported that the costumes were deliberately cut
too tight and left angry red weals all over her body at the end of
every shift. Only the bust was oversized, a deficiency most girls
remedied by stuffing it with plastic bags. They worked long hours,
sometimes without a break, and grabbed what they could to eat
from what was left on customers' plates. The club took half of
everything they made in tips and few of them were able to earn
anything like the $200 to $300 a week offered in the advertisement.
Steinem's first paycheck was $35.90.

Playboy executives did their best to dismiss the piece as biased
and inaccurate, but the Bunny would never again have quite the
same glamor in the eyes of the public.

At 232 East Ohio Street, there was deep suspicion that a knife
was being turned in a particularly painful wound. Why had *Show*,
ostensibly a magazine for the arts, published a muckraking exposé
of the Bunnies? Was it because a number of *Show*'s senior editors
were recently, and unhappily, in the employment of Playboy during a disastrous attempt by Hefner to extend his publishing interests with a new magazine called *Show Business Illustrated*?

5

The Best Party There Never Was

Hefner loved celebrities. He couldn't help it, it was the way he was. Actors, football players, dancers, boxers, singers, writers, racing drivers, comedians . . . it did not matter who they were; even if they were only modestly celebrated they were guaranteed a welcome at the Playboy Mansion. Although by the sixties he was a millionaire and something of a celebrity himself, fame could still dazzle him: he was a natural fan. There was, however, one name he cherished above all others. His hero, his *idol*, was Frank Sinatra. And when Frank Sinatra visited Chicago in the autumn of 1960 to sing at a benefit concert for the Urban League and accepted an invitation to the Mansion, Hefner was beside himself with happiness. On the big day, the great man arrived with his usual retinue of sunny chums and, seated in the ballroom, treated the shining-eyed publisher to the benefit of his views on the subject of magazine publishing, with particular reference to the editorial attitudes of *Variety* and the *Daily Reporter*, both of which had managed to cause him offense.

"Sinatra talked with Hef," Hefner wrote later in his scrapbook, "about the possibility of going into business together on a West

Coast show business newspaper. They plan to discuss it further after Frank returns to the West Coast."

No further discussions were actually recorded, but Sinatra had planted the seed of an idea. Hefner was attracted by the prospect of launching another magazine and re-creating the success of *Playboy*, which by the end of 1960 was selling more than one million copies every month. To a man infatuated with the stars, what could be better than a show business magazine? He visualized something slick, glossy, sophisticated, the kind of magazine that would reflect the fun and excitement of show business and, incidentally, give its publisher a legitimate entrée into the glittering world of entertainment. The more Hefner thought about it, the more he liked it.

At 232 East Ohio Street, his enthusiasm was not shared by either Preuss or Spectorsky. Preuss, ever the cautious accountant, thought the start-up costs of another magazine would put a dangerous strain on corporate funds already stretched by financial commitment to the opening of Playboy Clubs. Spectorsky argued that the editorial staff, Hefner included, was working all hours just to get *Playboy* out. How could they take on another magazine?

What Auguste Comte Spectorsky did not tell Hefner was that he *loathed* the idea of a show business magazine. He had come to terms with being in Chicago, and at *Playboy*, by slowly building the magazine's literary reputation. No one could question the editorial quality of *Playboy* magazine and Spectorsky was proud of that fact, took comfort from it. He was dismayed at the prospect of a "showbiz" magazine being pushed into the same stable. Although Hefner completely shared Spec's desire for *Playboy* to be a showcase of excellent writing, the two men had little else in common. Spectorsky was openly contemptuous of much about Hefner's lifestyle, his friends, and his parties. The people Hefner thought were glamorous, Spectorsky thought were tedious. He avoided the Mansion whenever he could and sneered at the Playboy Clubs, which he liked to say were "about as exclusive as the Red Cross."

His relations with Hefner remained cordial largely because he disdained to disagree, so when Hefner persisted with his plans for a show business magazine, Spectorsky put up no more than feeble opposition. Not long after Sinatra's visit to the Playboy Mansion, Spectorsky found himself in the first-class cabin of an airliner bound for New York, with orders to hire an editorial team for a magazine in which he had no confidence and no interest. The outcome was calamitous.

Hefner told Spectorsky he wanted the very best writers and editors to be found in New York; no expense was to be spared. Comfortably settled into a suite at the Plaza Hotel, Spectorsky began sounding out his contacts in publishing and journalism. He talked airily of the new magazine being something like a *"New Yorker of show business"* (a description that would have surprised Hefner), hinted at exciting prospects and unlimited funds. He appeared ready to make any promise, offer any reassurance, to attract top people. When over cocktails a senior editor at *Newsweek* confessed he really did not have any deep understanding of show business, Spectorsky told him not to worry, he could learn.

Spectorsky's choice of editorial director for the still unnamed magazine was Frank Gibney, a respected editor on *Life* magazine. Gibney was a graduate of Yale, a Japanese scholar, and the author of several books. Enthused by Spectorsky's promise of editorial freedom, Gibney talked about making the magazine the "voice of urban culture" and including between its covers features on such varied subjects as Kabuki theater, town planning, and Restoration comedy. Spectorsky said nothing to disabuse him.

Gibney brought in Len Jossels, from Time-Life Books, as art director and the rest of the team was quickly put together. Many of the candidates Spectorsky first approached had rudely expressed reservations about working for a "tits-and-ass" outfit like Playboy, but the appointment of Frank Gibney convinced them they had nothing to fear—he was not the kind of man to preside over a second-rate operation. William Ewald, *Newsweek*'s radio and television editor, joined along with his predecessor, Marvin Barrett; Sheward Hagerty came from the assistant managing editor's desk at the New York *Daily News*; Lee Gottlieb moved from *TV Guide*; and John Appleton, Gibney's book editor, joined from Harper.

They were, undeniably, the best people that Playboy money could buy. Predominantly Ivy League, their qualifications were impeccable; even Gibney's assistant, Margarete Sutton, was a graduate of Cambridge University. Spectorsky had carried out his orders to the letter.

On February 23, 1961, Playboy issued a press release announcing the birth of a new magazine. It was to be called *Show Business Illustrated*, would be published every two weeks, and would sell for 50¢. Hefner was quoted as saying: "We will stay far away from the cotton-candy press-agent pap of the fan book or the sanctimonious peeping tomfoolery of the exposé magazines."

Although the title did not exactly give a *New Yorker* impression, there was nothing in the press release to alarm the staff of the new magazine, most of whom were still in New York working out their notices. Neither were they particularly worried when it was announced that Huntington Hartford, heir to the A & P store fortune, was launching a similar magazine, called *Show*. They were confident that they could beat any competition, even though *Show* would have the advantage of being published in New York, a lot closer to the heart of the entertainment business than Chicago.

In April, the staff of *Show Business Illustrated* assembled in Chicago, on a floor at 232 East Ohio Street vacated to make way for them. The first shock was not long in coming and it arrived in the form of a long memorandum from the publisher, Hugh M. Hefner, in which he set out guidelines for the style and content of his new magazine. It read, in part, as follows:

SHOW BUSINESS ILLUSTRATED will bring all the thrills, the excitement, the humor, the pathos, the color and glamor of show business right into the home in the very pages of the magazine itself. Excitement is the word—excitement in words and photographs and art and design. We'll have a Show Business Beauty in every issue, but we mustn't count on this alone for our sex content. An additional pictorial feature of some kind should be included in almost every issue that has some kind of girl flavor or aspect to it. It doesn't necessarily have to have any nudity, but it should have meaningful sex impact . . .

Gibney was horrified. He had come to Chicago to produce a *New Yorker* and here was the publisher talking about sex content and Show Business Beauties! The memo continued in a lyrical vein:

Show business is at its best a wondrous fairyland (and I'm not referring to any of the sexual leanings of its inhabitants), a world of make-believe, of colored lights and tinsel and sequins—as sophisticated and corny in the same moment as Rodgers and Hart's first hit song "Manhattan," that permitted the incredibly wonderful imagery and internal rhyming that takes place within the song to stand side by side with ". . . the great big city can never spoil the dreams of a boy and goil . . ."

The memorandum was greeted with disbelief and consternation. At first some people thought it was a joke. Gibney appealed for calm and counseled patience; had he not been guaranteed editorial freedom? A few days later, most of the staff had their first opportunity to meet Hefner at an editorial conference. To the astonishment of everyone—they all believed they would be producing the magazine from scratch—Hefner produced a dummy cover, mock-ups of picture spreads, tables of contents, and a sheaf of feature ideas. He then delivered a dissertation on the kind of magazine he wanted, expanding on the notorious "sex content" memo.

The discussion that followed slightly allayed the worst fears of the staff. Hefner was charming and attentive, listened carefully to everything they had to say, and often appeared to agree. He sucked on his pipe, smiled and nodded a lot. He seemed to share their desire to produce a high quality magazine and appeared willing to let them have a relatively free hand. But the battle was not that easily won.

With the launch date set for August, work began immediately on detailed planning of the first issues. The staff clung determinedly to the *New Yorker* ideal, but any hopes they might have entertained that Hefner would let them pursue it were soon dashed. He padded through the office late at night like a malevolent wraith, scribbling comments on manuscripts, altering layouts, and leaving long, rambling memos. Work that an editor had left at the end of the day completed to his satisfaction, he would discover next morning reedited by Hefner. "It drove people crazy," said Lee Gottlieb. "You would spend all day getting something right, the way you wanted it, and next morning you would find some mysterious visitor had altered it."

Playboy staffers offered no support to the newcomers, whom they regarded with the deepest suspicion. The floor occupied by *Show Business Illustrated* was referred to in the *Playboy* offices as the "East Coast" and there was little socializing between the two. At lunchtime, *Show Business Illustrated* editors often went out to Navy Pier Park at the end of the street and played touch football; *Playboy* people thought such behavior demonstrated a lack of cool and exhibited a preference for expense-account restaurants where they could worry about the mixing of their martinis. Neither side understood the other.

As the relationship between Hefner and the *SBI* staff deteriorated, his comments and suggestions were increasingly ignored or ridiculed and his memos treated with open derision. "One day we got a fifteen-page memo," said Lee Gottlieb, "telling us how to use punctuation, commas, semicolons, and so on. We looked at it with disbelief." For his part, Hefner was daily more frustrated at his inability to get through to these snooty East Coast so-called hotshots, who, he suspected, were sneering at him behind his back. To be treated in such a cavalier fashion was a terrible shock to Hefner. The staff of *Playboy*, which had grown together, considered him to be an editorial genius. These newcomers from the East clearly considered him to be a *jerk*. One afternoon, at a meeting in Frank Gibney's office, he exploded: "Why won't you guys listen to me? Why won't you do it the way I want it? How can I run this magazine if you don't believe me?"

Hefner persisted in his belief that it was only a matter of time before Gibney came round to his way of thinking, but there were irreconcilable differences between them. During their first meeting, Hefner was genuinely surprised when, in the underwater bar at the Mansion, Gibney made a face at the back-lit pictures of nude Playmates which decorated one wall. "You might be surprised to learn," Hefner said, "that most of them are very nice women." "That makes it even sadder somehow," Gibney replied. Hefner concluded that Gibney had a very strange attitude toward sex.

Gibney vigorously resisted Hefner's attempts to get more girls into the magazine and as the enmity between them grew he took to referring sarcastically to Hefner behind his back as "Hughie," a name which did nothing for his stature around *SBI*.

Notwithstanding the dramas behind the scenes, the first edition of *Show Business Illustrated* went on sale on August 23, 1961. Its launch was marked by lavish parties in Chicago, New York, and Los Angeles and a nationwide promotion campaign. Advertisers were promised a circulation base of 350,000 copies. The disaffected staff could not but compare their own magazine with Huntington Hartford's *Show*, which appeared around the same time. *Show* featured Kenneth Tynan on Orson Welles; *Show Business Illustrated* offered Joe Hyams on Frank Sinatra. "He wanted Frank Sinatra in every goddam issue," said Gottlieb.

There was a faint hope among the staff that once the magazine was out the publisher might begin to take a little less interest. It was not to be. Hefner often said that he edited *Playboy* for himself and it soon became clear that he felt the same about *Show Business Illustrated*. The editors were mercilessly bombarded with nitpicking memos, many of them instructing the reviewers what to say about new movie and record releases:

> Let's give the new Henry Mancini album a nice review and mention that it includes a tasty small-group version of "Playboy's Theme."

> Should give the Judy Garland Carnegie Hall a rave review and five stars in the ratings. Really enthuse over it.

> Let's get somebody into the Playboy Club to catch vocalist David Allen and give him a good little review.

> Please don't give Sinatra's new LP "I Remember Tommy" five stars. Make it four. This one doesn't match his last release for me.

Sales returns from the first few issues of the magazine offered no one any encouragement. The magazine was only selling around 200,000 copies and the subscription pick-up was similarly disappointing. To broaden the appeal, Hefner decided *SBI* should offer saturation coverage of movie and record reviews. Two editors worked all night putting together seventy reviews of classic, pop, and jazz records. "What?" said Hefner the next day. "All you have are seventy reviews? I want three hundred." The only way of getting three hundred reviews in time for the next issue was to rewrite them from other magazines. The two unfortunate editors produced three hundred reviews for the following day and when the magazine was laid out it was discovered there was only space for forty.

Hefner also insisted that movies should be reviewed before release. When no one could get a prerelease viewing of *The Hustler*, starring Paul Newman, *SBI*'s Los Angeles bureau chief was told to ask people at the studio what they thought of the film. Their replies were not particularly enthusiastic, so *SBI* awarded it a mediocre two and a half stars. By the time the magazine was on the street, all the newspapers had published rave reviews and Hefner fired off another salvo of outraged memos demanding to know why *SBI* was the only publication in the United States to pan *The Hustler*.

When *SBI* came round to voting a film of the year, Hefner was not going to tolerate any more mistakes. The two candidates were steamy *La Dolce Vita*, which Hefner favored, and *L'Avventura*, a more artistic affair which the *SBI* staff favored. The vote was nine to two in favor of *L'Avventura*. When Hefner had counted the ballot papers, he looked round the conference table and said bleakly: "It's my million dollars *SBI* has lost. I say *La Dolce Vita* is the winner."

After only five issues, the *SBI* staff began to break up. Art director Len Jossels, tired of fending off the nude pictures Hefner constantly wanted to foist onto the magazine's pages, quit and went to *Look*. Three weeks later, Frank Gibney was fired. "Thank God," he was reported to have said, "I'll never have to read *Variety* again." Later he would tell the *Saturday Evening Post*: "There was one problem, pure and simple. Hefner wanted us to run a lot of stuff like nude showgirls in Las Vegas and the dirty footage cut out of European films by the censors. We wouldn't do it." Gibney was quickly followed by Sheward Hagerty, who returned to *Newsweek*, and Marvin Barrett, who joined Gibney at *Show* magazine.

At 232 East Ohio Street, Hefner held a crisis conference with his trusted aides—Lownes, Preuss, Spectorsky, and Art Paul. *SBI* was losing $75,000 a week, the circulation was flagging, and the advertising slipping away. They had got a magazine that was a ragbag of news, reviews, showbiz gossip, sex, and pale echoes of

The New Yorker. What were they to do? Lownes had a proposal. The only way to save the magazine, he said, was by putting in a lot more tits and ass. Hefner concurred. To economize, it was decided to make the magazine a monthly.

Spectorsky and Art Paul were given overall control of the magazine and the February issue displayed much of *Playboy*'s self-assurance. "With this issue, *SBI* is transformed into a monthly, the better to give our staff time for a deeper look into the realms of the performing arts and our pages finer pictures and graphics to gratify the discerning eyes of our entertainment-oriented readers. With what we hope is modest confidence, we believe *SBI* will be an even more satisfying and perceptive illustrated guidebook to the fascinating world of show business."

The reality was rather different. Preuss warned Hefner that unless the *SBI* cash hemorrhage was blocked, it would soon take the company under. Losses amounted to $3 million, the book value of the company, and the American National Bank was threatening to close Playboy's line of credit. Late in January, Hefner flew to New York to try and make a deal with Huntington Hartford, who was also losing money on *Show* magazine, but who had virtually unlimited funds at his disposal.

On February 2, 1962, a few days after the first monthly issue of *SBI* reached the newsstands with its message of "modest confidence," the *New York Times* carried a brief item:

> The competitive fight between Huntington Hartford, President of *Show* magazine, and Hugh M. Hefner, publisher of *Show Business Illustrated*, has been won by Mr. Hartford.
>
> Mr. Hartford announced late yesterday that arrangements had been completed for his magazine to absorb *Show Business Illustrated* for an amount in excess of $250,000. Mr. Hartford said the April issue would be the last issue of *Show Business Illustrated*.

Gottlieb, who had been promoted to managing editor, was given the job of firing thirty of the staff on the last day. "There was a lot of tears, a lot of trauma. We had tried so hard, put a lot of energy and hope into it, all for nothing."

Hefner presented a few favored members of the staff with a

bound volume of the twelve issues of *Show Business Illustrated* inscribed "To what might have been." It was hard for him not to be bitter about the whole episode and he had no doubts where the blame lay. "Instead of sticking with the guys I had, who could indeed have done this thing, I brought in a whole new staff. On paper it was an excellent staff, and individually, man by man, they were very talented guys, but we never really got them swinging together. I discovered I had hired a lot of square people to run a hip magazine."

No recriminations were directed against Spectorsky because Hefner was somewhat in awe of his epigrammatic editorial director, with his affected, world-weary nineteenth-century pose and vicious tongue.

Not long after the demise of *Show Business Illustrated*, Ol' Blue Eyes was back in Chicago. Hefner sent word to inquire if Frank would be inclined to attend a party in his honor at the Playboy Mansion and Frank sent gracious word back that he was so inclined, providing the party comprised no more than fifty guests, most of whom he would supply. "In other words," said Jodie McRae, who was appointed Hefner's personal valet in 1961 after joining the Mansion staff as a bartender, "he didn't want a lot of people he didn't know crowding into the place and gawking at him."

The Mansion was prepared for this event with an attention to detail that a royal household would be hard put to surpass. Regiments of cleaners scrubbed and polished the public rooms, while engineers checked the hi-fi systems and the pinball tables in the Games Room and the electronic gadgetry throughout the house. After discreet inquiries as to Mr. Sinatra's eating habits, the finest caterers in Chicago were called in to provide a cold banquet in the Italian style. Every bar was stocked with every drink Mr. Sinatra had ever been known to order. Twenty additional waiters and bartenders were hired.

Everything was ready by the time the party was due to begin at midnight. Waiters in white gloves were ranged behind the buffet. Two bartenders were on station at every bar, ice buckets filled, lemons cut, olives ready, glasses gleaming. In the ballroom, a trio from the Playboy Club had set up in the corner and was strumming

Mr. Sinatra's favorite melodies; a handful of favored Bunnies, selected to decorate the party, stood in a small group by the fireplace, giggling nervously. Mr. Hefner remained in his quarters, having left instructions for Jodie McRae to buzz him on the internal telephone the moment Mr. Sinatra's party arrived.

At one o'clock, no one had showed up. At two o'clock, no one had showed up. Some of the Bunnies went to bed. At three o'clock, there was a ring on the front door bell. McRae hurried to the door and found Phyllis Diller standing outside. He explained that they were waiting for Mr. Sinatra and his friends to arrive for a party.

"Don't hold your breath, honey," said Miss Diller. "Those assholes are down the street and they ain't going anywhere. Dean Martin's crawling around on all fours." It transpired that Mr. Sinatra and his friends were having a party at the Ambassador Hotel, just four doors south of the Mansion, and were in no condition to travel.

Jodie McRae chose not to advise Mr. Hefner of this development, since he knew that Mr. Hefner did not respond kindly to negative information. Mr. Hefner continued to wait in his quarters, while Phyllis Diller entertained Jodie McRae with show business stories in the underwater bar. She departed after about half an hour.

At seven o'clock in the morning, with still no sign of Mr. Sinatra and his friends, Jodie judged it safe to dismiss the staff. "I guess you could say," he remarked with a wry smile, "it was the best party there never was."

6

What the Hell Was I Supposed to Go Out For?

It was a little more than a mile from the Playboy Mansion on North State Street Parkway to the Playboy offices on East Ohio. When he first took up residence in the Mansion, Hefner used to set out for work at about five o'clock in the afternoon at the wheel of his 150-mph Mercedes 300SL. Yearning for the autobahns, the car spluttered and burbled in the stop-start traffic for thirteen blocks down State Street, made a left onto Ohio, crossed Michigan, and stopped outside 232 East Ohio at about the time most of the publisher's employees were preparing to go home.

When the novelty of driving a foreign sports car palled, as it soon did, Hefner acquired a chauffeur and a $30,000 Mercedes limousine, license plate HMH-1340, equipped with a color television, cocktail bar, telephone, and the day's newspapers to provide him with some diversion during the journey to and from work. Two little orange pennants, embroidered with the Bunny logo and fluttering from chrome flagstaffs, indicated his illustrious presence on the leather upholstery in the rear.

The passing of the Playboy limousine with its flags flying was quite a sight, but one to which the citizenry of Chicago had little opportunity to become accustomed, since the novelty of traveling into the office each day also began to pall. Hefner became enamored of the idea of reversing the customary commuting pattern. Instead of his going to the office, he decided the office would come to him.

From the summer of 1962 onward, the same summer *How to Succeed in Business Without Really Trying* won a Pulitzer prize for drama, Hefner's appearances at 232 East Ohio became less and less frequent. He had an office suite created for himself in the Mansion, connected to his private quarters by a spiral staircase, and a secretary moved in, and the Playboy limousine, minus its flags, was employed to shuttle the editorial mountain to Mahomet in order to produce a magazine each month.

Hefner found this to be an extremely convenient and agreeable arrangement, so much so that it seemed perfectly logical to take it a step further: if he did not have to go out to work, why did he have to go out to *play*? In truth, everything he wanted from life could be found within the Mansion: girls galore, fun and games, parties, movies, toys, celebrities. "What the hell was it," he asked himself, "I was supposed to go out for?" As he could not think of an answer, he simply stopped going out.

For most of the sixties, Hefner remained closeted in the Playboy Mansion with the windows shuttered and the curtains drawn, heedless of day or night or the passing of the seasons. Sometimes he would not see daylight for months on end. A wag suggested giving him seven pairs of pajamas with the day embroidered on each of them in reversed writing so that when he looked in the mirror to shave, he would at least know what day it was.

Only under the most exceptional circumstances would he agree to leave the house. One such occurred in the summer of 1963, when a judge signed a warrant for his arrest on a charge of publishing and circulating an obscene magazine. The June 1963 issue of *Playboy* carried pictures of Jayne Mansfield in bed and in a bubble-bath and caused offense to Chicago's Catholic hierarchy. Four officers from the vice squad literally dragged Hefner out of the Mansion and carted him off to South State Street Court for arraignment. At the trial, the jury failed to agree.

One winter when Chicago had an exceptionally heavy snowfall, Hefner, ever the romantic, went out for a midnight walk with a girlfriend. The word spread through the house as if a miracle had happened: "He's gone out! Hef's gone *out!*" And the staff rushed to the windows to witness this remarkable event, in time to see Hefner and his date building a snowman in the front garden by the light of the street lamps.

Hefner liked to describe the Mansion as a "controlled environment," by which he meant he lived in a world that revolved entirely around himself. Whatever was happening outside 1340 North State Street Parkway was largely irrelevant, and usually out of "synch" with what was happening inside. The day began when he got up, ended when he went to bed; nothing else was certain. Swallowing innumerable amphetamines to scramble his body clock, his working day could easily stretch to sixty or seventy hours. If, at the end of it, he wanted a party, party-time was declared and the house filled with instant revelers. If he wanted his lunch at three o'clock in the morning, it was considered to be lunchtime. That an outside world existed at all he recognized only through the media, on which he relied to keep in touch with his fellow man.

Hordes of newspapermen trekked to North State Street Parkway to report on the curious phenomenon of the publisher as swinging recluse. Hef had plenty to say about the joys of his lifestyle and he said it over and over again. "Man is the only animal capable of controlling his environment," was a favorite phrase, followed by: "What I've created is a private world that permits me to live my life without a lot of wasted time and motion that consume a large part of most people's lives." He would pose for photographs on his already famous round bed and demonstrate how he could rotate it and create four—yes, four—different environments for himself in that *one room.*

The more seriously Hefner talked about "life," the more he became convinced he had something profound to say and toward the end of 1962 he judged the time had come for him to share his thoughts with the readers of his magazine. Lesser editors might have approached such a project with a certain diffidence, perhaps presenting the material under a headline like "Viewpoint" or "Opinion." But that was not *Playboy*'s style. In December 1962, the magazine carried the first lengthy installment of the "Playboy Philosophy," no less.

Before it ended—and there were some *Playboy* editors who

thought that it would never end—this sententious opus rambled through 250,000 words and spread over twenty-five issues of the magazine. Its writing occupied most of Hefner's time in the Mansion for more than two years and exposed him to a barrage of sneers and ridicule, from the media at least. "It is couched in the royal 'we,' " a woman journalist reported, "reeks of defensive pomposity, is numbingly serious and breathtakingly naïve." *Life* magazine called it a "pretentious marathon outpouring."

"Hef got kidded about it a lot," says Art Paul, "but the people who did the kidding never really read it. Some people thought it was boring, but it was actually a kind of interesting thesis on censorship and sexual repression, if you could take the time to sit down and read it."

Hefner wanted the Philosophy to provide a learned answer to *Playboy*'s critics, of whom there was no shortage. Harvard theologian Harvey Cox accused the magazine of feeding on the existence of a repressed fear of involvement with women. Writing in *Christianity and Crisis: A Christian Journal of Opinion*, he said, "*Playboy* and its less successful imitators are not 'sex magazines' at all. They are basically anti-sexual. They dilute and dissipate authentic sexuality by reducing it to an accessory, by keeping it at a safe distance."

Few clergymen disagreed. They spoke of the magazine's emptiness as a bible for the upwardly mobile male and its failure to nurture insight or understanding. But the most devastating attack came from Benjamin De Mott, a professor of English at Amherst, in the August 1962 issue of *Commentary*, an intellectual journal sponsored by the American Jewish Committee. "The *Playboy* world is first and last an achievement in abstraction: history, politics, art, ordinary social relations, religion, families, nature, vanity, love, a thousand other items that presumably complicate both the inward and outward lives of human beings—all have been emptied from it. In place of the citizen with a vote to cast or a job to do or a book to study or a god to worship, the editor offers a vision of the whole man reduced to his private parts."

On the entirely reasonable hypothesis that if he was going to be damned, he would rather be damned for what he really believed than for what other people thought he believed, Hefner embarked on the Philosophy, otherwise known as a monthly statement of *Playboy*'s guiding principles and editorial credo: "Some people seem to feel that a happy, even frisky and romantic attitude toward life, and a savoring of its material pleasures, preclude seriousness, work, sensibility, a viable esthetic . . ."

Early installments of the Philosophy underscored Hefner's concern for the rights of the individual in a free society, but he also laid into organized religion, which he believed exercised a pervasive and noxious influence on society. The puritan tradition, he claimed, emasculated the Bill of Rights and repressed healthy heterosexuality.

Reader response was encouraging, if the letters published in the magazine were any indication: ". . . as the wife of a recent *Playboy* subscriber, I must congratulate Hugh Hefner on his superbly written editorial, the Playboy Philosophy. In trying to decide how to describe the all-encompassing material discussed and clarified so perfectly I can say nothing better than 'brilliant.' "

Most of the other letters were in the same vein, although the magazine did have the grace to publish a heartfelt plea from one young man who wrote: "Gee whizz! Do we *have* to have a Philosophy?"

Hefner had hoped that his attack on the Church would produce an avalanche of mail from theologians. Only a trickle arrived and so he summoned Anson Mount, the magazine's promotion manager, to the Mansion and ordered him to prod a reaction out of the clergy. Hefner was certainly not going to allow his philosophy to be *ignored*.

Anson "Smokey" Mount was a cheerful Southerner from Tennessee who was working part-time as a cab driver in Chicago and studying for an M.A. when he was hired as Victor Lownes's assistant in the mid-fifties. One of the little irritations about working for Playboy in those days was that Mayor Daley's police officers vigorously enforced parking regulations outside Playboy's offices on East Superior Street, almost to the point of persecution. Cars belonging to Playboy staffers were sometimes towed away while others were blithely ignored. One day Mount took it upon himself to point out to two policemen enthusiastically writing tickets outside 11 East Superior that the Archbishop of Chicago's limousine was illegally parked on the other side of the street outside the Holy Name Cathedral. When one of them inquired, with heavy sarcasm, if Mount wanted to lodge an official complaint, Mount said yes, he did. Ten days later he was visited in his apartment by plainclothes officers who demanded to know what he had against the archbishop and proceeded to beat him up.

This incident persuaded Mount to drop his complaint, which was perhaps just as well since he would eventually be appointed *Playboy*'s religion editor after demonstrating his ability to manipulate the clergy in the matter of the Philosophy. A man of considerable ingenuity, he did not consider Hefner's instructions to be in any way taxing. First he sent his secretary to the library at the University of Chicago Divinity School and told her to find the names and addresses of all the clergymen teaching at divinity and theological schools throughout the country. It took her two weeks. Using this information as a mailing list, Mount sent out hundreds of reprints of the third installment of the Philosophy with a cover letter saying that "a friend" had suggested the recipient might be interested. The letter politely invited comments.

Blissfully unaware that they were being set up, the good clerics replied at length. Fundamentalists by and large said that the Philosophy would lead the younger generation straight to hell and that Hefner was clearly an agent of Satan. But most of the opinions were less extreme and there were plenty of letters making constructive or favorable remarks. These last, suitably edited, were immediately printed in *Playboy*, sometimes to the horror of their authors. A lot of professors, Mount admitted, got "their ass in the wringer" as a result. But Hefner got what he wanted: recognition as a contemporary philosopher worthy of being taken seriously by no less venerable an institution than the Church.

Thereafter, the Playboy Philosophy triggered off a virulent debate within the Church, with Hefner attracting a surprising amount of support. "The average Minister's sermons would be more relevant," said a Minister of the United Church of Christ in Pittsburgh, "if *Playboy* were required reading." The magazine's position, a Wesley Foundation Minister told students at Indiana University, was "more authentically Christian than much that is heard from pulpits today."

Harvey Cox, who had attacked *Playboy* for being "basically anti-sexual," became a regular contributor, a conversion sarcastically described in the *National Review* as the "most remarkable since Saul set out for Damascus." The Chaplain of Southern Methodist University, writing in the *Catholic World*, suggested comparing the Playboy Philosophy with the First Epistle of John: "It may surprise the reader to know that John was wrestling with many of the same problems which *Playboy* confronts in the contemporary world." And a contributor to a journal published by the Lutheran Theological Seminary in St. Louis dared to conclude: "*Playboy* has performed a service for the Christian Church in emphasizing the fact that the Ten Commandments and the 'marriage' of Adam and Eve are no longer generally accepted as the basis for sex relationships."

Spurred on by the attention, Hefner toiled at his typewriter in the womb of the Mansion. He wrote in frenetic bursts, sometimes going for thirty or forty hours without rest, keeping himself awake with Dexedrine and Pepsis and producing thousands and thousands of words. Writer Tom Wolfe visited the Mansion around this time and reported: "The white wall-to-wall in the living room of Hefner's bedroom suite is covered with great hummocks of research material, marked 'Sodomy,' 'Homosexuality,' 'Adultery,' and so forth. He clodhops through it all and works away on a streamlined typewriter, sitting there in his pajamas and bathrobe. The Philosophy imputes deep moral purpose to his enterprises, legitimizes them." Wolfe dubbed Hefner "King of the Status Drop-Outs" and added that the Philosophy, to East Coast intellectuals at any rate, seemed like a naïve and tedious set-to with a colossus somebody or other must have killed off forty years before.

When Hefner was working, a mantle of sepulchral reverence descended on the Mansion: the staff crept about as if in church and whispered to each other in awed tones, "Hef's working on the *Philosophy*." Churned out to meet unforgiving deadlines, much of it was hopelessly muddled and repetitive. From the start, he had no clear idea of what he wanted to say, so the ideas poured out haphazardly, clogged by dauntingly long quotations and confused by qualifications appearing months after the original statement. "This direct, organic approach suits our purpose," he explained, "since the Philosophy is intended as a living statement of our beliefs, our insights and our prejudices."

Sparkling prose was not, in any case, the Philosophy's strong point: "If any of us were ever in serious doubt about the relative merits of group-oriented collectivist socialism or communism versus self-oriented, individual initiative, free enterprise capitalism . . ." It was heavy going for a magazine that featured cartoons endlessly depicting the ravishing of buxom young ladies by men saying things like "Why talk about love at a time like this?"

As a philosopher, Hefner's views were hardly revolutionary and not particularly original (John Stuart Mill said much the same a hundred years earlier in his essay *On Liberty*), but he presented them with a touchingly triumphant air, as if stumbling across astonishing truths previously concealed. Flailing about from one subject to another, he argued in support of the separation of Church and State, the body as a source of pleasure, free enterprise, and individual freedom. He opposed censorship, prejudice, and puritanism in all their forms and persistently nagged for the repeal of America's archaic obscenity laws.

The one passage that caused a real stir, and would be waved about by anti-*Playboy* protesters in the years to come, was his cautious defense of sex for its own sake. "Being a romantic fellow ourself," (the "editorial we" played havoc with Hefner's syntax) "we favor our sex mixed with emotion. But we recognize that sex without love exists, that it is not in itself evil and that it may sometimes serve a definitely worthwhile end." This viewpoint, variously repeated, never failed to purse lips across the nation.

While the pro-*Playboy*, anti-*Playboy* debate continued in the Church, the Reverend Roy Larson proposed in *Motive*, the magazine of the Methodist student movement, that since the Philosophy had become a sort of substitute religion for the readers of *Playboy*, they ought to have their own Ten Commandments. He suggested the following:

> Thou shalt not wear double-breasted suits
> Thou shalt not swing and sway to Sammy Kaye
> Thou shalt not drive a Dodge
> Thou shalt not serve a breakfast coffee after dinner
> Thou shalt not attend the P.T.A.
> Thou shalt not eat Velveeta cheese
> Thou shalt not be crude or cavemanish in love-making
>   and above all, thou shalt not be guilty of chastity

Thou shalt not travel by bus
Thou shalt not be stuffy and intellectual
Thou shalt not read the *Reader's Digest*

If Hefner ever doubted the need for his Philosophy—there is no evidence he ever did—he had only to turn the pages of his own magazine, to the Playboy Advisor column, for an insight into the neuroses, insecurities, and anxieties that plagued male America in the early sixties.

The idea for the Advisor came from a parody of the Ann Landers column submitted by a free-lance contributor sometime in 1960. Hefner liked Ann Landers and did not want to run the piece, but suggested instead that the magazine should begin its own advice column for men. The first letters were all written and answered by *Playboy* staffers and covered everyday problems like how much to tip in a restaurant, what tie to wear with tweeds, and "What do you think of those martinis and Manhattans that come in those little plastic bags?" Answer: "We think they should remain in those little plastic bags."

The column generated sixty-three genuine queries—at the time, an encouraging response—and set up a fascinating dialogue that over the years revealed the *Playboy* reader to be far removed from the suave man-about-town to whom the magazine was supposed to appeal. On the contrary, it appeared he was a perplexed and unhappy figure, singularly lacking in confidence. Not only did he need guidance on basic points of etiquette, like whether to answer the telephone in the middle of sex, but he was also excessively troubled by the size of his cock.

Among the shoals of letters asking when a Windsor knot was acceptable and if venereal disease could be caught from lavatory seats, there would always be dozens of anxious inquiries about the average size of the penis. It was the one subject that dominated the correspondence and no amount of reassurance that size was not related to performance stopped readers fretting that theirs was not big enough. If ever the debate wilted, *Playboy* had only to publish letters like "Mine is twelve inches but my girlfriend thinks it is small" for the rulers to come out and the Advisor to be swamped with letters from men pleading to be told they were *normal*. The claims of the "big cock society" that big was better were consistently decried by the magazine as being without scientific basis. A prostitute with twenty years' experience wrote in to say that she was familiar with penises of "all types and sizes" and that size had no bearing whatsoever on ultimate pleasure. "This nonsense about big breasts and big penises is just part of the great American bigness fixation," another correspondent claimed, probably with justification.

When the Advisor was first published, only a few readers had sex on their minds: for every letter asking advice about sex, there were seven or eight asking about wine or cuff links or sports cars. Sex questions were largely concerned with dating etiquette and deflowering virgins, and answers were obtained by an editor wandering around the office asking "Anyone know anything about this?" By the end of the decade, a team of experts was required to provide the answers and up to one thousand readers were writing in each month with queries on obscure subjects like fist-fucking and the caloric content of sperm.

Hefner liked to describe what happened in the sixties as the "decontamination" of sex and claimed much of the credit. "A lot of people are starved for fresh air," he told *Life* magazine in 1965, "and there's pure oxygen coming from this corner. It's no wonder people are pressing close to the ventilator."

Certainly it was impossible not to recognize that attitudes toward nudity and sex were changing rapidly. In 1964, bare breasts blossomed in fashion magazines when Rudi Gernreich introduced his outlandish "topless look," much favored by starlets at Hollywood premieres. The mini-skirt arrived the following year in a flurry of thighs and became the micro-skirt, also vulgarly known as a "pussy-pelmet." There were long lines everywhere outside movie houses showing *I am Curious (Yellow)*, the first widely distributed movie in America to portray explicit sex. And on the New York stage, the cast of *Hair* briefly removed their clothes at the end of the first act, paving the way for *Oh! Calcutta!*, the first show in the history of theater with a nil budget for costumes.

Those poor souls unable to decide how to react to these events could always ask the Playboy Advisor for guidance. It became the second most popular feature in the magazine and a source of considerable comfort to men who were apparently unable to take their problems elsewhere—every letter was answered and in its early days the column established a reputation for honest, accurate, and unequivocal answers. ("Should I wear an ascot?" "No, only assholes wear ascots.") So well known did the feature become that James R. Petersen reported the following exchange with a woman in a Chicago bar soon after he had taken over as editor: "Hi, what do you do?" "I write the Playboy Advisor." "That's neat. I have a friend who writes the Playboy Advisor all the time. What's your problem?"

In 1963, the Playboy Advisor was joined by the Playboy Forum, a companion feature intended to offer a platform to readers for the exchange of ideas raised by the Playboy Philosophy. Anson Mount, whose contribution to promoting the Philosophy had not gone unnoticed, was appointed editor of the new feature and immediately decided that most of the letters passed to him for possible publication were either too long or too boring or both. It did not worry him at all.

No one could complain the Playboy Forum was boring when it made its debut in June 1963. Indeed, the ideas being exchanged were astonishing for the times: there were outrageous letters from young girls describing the pleasures of group sex, advice from priests on the benefits of premarital sex, wild stories from Southern sheriffs. All of them were written by the Forum's ingenious editor and signed with names chosen at random from the telephone directory.

It was a technique that so alarmed his fellow editors he was removed after a couple of months and returned to the promotion department, where he was given special responsibility for maintaining the liaison between the magazine and the clergy. But by then the genuine letters that were pouring into the Playboy Forum were quite as extraordinary as those dreamed up by Anson Mount. Readers became involved in uninhibited discussions about matters rarely aired before in public—masturbation, buggery, penis envy, lesbianism, impotence, abortion. One girl wrote from Boulder, Colorado, to announce that she had resolved the conflict between the teachings of the Catholic Church and her desire for sex by thrusting a crucifix up her vagina, a solution that would probably never have occurred to Anson Mount in the wildest of his dreams.

A gentleman from Iowa wrote to describe a memorable orgasm achieved in the bath when he removed the wings from a fly and somehow persuaded it to trudge around the tip of his penis.

No subject was debarred from the Forum and it was used by readers to debate everything from breast feeding to civil rights, from the imprisonment of sex offenders to the war in Vietnam. It was well established as a regular feature in the magazine when Anson Mount resurfaced in 1965 as the newly appointed religion editor. It was announced that he was being sent to the Episcopal Theological Seminary in Sewanee, Tennessee, to study moral theology, contemporary theology, and Church history, the better to understand and interpret the theological implications of the Playboy Philosophy.

This was seen by Hefner as a very important and serious move, and *Playboy* staffers were discouraged from making frivolous jokes about "sermons on the Mount." When he arrived at the seminary, Mount discovered he was the only student in the course who was not an ordained Minister. Thoroughly unabashed, he rented a large house and invited fellow students to drop by for cocktails and theological discussion, every night.

Theologically fortified by his summer in Sewanee, he set out on the lecture circuit to spread the gospel according to Hefner, frequently proclaiming en route that Hefner was the "hottest thing since Martin Luther." In between speaking engagements, he kept up a running debate, by correspondence, with as many as two thousand clergymen of different denominations and could regularly be seen wining and dining visiting clerics and divinity students at the Chicago Playboy Club.

A few selected "celebrity" ministers were even invited to the Mansion to meet Hefner himself. Martin Luther King came and stayed until four o'clock in the morning, rapping with Hef in the ballroom about civil rights, the role of the Church, sex, and morality. The Reverend Malcolm Boyd, author of *Are You Running With Me, Jesus?*, also received an invitation and confessed to a curiosity to meet the resident Bunnies. "One girl, freckle-faced and sweet-looking," he noted later, "had recently had the distinction of appearing in the celebrated centerfold of *Playboy* stripped to the buff. Another, who wore the falsest eyebrows in memory, brushed back her long blonde hair and purred, 'Do you like sex?' "

Although the good reverend neglected to record his reply, it was clearly an encounter that made a deep impression, understandably perhaps, since false *eyebrows* could not have been widely worn, even in the Playboy Mansion.

Martin Luther King made an appearance in the pages of *Playboy* magazine some time before he visited the Mansion: he was an early subject for the Playboy Interview in January 1965. The interviewer was another black man, Alex Haley, who would later write an enthralling saga of his own family and call it *Roots*.

Widely applauded for its consistent intelligence and depth, the Playboy Interview was, indisputably, the magazine's single most important contribution to American journalism. Through the medium of exhaustingly long and probing question-and-answer sessions, the readers of *Playboy* were introduced to widely divergent views on important issues of the day and given an insight into the hearts and minds of an extraordinary variety of people, from Fidel Castro to Timothy Leary, from Albert Schweitzer to Dolly Parton.

Haley conducted the first Playboy Interview in 1962, when he was struggling to make his way as a writer after twenty years' service with the U.S. Coast Guard. It began as a commission for *Show Business Illustrated*. They asked Haley to try for an interview with Miles Davis, the jazz trumpeter. Davis was a recalcitrant, prickly character with no love for journalists, particularly white journalists, but the *SBI* editors hoped he might feel some kinship with Haley.

It was the kind of assignment a writer less desperate than Haley might have given up. Davis wanted nothing to do with an interview. Haley approached his press agent, his recording company, even his wife, and was rebuffed by them all. When he heard that Davis was playing at the Village Vanguard in New York, he went there every night and tried to ask questions during breaks in the music. Davis replied with monosyllabic, overtly hostile answers. Haley waited outside by the stage door to try to speak to him at the end of the concert and was brushed aside as the trumpeter swept out.

Then someone told Haley that Davis boxed most afternoons at a gym in Harlem. Haley found the place, on 135th Street, and as he opened the door he saw Davis standing in the ring in boxing gear. At that moment, the musician was looking around for a sparring partner, and when he spotted the writer who had been pestering him at the Village Vanguard he cocked his head and told him to get into the ring. Haley was no fighter: he was small, short-sighted, and gentle by nature, but he took off his glasses, ducked under the ropes, and pulled on a pair of gloves.

Davis began to pepper him lightly with punches and Haley did his best to defend himself while gamely trying to get in a couple of questions. In a clinch, Haley grunted something about reporters being a hateful, untrustworthy lot and Davis laughed out loud. They began talking in the shower stalls and Davis eventually invited the other man back to his house on West 77th Street where Haley got his interview. A few weeks later, he proudly delivered his copy to *Show Business Illustrated* in Chicago, only to be told the magazine was folding.

After the *SBI* editors had returned, thankfully no doubt, to New York from whence they came, Spectorsky asked Murray Fisher, an associate editor on *Playboy*, to rummage through the *SBI* files and dig out any manuscripts worth saving. There was not, in truth, a great deal of material to interest *Playboy*, but Fisher was struck by Haley's interview with Miles Davis, in particular because the trumpeter spoke with bitter passion on the subject of racial prejudice. Here was an articulate, successful, and angry man, haunted by the shadow of Jim Crow, talking about the harsh reality of being black in white America, two years before the passing of the Civil Rights Act.

The black struggle for civil rights was a burning issue in 1962: many of the Southern states were in a turmoil, black churches were bombed, the Klan rallied behind its infamous burning crosses, and three thousand troops were needed to quell the riots sparked off by the admission of a black student, James Meredith, to the University of Mississippi. There was no better time to publish the views of Miles Davis.

Fisher took the piece to Spectorsky, who took it to Hefner, who agreed it should be published. It was Hefner's idea to run it in a question-and-answer format, with the questions being posed anonymously by the magazine. When his interview appeared in the September 1962 issue of *Playboy*, the luckless Haley's name was nowhere to be found.

Thereafter Murray Fisher was assigned to take charge of the Playboy Interview, lining up suitable subjects with something interesting and relevant to say and pressing writers to probe deeper, to keep asking questions and to ask things no one had dared to ask before. It was not easy at first to persuade prominent Americans to appear in the company of a Playmate and Fisher often had to look for candidates abroad, which was one of the reasons why Bertrand Russell, Jean Genet, and Jean-Paul Sartre were early subjects.

Malcolm X, Haley's second assignment, had no inhibitions about appearing in *Playboy* but he was not a great deal easier to talk to than Miles Davis. They met in a Harlem restaurant owned by the Black Muslims and at first Malcolm X would talk of nothing but the Muslim movement, constantly taunting Haley that the "white devils" would not publish his views. He was nearly right. Spectorsky was adamantly opposed to the interview, but was overruled by Hefner. The interview appeared in May 1963, although Spectorsky ensured that the readers knew *Playboy* did not approve of what the Muslim leader had to say. The feature was introduced as a "damning self-indictment of one noxious facet of rampant racism."

While Haley was working on the Malcolm X piece, he was also trying to get Martin Luther King to agree to be interviewed. King was worried about the suitability of *Playboy* as a forum for the discussion of civil rights, but Haley won his agreement with figures. At that time, *Playboy* was selling nearly three million copies every month. Haley gave one of King's advisers a demographic breakdown of the readership. "I told him the readers were crucial to King's cause, and that whatever he thought about the nude photography, he couldn't ignore the audience."

The interview took place in King's office behind the Ebenezer Baptist Church in Atlanta, Georgia, not long after his famous "I have a dream" speech to the 200,000 civil rights marchers at the Lincoln Memorial in Washington had so stirred the nation's conscience. King's schedule was so hectic that he could only find time to sit down with Haley at night, after a church barbecue supper.

He talked for hours, far into the night, until he nodded off at his desk, totally exhausted.

Publication of the Martin Luther King interview was fortuitously timed. A few weeks before the issue was due on the streets, he received the Nobel Prize for Peace. His acceptance speech in Oslo made headlines around the world. "I accept the Nobel Prize at a moment when twenty-two million Negroes of the United States of America are engaged in a creative battle to end the long night of racial injustice. . . . Yet when the years have rolled past, men and women will know and children will be taught that we have a finer land, a better people, a more noble civilization because these humble children of God were willing to suffer for righteousness' sake."

King's rhetoric in *Playboy* was perhaps less stirring, but no less eloquent or sincere. It was the longest interview he had ever given to any magazine and he told Haley later it was the best. A few months later Haley was handed another commission, one which would result in the most bizarre encounter in his career. He was sent to interview George Lincoln Rockwell, self-appointed "Führer" of the American Nazi Party and "Messiah of White supremacy."

When Haley telephoned Rockwell and asked if he would be willing to be interviewed by *Playboy*, Rockwell only inquired if Haley was a Jew. No, he said, I'm not. Five days later, Haley stepped out of a taxi outside Rockwell's "International Headquarters"—a red brick and white frame house in Arlington, Virginia, with a sign on the roof saying: WHITE MAN FIGHT—SMASH THE BLACK REVOLUTION. He was greeted at the door by a uniformed guard whose mouth dropped in amazement.

While a hurried telephone call was made to Rockwell, Haley was instructed to wait in the Shrine Room. This was a gloomy living room painted black, lit by flickering red candles and decorated with the American and Nazi flags and portraits of Hitler, George Washington, and Rockwell.

After a few moments, two "storm troopers" entered the room, delivered themselves of Nazi salutes, and told Haley there was a staff car outside to take him to Commander Rockwell's personal headquarters. He was bundled into the back of the car and driven down a narrow, tree-lined road, passing a No Trespassing sign and a slavering Doberman guard dog, to a large farmhouse hung with red Nazi flags. An armed storm trooper frisked him at the door, then ushered him into a spacious room where Rockwell was standing underneath another portrait of Adolf Hitler. The two men stared at each other in silence. Then Rockwell motioned Haley to a chair, sat down himself, took out a pearl-handled revolver and placed it ostentatiously on the arm of his own chair. "I'm ready if you are," he said.

As they began talking, Rockwell explained that although it was nothing personal, he called people of Haley's race "niggers." Haley replied that he had often been called a nigger, but this was the first time he was being paid for it, so the Commander should feel free to go right ahead. This exchange set the tone for the interview, with Haley, the sweet voice of reason, calmly probing while Rockwell explained how, after his election as president in 1972, he would ship all niggers back to Africa where they belonged, isolate "queers" on some off-shore island, and exterminate the Jews.

Many years later, when Haley's best-seller *Roots* was adapted for television, the interview was included in the script, with Marlon Brando playing the part of Rockwell. In real life, Haley brooded unhappily about his *Playboy* interviews, believing them to have been cursed in some way since three of his subjects were assassinated before the end of the decade.

Malcolm X was shot in February 1965, at a rally of his followers at the Audubon Ballroom in Washington Heights. His life story, *The Autobiography of Malcolm X*, written largely by Haley, was published a few months later.

Rockwell was shot at his Arlington headquarters in 1967, one year after his Playboy Interview was published.

Martin Luther King was shot on a motel balcony in Memphis, Tennessee, on April 4, 1968. The photograph of his followers pointing frantically at the fleeing assassin was as haunting as that taken in Dallas in November 1963 of a young woman in an open car cradling her dying husband in her bloodstained lap.

7

Godzilla
of Sleepy Hollow

"**T**here's been an *incredible* fuck-up!" Hefner was on the internal telephone in the Mansion, talking to Bobbie Arnstein, his personal assistant. It was a phrase she got to know well: an *incredible* fuck-up. What could it be? Was the magazine being sued for libel? Were the police massing to raid a Playboy Club? Had a Bunny been discovered in a whorehouse? No, nothing like that, but something very important to the editor-publisher had gone badly wrong: his gravy was lumpy, *again*.

It was a tradition at the Playboy Mansion that guests could ask for anything they wanted in the way of food and drink, and get it. Staying in the Mansion was rather like traveling first-class in the heyday of the great transatlantic liners: the kitchens were manned round the clock and were geared to produce virtually any dish, no matter how exotic, at any time of the day or night. Show business personalities, staying over while appearing in Chicago, liked to test the chef's mettle when they got back from the theater by ordering truffles and salmon in aspic and venison and cheese soufflés. Even the resident Bunnies regularly chomped lobster thermidor.

It was, therefore, a source of considerable irritation to Hefner when the duty chef failed to accommodate his own extremely modest demands. Virtually all he asked was for his sandwiches to be made with fresh Wonder Bread, for his chicken to be juicy and succulent, and for the gravy with his pot roast not to be lumpy. Was it any wonder that he considered failure to meet these not-very-exacting standards to be an incredible fuck-up? Angry memos were dispatched whenever he was dissatisfied with the food or service in the Mansion. "I have a twenty-four-hour kitchen," he would often begin, as if its ceaseless operation was of some deep significance, "why can't I have chicken like they make at Kentucky Fried Chicken?"

Jodie McRae devoted a great deal of his attention to Mr. Hefner's diet and in particular to the problem of Mr. Hefner's gravy. When Hefner's elderly mother visited the Mansion, Jodie sought her out and asked her *exactly* how she made his gravy when he was a little boy, hoping for an infallible recipe that would finally defeat the recurring lumpy-gravy crises. This information was passed to the kitchen and incorporated into the detailed book of instructions on how to prepare Mr. Hefner's meals.

By the mid-sixties, Hefner was an extremely rich man—certainly rich enough to fret about lumpy gravy if he wished. He was worth around $100 million. In 1965, the magazine grossed $28,400,000, the thirteen Playboy Clubs brought in $19,667,000, and the sale of Playboy products added another couple of million to the pot. In addition, he owned a hotel in Jamaica (in Bunny Bay), a model agency, and a movie theater in Chicago. A Playboy book division was doing well, selling anthologies from the magazine, and plans were well advanced for the construction of a $9 million Playboy resort at Lake Geneva, Wisconsin.

The chairman of this burgeoning empire candidly admitted that business bored him. He still loved his magazine, of course, but he was becoming increasingly obsessed with the minutiae of his life and the mechanics of the capsule in which he was living. Since he never went out, whatever was happening within the Mansion, no matter how insignificant, assumed a sometimes farcical importance. When he complained that the pink and white satin sheets custom-made for his round bed exhibited an annoying tendency to rumple, his executive assistant, Dick Rosenzweig, convened a solemn conference around the bed to discuss, with other executives and secretaries, ways and means of solving the problem.

When a butler took Hefner's St. Bernard, Humphrey, out for a walk, he was required, on his return, to fill in a report in the "Humphrey Book," a red loose-leaf file that documented Humphrey's adventures and bowel movements. "Hef's very detail oriented," Rosenzweig explained.

In the entirely artificial world of the Mansion, populated by courtiers and propped up by an elaborate infrastructure of myriad flunkeys, Hefner was indisputably king. New staff at the Mansion were warned never to say no to him. "On my first day," said Shirley Hillman, the social secretary, "I was told that if he asked for something, you were to say you would see to it as soon as possible. You were *never* to say that something could not be done, even if you knew it was impossible."

Shirley Hillman was an attractive young Englishwoman, married to an American. As social secretary, one of her primary duties was to pack Playboy parties with enough pretty girls to heavily outnumber the men: Hefner liked a ratio of at least two to one. It was not always easy, as Shirley explained. "People imagined that every girl in America was dying to get invited to a party at the Mansion. That was the myth. The reality was me traipsing around Chicago, desperately trying to find enough girls *willing* to go. One of the problems was that girls who had been to the Mansion expecting to meet lots of glamorous celebrities came back and told their friends that there was no one there but a bunch of middle-aged lechers.

"Hefner liked to have lots of girls around the place because he was always hoping to fall in love. He often said he was a romantic and it was true. He was like an adolescent. He imagined at every party that he would see a girl across a crowded room, their eyes would meet, violins would start to play, and he would feel that pit-a-pat. It was what he wanted out of life more than anything: lots of pit-a-pat."

Sometimes Shirley would pluck up sufficient courage to stop girls in the street. She might be shopping on Michigan Avenue and suddenly see the kind of girl Hefner could easily fall in love with—a fresh-faced ingenue, cheerleader-pretty, blonde, with a T-shirt stretched over thrusting breasts. She would tap her lightly on the shoulder and say: "Excuse me . . ." When all else failed, Shirley looked for girls on Oak Street beach, along the lake shore, usually trailing her small daughter along with her so she did not look too much like a procuress.

Parties were held twice a week, on Fridays and Sundays. The guest list was handled by Benny Dunn, a former vaudeville comedian who had been hired as a public relations man. Benny worshiped Hefner, wore the same clothes as his idol, and frequently declared: "Hef's the most wonderful man I've ever known in my whole life." When Benny was out and about in the Playboy limousine, he often used to telephone his mother. "Hi, Mom. This is Benny. Just thought I'd let you know I'm with Hef in the limousine on the way back to the Mansion. Hef says hello. He's a little busy to talk to you himself right now." These conversations would take place while Benny was entirely alone in the back of the limousine and the chauffeur was clenching his teeth to stop himself from laughing.

It was Benny's job to keep tabs on which celebrities were in town and to ensure they all received a telegram invitation to the next party. His success could be measured in the pages of the Mansion guest book, which contained an astonishing variety of names. As well as predictable Playboy party-goers like Sammy Davis, Jr., and Tony Curtis, there were names like Margot Fonteyn and Rudolf Nureyev, James Baldwin, Joseph P. Kennedy, and Yevgeny Yevtushenko. Benny would have had not the slightest hesitation in inviting the Pope to a party at the Playboy Mansion, had His Holiness been in Chicago.

Guests began arriving for the Friday night parties at around midnight, wheezing out of their limousines on North State Street Parkway and licking their lips at the hopeful prospect of the Rabelaisian revels within, for it was well known that there were always plenty of unattached Bunnies and Playmates at Hefner's parties. And while Hef naturally served the finest food and the bartenders could mix any known cocktail and all the astonishing facilities of the house were at the disposal of the guests, it was the presence of the Bunnies and Playmates, those most potent symbols of the American wet dream, who made an invitation to the Mansion so prized. Sometimes there were as many as five hundred guests at Friday night parties, eating, ogling, drinking, dancing, and hoping, oh bliss, to end the frolics getting laid by a beautiful, blonde, big-breasted, blue-eyed Bunny!

It was certainly a wonderful house for a party. You could watusi with a Bunny in the ballroom, slide down the fireman's pole into the underwater bar, swim in the pool, steam in the sauna, sunbathe in the solarium, wrestle with the pinball machines in the Games Room, bowl in the bowling alley, canoodle in the Woo Grotto. This last facility could only be entered by swimming through a waterfall softly splashing between the thatched huts and fake palm trees designed to create a South Sea Island setting for the swimming pool underneath the ballroom. A secret button lifted a trap door in the floor of the ballroom above the Woo Grotto. It was Hefner's little joke: couples canoodling on the grotto's plastic cushions would suddenly find a square hole, rimmed by leering faces, had appeared in the roof.

Norman Mailer stayed at the Mansion when he was in Chicago to cover the Liston-Patterson fight and recorded his impressions in *The Presidential Papers*:

The party was very big and it was a good party. The music went all the way down into the hour or two before breakfast, but no one saw the dawn come in because the party was at Hugh Hefner's house which is one of the most extraordinary houses in America and the living room where much of the party was going on was sixty feet long and more than thirty wide, and almost twenty high, yet there were no windows, at least I never saw the sky from that room, and so there was a timeless, spaceless sensation . . . the peace when empty of the house was profound, one never saw one's host except for once or twice in some odd hour of the night. He had a quality not unlike Jay Gatsby, he looked and talked like a lean, rather modest cowboy of middle size; there was something of a mustang about Hefner. He was not the kind of man one would have expected to see as the publisher of his magazine, nor the owner of the Playboy Club, nor certainly as the undemanding host of his exceptional establishment. Timeless, spaceless, it was the outward bound. One was in an ocean liner which traveled at the bottom of the sea, or on a spaceship wandering down the galaxy along a night whose duration was a year.

Hefner very much liked Mailer's essay and would quote it often in years to come, always happy to see himself as the enigmatic Great Gatsby, outward-bound in his timeless spaceship. He was less enthusiastic about novelist Nelson Algren's portrayal:

> The great baronial hall was serving as a guest room for a gaggle of humans wearing all the clothes anyone could possibly need to break into society once they found a society to break into. This plainly wasn't it. This was high schlockhouse . . . If what was going on here was high society, Caroline Kennedy is president of the Veteran Boxers' Association.

Algren, author of *The Man with the Golden Arm*, was banned from the Mansion for a while because of his hurtful comments. Word was put out that he was not welcome because he misbehaved, getting so drunk that he could be found talking to the suits of armor flanking the entrance to the ballroom. Algren retorted that there was no one else at Playboy parties worth talking to, earning for himself an even longer banishment.

Hefner did not always make an appearance at the Friday night parties, sometimes preferring to stay in the solitude of his own quarters, with the doors locked to keep out straying merrymakers. Next day he'd ask Jodie McRae how the party had gone. If there were celebrities around he would normally show up at least long enough to be photographed with them by the *Playboy* staff photographer who was always present, but the moment the festivities began to flag he would be gone, back into his white-carpeted bolt hole, without so much as a farewell. The Mansion had a number of secret doors and passages, installed by Hefner because he thought it was the kind of house that *should* have secret doors and passages, thus he was able to disappear as if by magic.

Speculation about what went on at Playboy parties was a popular pastime in Chicago and it was generally agreed that whatever it was, it was probably disgusting. There were endless rumors of orgies, wild debauchery, and all kinds of sinful revelry with the Bunnies. Such was the Mansion's reputation that when *Chicago*

Daily News columnist Mike Royko reported that there was less whoopee at a Playboy party than at an over-thirty dance at any neighborhood ballroom, some people found it hard to believe. Most of the guests, said Royko, stood around trying to look cool and worldly and worrying that they did not look cool and worldly enough. An orgy it was certainly not. Indeed, the most risqué encounter anyone could recall at a Friday night party was the night the cast of *Hair* arrived and took off their clothes and danced in the swimming pool. But as they took their clothes off every night on stage, it could hardly be described as a particularly noteworthy or titillating event.

Hefner was amused by the gossip, rather than upset, and never felt he had anything to hide. When a Canadian film team making a documentary about him asked if they could film at a Friday night party he agreed without hesitation. The film was devastating, not because of what it revealed about a Playboy party, but because it exposed Hefner's vulnerability to ridicule. Years later, audiences would still hoot with laughter when he turned to the camera, with his party guests twisting furiously in the background, and admitted: "Genius is a funny kind of word . . . I suppose by definition I consider myself one, both intellectually and in terms of creativity."

Undoubtedly it was the presence of the live-in Bunnies that largely fueled salacious rumors about what was going on in the Playboy Mansion. Twenty-five Bunnies occupied the austere dormitories on the top floor, the first girls having moved in shortly after the opening of the Chicago Playboy Club. It was an arrangement that suited both parties admirably. For the girls, the Mansion offered cheap accommodation and food ($50 a month rent, $1.50 for dinner), the chance to meet celebrities, and plenty of entertainment. If they could forget their bunk beds, lockers, and communal washrooms, the Mansion was a glamorous place to be.

For Hefner, the Bunnies primarily provided decoration for his home and valuable promotion for his magazine, since their presence attracted so much attention. They were constantly available and completely undemanding companions for him and his friends, often for nothing more dissolute than a game of Monopoly. Although many of them were undoubtedly willing to sleep with Hefner and his house guests, none was pressured to do so and they were never "offered" as part of the hospitality. (One of the most common rumors was that when a guest was shown to his room, he was asked by a butler if he "wanted a Bunny.") If a guest could strike up a relationship with a Bunny and get her into his bed, that was his good fortune. If he could not, that was his bad luck.

"Obviously some of the Bunnies were promiscuous to start with," said Milda Bridgewater, a bouncy little blonde who was employed at the Mansion to collate Hefner's scrapbook, "but also a lot of them became promiscuous while they were there. The atmosphere in the Mansion could be a traumatic experience for a girl from a small town. She would arrive sweet, naïve, and innocent, but she would not stay that way for long because it was very difficult to separate fantasy from reality in that place. If a girl was a bit of a prude, she'd probably leave of her own accord or be eased out. You know, she wouldn't be invited to the parties and suggestions would be made that she'd probably be happier elsewhere."

Hefner ensured that Bunnies were always around when he was entertaining celebrities by dictating frequent memos to Bobbie Arnstein on the subject: "Please get word to all the girls in the House, plus all of the Bunnies in the Chicago Club, that Anthony Newley will be my houseguest here Wednesday and Thursday, and we would enjoy having as many of the girls hanging in in the evening, and after work, as possible. . . ."

Off-duty Bunnies were also always present at the Sunday night parties, when a newly released movie was screened in the ballroom for an eclectic gathering of friends, celebrities, *Playboy* editors, and secretaries. Guests assembled around six o'clock for cocktails and champagne and a lobster buffet was served at seven. Hefner never made an appearance until sometime after eight o'clock, but his arrival was the signal for the movie to begin instantly. As he stepped down into the ballroom, a huge screen unfurled silently from out of the cornice on the left-hand side of the room and the lights began to dim.

Hefner and his date occupied an orange-upholstered couch—the "love seat"—set alongside the stereo console and in the front row, naturally. Next to him was an identical couch reserved for a best friend and his girl: this was often his younger brother Keith, or John Dante, a former bartender at the Chicago club who had become very close to Hefner. If there was no best friend present, this couch was left unoccupied. Everyone else sat on the chairs or cushions, their status clearly determined by their proximity to Hefner.

For more than three years, Hefner shared his love seat at the Sunday night movie with the same girl—Mary Warren, a tall blonde with classic good looks, not unlike Grace Kelly. She was still a teenager and working as a Door Bunny at the Chicago club when Hefner first saw her and felt that familiar pit-a-pat. He put her on the cover of *Playboy*, gave her a job in the magazine's personnel department, and invited her into his bed, probably not in that order. Many people privy to the claustrophobic world of the Playboy Mansion predicted Mary would be the second Mrs. Hefner. Hefner was unquestionably besotted with her and they played mummy and daddy roles to Humphrey, the St. Bernard, when he was a puppy. Mary had him put in a playpen in their bedroom and christened him Baby.

But Mary found it as difficult to interest Hefner in monogamy as her legion of predecessors. One day she was sitting in the ballroom talking to her friend Milda Bridgewater, when she actually *saw* another girl creeping guiltily out of Hefner's quarters. "That goddam pig!" she snapped. Milda wondered if she was talking about Hefner or the girl. Not long afterward, Mary told Hefner she had had enough and left the Mansion for good. Later, Milda helped her sneak back into Hefner's apartment to retrieve the film Hefner had taken of them making love.

Milda knew more than most about what was going on in the Mansion since she had discovered where Hefner kept his blue-covered logbook of conquests. It was underneath a lot of other papers in the middle drawer of the desk in his study. Milda and Bobbie Arnstein and Shirley Hillman liked to look through it and giggle over the names and comments. They never had time to count the entries, but they all agreed the book probably contained more than one thousand names. On one dog-eared page compiled in the early years, they found the name of an extremely plain and plump woman accountant, still working for Playboy, and screamed with laughter at the prospect of her in bed with Hefner.

Names were added to the book with startling frequency after

Mary Warren's departure, as Hefner sought to console himself with a veritable procession of young ladies, each briefly straddling the famous round bed before being dispatched. Staff at the Mansion were able to keep track of the master's amorous activities by his Homeric consumption of Johnson's Baby Oil. At one point, Bobbie Arnstein complained to Rosenzweig that ordering the stuff was becoming an embarrassment—crates containing fifty economy-size bottles were regularly humped into his quarters by the housemen, manfully trying not to smirk.

"Every girl who slept with Hefner thought they would be the one to land him," said Milda. "None of them could accept that to Hefner they were just another girl."

One day Milda was surreptitiously checking out the blue logbook when she noticed the latest entry was a name entirely unfamiliar to her. In the comments column Hefner had written "Friend of Christie's."

Hefner had not had much contact with his children since his divorce from Millie in 1959, but when Christie was sixteen, he hosted a Sweet Sixteen party for her at the Mansion. She was allowed to invite ten of her school friends for a sit-down dinner in the ballroom with printed menus and all the trimmings. Hefner enjoyed playing the role of indulgent father, just as he enjoyed making love to one of the guests a few days later. The girl telephoned him after the party and said she would like to see him again. Hefner guessed what she wanted and briefly agonized—he asked Bobbie Arnstein what he should do—about the seemliness of bouncing a friend of his daughter on the round bed. In the end, the temptation proved too much.

Hefner's reluctance to leave the Mansion did not in any way affect the success of his business. In 1966, Playboy reported profits up by an astonishing 58 percent. H.M.H. Publishing grossed $40,215,000, an increase of 42 percent over the previous year; Playboy Clubs, International produced $24,860,000, an increase of 26 percent. *Playboy* magazine, by then selling more than 3,500,000 copies every month, turned a profit on its newsstand sales alone, a phenomenon in American publishing. Hefner liked to refer to the magazine's handsome advertising revenue (a four-color page cost $27,000) as gravy. And advertisers loved *Playboy*, since its readers were prodigious spenders; media surveys indicated 52 percent of reader households chalked up annual incomes in excess of $10,000 and more than 22 percent were members of country clubs.

Time magazine devoted a cover story to Hefner in 1966 and described Playboy as a "major American business success story," an accolade perhaps soured by a surprising attack from *Time*'s popular stablemate, *Life*, in a piece by Diana Lurie, which went straight for Playboy's underbelly. "In Hefnerland," Miss Lurie wrote, "a woman is simply another aspect of the status symbol mania that is stamped all over Playboy. She is no more or less important than the sleekest sports car or the most expensive bottle of Scotch. A woman becomes depersonalized, an object for man's pleasure, something to pour his drinks, inflate his ego, and look gorgeous on his arm as he parades in front of his pals."

But this was years before the rise of the feminist movement, and there were plenty of women in America who could see absolutely nothing wrong with pouring a man's drinks, inflating his ego, and looking gorgeous. *Playboy*, guided by an editor who described it as "a projection on the wonderful world I dig," could do no wrong: even increasing the cover price from 75¢ to $1.00 did not dent the soaring curve in the circulation graph. Hailed everywhere as a polished and literary package, it could sit proudly on the nation's coffee tables along with *Esquire* and *The New Yorker* and should an eyebrow be raised, its existence could be perfectly justified by the quality of writing to be found under the voluptuous cover girl.

In 1967, as tangible proof of its success, Playboy moved into one of Chicago's most venerable skyscrapers—the thirty-seven-story Palmolive Building on North Michigan Avenue. Preuss negotiated the purchase of a sixty-three-year lease for $2,700,000. A clause in the lease prevented the name of the building being changed without the permission of the owners, the Prudential Insurance Company, and Preuss was warned that if he asked for such permission, it would probably be refused. "I thought the best thing to do," he said, "was not to ask." Workmen could soon be espied clinging to the upper flanks of the building to fix the word PLAYBOY in huge white letters onto the gray stone façade. Thereafter, it was the Playboy Building.

Similarly, the Lindbergh Beacon on the roof was rechristened, with breathtaking insouciance, the Bunny Beacon. This two-billion-candlepower revolving searchlight swept the heavens at night and was visible to pilots approaching Chicago from as far as five hundred miles away. It was originally named to commemorate Charles Lindbergh's historic flight across the Atlantic in 1927. Clearly Playboy thought this feat paled to insignificance beside the invention of the Bunny.

Each of the fifteen floors occupied by Playboy in the new building was decorated in a style befitting the magazine. Masculine tweed carpeting covered the floors, the walls were rough-textured and hung with original artwork, office furniture was in marble and oiled teak, and linen drapes could be pulled across the windows should the view pall. When the elevator doors of burnished walnut, decorated with Art Deco reliefs, opened on each floor, the first sight to greet the visitor was a beautiful receptionist sitting at a marble-topped desk.

Hefner did not bother to look around the Palmolive Building before he bought it, neither did he visit it after his staff had moved in. Preuss kept him informed of the negotiations for the lease and he approved all the designs for the interiors, but he had not the slightest inclination to see the place for himself, until one night he suddenly decided, for no apparent reason, that he would take a walk. It was two o'clock in the morning, cold and raining, when he got outside and for a moment he was unsure where to go. Then he had the bright idea of taking a look at the Playboy Building, which was only a few blocks from the Mansion.

Pulling his coat tightly around him and turning up the collar to keep out the rain, he set off down North State Street Parkway. In five minutes he was outside the Walton Street entrance to the Playboy Building, rattling the doors and punching the night bell. Thirty-seven floors up, the Bunny Beacon whirred round and round, blinking its beam across the blackness of the Great Lakes.

No one blamed the security guard for not letting Hefner into the building. All the guard could see by the dimmed lights of the lobby was a thin, scruffy-looking man, unshaven, with unkempt hair plastered against his head by the rain. Sure, he said he was Hugh Hefner, but everyone knew Mr. Hefner never left his Mansion, so who was this kook trying to kid?

After some considerable time, Hefner managed to convince

the guard who he was and he was let in, but the guard followed him around the whole time he was in the building, just in case. Hefner trudged slowly along the carpeted reaches of his deserted headquarters, leaving damp footprints in his wake. He opened the doors of the executive offices, looked at manuscripts and layouts on desks, admired the fittings, and left after about half an hour to disappear into the night, with the guard still wondering if he had been hoaxed.

Throughout the years he spent cloistered in the Mansion, Hefner never relinquished control of Playboy despite the curious fact that he could be found slumbering in his round bed, deep in the innards of the Mansion, for most of the time his staff was at work. He hated to delegate responsibility, valued his own judgment above that of all others, and wanted to make all the decisions himself. In 1967, Spectorsky was earning considerably more than the President of the United States, but he still had to get Hefner's approval before an engraved letterhead could be ordered for a new editor.

Hefner managed by meeting and memo, both at inordinate length. Night after night he would sit on his bed, feeding belts into the Dictaphone machine built into the curved headboard and dictating hundreds of memos, sometimes up to thirty pages long. Don Myrus, head of the book division, proudly claimed to be the recipient of Hefner's longest-ever memo—39,000 words covering forty pages on what action he should take to develop his division. Three typists, working on shifts round the clock, were required to keep pace with Hefner's prodigious flow of paperwork.

No detail was too unimportant to occupy his attention. "The first sentence of the review of 'How to Succeed with Women' has me thoroughly puzzled and yet I'm sure this was read and reread and proofread, so it must be correct. Shouldn't it read 'The hip, hilarious series *has* . . .' Doesn't the word 'series' take the singular, the same as 'group' or 'collection' or any similar noun? I recognize that the word 'series' can be either singular or plural, but it is hard for me to understand how it can be used in the plural here."

At editorial meetings, too, Hefner was capable of devoting hours to the most trifling niceties. *Playboy* editor Frank Brady recalled one such meeting, which began at five o'clock in the afternoon: "I was still sitting at the conference table with Hefner ten hours later as he rewrote an answer to a letter to the editor that was scheduled to be published. He kept talking about the letter, concerning some ludicrously trivial matter, until I was ready to scream or walk out."

Brady was lucky. Myrus, recipient of the record memo, maintained that his three meetings with Hefner to discuss the book division each broke existing records for longevity: the first was twelve hours, the second eighteen hours, and the third a marathon twenty-six hours. Hefner kept himself going with amphetamines and Pepsi; Myrus chose Dom Perignon champagne.

After a meeting at the Mansion, Spectorsky often returned to his office in the Playboy Building fuming at the time he had had to spend with Hefner working over a single sentence, sometimes a single phrase. "Spec" never made any secret of his feelings about Hefner's lifestyle and the Mansion, which he often referred to as "the bunker." He liked to say it was as personal as a "hotel lobby decorated in early garish" and its owner he described as "Godzilla of Sleepy Hollow."

But his attitude toward Hefner as a man was often ambivalent. "To me, Hef's unique, a brilliant walking paradox," he once told the Reverend Malcolm Boyd. "He can be bonehard selfish, egocentric, anally retentive, suspicious, almost paranoid; he can also pour out love, humanity, act out all the beautiful clichés that cynics no longer believe possible. He is a profound, practical psychologist and at the same time he can be completely fooled by people who are transparently obvious to everybody else."

Spectorsky certainly found working with Hefner a source of considerable frustration, since it was not easy to produce a magazine each month when the publisher was largely inaccessible to his staff, when he was obsessed with editorial minutiae, and when he lived 180 degrees out of synchronization with the rest of the world. Editors could not even telephone Hefner: he never accepted calls, only returned them—selectively. One editor, desperate for a meeting with Hefner, hung a huge sign on the glass doors separating Hefner's apartment from the rest of the Mansion.

Hefner insisted on final approval of virtually everything in the magazine with the exception of the fiction, which he left to Spectorsky and often did not bother to read. He always selected the Playmate, chose the cartoons, and edited the Party Jokes page.

When proofs came in, he was perfectly capable of fussing over the use of a semicolon or fretting about the color of the reflection in the Playmate's eyes. He was the worst bottleneck in the magazine's production system and delays cost the company hundreds of thousands of dollars at the printers for overtime and waiting charges. Once Preuss crept into his bedroom to retrieve a layout that was holding up production; Hefner woke up and was furious at the intrusion, but the phlegmatic Preuss pointed out later that at least that particular issue came out on time.

By 1968, Hefner had been sequestered in the Mansion for more than five years and it was clear from his appearance that his health was beginning to suffer. His weight had dropped from 175 to 135 pounds, making him look more gaunt than ever; his eyes were sunken, and he was deathly pale, almost etiolate, from lack of exposure to natural light; he had developed an alarming tolerance for amphetamines, swallowing them by the handful scooped from a mug on Bobbie Arnstein's desk; he ate irregularly, never exercised, and the twenty-five bottles of Pepsi he swilled every day were rotting his teeth.

When his mother visited the Mansion she scolded him for not taking care of himself, told him he looked like a skeleton, and insisted on taking a photograph of him so that he could see for himself how ill he looked. Hefner's doctor also warned him that if he continued to neglect his health he would never reach the age of fifty. He was then forty-two.

Hefner did not much care for this advice, but he did start to think about the way he was living. What had happened to all the proud talk, earlier in the sixties, about being in control of his own environment? To all intents and purposes, it now appeared that his environment was in control of *him*. He was working at a frenetic pitch simply to keep pace with the growth of his business, and the Mansion was functioning like some great heartless machine, routinely providing parties, entertainment, hospitality, and facilities for those marathon meetings.

Although screened by the diligent duo of Arnstein and Rosenzweig, he was still under constant pressure—deadlines and schedules and mountains of paper ruled his life. Even his bedroom, that fabled love chamber, was awash with paper stacked in untidy heaps all over the ankle-deep carpet.

It became clear to Hefner that something had gone wrong with his life, although the magazine blithely continued to promote him as the man who had it made. One issue included a cartoon which showed a weary traveler climbing a mountain to be told by a bearded guru at the summit: "In a place called Chicago, there is a man who lives in a mansion full of beautiful women and wears pajamas all the time. Sit at his feet and learn from him, for he has found the secret of true happiness."

The spur that prompted Hefner to end the years of reclusion was a timely offer from Los Angeles to host another television series, provisionally titled "Playboy After Dark." Hefner regarded his first series as an unmitigated success, despite the losses incurred and the acerbic reviews, and he had few qualms about undertaking a second, particularly as it provided a rationale for getting away from the Mansion at a time when he suddenly felt a need to escape.

Once the decision had been made, the resurrection of Hugh M. Hefner proceeded at a rapid pace. Hefner called Jodie McRae into his bedroom and said: "We're going to start traveling." A complete new wardrobe—$15,000 worth of Edwardian suits— was ordered from Chicago tailor George Mashbitz, sadly without reference to the Playboy Advisor, which would have undoubtedly warned Hefner that the vogue for Edwardian suits was waning. A penthouse apartment was prepared for him on the top floor of the office building on Sunset Boulevard in Los Angeles that accommodated Playboy's West Coast headquarters.

Since he was resolved to discover the joys of traveling, Hefner decided he needed personal transport in keeping with his image and so he placed an order with McDonnell Douglas for his own DC-9 airliner, only hesitating when he learned he would have to wait eighteen months for it to be delivered. It cost a little over $5 million—a trifling amount for the publisher of *Playboy*.

In August 1968, an extraordinary incident occurred in the Mansion: the noxious stink of tear gas seeped through its shuttered windows.

It was obvious from the start that there would be trouble at the 1968 Democratic Convention in Chicago. Nearly ten thousand young people wearing beads and long hair descended on the city to protest against the war in Vietnam and profess their belief in peace and love. Some of them proclaimed themselves to be members of a New Left group, the Youth International Party, and described themselves as Yippies.

Opposition to the war had been building for some time, fostered by ghastly pictures on television of children with burning skin, clattering helicopter gunships on search-and-destroy missions, and marines with terrible staring eyes sitting in muddy foxholes. *Playboy* magazine's first Vietnam coverage was of a morale-raising visit to the boys by the Playmate of the Year, Jo Collins, organized as a promotion stunt after a second lieutenant had written from Bien Hoa enclosing a lifetime subscription and asking if there was any chance of a Playmate delivering the first issue, as he understood happened back home.

That was in January 1966, when Vietnam was still viewed by many Americans as a glorious crusade against the spread of godless Communism. But as the mood of the country changed, *Playboy* began to give more and more space to the voices of liberal dissent, publishing fine anti-war polemic by names like John Kenneth Galbraith, Senator William Fulbright, and Allen Ginsberg. It did nothing to harm the magazine's popularity with the American forces in Vietnam, and Hefner was tickled when someone told him that the quickest way to know how long a unit had been in Vietnam was to count the Playmates pinned to the wall of the base recreation room.

After the assassination of Robert F. Kennedy, the contest for the Democratic presidential nomination in 1968 was between Eugene McCarthy, the "peace candidate," and Vice President Hubert Humphrey, who enjoyed the vigorous support of Mayor Richard J. Daley, the political boss of Chicago. Daley was not the kind of man to tolerate the streets of his town being taken over by young peace campaigners and he ordered his police to restrict protest activities severely.

Trouble began with a few inevitable taunts and jeers and some stone throwing. Then, without warning, the police went berserk, turning brutally on the young people with nightsticks, tear gas, and mace. Bloody clashes spread through the streets and there was further violence in the convention hall itself, where newsmen and delegates were beaten up on the floor of the hall by helmeted police, while Mayor Daley, purple with rage, bellowed obscenities at a senator who had declared in the middle of a speech supporting McCarthy: "With Eugene McCarthy we wouldn't have Gestapo tactics on the streets of Chicago."

This astonishing performance and the mayhem on the streets were watched in fascinated horror by a nationwide television audience, including the house guests at the Playboy Mansion, which Hefner had put at the disposal of visiting celebrities for the duration of the convention. When they could actually smell the tear gas coming in off the streets, Hefner and two friends—cartoonist Jules Feiffer and columnist Max Lerner—decided to venture out and see for themselves what was going on.

For a while it seemed fairly quiet, but on Wells Street they came upon a crowd of young people being chased by the police, many of whom had taken off their identification tags. The police were shouting and screaming, completely out of control, and were clubbing the demonstrators into submission with unrestrained fury. Hefner and his two friends were sickened and turned to leave but, as they did so, a squad car screeched to a halt close by and five armed policemen with their bloodlust up jumped out. Feiffer and Lerner scurried off in different directions.

"Get on home," one of the cops shouted at Hefner. "That's what I'm trying to do," he replied, but he apparently did not move himself quick enough. The cop swung his nightstick and gave one of the city's biggest taxpayers a vicious whack across the rump.

It was an incident which would be widely interpreted as a catalyst in his life. Hef's friends liked to kid him that they detected a distinct drift to the left in his political attitudes after the 1968 Democratic Convention and his painful experience on the streets. And when it was revealed he was intending to end his long years of hibernation in the Mansion, deep significance was attributed to the rap on his backside.

The truth was that his views were no more radical after 1968 than they had been before, and he had made a decision to change his lifestyle some months before venturing out onto Chicago's troubled streets during the convention.

"I just had a strong feeling," he explained, "that there were things I wanted to get out and do. One of them was that I wanted to fall in love."

8

Pit-a-pat, Pit-a-pat

Twenty-four hours after his unhappy brush with the red-eyed and maddened officers of Mayor Daley's police force, Hefner left Chicago for Los Angeles, where he was to tape the first of the "Playboy After Dark" shows. On the way to O'Hare airport in the Mercedes 600 limousine, Jodie McRae turned to Hef and asked if it had taken a lot of will power to start traveling again after so many years shut up in the Mansion. "He put down his Pepsi," Jodie recalled, "looked left and right with his eyes all sunk and said: 'Jodie, I was killing myself. I had to get out of there.' "

As "Playboy After Dark" was due to run for twenty-six weeks, a $35,000 set had been built for the show at the CBS-TV studios in Hollywood. It incorporated a den, a living room, and a rumpus room, all designed to look as if they had been ripped from the pages of the magazine, and the idea, as in Hefner's previous television series, was that each show would resemble an impromptu party. Celebrities would drop by to talk or entertain and a handful of young and pretty girls would stand around in the background and pretend they were having fun.

"Playboy After Dark" was trailed, with typical lack of restraint, as a "gathering of the most attractive, talented, accomplished, and involved people in contemporary society." It was better in every way than Hefner's first foray into television and the ratings were good, but the critics were generally only luke-warm. "As an actor," *Time* magazine reported, "Hefner makes a pretty good magazine publisher." He was portrayed, predictably, as "wooden," sitting awkwardly in his tuxedo and clipped-on bow tie, asking shallow cue-card questions of his guests. Hefner was unabashed. "I know how good the show is," he told *Time*. "It's better than the Johnny Carson Show and I do a better job of hosting than Ed Sullivan does."

Among the girls hired for the taping of the third show was a fresh-faced UCLA co-ed, eighteen years old, by the name of Bar-bara Klein. Only five-feet-three-inches tall, Barbi—as she pre-ferred to be called—was the epitome of the idealized American teenager who could always be found grinning from toothpaste advertisements. She had shining, healthy, innocent good looks, clear green eyes, a heart-shaped face and a cute little snub nose, thick curly hair, and a pubescent body boys described as well stacked. In her home town of Sacramento, she was a high school cheerleader and a contestant in the Miss Teenage America contest; as a premed student at UCLA, she was soon noticed and offered modeling jobs after school—it was this connection that led her to the "Playboy After Dark" set. The moment Hefner walked onto the studio floor, his eyes alighted on her and his forty-two-year-old heart went *pit-a-pat*.

They began talking while the lights and cameras were being set up and Hef asked her if she would like to join him and a few friends at The Candy Store, a local discotheque, after the show. "I already had a date," Hefner confessed, "but that night I only had eyes for Barbi." His ardor did not go unremarked by his friends and one of them asked Barbi, with a wink, if she ever dated older men. "I've never dated anyone older than twenty-four," she replied brightly. "That's okay," said Hef, "neither have I." She laughed and agreed, later, to see him again.

Barbi was a nice, sensible Jewish girl and a virgin. She was not at all sure she wanted to get involved with a man with Hefner's reputation, she was worried what her parents would say if they found out (her father was a doctor), and she had a regular boy-friend at college. But Hefner was charming, considerate, apparently unaffected by his success and his money, and she could not stop herself from liking him.

When he arrived in a chauffeur-driven limousine to pick her up at her college dorm for their first date, Barbi was more embarrassed than she was impressed. Her friends stood giggling helplessly behind the windows as she ran out to meet him, and after that she insisted on driving her own car to see him. Hefner liked that about her, respected her independence and her determination to remain a virgin. She avoided being alone too much with him, fended off his gentle approaches, made it quite clear that sex was out of the question, and allowed him no more than a chaste goodnight kiss. Hefner, starry-eyed, desired her all the more.

During the taping of "Playboy After Dark," two shows at a time, Hefner commuted between Chicago and Los Angeles, where he spent all his spare time with Barbi. Inevitably, they were seen out and about together and Barbi began appearing in Hollywood gossip columns as Hefner's latest "companion." Her parents in Sacramento were far from pleased, but by then she was thoroughly enjoying Hefner's attentions and had no intention of breaking off their relationship which was still, at her insistence, purely platonic. Hefner remained a perfect gentleman, although an ardent suitor.

Within the Playboy organization word quickly spread that Hef was in love again and that this time it was serious. "You could always tell when Hef was in love," Dick Rosenzweig explained, "because he'd be very bright, very *up*. You'd get the feeling that he thought life was good and all was right with the world."

It was also common knowledge at all levels of the business—there was an effective grapevine—that Barbi had so far resisted Hefner's advances. When they went to Las Vegas for the weekend, the incredible word was transmitted to Chicago that *separate* rooms had been reserved for them in a hotel. When they went skiing in Aspen, they stayed with Hef's brother, Keith, who had a house in the mountains, and it was whispered in Chicago that Barbi had insisted on her own bedroom.

It was assumed, correctly, that Barbi's virginity was unlikely to withstand a determined assault by Hefner for very long and her resistance to his amorous advances weakened inexorably. During the early summer of 1969, Barbi visited Hefner at the Playboy Mansion in Chicago and finally succumbed, on the famous round bed, like so many pretty young things before her. After performing the deed Hefner could not wait to spread the glad tidings. While Barbi was still sleeping, he slipped out of bed and up the spiral staircase to the office shared by Bobbie Arnstein and Shirley Hillman.

"He came in in his pajamas, grinning all over his face," Shirley Hillman recalled, "and said 'I did it! I just made love to Barbi!' Bobbie looked at him and said, 'What do you want me to do? Send up the news on the Goodyear blimp?' "

Thereafter, it was Hef and Barbi, the love story. Barbi abandoned her UCLA studies and moved into the Mansion and they went everywhere hand in hand, cuddling and canoodling and staring into each other's eyes. To please Barbi, Hef organized little outings for her entertainment, the idea that the Mansion contained all the possible sources of pleasure being now forgotten. "I remember one trip we took to Acapulco," he said, "soon after our romance got going, when some of the gang decided to go kiting over the bay. Naturally, Barbi had to be the first one to try it and, romantic fool that I am, not to be outdone by my new girlfriend, I decided to try it, too. So there I was, high above Acapulco Bay, hanging on to that kite for dear life, wondering if the motor boat that was pulling the kite would be able to put me down safely on the little raft where I'd started. From that height, the raft looked about the size of a postage stamp, and I can't swim a stroke. My life is too sweet to be risking it with such daredevil foolishness, but there I was, just the same. I was crazy—love crazy."

The visit to Acapulco was so successful that Hef next took Barbi on a month-long holiday to Europe, visiting London, Paris, Rome, and Copenhagen, accompanied, as always, by Hefner's entourage of buddies and his faithful valet, Jodie McRae. They were in Paris in July when they heard that America had landed a man on the moon. Barbi wanted a little trinket to commemorate this historic event, so Jodie took her out shopping and paid for the $2,000 charm bracelet she selected. "I took care of all the tips and everything the entourage wanted," Jodie said. "If Barbi wanted to buy something, I just put it on my expense account." A few days later they were all at a discotheque in London, with film director Roman Polanski, as wire services around the world were clattering with the news of a frightful discovery in a rented house in Benedict Canyon, outside of Los Angeles—the slaughtered bodies of actress Sharon Tate, Polanski's pregnant wife, and her four house guests, all victims of self-proclaimed messiah Charles Manson and his "family."

In the same month that a man landed on the moon, Barbi made her debut in *Playboy* magazine as "Rising Star Barbi Benton" (Hefner decided she needed a new name), the first of many opportunities for readers to examine her nubile body. With their affair now entirely public (she was always described in the magazine as Hefner's "constant companion"), there was much speculation about the propriety and wisdom of a forty-two-year-old man romancing a teenager not much older than his own daughter. It was gossip that both mystified and irritated Hefner, particularly when it was suggested that he was frightened of more mature, challenging women.

"I simply find younger women more attractive physically than women of my own age," he explained forlornly. "Maybe it's partly because of the need to be able to escape to an emotional island away from the demands and problems of work. There's also something nice about an affair that's the first serious relationship in a girl's life; it permits you to recapture your own early responses. It's a way of holding on to your youth and the enthusiasm you first felt about love and life.

"Obviously, you're not going to get any real intellectual drive from young girls, but I don't look for the same intellectual stimulation from women as I do from men. And besides, I'm not romantically attracted to the women I find most intellectually exciting."

Gloria Steinem met Barbi when she visited the Playboy Mansion to interview Hefner for a piece in *McCall's*. (Hefner could never bear a grudge for long and soon forgot Steinem's devastating exposé of the Bunnies in the early sixties.) When Barbi left the room, Steinem said, "She's so *young*," and Hefner could not get her remark out of his mind. During the interview Steinem told Hefner that a woman reading *Playboy* felt a little like a Jew reading a Nazi manual, but that didn't bother him in the slightest. "Why did she have to say that about Barbi?" he repeatedly asked his friends later. "Why couldn't she have said, well, *fresh*?"

In November 1969, Hefner took delivery of the "Big Bunny," a stretched DC-9 airliner painted entirely in black, except for a white Bunny logo on the tail. Even by Playboy's sybaritic standards, this was a wondrous and expensive new toy—it cost $5,336,812. Hefner, who recognized the value of facetious understatement, liked to refer to the aircraft, off-handedly, as "basically, just a convenience." *Newsweek* begged to differ, describing it as "the most mind-boggling display of sensual opulence ever assembled in a flying machine."

The interior of the only black jet in the world had been re-modeled at Hefner's behest—and at a cost of $510,000—so that it resembled, insofar as it was possible, an airborne Mansion. "It's got everything," Hefner joked, "except a swimming pool and a bowling alley." At the front of the aircraft there was a dance floor and discotheque connected to a conference room, lounge area, and bar with upholstered seats grouped around tables with inset back-gammon and Monopoly boards. The galley was equipped to pro-vide gourmet meals (lobster and roast beef carved at the table were standard fare) and stocked with the finest wines. There was enough silver, china, and crystal on board to serve thirty-six passengers. Seven built-in video screens provided a selection of in-flight mov-ies and there were skyphones throughout the plane to provide communication with the cockpit or the ground.

Hefner's personal quarters were at the rear and included a six-by-eight-foot elliptical bed upholstered in black Himalayan goat-skin, covered with white silk bed sheets and a spread of Tasmanian opossum pelts. A belt was strapped across the bed during take-off and landing so that Hef and his companion of the moment need not be unnecessarily roused. Alongside the bed was a control panel that enabled Hefner to talk to the crew, darken the windows to watch a movie, listen to the radio, or play his favorite audio tapes. Leading off the bedroom was a sunken roman bath and shower and a study with a desk, telephone, tape recorder, and lightbox to examine color transparencies.

Two crews of six, one based in Chicago, the other in Los Angeles, were hired to fly the Big Bunny wherever Hefner wanted to go. The cabin staff were selected from the brightest and best of the Bunnies. Trained by Continental Airlines, they were hence-

149

forth known as Jet Bunnies and equipped with striking $500 ward-robes—wet-look black nylon uniforms with mini-skirts, thigh-length boots, and white silk scarves. The Bunny logo was em-broidered on their scarves and in the center of the wings sewn on each arm of their tunics and trench coats.

It was initially planned to offset the Big Bunny's daunting operating costs by offering it for charter, but a later analysis, in harder times, would reveal that Hefner traveled on all but three of its 191 flights. Total operating costs were $4.2 million but in the heady days of the early seventies no one at Playboy cared about costs; the fifteenth annual report showed profits up to a new record of $6.8 million and a single issue of the magazine was capable of bringing in more than $3 million in advertising revenue.

Although the Big Bunny was equipped with long-range fuel tanks so that it could fly anywhere in the world, it was at first employed for nothing more adventurous than to ferry Barbi, Hef, and his friends back and forth between Chicago and Los Angeles, the hingepins of Hefner's world. Hefner possessed no desire to travel to faraway places; he could see little virtue in visiting coun-tries where he could not understand what people were talking about and the fried chicken was not cooked the way he liked it. But Barbi was different. She was young, adventurous, and longed to see the world; it seemed a shame to have the Big Bunny and not go anywhere. No more needed to be said. Barbi was Hefner's princess—whatever she wanted was hers.

Thus was the Grand Tour, Playboy-style, conceived. It was to be, Hefner decreed, the trip of a lifetime: a whole month away, hopping in the highest possible style from Hilton to Hilton across Europe and Africa. If Barbi had entertained any hope that they might be traveling as a romantic twosome, she was to be disap-pointed. Hef invited along all his closest buddies: John Dante, Gene Siskel, the movie critic of the *Chicago Tribune*, Leroy Neiman, Shel Silverstein, Nelson Futch, his brother Keith, the *whole damn gang*. Alexas Urba, a Playboy photographer, was to be there to take pictures of them all having fun and Jodie McRae was to look after the details. When Africa was added to the itinerary, Hefner told Jodie to go out and buy him some dashing white-hunter safari suits. "You want me to get you safari suits in *Chicago*?" Jodie asked.

On the morning of Tuesday, July 28, 1970, a fleet of limousines assembled outside the Playboy Mansion to transport the holiday-makers to the Big Bunny, waiting at the Butler Aviation terminal at O'Hare airport and stocked by the diligent Jodie McRae with dozens of crates of Pepsi Cola. As the black jet climbed up into the pale blue skies over Illinois and headed east, furious backgammon tournaments were already in progress on board, tournaments that would continue, both in the air and on the ground, for the entire trip. Barbi had brought along a self-improvement book full of interesting new words. "Did you know," she asked Alexas Urba, "that triskaidekaphobia is a phobia about the number thirteen?"

The first stop was London, where a fidgeting crowd of reporters and photographers was waiting at Heathrow airport to greet them and ogle the Big Bunny. Hefner said a few words at a press conference in the airport, the same few words he would say at every press conference at every stop. From the Hilton in London they flew to the Hilton in Marbella, on Spain's Costa del Sol, where the itinerary allowed them two days "at leisure," most of which they devoted to noisy backgammon games played by the hotel swimming pool. From the Hilton in Marbella they flew to the Hilton in Nairobi, Kenya, where they went on a safari in the Uaso Nyira game reserve, before moving on to Tanzania to observe the wild life migration in the Serengeti National Park.

From the Hilton in Nairobi, they flew to the Hilton in Athens, where, the itinerary pointed out, "typical American breakfasts and hamburgers are available in the hotel's Byzantine coffee shop." This was a relief to Hefner, who was already vexed by a critical shortage of Wonder Bread for his sandwiches. Urgent messages had been dispatched to Chicago to arrange for fresh supplies to be flown over, but the logistical problems involved in flying Wonder Bread across the Atlantic and keeping it fresh had proved insuperable. Three days were allocated to cruising the Greek islands in a chartered yacht, then it was off to Rome, Venice, Munich, and the Hilton in Paris.

The highlight of their stay in Paris was to be dinner at Maxim's, one of the most famous restaurants in the world and a citadel of haute cuisine. By then, said Hefner, he was "horny for some home-cooked chicken" so Jodie was sent to the restaurant in advance with instructions to explain how Mr. Hefner liked his chicken fried. In Maxim's famous kitchens, with an astonished chef in attendance, Jodie solemnly washed a chicken joint, dredged it in flour and salt and fried it in butter. "I gave them the recipe," said Jodie, "but I don't know whether they kept it or not."

After the meal, the chef emerged to inquire, with only the faintest hint of sarcasm, if M'sieur 'Efner had enjoyed his fried chicken. Sure, said Hef, it was fine. With a helpless shrug, the Frenchman turned on his heel and retreated to the kitchen. "I was sure," said Urba, "that he was going to blow his brains out."

The last stop of the tour was the Hilton at Rabat in Morocco, where Hefner and his friends were deemed sufficiently important to be the guests at an official alfresco banquet. Carpets were laid out on the desert sand and native dancers performed by the light of flickering torches while Arab horsemen in flowing robes demonstrated their shooting skills and Hef's friends tucked into a five-hundred-pound dish of caviar. Jodie said the scene was like something out of the Arabian Nights.

On August 28, the Big Bunny returned to Chicago and the intrepid travelers wound up their backgammon and Monopoly tournaments. Hefner, whose dislike of foreign parts had been amply confirmed, was glad to be home, back in the Playboy Mansion, where the Wonder Bread was always fresh.

Barbi, being a California girl, was not entirely happy in Chicago and harbored ambitions for a career of her own in show business. Doggedly plugged in the magazine as a "rising star" (she featured on the cover three times), she landed a job as the kissable girl with the sweet breath in a Certs toothpaste commercial ("If he kissed you once, will he kiss you again?") and a bit part in an unsuccessful movie presciently titled *How Did a Nice Girl Like You Get Into This Business?* But she felt that if her career was ever to take off, she needed to be in the center of things, in Los Angeles.

Hefner was sympathetic. Playboy, awash with corporate funds, had begun to invest in film production, a diversification that provided a convenient, if thin, excuse for Hefner to spend more and more time on the West Coast and thus please Barbi. They always stayed in the penthouse on top of the Playboy Building on Sunset Boulevard, but it was hardly a suitable place to rub shoulders with the stars (which for Hefner was one of Los Angeles's primary attractions), and early in 1971 Barbi began looking for a house in Beverly Hills where they could entertain in a manner befitting the owner of Playboy.

After several disappointments—Sonny and Cher got Tony Curtis's house in Bel Air and George Hamilton's place was snapped up by Bernie Cornfeld—they found Holmby House, a mock Victorian-Gothic stone mansion with thirty rooms, in five landscaped acres on Charing Cross Road, only a block from Sunset Boulevard. Hefner wanted it the moment he laid eyes on it. The price was $1,050,000, a paltry matter. Playboy paid cash, balking only at the $30,000 asked for a collection of rare orchids that filled three greenhouses on the grounds. "Thirty thousand dollars," Hefner expostulated, "for a lot of *flowers?*"

Holmby House was constructed in 1927 for a rich Californian industrialist and was said to be a replica of an English country house with the same name, although no records exist in England of such a house. Clearly built without regard for expense, it featured floors of Botticini marble, hand-carved oak paneling, and an Aeolian pipe organ (which could play *Moonlight and Roses*) set into a wall in the living room. Before it came on the market it had been variously used as a country club and an unofficial hospitality residence for important visitors to Los Angeles—the King and Queen of Thailand stayed there during their visit to the city.

After many years cloistered in the Playboy Mansion in Chicago, heedless of night or day, Hefner thought he had found his Shangri-la at Holmby House. Although the house was suitably imposing, it was filled with warmth and sunlight and was entirely screened from the neighbors by luxuriant tropical gardens stocked with exotic trees and flowering shrubs. Brightly colored birds nested in the trees and butterflies dithered around great heaps of blossoms that filled the air with a heady fragrance.

It was a veritable paradise, but not quite a Playboy paradise since it lacked the necessary facilities for fun and games. Hefner called in the services of Ron Dirsmith, a Chicago architect who had supervised the remodeling of both the Playboy Mansion and the interior of the Big Bunny, to devise at Holmby House a playground more in keeping with the fantasies entertained by the readers of *Playboy* magazine. Soon bulldozers were reshaping the contours of the ground to clear space for a tennis court and a marvelous water-garden complex, which included a fish pond, swimming pool, lagoon, artificial waterfalls, and a grotto, all contrived to look like natural features of the landscape. Even in the most lavish Hollywood productions, Dorothy Lamour never splashed in a more glamorous lagoon than that created at Holmby House, soon to be renamed Playboy Mansion West. Underground cables were laid throughout the property to pipe music to fake rocks made of polyester resonants, a feature of which Dirsmith was particularly proud. A bathhouse, barbecue, and aviary were constructed from stone matching the house and an existing building was converted into a Games House to accommodate Hefner's pinball machines. By the time the exterior improvements had been completed, nearly $5 million had been spent.

Inside the house there was less to do, although the total bill for furnishing and refurbishment accounted for another $2,500,000, most of which was spent on the master bedroom suite soon to be occupied by Hef and Barbi. Hefner was thrilled with Playboy Mansion West and never tired of showing people around the place. As the Big Bunny droned west over the American heartland on its regular shuttle between Chicago and Los Angeles, he would endlessly describe the Mansion to friends visiting for the first time. "Just wait until you see it," he used to say, "just wait . . ."

Hefner's arrival as a part-time resident of Beverly Hills was largely welcomed by the movie community, since the regular parties at the Playboy Mansion West brought back memories of the grand days of Hollywood, when studio moguls and the stars entertained in an extravagant style long since abandoned. Who else but Hefner, or rather Playboy, could afford to throw ritzy parties *twice a week*, invite everyone who mattered, serve the best food and wine, and never count the cost? Playboy picked up the tab for all entertaining at the Mansion as a promotion expense: the Friday and Sunday parties usually cost between $1,000 and $7,000, but the bigger affairs (on New Year's Eve, Hef's birthday, and midsummer night) never cost less than $25,000, sometimes considerably more.

Both mansions were owned by Playboy and Hefner paid a modest rent for their use—just $650 a month, inclusive of food, drink, staff, entertainment, maintenance, everything. It was a bargain that would eventually be drawn to the attention of the Internal Revenue Service and the Securities Exchange Commission, but for the time being no one saw fit to question whether $650 a month was a suitable rent for a property that cost about $100,000 a month to run.

Hefner was certainly the most generous of hosts and never seemed to worry if his guests glugged sixty-dollar bottles of wine or stuffed their pockets with his cigars. Tales of abuse of Playboy's hospitality were legion: there were stories of guests going into the kitchen and ordering a pile of lobster sandwiches to take home; of friends bringing crowds of their own friends to the Mansion every day to eat and drink at Playboy's expense. One "friend" of Hefner tried to persuade a butler at Playboy Mansion West to work for him during the periods when Hefner was away in Chicago. "What happens when Hefner comes back?" the butler asked. "That's okay," the guest replied, airily. "I don't need a butler when Hef's around because I get everything I want at the Mansion."

Although Hefner still felt the need to spend a great deal of time in Chicago, Barbi settled in happily at Playboy Mansion West. When he was away, Hefner telephoned her every day to tell her he loved her and missed her and Barbi was content. She was beginning to pick up work as an actress and a singer—often as a result of meeting producers at Mansion parties—and felt she was making progress with an independent career.

When she was not working, there was plenty to keep her occupied. She decorated the guest cottage in early American style, choosing all the furniture and color schemes and the cheery red gingham curtains. She liked to sew and gave a needlepoint to Hef as a present, which he had framed and hung in the library. Also in the library was a Frank Gallo epoxy bust of Barbi, in the style of a ship's figurehead, which somehow emphasized the security of her position.

Her presence, in pictures and personal touches, could be discerned everywhere in the Mansion and she was happy to be so much a part of Hefner's life. What Barbi did not know was that while Hef was in Los Angeles, he telephoned the Playboy Mansion in Chicago every day to tell a girl called Karen Christy how much he loved and missed *her*.

Hefner's best friend, John Dante, had taken charge of Bunny recruitment for Playboy Clubs, an undemanding job that required
him to travel the country on "Bunny Hunts," interviewing girls
who had answered newspaper advertisements offering a glamorous career with Playboy. In May 1971, he was at the Statler-Hilton
hotel in Dallas, and Karen Christy was among two hundred girls
in bikinis who paraded before him at the audition.

Karen was nineteen years old, a peroxide blonde with green
eyes, buttermilk skin, and large, round, firm breasts. Orphaned
at the age of thirteen—her mother died from kidney disease when
Karen was only three and her father was shot in a hunting accident—she was brought up by relatives in rural Abilene and was
working as a secretary when she decided to apply for a job as a
Bunny. Three weeks after her audition she received a letter telling
her she had been accepted. Enclosed in the envelope was an airline
ticket to Chicago and an invitation to stay at the Playboy Mansion
while she was in training.

Like hundreds of small-town girls before her, Karen arrived
at the portals of 1340 North State Street Parkway literally trem-
bling with nerves. A butler took her straight up to the Bunny
dormitory on the top floor where she was shocked to see most of
the girls walking around with little or no clothing. She was assigned a bunk and a locker and, when she took off her coat, a
Bunny painting her fingernails on an adjoining bunk eyed Karen's
brassiere and drawled: "We don't wear those around here, honey."
Karen smiled and said nothing, convinced that *she* would never
walk around without a bra. Such brazen behavior would never
have been tolerated in Abilene.

Later, Karen and a few of the other girls went downstairs to
the ballroom, where almost the first person she saw was John
Dante. He remembered her, was friendly and welcoming, got her
a drink, and asked her if she would be interested in a conducted
tour of the Mansion. A lot of guys liked to show new girls around
the place because it was always amusing to see the way they
reacted, and it was a chance to get to know them and perhaps
stake a claim before someone like Warren Beatty showed up for
a party and ruined the chances of lesser mortals.

Dante, like Hefner, was in his forties and looked like a man
who read *Playboy*—he had rugged good looks, a rakish moustache,

and wore a silk shirt and a gold medallion around his neck. With one hand lightly guiding Karen's arm, he took her down to the swimming pool and showed her the Woo Grotto on the other side of the waterfall, pointing out the trap door in the ceiling. He showed her the solarium and the sauna, the underwater bar with the brass fireman's pole, the games room, and the bowling alley.

At the end of the tour, Karen shyly asked if it would be possible to see Hefner's quarters. Dante said he would ask, but warned her that Hefner had only returned from Los Angeles earlier that day and might still be asleep. Telling her to wait in the gallery over-looking the ballroom, Dante disappeared through the double glazed doors leading to Hefner's bedroom and returned after a few minutes to say it was okay; Hef would be glad to see her.

Hefner was sitting in the center of the round bed, eating fried chicken, swilling a Pepsi, and checking page proofs of the magazine when Dante and Karen walked in. He looked up, swallowed, scrambled immediately from the bed, paced across the white carpet, and took her hand. Yes, it was the real thing, *again: pit-a-pat.*

Hefner offered to show Karen around personally, starting with a demonstration of how the round bed vibrated and revolved. She was struck by his boyish enthusiasm and pleased that he seemed to like her. When there appeared to be nothing left to show her, he asked her if she would care to join him later when he would be playing pool with Hugh O'Brian and a few of the other guests.

Dante waived any plans he might have had for Karen when he saw that Hefner was interested; competing with Hef for a girl's favors would have been unthinkable. Throughout the evening, Hefner paid exuberant court to the new Bunny, making little jokes for her benefit while he was playing pool, winking at her when he played a good shot. After supper, which the guys devoured from trays in the games room without interrupting their various tussles with the pinball machines, a few of them went down to the underwater bar for drinks. Hef and Karen sat closely together talking quietly and the others in the party began to drift away, sensing that the pair wanted to be alone.

As the sun rose above the eastern horizon of Lake Michigan and the irritable rush-hour traffic began its inexorable build-up along Lake Shore Drive, in the timeless depths of the Playboy Mansion, Hugh Hefner could be found removing Karen Christy's brassiere and reaching for the Johnson's Baby Oil. Any faint disappointment he might have felt a little later to discover that she was not a virgin was more than compensated for by her startling, enthusiastic, and uninhibited virtuosity on the round bed. Although only nineteen years old, she was as exciting a lover as any woman he had ever known.

Karen never had to face the rigors of being a Bunny; instead Hefner selected her as a Playmate (she was Miss December 1971) and moved her from a bunk in the Bunny dormitory to her own apartment safe within the Mansion. Her swift and remarkable elevation in status prompted a great deal of bitchy gossip among the Bunnies, many of whom considered themselves eminently more worthy of her position as Hef's lover. But there was no doubting his genuine affection for her, an affection he demonstrated by showering her with presents: a diamond-studded watch, a full-length white mink coat, a white Lincoln Continental, and a Persian kitten, which Karen ill-advisedly decided to call Pussy. She gave Hef a photograph of herself and signed it "From Karen and her Pussy"—delicious news that soon traveled the Mansion's corridors, causing considerable hilarity.

Every other week, Hefner kissed Karen good-bye and headed for Los Angeles, where Barbi was anxiously awaiting his arrival. Karen knew all about Barbi: she had read of her relationship with Hefner in the gossip columns long before she arrived in Chicago and Hefner had never made any attempt to conceal the fact that he was involved with another girl in California. Whatever anguish Karen suffered during Hefner's absences was often aggravated by jealous Bunnies who liked to tell Karen that Barbi was Hefner's *real* girlfriend. "You're just someone he fucks," a Bunny once told her bitterly.

Karen was painfully vulnerable to ridicule since she had little taste and less style. Out and about in Chicago in her white mink coat and her white Lincoln Continental and her white candy-floss hair, teased into a billowing bouffant, she looked, someone said, "like the abominable snowman."

As Christmas 1972 approached, the luckless Karen tried to discover what Hef was giving Barbi as a present. Hefner's social secretary, Shirley Hillman, knew that Barbi was getting a $35,000 Tiffany lamp. "I felt sorry for Karen," said Hillman, "so when she asked me what Barbi was getting, I told her it was just a lamp. She was thrilled." Karen got a $13,500 diamond ring that Christmas. "Do you like it?" she would ask the Bunnies in the Mansion. "It's my Christmas present from Hef. *She* only got a *lamp.*"

For all her breathtaking naïveté, Karen unquestionably pleased Hefner, and not only between his silk sheets. She was an undemanding, uncritical companion always eager to please him, a pretty doll he obviously enjoyed having on his arm. When *Tie a Yellow Ribbon Round the Old Oak Tree* was on the hit parade, Hefner returned from Los Angeles to find that she had tied yellow ribbons around all the trees in North State Street Parkway to welcome him home. It was the kind of silly, romantic gesture guaranteed to make him dewy-eyed.

It was Karen, also, who had the idea of getting a special Monopoly set made for him, with little figurines of the regular players. The money was printed with etchings of the two Playboy mansions on one side and a Lincoln-style likeness of Hefner on the other. On the dice, tiny Playboy logos replaced the dots. Hefner was delighted with it. Karen learned to play Monopoly well enough to match Hefner. One day they were halfway through a game when a butler came to tell Hefner he was due to leave for the airport. Giggling like a couple of kids, they promptly carried the board out to the limousine and continued playing, eventually finishing the game on the Big Bunny, where Hefner noticed that Karen was barefooted—she had not even stopped to put shoes on.

Karen was not, of course, allowed to visit Playboy Mansion West; but she often traveled with Hefner in the Big Bunny to Los Angeles, returning immediately and uncomplainingly on a scheduled flight. Alternatively, she would fly out to meet him at Los Angeles Airport in order to return with him in the Big Bunny. Once Hefner chartered a Lear jet, for $10,000, to pick her up from Texas, where she was visiting her family, and bring her to Los Angeles just so she could join him for the four-hour flight back to Chicago. Barbi remained happily unaware of these various clandestine arrangements.

No matter what others thought about Hefner's predilection for young, unsophisticated girls like Karen Christy and Barbi Benton, he certainly considered himself fortunate to have two such wonderful women in his life simultaneously; although there were, of course, other girls, lots of them, none was treated with the same romantic reverence accorded to Barbi and Karen. When either of them was out of the way, Hefner liked to play, dabbling on the dark side of the alternative lifestyle he promoted so vigorously. Many girls drawn into this orbit found the world of Playboy was not a pretty place, as Bunny Bee-Jay of the Los Angeles Playboy Club would readily confirm.

I was twenty-three when I arrived in Los Angeles, hoping to become an actress. Back home in Virginia I had won a lot of beauty titles—I was Miss Virginia 1971—and I'd got a bit part in a Jack Nicholson movie, *The Last Detail*. I thought if I was going to be a star, I ought to be in Hollywood, but the only regular work I could find was as a Bunny. I saw an advertisement in *Variety* for Bunnies to work in the new Playboy Club in Century City and I applied.

I hadn't been working for Playboy long before I was invited up to the Mansion for a barbecue one Sunday. I didn't know what to expect, I thought there might be a lot of people running around in the nude, so I didn't go. Then some of the other Bunnies told me it was real nice, that they just showed regular movies, not filthy stuff you wouldn't want to see. In the end I said I'd go. I thought it was terrific at first. I still wanted to be an actress and I thought it would be a great place to meet producers. I wanted to be part of that life.

After that first party I went home with one of Hefner's best friends and went to bed with him. There did not seem to be any reason not to. Then I started sleeping around with other guys, scores of them. I am amazed I didn't get v.d., but I didn't. I couldn't seem to say no anymore. It wasn't that any pressure was being put on me, but the atmosphere at the Mansion was that sex was free and everyone was doing it. The Playboy Philosophy is that promiscuity is okay and that your body is your own to do what you like with so there was no reason not to have sex with complete strangers. It was as if there was nowhere to draw the line.

I was at the Mansion one afternoon when Cher, the singer, telephoned and said she was coming over. Hefner turned to

his cronies and said, "You know who I'd like to have? Chastity!"
I suppose he was making a joke, but I was repulsed. Chastity
was Cher's ten-year-old daughter.

One night I was invited to a special party at the Mansion
with my roommate, Libby, who was also a Bunny and who
had told me about the orgies she had taken part in in Chicago.
I didn't know it at the time but we were being invited to an
orgy.

When we got there, Hef and two other guys were watching
Gone With the Wind in the living room. Two girls had already
arrived; I was told later that they were hookers. After the movie
we all went to the Grotto to swim in the nude. The guys
wanted us to touch each other, to put on a show for them,
but I didn't want to do that. Hef was sitting with me and I
tried to tell him that I would rather be alone with him. He just
said, "We'll see."

After a while in the Grotto, we all put on robes and went
up to Hef's bedroom. I had never been in his bedroom before.
We sat around in the nude and watched *The Devil and Miss
Jones* and then everyone began having sex. I was with Hefner
on the bed, with my roommate and another guy. The third
man was with the two other girls on the floor. It was the first
time I had had anal sex, which was what Hefner wanted. It all
seemed very unreal. I had the strangest feeling that the two
other guys were waiting for Hefner to orgasm before they did,
I don't know why. The thing I remember most is that I kept
my sunhat on the whole time; I think I felt no one would see
me if I kept my hat on.

When we were driving home the sun was coming up over
the valley. I felt dirty, disgusted with myself. I couldn't believe
what I had done. After that, nothing seemed to matter very
much. I felt there was so much moral decay about the place
that it did not matter what I did.

I got a couple of bit parts in movies by taking the casting
couch route, then I got a job doing film reviews for a local
television station, KTTV-TV. I was very pleased about it because I didn't have to sleep with anybody to get it. But then
I was told I ought to get some jazzy Hollywood glasses—my
contact lenses made me blink too much in the lights—and so

I slept with this really repulsive guy in exchange for a $500 pair of glasses.

I was still working full-time as a Bunny and going up to parties at the Mansion, but I began to realize that as far as Playboy was concerned I was completely expendable, no more than a plaything. No one at the Mansion wanted to know what kind of person was inside my body, no one cared what kind of person I was, what thoughts I had. I could have been a doll. I don't think Hefner thought having anal intercourse with me counted for anything at all.

I was such a mess I tried suicide a couple of times. To me, there was no purpose to the kind of life I was leading. In the end, I went back home to Virginia, completely burned out. For a while I was in a mental hospital and I was under psychotherapy for a long time, but I eventually got over the experience.

I always think that if I stayed around Playboy I would have become a lesbian to avoid the kind of men I met at the Mansion. *Playboy* magazine should have a warning on it like cigarette advertising: this Philosophy can be hazardous to your health.

Prominent among the regular guests at Playboy parties in 1973 was Linda Lovelace, star of the film *Deep Throat*, which had outraged puritan America and was playing to packed houses wherever movie houses dared to show it. The film's improbable plot revolved around a girl who had made the startling discovery that her clitoris was in her throat and thus achieved memorable orgasms by fellatio. As editor-publisher of *Playboy*, Hefner saw himself in the vanguard of the sexual revolution and what he liked to describe as the decontamination of sex, and proudly claimed a role in creating the kind of climate that enabled films like *Deep Throat* to be shown in public.

Linda Lovelace was first invited to stay at the Mansion when she agreed to pose for a nude photo spread in the magazine. Her appearance, when she arrived, was something of a shock. Instead of the glamorous porn queen everyone expected, a wan, dispirited young woman with lank, mousy hair stepped from the limousine. In her cheap jeans and T-shirt, she looked like a tired housewife just back from the supermarket. She was accompanied by a tall, muscular man with a domineering manner and a loud mouth—Chuck Traynor, her husband and manager.

The photo session lasted three days and was a success, thanks in no small part to the skill of the hair-stylist and make-up artist. Linda posed in and around the house and grounds, draped in yards of antique lace, a play on her name that was to be the theme of the pictures. When she was packing up to go, Hefner's West Coast secretary, Joni Mattis, knocked on the door of her room and asked her if she would like to come back for a party later that night. It was just a regular get-together, she said, a buffet and a movie with a few friends. Linda looked at Traynor.

"You can tell Mr. Hefner," he said, "we'd be delighted." Joni looked disconcerted and said she was sorry but the invitation was just for Linda. "She doesn't go anywhere without me," Traynor growled. "If I don't go, she don't go." Joni hastily left the room, mumbling something about having to check it out and she returned after a few minutes to tell them it was fine, they were both welcome.

Linda enjoyed the party, but remembered nothing of the movie. No sooner had she taken her seat in the living room when Clint Eastwood walked into the room and casually sat down in the chair next to her. She could hardly believe it. When she was growing up in Florida there were pictures of Clint Eastwood all over her bedroom wall. He didn't say a word to her, but she didn't care; the movie rolled in a blur in front of her eyes.

Afterward, Joni said that Hef would like to meet them. Linda had seen him around the place a couple of times during the photo session, but he had said no more than a polite hello. Joni led the way to the library, where Hef was sitting in his silk pajamas on a leather chesterfield sofa. He got up immediately and shook hands with them both. Linda found him very engaging; he told her she was much prettier than she appeared on the screen and how much he had enjoyed *Deep Throat*, which he had shown several times at Mansion parties. She blushed and smiled and said little. Hef and Traynor appeared to have a lot to talk about and the conversation drifted around to Hef's private collection of pornographic movies; Linda looked around the room admiring the books and the pictures and the striking bust of Barbi Benton. After a little while, she became aware, with a sinking heart, that Traynor was telling Hef how much she liked sex with dogs. She felt that familiar nausea rising. . . .

Linda and Chuck had only been together for about two years, but much had happened in that time. When they met, she was a wayward twenty-one-year-old living with her parents near Fort Lauderdale and bored with small-town life. He was a vicious small-time hustler running a bar, with girls and drugs on the side. Only weeks after she had moved in with him, she was working for him as a hooker. Her first trick was a gang-bang in a Holiday Inn. When she demurred at some new perversion, he beat her. When she failed to satisfy a john, he beat her. When she tried to escape from him, he beat her. After a year together, she had suffered every conceivable kind of sexual humiliation. Traynor ceased to use her name in conversation: he called her cunt. To secure her cooperation in making a pornographic 8 mm movie with a dog in New York, Traynor laid a gun on a table and told her he would kill her if she did not do it. She did it. Nothing, she recalled later, matched that degrading and loathsome experience. Throughout, she had to look as if she was enjoying it.

Thereafter, Traynor did not need to use physical violence to keep Linda in line. He bought a dog. At the Humane Society dog pound in Miami he found a lumbering mutt called Rufus, a cross between a Bloodhound and a Great Dane. The presence of Rufus was a guarantee of Linda's cooperation, since she lived in perpetual fear that Traynor would drag the dog into the house, tell her to take off her clothes, and get down on her hands and knees. Chatting with Hef in the library at Playboy Mansion West, Chuck was saying how Linda was great with animals, how they had this dog back home in Florida called Rufus and Linda just couldn't get enough of him. Hef said he'd seen Linda's dog movie, he had a copy of it in his collection.

Linda and Chuck became regular guests at Playboy Mansion West, one of the few privileged couples who would automatically be afforded entry, even if their names were not on the List. Traynor thought that Playboy would give them an entrée to the big time, and he decided that Linda's sexual services should be reserved exclusively for Hefner as a way of currying favor. It was a decision that improved Linda's lot immeasurably and Traynor diligently protected her dubious virtue at Playboy parties, always stepping in if another guest looked as if he might be getting a little too familiar.

Hefner did not show much interest in Linda until one night there was an impromptu orgy in the Grotto after Barbi Benton had gone to bed. Hef was frolicking in the water with his economy-size bottle of Johnson's Baby Oil, gently massaging all the girls. Linda thought there were about fifteen guys present, all Hef's regular cronies, but fewer girls. One of them she knew as Lila, a seventeen-year-old high school student from Santa Ana, whose startling sexual precocity made her a popular participant at orgies. Lila took Linda's hand and together they put on a little lesbian show; the others gathered round to watch and offer suggestions. It reminded Linda of those old-fashioned Fred Astaire and Ginger Rogers movies, when the other dancers on the floor stopped and formed a circle around the star turn. Then Linda was held out of the water and Chuck demonstrated how he could insert his whole fist into her body, finger by finger. This performance produced muted cheers and Lila tried the same trick. The fun ended with Hef having anal intercourse with Linda. Chuck was delighted.

Not long afterward, Linda was appalled to learn that Rufus had arrived at Playboy Mansion West. He had apparently been collected from their house in North Miami, flown to Los Angeles, picked up in a Playboy limousine, and installed in a kennel at the Mansion, where he sat day after day, howling mournfully. "I began to dread going up to the Mansion after that," she said. "I knew what was going to happen and every time I would think 'God, is this the night?' "

Rufus quickly wore out his welcome at the Mansion. Linda neither knew nor cared what happened to him, but one day he was not there anymore; someone told her that the neighbors had been complaining about his howls in the night.

A few months later, Linda Lovelace left Chuck Traynor. When she heard that he was searching for her with a gun and threatening to kill her, she sought refuge at the Playboy Mansion, which was protected by armed security guards. Hefner was kind and understanding: he told her she was safe at the Mansion and that Chuck would not be allowed on the property. He also, Linda claimed, apologized to her, saying he had not realized her situation.

Hefner never really believed Linda's story that she had been forced into pornography by Traynor against her will. Harry Reems, the male star of *Deep Throat*, was a friend of Hefner's and said often enough that it never seemed to him, while they were making the movie, that Linda was doing something she didn't want to do. Hefner also denied that there was any significance in Rufus's arrival in the Mansion; he said he was just doing them a favor, looking after the animal while they searched for a house in Los Angeles.

Linda Lovelace eventually remarried happily, had children, and found merciful obscurity in a small, neat house on Long Island. The only noticeable scar from her years in pornography is that she cannot bring herself to say the word dog, nowadays: she has to spell it out, *d-o-g*.

In July 1973, Hefner's domestic bliss was discomposed by an eventuality that might, perhaps, have been anticipated. Under a headline "Adventures in the Skin Trade," a story in *Time* magazine revealed his unusual rooming arrangements: "Long a two-of-everything consumer, Hefner has lately extended the principle to his romantic life. Former Playmate Barbi Benton, his longtime escort, lives in the California mansion: blonde Karen Christy, an ex-Bunny in the Chicago Playboy Club, is ensconced in his Chicago quarters." Accompanying the feature was a picture of Hef being cuddled by Barbi in Los Angeles and another picture of Hef canoodling with Karen in Chicago. "Somehow," *Time* added, with a hint of bewilderment, "the arrangement continues to work."

Barbi Benton read the story, packed her bags, and roared off in her Maserati (a present from Hef) without a word to anyone. Although she had not dared to hope that Hef was faithful to her while he was in Chicago, Barbi was dismayed to learn from *Time* that Karen Christy was considered to be her counterpart, the châtelaine of the Chicago Mansion. When Hefner telephoned from Chicago to tell her how much he loved and missed her, a secretary nervously broke the news that Barbi appeared to have gone. Hefner was distraught: he *loved* her, how could she do this to him? Pausing only long enough to persuade Karen of the urgent need for him to go to Los Angeles, and assuring her that he loved her and that he would telephone every day to tell her how much he missed her, Hefner summoned the Big Bunny to fly him to the West Coast to look for Barbi.

By the time he arrived at Playboy Mansion West, Barbi had been located at a hotel in Hawaii. Hefner telephoned her immediately to plead for her understanding and forgiveness. They talked for a long time, but Barbi insisted on her need to get away from the Mansion to think things over and said she was going to stay in Hawaii for at least a week. Hefner waited unhappily for her return, telephoning constantly. When she got back there was an emotional reunion, but Barbi announced that she was going to find her own apartment in Beverly Hills so that she could have some independence, although she promised not to date other men. She said she still loved him and would move back into the Mansion in time. With this, Hefner had to be content.

Leaving instructions for flowers to be sent to Barbi's new apartment every day, he returned to Chicago, to discover Karen was strangely cool and remote. She was finding it increasingly difficult to cope with the stress of competing for Hefner's affections and the loneliness of the Mansion when he was away. She desperately wanted to believe that she was the most important person in his life, that she was the one he preferred, but it was hard to forget that bitter jibe: "You're just the one he fucks!"

After the kidnapping of Patty Hearst, Hefner insisted that a security guard accompany Karen every time she left the Mansion, a sensible precaution, no doubt, which also enabled Hefner to keep tabs on what she was doing and where she was going. One day, Karen slipped out of the Mansion unobserved and disappeared. Her absence was not noticed until evening, when Hefner came out of an editorial meeting and could not find her. The Mansion was searched room by room, but by midnight she had still not been found. Hefner was stricken.

Someone said she might have gone to see her friend Nanci Heitner, a Bunny who lived in the Lincoln Park area. Hefner put a coat on over his pajamas and set out in a limousine, with two guards, for Lincoln Park. There were no names on the bells outside the apartment building where Heitner lived. Hefner rang them all and when the front door buzzed and clicked open, he went inside and shouted up the stairwell. "This is Hugh Hefner. Is Karen

Christy up there?" When there was no response he began banging on each of the doors. He found Nanci Heitner on the second floor—she was alone.

Karen telephoned her friend Nanci a few minutes later and said she had to talk to her. They arranged to meet in a nearby bar, the "Four Torches," where Karen sobbed for two hours over Hefner. Nanci's advice was to leave him; it was clear, she said, there was no future in their relationship. Karen tearfully agreed but as they walked back to Nanci's apartment, Hefner stepped from his limousine, which was parked outside, and ran across to her with tears in his eyes. Karen began to cry again as they hugged each other and Hefner gently led her back to the limousine. Nanci Heitner shrugged and returned alone to her apartment.

After this incident, Hefner did his best to convince Karen to stay. He took her on a holiday to Acapulco and when she went back to Texas to visit her family, he offered to fly down to Dallas in the Big Bunny to pick her up and meet her folks, a gesture designed to reassure her of his sincerity. Karen gathered various aunts, uncles, and cousins at Dallas airport to await the arrival of the great black jet. As it circled out of the sun and touched down with a faint puff of smoke from each wheel, a sizable crowd had assembled to gawk at this famous airplane and speculate at the nature of the revels that undoubtedly occurred within its sleek, black body. Hefner jumped down the steps as soon as the jet stopped and walked across the tarmac to where Karen was waiting in a skimpy mini-skirt and T-shirt. He shook hands politely with her assembled relatives, chatted amiably for a bit, posed for a picture, then walked her back to the plane, which hauled up its steps and turned back toward the runway.

All Hefner's efforts were to prove fruitless. Karen had met a young man in Dallas and the prospect of a simple, straightforward relationship of the kind ordinarily enjoyed by girls of her age highlighted her unhappiness and disaffection with her life in the Playboy Mansion. Back in Chicago, she began secretly packing up her possessions and sending them home to Texas. She "lent" the white Lincoln to a friend for a couple of days. One afternoon she said she wanted to go shopping. A chauffeur brought a limousine around to the front door and Karen stepped out into North State Street Parkway with a security guard at her side. First stop was a boutique in Rush Street. While the guard and the chauffeur waited outside Karen went into the shop and out through a back door, along an alley to a parallel street, where she hailed a taxi. An hour later, Karen Christy and her friend Nanci Heitner were far from Chicago, heading south in the white Lincoln on Route 57, bound for Texas.

None of these dramas was mentioned in the pages of *Playboy* magazine, which continued to present Hef as the man who had discovered the secret of eternal enjoyment. In the twentieth anniversary issue of the magazine, published in January 1974, Hefner was the subject of the Playboy Interview, an assignment that apparently occupied the interviewer—free-lance writer Larry DuBois—no less than six months.

The result was *Playboy* at its self-indulgent worst. The editors proclaimed themselves well pleased with Mr. DuBois's efforts. "He saw," they unblushingly noted, "all this complex man's facets and explored, more thoroughly than we dared hope, his thinking."

Mr. DuBois himself, in the preamble before the interview, despaired of finding the words to describe the ineffable bliss of being in the presence of the editor-publisher. Being around him, he recorded, was a "forceful, funny, absolutely extraordinary experience. Like his legend, Hefner is larger than life . . . an elusive, contradictory, sometimes maddening, sometimes just mad genius." He had "all the facility and polish of an uncommonly shrewd politician" and, but for his "tremendous reserve," he "could be a very successful stand-up comic." Moreover, "in many ways he is an even more remarkable figure than his legend . . . the man is 47 but his energy is staggering . . . his powers of concentration are—well—overwhelming . . . His mind is so quick, so totally focused . . . an incredibly compelling personality . . ."

This genius, this paragon, this muse, was going to need all of his many talents during the next couple of years.

9

The Pubic Wars

In the summer of 1969, *The New York Times*, the *Chicago Tribune*, and the *Los Angeles Times* all carried full-page advertisements showing the famous Playboy Bunny logo in the cross-hair sights of a rifle. Underneath was the warning: "We're going rabbit hunting." The advertisement announced that *Penthouse* magazine, previously published only in Europe, would be available on the newsstands in America from September onward. In a further, scarcely veiled dig at *Playboy*, it added that *Penthouse* would offer its readers the "pin-ups without the hang-ups" and "the pictures without the lectures."

At the Playboy Building on North Michigan Avenue, the news was greeted with some amusement and considerable disdain. *Playboy* had spawned dozens of imitators over the years without its preeminence ever being remotely threatened. There was *Nugget*, *Dude*, *Swank*, *Gent*, *Rogue*, *Fury*, *Caper*, *Cavalcade*, *Gay Blade*, *Scamp*, and many, many more, yet none of them had ever approached *Playboy*'s circulation. In 1969 *Playboy* was selling around 4.5 million copies every month; its closest competitor, *Cavalier*, could manage no more than 110,000 a month. There was every reason not to be concerned by the arrival of yet another title.

We're going rabbit hunting.

If you catch a rabbit once, you can catch him again.

Penthouse is the magazine that caught him in England and France. Our English edition outsells him 3 to 1.

Now the hunt is on in the rabbit's own backyard. Our American edition, edited in New York, will be on the stands August 12.

What today's male likes about Penthouse is its unique international outlook. We give our readers the pictures without the lectures. The pinups without the hangups. Writers yes, philosophizers no. Adult entertainment ranging from outspoken, contemporary comment to stunning photographic essays.

And advertisers can buy our 100% newsstand circulation for a lot less lettuce than the bunny wants.

The way to catch this rabbit is to give you a better run for your money.

PENTHOUSE

The International Magazine for Men
Published by Penthouse International, Ltd.
110 East 59th Street, New York City 10022
For information call
New York Miss Kathy Keeton, (212) 421-4080
Los Angeles, I E Publishers Representative Co., (213) 663-5841
Chicago, The Bill Pattis Group, (312) 679-1100

Holiday Issue: September, 1969
On sale: August 12
Closing (scotch prints): June 23

But the editor-publisher of *Penthouse*, true to his Sicilian origins, was not the kind of man to issue idle threats. Robert Charles Edward Sabatini Guccione was a tall, flamboyant character with dark, curly hair, heavily lidded eyes, and a swashbuckling wardrobe: he liked to sport tight leather trousers tucked into boots and shirts slashed to the waist to disclose five or six thick gold chains around his neck. Among the jeweled trinkets burrowing in the hairs of his chest could always be found a gold penis, which, he liked to say, with a slow smile, was "life-size."

He looked something like a latter-day pirate, which was entirely appropriate, since he displayed typical buccaneer cunning when he set out to plunder *Playboy*. The rabbit hunting advertisements, apparently no more than harmless cheek, were in reality the opening moves in a carefully planned and elaborate campaign to topple *Playboy* and make *Penthouse* the biggest men's magazine in America. Ludicrous caricatures of the Bunny, drawn by Guccione himself, kept cropping up in subsequent trade advertisements. There was a Bunny with a twisted grimace over a headline "What Bugs Bunny?" A wizened and elderly Bunny appeared with a suggestion "Give the old man *Playboy* for Christmas." And a drawing of a Bunny avidly reading *Penthouse* was accompanied by a single, telling phrase: "Penthouse Envy?"

It was a brilliant strategy, which created an illusion that *Penthouse* was a serious competitor to *Playboy*, when in reality it was still struggling for a viable circulation. The print order for the first issue of *Penthouse* was only 350,000 and a 60 percent sale was needed to break even. The figures came in at 62 percent. "It was a big crap shoot," said Guccione. "We just slid in under the wire.

"Although we were not selling anything like *Playboy*, we *were* the second biggest magazine so we could make it look as if we were battling it out with *Playboy*. It was like guerrilla warfare. I used *Playboy*'s power against them, creating a fight when a fight did not exist. We were Hannibal assaulting Rome, attacking, disappearing into the night, and attacking again from another point.

"I signed the Bunny drawings in the advertisements, so they would know I was doing them personally. That really pissed them off."

Playboy remained aloof, refusing even to acknowledge the

existence of Guccione or his magazine. There was a brief discussion at the Mansion about suing for trademark infringement, but it was decided that the best way to deal with *Penthouse* was to ignore it.

Guccione did not imagine Hefner would be "dumb enough to sue," but he had no intention of being ignored. He decided that *Penthouse* would be the first men's magazine in America to risk *going pubic.*

Guccione often liked to say, because he hoped it irritated Hefner, that *Playboy* taught him everything he knew about magazines. It was largely true.

The Gucciones hailed originally from Sicily—all Robert's grandparents were born there—but by the time he arrived in the world, in 1930, his father was a prosperous accountant in Brooklyn. Young Robert attended a private boarding school in Blairstown, New Jersey, where he was remembered in the yearbook for his magnetic personality, wit, and colossal egotism. "He regards himself as a sort of modern Messiah," the yearbook recorded, "and considers the academy unbelievably fortunate to be able to entertain him."

After graduation in 1948, he skipped college and sailed for Europe to seek his fortune as an artist. In this ambition he was notably unsuccessful, so he bummed around from country to country, taking odd jobs here and there and living off the regular checks that arrived from his extraordinarily indulgent father. He married twice and sired five children. At one point, he could be found working the cafés in the south of France with his second wife, an English girl he met in Tangier, where she was singing in a nightclub: he offered instant pencil portraits for 1,000 francs and she read palms for the same price.

By the mid-sixties, Guccione had drifted to London and had developed a little business selling pinup pictures by mail order and peddling back issues of American skin magazines. He was at this time a regular reader of *Playboy*, which sold around 120,000 copies a month in Britain. Guccione thought *Playboy* was terrific and he could not understand why there were no similar magazines available in Britain. He soon began to mull over the idea of starting a

The old grey hare just ain't what he used to be.

B.O.
(BURNT OUT)

Guess who's been stretching the truth?

magazine of his own and as he knew nothing about magazines, he resolved to copy *Playboy*'s clearly successful format. Nothing could have been simpler.

He thought he would call his magazine *Playgirl*, but was warned by a lawyer that *Playboy* might sue for trademark infringement, so he decided on *Penthouse*, which had a nice swinging bachelor ring about it. Instead of a Playmate of the Month, he would have a Pet of the Month. Although Guccione had never taken a photograph in his life, he considered his background as an artist eminently qualified him to photograph the first centerfold, particularly as he had a friend who offered to lend him a Rolleiflex. To find a model, he positioned himself in the King's Road, Chelsea, outside an employment agency that was offering secretarial jobs at five pounds a week and began stopping likely looking girls passing by and asking them if they would be photographed nude for a new magazine for five pounds an hour. After a number of rejections from girls who clearly thought he was a pervert, this tactic eventually proved successful—it was, after all, the days of "Swinging London." Guccione was somewhat short of ready cash, and so speed was paramount when the first girl arrived at his apartment to pose for *Penthouse*—he completed the session in forty-five minutes flat. The girl was paid pro rata and received £4 5s for her trouble.

Timing was also rather critical when it came to paying for a color brochure he had designed to tout for subscriptions. Already overdrawn at the bank, he was able to delay writing a check for the printer until after the banks had closed on a Thursday, knowing that it would not be cleared until the following Monday. By then, he prayed, sufficient subscriptions would have arrived to cover it. Monday morning found Guccione sitting in his car outside the bank, tearing open envelopes, pulling out cash, postal orders, and checks and stuffing them into a bag. He just made it.

The brochure Guccione mailed to potential subscribers featured eight of the naughtiest nudes culled from his pinup collection and the promise that *Penthouse* would be "a magazine that separated the men from the boys . . . jam-packed with beautiful girls, controversial articles, intimate stories, and delectable lashings of bedside humor." As his mailing list was somewhat eclectic, the brochures were addressed to a wide variety of "potential subscribers," including schoolgirls, priests, wives of Members of Parliament, and members of the Townswomen's Guild.

A few days later, an angry Member of Parliament stood up in the House of Commons, waved a bunch of *Penthouse* brochures, and demanded what was going to be done to stem this new wave of pornography. Guccione was very grateful for the publicity and was similarly happy to be charged under an obscure section of the Post Office Act with sending obscene material through the mail. He went into hiding at his house in Chelsea and completed arrangements for the launch of *Penthouse* by telephone and mail, with two police officers sitting in a car outside waiting to serve the summons the moment he emerged. When everything was ready, he telephoned the newspapers and stepped outside to be handed a summons. All of these events were well-reported, which virtually guaranteed a sellout for the first issue of *Penthouse*. One of Guccione's sweetest memories was of leaving the court after being fined a bargain £110 and finding evening newspaper placards on the street shrieking: SEX MAG MAN IN COURT.

The initial print order for *Penthouse* was 120,000 copies. They were gone in five days. "When I held the first copy in my hand," said Guccione, "I knew I would have to take it to America."

In 1969, *Oh! Calcutta!* was playing on the New York stage, teenage hippies had been filmed joyfully gamboling in the nude at Woodstock, and there were strip joints in every major city of the United States, but it was still taboo in the skin magazines to show pubic hair. Most of them accepted an unwritten rule that the difference between erotic photography and pornography was to indicate to their readers that pin-ups had hair between their legs.

Playboy had nervously tested the water that year with a couple of pictures faintly hinting at the existence of pubic hair; a tantalizing glimpse, no more, either hidden in deep shadow or fuzzily out of focus. As the heavens did not fall, Hefner was encouraged, in November, to approve an artistic spread of pictures of Paula Kelly, a dancer in the musical *Sweet Charity*, shot with a strobe-lit time exposure. There were seven images of Miss Kelly, totally nude, leaping across the page and in two of them her pubic hair was clearly visible.

Perhaps there would have been no fuss had Miss Kelly been

white, but she was not, she was black. Sensitive civil rights leaders immediately accused *Playboy* of racism, because a black woman had been chosen to introduce pubic hair into the magazine. It revived all the barely dormant suspicions about black women being used for white men's delectation and Hefner, who was the least racist of men, realized he had made a tactical mistake. After this, *Playboy* lost heart and returned to using an airbrush to remove any stray strands of pubic hair that inadvertently sprouted into view.

But Guccione had devised what he described as the perfect rationale for going pubic. It was a loquacious argument about accepting Judeo-Christian principles of God creating man in his own image and therefore no part of the human anatomy could be, of itself, an obscenity and therefore denying the existence of pubic hair was an offense against God and therefore. . . . It was a very long discourse.

His lawyer told him it was a nice argument but, before he would have an opportunity to air it, his magazines would be seized all over the country. The lawyer warned him he might be in court for two years. Guccione was undeterred. "It was a big gamble, but one I was willing to take."

In February 1970, *Penthouse* published a color picture of the reigning Miss Holland with a soft halo of pubic hair clearly visible in profile. When advance copies of the issue arrived at the Playboy Building, most Playboy executives declared themselves in agreement with Guccione's lawyers; after studying the picture of Miss Holland with some awe, the consensus was that Guccione had gone too far. They waited, not without satisfaction, for Guccione to be arrested. Nothing happened. Two months later, *Penthouse* did it again, publishing a frontal view of a girl, who, although she had her legs crossed, also clearly possessed a frizzy bush of pubic hair. Again, nothing happened. The issue, 500,000 copies, sold out.

"From that moment on," said Guccione, "*Playboy* allowed the leadership to fall into my hands. We became the magazine standing at the cutting edge of what was permissible. We were the adventurous, progressive magazine. We were what every young man in America wanted."

In September 1970, the President's Commission on Obscenity

and Pornography, set up under Lyndon Johnson, issued a surprising report asserting there was little evidence that pornography was harmful and urging government restraint in attempts to "interfere with the rights of adults who wish to do so to read, obtain, or view explicit sexual materials." Organizations like Citizens for Decent Literature immediately expressed outrage, as did J. Edgar Hoover, director of the FBI, who had long contended there was a direct link between pornography and crimes of violence, particularly rape.

President Richard Nixon condemned the report as "morally bankrupt" and accused the Commission of performing a "disservice" to the nation. "So long as I am in the White House," Nixon said, "there will be no relaxation of the national effort to control and eliminate smut from our national life."

That same month, *Penthouse* appeared on the nation's newsstands with pictures of a freckle-faced girl called Tina McDowall displaying more pubic hair than had ever been seen in any magazine available over the counter in the United States. The pictures were taken by Guccione on a beach in Yugoslavia (where *Penthouse* had opened a casino) and in Richmond Park, London, where Tina McDowall was obliged to crouch under a coat every time someone walking a dog came close to the leafy glade in which she posed. In one of the pictures she could be seen stretching catlike up against a tree as if sharpening her claws. In others, she was touching herself with soft, erotic caresses.

At the Playboy Mansion in Chicago, Hefner flicked through the September *Penthouse* at a meeting with Preuss, Rosenzweig, and Stephen Byer, the marketing director, and pronounced Guccione's pictures to be "cheap, pornographic crap." Hefner still refused to take *Penthouse* seriously, dismissing it as just another magazine in the legion of lesser competitors, and swore he had no intention of following *Penthouse* by showing pubic hair in *Playboy*. Only a few weeks earlier, Rosenzweig had rushed in with a proof of a cartoon depicting a nudist colony in which the only pubic hair visible belonged to a black girl. Hefner pondered the cartoon for two full minutes before delivering his judgment: "Tell Spec to rub out the pubic hair."

Outside Hefner's immediate circle of courtiers, who would never disagree with Hef, there was little support for the view that

Guccione's pictures were crap. Both Art Paul and Vince Tajiri, the men who headed the art and photo departments, made no secret of their belief that Guccione showed considerable talent as a photographer. His soft-focus pictures had an intimate, sensual realism that made Playmates look like plastic dolls.

Guccione's technique was to use the camera as a voyeur, catching a girl, apparently unaware, at an unchaste and private moment, when she might be dreamily stroking her body with a wisp of antique lace, or gazing into a mirror, lost in a concupiscent reverie. *Penthouse* girls were constantly examining themselves, as if preoccupied with their own sexuality, although *Newsweek*, never fond of the skin magazines, formed the opinion that they fondled themselves as though "they were looking for lumps."

Hefner publicly sneered at Guccione, likening him to a "Victorian peeping Tom," but privately he was alarmed at what he perceived as the inability of his own photographers to produce pictures with the same libidinous appeal. Bill Arsenault, a *Playboy* photographer, recalled a crisis meeting at Playboy Mansion West to discuss the *Penthouse* threat. "The meeting consisted of Hefner waving copies of *Penthouse* and saying 'Why can't we have pictures like this?' No one told him the reason was that he always chose the centerfold and he always chose the same kind of girl and the same kind of picture."

Certainly, the *Penthouse* Pet did not look like the girl who lived next door, which was where the corn-fed, all-American Playmate could still be found, out shopping with her folks, riding on the beach with her hair tangled by the wind, whipping up an omelette in the kitchen, or playing Ping-Pong with her kid brother. Innocent, implausibly perfect, untouchable, and unbelievable, she pouted coyly from *Playboy*'s centerfold every month and denied that the world was changing. The "permissive society" had arrived and the Playmate had not noticed, whereas the Pet looked as if she was enjoying it. "They were still fighting the sexual revolution," said Guccione. "Our starting point was that the revolution had already been won."

Playboy and its Playmates also came in for harsh criticism from psychiatrist Rollo May in a book called *Love and Will*, published soon after *Penthouse* appeared in America. May claimed that *Playboy* espoused a form of "new puritanism" which in American men derived its dynamic from a repressed anxiety about impotence, underlying a fear of involvement with women. "You discover the naked girls with silicated breasts side by side with articles by reputable authors, and you conclude on first blush that the magazine is certainly on the side of the new enlightenment. But as you look more closely you see a strange expression in these photographed girls: detached, mechanical, uninviting, vacuous—the typical schizoid personality in the negative sense of that term. You discover that they are not 'sexy' at all but that *Playboy* has only shifted the fig leaf from the genitals to the face."

No one was happier than Guccione to hear Playmates described as "typical schizoid personalities"—his feelings precisely. The burgeoning women's movement was similarly heartened by Dr. May's attack, since *Playboy* was anathema to feminists, who charged that women were treated within its glossy pages as objects of consumption no more or less important than the latest stereo or sports car, and objects that became useless with age.

The women's movement, fired by Betty Friedan's seminal book *The Feminine Mystique*, became increasingly militant with the dawning of the seventies, a militancy fatuously symbolized by bra-burning. In Atlantic City, women crowned a sheep as Miss America and threw copies of *Playboy* onto liberation bonfires. They infiltrated the Playboy Mansion in Chicago and plastered the paintings in the ballroom with anti-Playboy stickers. There were demonstrations outside Playboy Clubs and at Grinnell College in Iowa, half a dozen male and female students stripped during a visit by a *Playboy* representative and invited him to do the same. He refused, shamefacedly.

Hefner did his best to defend his position against feminist brickbats, claiming that *Playboy* had helped women by decontaminating sex. "The feminists who criticize us don't realize how *Playboy*, far more than the women's magazines, is responsible for the nongirdle look, the bikini, the mini-skirt, the openness to nudity." Feminist critics of the magazine often missed the point of what it was all about. *Playboy* was a celebration of sexuality, not an exploitation of sexuality. "I don't understand why feminists aren't grateful to us," he groused to a deeply unsympathetic Gloria Steinem. Perhaps it was because the magazine was still packed with dispiriting evidence of the most rabid male chauvinism—"Our Unabashed

Dictionary defines assault as what every woman likes to be taken with a grain of."

Any faint hope he might have retained of earning the gratitude of feminists was totally destroyed toward the end of 1970 when a secretary at the Playboy Building, a covert feminist sympathizer, secretly copied a Hefner memo and smuggled it to a local women's group, which sent copies to all the major newspapers. The memo aborted the magazine's plans to publish an objective feature on the women's movement, commissioned from a free-lance writer called Susan Braudy.

Hefner did not want any "objective" reporting about the women's movement in his magazine. "What I want," he pointed out in the long memo to Spectorsky,

> is a devastating piece that takes militants apart. . . . What I'm interested in is the highly irrational, emotional, kookie trend that feminism has taken. These chicks are our natural enemy. It is time to do battle with them and I think we can do it in a devastating way. . . .
>
> The only subject related to feminism that is worth doing is on this new militant phenomena [*sic*] and the only proper *Playboy* approach to it is one that devastates it. If you analyze all of the most basic premises of the extreme form of new feminism, you will find them unalterably opposed to the romantic boy-girl society that Playboy promotes. It is up to us to do a really expert, personal demolition job on the subject. . . .

The secretary who leaked the memo was fired, but the fat she had thrown onto the flames sizzled furiously for weeks. The women's movement was a hot story at that time and the media were happy for a new angle that offered a little light relief at *Playboy*'s expense. Hefner went on the Dick Cavett show to defend himself but put up an unimpressive performance against the women invited to debate feminism with him. The audience cheered wildly when Susan Brownmiller, asked to define sexual equality, snapped: "When Hugh Hefner comes out here with a cotton tail attached to his rear end, then we'll have equality."

Susan Braudy wrote a piece for *Glamour* magazine, entitled

"The Article I Wrote on Women That Playboy Would Not Publish," and took the opportunity to settle the score: "Why can't a magazine written to titillate men present a full picture of real women to those big, brave men? Why must she be a fantasy figure so dehumanized as to be really desexed—hairs plucked, smells replaced, pores filled with make-up, smoothed to unthreatening blandness? Is the Playboy male so weak, so ultimately unable to cope with reality and real women that the fantasy creature of his glossy Playboy-inspired reveries must be mechanized, passive, manipulable, and controllable?"

While *Playboy* was embroiled in this unhappy tussle, battered by feminists who presented such a startlingly different image of womanhood to that found within the magazine, the news from the competition was still bad: the *Penthouse* centerfold had gone pubic, *full frontal*, and its circulation was up to 1,500,000. Hefner decided that *Playboy* could no longer afford to ignore this feisty opponent. Thus began a contest between Hefner and Guccione to see who could produce the raunchier magazine. It was a battle for circulation that became known in the trade as the "Pubic Wars."

Playboy took the decision to go pubic painfully and protesting all the while it had nothing to do with *Penthouse*. In truth, the first pubic Playmate pictures were shot by accident. Alexas Urba was photographing a pneumatic blonde, Liv Lindeland, in Chicago for the January issue. "She was sitting on a bed in the studio and I asked her to raise her right leg a little to improve the pose," said Urba. "I didn't notice her pubic hair was showing until the film was developed."

The full set of pictures was sent over to the Mansion for Hefner to make the final selection, as usual. Poring over a lightbox with an eyeglass, Hefner minutely examined Miss Lindeland's pubic hair and pondered the issue. Were his readers, or perhaps more importantly, his advertisers, ready for this? Was *America* ready? Finally he turned to production manager John Mastro and said: "Let's do it." Mastro immediately telephoned photo editor Vince Tajiri with the momentous news: "We're going pubic."

"I was very, very unhappy about it," said Tajiri. "I felt we were chasing an upstart. There had been competitors before and they had never bothered us. I thought if we were going to move in that direction it should be at our own pace. I didn't think we should be pushed by *Penthouse*. But Hefner began to take the challenge from *Penthouse* very seriously—he'd been counting the number of pubic hair pictures in every copy."

When Tajiri saw the proofs in Mastro's office, he and Mastro fretted about the extent to which Miss Lindeland's pubic hair was highlighted and both of them agreed that the highlights would have to be "knocked down." The final decision was, of course, deferred to Hefner. He got his eyeglass out again and considered Miss Lindeland's loins anew. Rarely could a girl's private parts have been so thoroughly scrutinized before being made public. "Leave the highlights as they are," said Hefner slowly, aware that history was being made.

Playboy's first pubic Playmate went generally unremarked by the nation at large, although the *Atlantic Monthly* expressed deep disapproval some months later in a feature headlined "The Business of Sex":

> Playboy has not, until very recently (and then very timidly) admitted pictorially the existence of pubic hair, partly because Playboy needs desperately to be accepted by reader and advertiser alike as an unobtrusive, overground publication that is part of the system, and partly because Playboy's sick male-chauvinist philosophy cannot admit the existence of a woman's sexual power, as signified visibly by pubic hair. In fact, Playboy's central marketing strategy is to sell fantasies of women as powerless, grateful sexual slaves to men who have found women far otherwise—strong, demanding and frightening—in real life.

There was much chortling in the Guccione camp when it was observed that *Playboy* was being forced to follow the lead set by *Penthouse*, as if it had a ring in its nose. The first pubic Playmate appeared a full five months after the first pubic Pet. *Penthouse* came out with a full-frontal centerfold in August 1971; *Playboy* followed suit in January 1972. Hefner agonized about taking this step and asked for two sets of proofs to be prepared: in one, the girl, Marilyn Cole, held an arm demurely across her body to conceal her pubic hair; in the other, she held her hands at her sides. Only at the last minute, when the presses could not any longer be delayed, did Hefner okay the full-frontal version.

In the month that Miss Cole revealed all to the saucer-eyed readers of *Playboy*, Guccione and Hefner met for the first, and last, time. Guccione was spending the New Year holiday with his friend Bernie Cornfeld, the colorful head of Investors Overseas Services. Bernie was not yet facing the welter of problems that would lead to the rapid collapse of IOS and was living in high style in Beverly Hills. A man of notoriously lascivious inclinations, his house guests were all girls except for Guccione. On New Year's Eve, Bernie threw a noisy party for around two thousand close friends and at one point in the evening he grabbed Guccione's arm and led him through the crowd, mischievously promising that someone had arrived whom Guccione just had to meet—it was Hugh Hefner, with his pipe in his mouth and Barbi Benton on his arm.

"Hefner looked at me," said Guccione, "licked his little pink lips and gave me a limp hand and muttered something which I took to be hello. I said 'Hi, how are you?' and I said hello to Barbi and that's all I said. He was much more embarrassed than I was."

Next day, Bernie and his house guests had been invited over to Playboy Mansion West for a buffet and a screening of *Clockwork Orange*. At about twelve noon, Hefner's secretary telephoned Bernie and said Hef would prefer it if Bernie did not bring Guccione because Hef "didn't think Guccione was a very nice person." Cornfeld slammed down the telephone and said, "That son of a bitch. That's it. We're not going."

But Guccione assured Bernie that he was happy to stay behind and said he should not disappoint the girls. He persuaded Bernie to go and deliver a personal message to Hefner. "Tell him that when I was on the Merv Griffin show I said that I would give him another four years as number one. Well, he doesn't have four years anymore. Because of this, I'm only going to give him three." When Cornfeld returned home later that night Guccione asked if Bernie had given Hefner the message and what was his reaction. "He said fuck you," Bernie reported, with a grin.

Although the circulation of *Penthouse* was rising fast, it still appeared that *Playboy* was inviolate. A "Memo to Advertisers" inserted inside the front cover of the January 1971 issue announced "Another Year of Bountiful Bonuses" and gave a breakdown of the magazine's circulation during the previous year: every month *Playboy* had sold at least a million extra copies over its circulation base rate of 4,800,000. Later in the year, the September 1972 issue of *Playboy* broke all previous circulation records by notching up a sale of 7,012,000. But not all Playboy executives exhibited the confidence that the figures might perhaps have prompted. "By then," said *Playboy*'s marketing vice-president, Robert Gutwillig, "my attitude had changed from one of concern to alarm."

Gutwillig knew Guccione better than anyone at Playboy. When Guccione launched *Penthouse* in the United States, he was able to raise finance through the Times-Mirror company in New York, whose subsidiary, the New English Library, distributed *Penthouse* in Britain. Gutwillig was a Times-Mirror executive and was appointed as "Bob's keeper" to watch the way he used the credit; they were given adjoining offices in the Times-Mirror building.

"I was very, very impressed with his energy and his nascent publishing ability," Gutwillig recalled. "I felt it was likely, given the backing, that he would launch the first credible challenge to *Playboy*."

A year later, Gutwillig joined Playboy to manage its ailing book division. Then in his late thirties, he had spent his whole career in publishing and was once Spectorsky's book editor at McGraw-Hill. In his conservative gray flannel suits and button-down shirts, he was hardly the picture of a Playboy swinger, but he was very bright, ambitious, and full of ideas. He made such an impression as a supercharged go-getter that there was soon talk of his being groomed as Hefner's eventual successor; certainly his promotion was nothing less than meteoric—by 1972 he was ranked with Hefner, Preuss, and Rosenzweig as one of the four men running the company.

By the time I arrived at Playboy I considered Guccione and his magazine to be a hell of a threat. I knew that Guccione had a single-minded mission to eclipse *Playboy*. I kept saying "The redcoats are coming, the redcoats are coming," but they just put it down to my overall pessimistic demeanor. Because I was a newcomer, I was not thought to be a true believer in the Playboy mystique.

When *Penthouse* passed one and a half million, people began to look a little worried. We would have all these silly meetings at the Chicago Mansion, where we would conjoin to discuss the latest *Penthouse* figures or the latest *Penthouse* pubic pictures, but they never reached a consistent strategy to do anything about it.

Hefner conducted himself like the steady commander at the tiller, keeping calm while everyone about him was losing his head. We would all be shooting off our mouths and Hefner would be sitting there in his bathrobe with a Pepsi in his hand and a faint air of preoccupation. He gave the impression of putting up with it to give the guys a chance to blow off steam, then he could get back to his pinball machines and his girls and not have to listen to it for another month or two.

In the spring of 1972, Gutwillig heard that Guccione was planning to bring out a second men's magazine in conjunction with Daniel Filipacchi, publisher of *Lui*, a French magazine with a remarkable similarity to *Playboy*. "If there's going to be three magazines cutting up the market," Gutwillig told Hefner, "we'd better be the company with two." Hefner agreed.

Although Guccione's negotiations with Filipacchi were well advanced, Gutwillig stepped in, dazzled the French publisher with the prospect of a deal with Playboy, and cut Guccione out. "I guess you could say Guccione was acutely displeased," Gutwillig confessed with a thin smile. The agreement was that *Lui* would be licensed to publish *Playboy* in France and Playboy would be licensed to publish *Lui* in America. Hefner didn't like *Lui* as a title and decided to change it to *Oui*, which he felt reflected the continental flavor of the magazine. (*Oui* would initially cause widespread head-scratching among customers unfamiliar with French and uncertain how to go about wrapping their tongues round three vowels.)

Playboy hoped that *Oui* would wipe out *Penthouse*. First, it would feature girl pictures as erotic and explicit as those found in *Penthouse*; second, it would have a similar European character and it would be a slick and sophisticated product aimed at a younger readership—*Penthouse*'s readership. (The irony of Playboy copying a magazine which had originally copied *Playboy* did not go unnoticed on the editorial floors in the Playboy Building, although it was not the kind of thing mentioned in Hefner's presence.) With *Oui* in its stable, *Playboy* would then be freed from the distressing necessity of slugging it out with *Penthouse* to see who could produce the raunchier magazine. This was the theory.

Oui was launched in September 1972 and was an immediate success. The print run for the first issue, 750,000 copies, was virtually sold out in the first two weeks. *Penthouse* tried to steal the new magazine's thunder by suggesting that its first centerfold, a delightful French girl by the name of Florence Fossorier, was actually an Austrian girl by the name of Lotte Gunthart who was a *Penthouse* Pet back in March 1971. There was indeed a remarkable similarity between them; nevertheless, nothing could detract from the fact that *Oui* looked like a winner, even if half its readers did not know how to pronounce the title.

What happened next, no one anticipated. The market was suddenly flooded with skin magazines in the *Playboy/Penthouse* mold. A month after *Oui* made its debut, *Gallery* appeared, looking so much like *Playboy* that Hefner described it, with good cause, as a blatant rip-off. *Gallery* used the same logo typeface as *Playboy* and copied the *Playboy* formula line by line, page by page, party joke by party joke. The Gallery Interview was with Jack Anderson, who, by coincidence, was the subject of the Playboy Interview that same month. "You may expect a Hefty supply of dressed and undressed ladies," the publisher's letter promised, although the magazine declared its intent not to enter the "current publishing contest to see who can print the most daring display of pubic hair."

Gallery was backed by Ronald L. Fenton, an entrepreneur from Ohio who had made a fortune selling computers. He found offices for his magazine in Playboy's lap—on North Michigan Avenue, right across from the Playboy Building—and moved into a large house that he called the Gallery Mansion. It was on North Astor, just a block from the Playboy Mansion. Mr. Fenton had no reservations about candidly admitting that *Gallery* was a rip-off of *Playboy*. "What do you expect me to do?" he would ask. "Copy a loser?"

Close on the heels of *Gallery* came *Genesis*, financed by Rocki Aoki, owner of a string of successful Japanese restaurants in the

United States, and edited by *Gallery*'s former associate publisher. *Genesis* offered its readers an inspired innovation—*two* centerfolds. After *Genesis* came *Coq*, put together by photographer George Santo Pietro, whose "Mansion" could be found in downtown Chicago next to a disused warehouse. Mr. Pietro was careful to point out that the name of his magazine was pronounced "coke."

Women's magazines also pitched into the pubic wars. *Cosmopolitan* published its first male nude pin-up—Burt Reynolds—in 1972 and sold out the entire issue. *Playgirl* magazine was launched in California and promised a male centerfold every month. Guccione brought out *Viva*, a glossy, sex-orientated magazine for women, and held a launch party at the Ambassador West Hotel in Chicago, just two doors from the Playboy Mansion. *Viva*, "edited by men who really love women for women who really love men," was derided in the Playboy Building as "*Penthouse* in drag."

The last remnant of the centerfold's beleaguered modesty was ripped away with the arrival of *Hustler*, a monumentally lowbrow magazine that offered its readers a gynecologist's eye view of the nude. *Hustler* was the tasteless brainchild of Larry Flynt, a pudgy thirty-year-old opportunist who ran a string of go-go bars in Ohio. Flynt grew up on a hardscrabble farm in Kentucky and had no pretensions about his beer-belly macho magazine: all he wanted was to make money. He was described at various times by *Chicago Sun-Times* columnist Bob Greene as "El Scummo"; a pervert, degenerate, and trash. He never complained.

While most of the new contenders in the pubic wars scratched around for circulation without ever offering a serious challenge either to *Playboy* or *Penthouse*, the outrageous *Hustler* hogged attention. Flynt got hold of some grainy photographs of Jackie Onassis sunbathing in the nude in Greece and immediately splashed them in his magazine, creating a fine old furor. When the circulation of *Hustler* passed the million mark, Flynt celebrated by buying a twenty-four-room mock-Tudor mansion in Columbus, opposite an expensive private school for girls. There were immediate objections to his undesirable presence—he responded by promising to stand outside his mansion handing out lollipops with his picture inset in the candy to tempt girls inside. Flynt's talent for self-publicity was quite as well developed as that of Hefner and Guccione, and *Hustler* survived when most of the other contenders in the Pubic Wars capitulated to the market supremacy of *Playboy* and *Penthouse*.

Early in 1973, *Playboy*'s circulation began to fall, little by little, causing some disquiet in the soft-carpeted corridors of the Playboy Building. From a peak of 7 million plus in September 1972, sales slipped to 6.7 million in the spring of 1973 and showed every sign of dropping still more. It had never happened before in the history of the magazine. Hefner tended to blame the sluggish economy, while other executives admitted that the competition was beginning to hurt. But there were many *Playboy* editors who believed the real problem was sitting on their own doorstep: *Oui* magazine.

Up to a healthy circulation of 1,500,000, *Oui* was doing fine, except that it was apparently taking readers from *Playboy* rather than *Penthouse*. No other conclusion could be drawn from the figures: *Playboy* was down, *Penthouse* was up. Guccione now claimed a circulation for *Penthouse* of more than 4 million and said it was increasing by an alarming 300,000 copies every month. He gleefully taunted *Playboy* with more disparaging advertisements, showing the rabbit hiding behind a rock or being flattened in a fistfight by a muscular tortoise, a symbol Guccione had adopted with an eye to Aesop's fable.

Playboy gloomily faced the failure of the *Oui* strategy in a memo circulated to staff on May 28, 1973: "You realize, of course, that we're in a tight circulation bind right now, and it will get worse before it gets better. *Playboy, Penthouse, Gallery,* and *Oui* are all fighting for the same buck . . . only *Penthouse* isn't hurting. We've all done some pretty deep analyses of *Penthouse,* and there's no getting away from the fact that one of their greatest appeals is an unabashed preoccupation with sex. Without imitating them, or even trying to compete with them in the magnitude of their preoccupation, I think we've got to get into sex in a major way."

Slowly, the girls in *Playboy* lost their innocence. Instead of lounging elegantly, they *sprawled*, with increasingly unchaste abandon. They touched themselves in ways that Playmates never did. They shamelessly opened their legs for what photographers described as the beaver shot. They began to wear kinky lingerie, leather, impossibly high heels, and net stockings, to catch the eye of the fetishists. Regular features were heated up, too, in particular the Playboy Advisor, which started to tackle subjects like anilingus and bondage.

In June 1973, it looked for a moment as if the U.S. Supreme Court would call a halt to the Pubic Wars. Chief Justice Warren Burger ruled that henceforth local communities would be permitted to judge for themselves whether or not a publication was obscene and therefore open to prosecution. Hefner called it "a preposterous and devastating decision," although he did not anticipate *Playboy* ever being considered obscene. Guccione reacted with a fine display of Churchillian truculence, offering to provide financial support to any retailers who ran foul of local vigilante groups, setting up a subscription service to mail magazines to customers unable to buy them locally, and promising that the next cover of *Penthouse* would be the "nudest yet." At a press conference in Manhattan, he vowed to fight any attempts to restrict circulation of his magazine, by breaking the law if necessary. "If I have to go to jail," he said, "that's okay with me."

Surprisingly, the Burger ruling did not provoke many "communities" to mount an attack on the skin magazines; there were a few brushfire distribution battles, mainly in the Bible Belt, but otherwise the Pubic Wars continued. Indeed, Guccione was so confident that he was soon threatening to "go pink" (show the parted lips of the vagina). This intelligence was greeted with consternation at the Playboy Building, where there was already a distinct lack of enthusiasm for the policy of meeting the *Penthouse* threat by matching smut with smut. A number of photographers, including Alexas Urba, had resigned in disgust. "I wanted to shoot beautiful pictures of beautiful women," explained Urba. "I didn't want to shoot pornography."

Hefner did his best to make light of the Pubic Wars in the Playboy Twentieth Anniversary Interview, published in January 1974:

PLAYBOY: How do you feel about the proliferation of *Playboy* imitators in the last year or two, and the fact that some of them are obviously trying to copy more than your magazine?
HEFNER: They say that imitation is the sincerest form of flattery, so I guess I've been flattered more sincerely—and more blatantly—than any other magazine publisher in history . . .

PLAYBOY: Considering the debt that *Penthouse, Gallery, Genesis* and the rest owe to *Playboy,* how do you react when their publishers tell interviewers that *Playboy* is old-fashioned and that their own magazines are more in tune with contemporary standards?

HEFNER: I think it's very funny, but what else can you expect them to say?

In 1974, the Pubic Wars spilled into the courts. *Playboy* suspected that *Penthouse* was inflating the circulation figures it filed each month with the Audit Bureau of Circulations, and challenged the 4,637,933 copies *Penthouse* claimed had been sold in December 1973. An ABC investigation revealed, to Guccione's embarrassment, that the figure was too high by 613,416 copies. He blamed the discrepancy on miscalculation of sales projections.

Following this gaffe, an advertising sales manager on *Oui* circulated a letter to a number of advertisers, claiming that *Penthouse* had not met its circulation guarantee. This was a ludicrous charge, since even after deducting the extra copies, *Penthouse* was selling well over its guaranteed figure of 3.5 million. Guccione immediately sued, alleging *Playboy* had disseminated "false and fraudulent information" and claiming damages of $40 million. *Playboy* counterclaimed, alleging *Penthouse* had infringed its trademark in advertising. All the suits foundered on technicalities. "It was very unfortunate," said Guccione. "I should have had an open and shut case for libel."

Heating up *Playboy* did nothing to arrest the slide in its circulation and it was hovering close to 6 million at its darkest hour in the battle with *Penthouse*. "Our lowest point," Dick Rosenzweig averred, "was unquestionably the month we published a cover picture of a girl with her hand in her knickers."

She was posed to illustrate a feature on "Sex in the Cinema" and was sitting on a cinema seat with her legs spread wide, her skirt pulled up, apparently masturbating while gawping at some unknown movie. There was an uproar after it appeared on the newsstands and a great deal of disapproving coverage in the media. *Newsweek* nicely described the cover girl as a "concupiscent young cineaste who—to give her the benefit of the doubt—seems to be plumbing the depths of her bikini pants for a stray kernel of pop-corn."

It was the turning point for *Playboy*. No one liked that cover, least of all the advertisers, but it served as a catalyst by highlighting how far *Playboy* had been pushed into the salacious mire in its attempt to compete with *Penthouse*. "We definitely overreacted," said Art Paul. "For a while, we lost our way, lost confidence. Hef was uncertain about what we were doing; we all were."

It was the end of the Pubic Wars. Hefner conceded the contest, to the general relief of his editors, and sent a memo round saying that *Playboy* would get back to what it knew best, and thereafter forbear to compete for readers primarily interested in looking at gynecologically detailed pictures of girls.

"At present there are some thirty-seven publications vying for a share of the male market," Hefner noted in the 1975 annual report, "and none approaches *Playboy* in covering the full scope of interests of the contemporary male. Generally, they focus on only one of those interests—sex—often exceeding the bounds of the most liberal of contemporary tastes. In these matters, our standards will be our own and will not be dictated by competitive pressures."

There was a curious postscript to the episode that somehow seemed to confirm the wisdom of his decision. When peace had been negotiated in Vietnam and the American prisoners of war returned home, they were asked what changes they observed in America, undoubtedly in the expectation of some profound comment on social change. One after another, they professed amazement that pubic hair could be seen in the *Playboy* centerfold.

A boyish Hef and a winsome Victor A. Lownes III face the press with a model of the first Playboy Club and a model wearing the first Bunny costume.

Some of the gang at a late-night meeting to discuss the expansion of the Playboy empire. From the left: Dick Rosenzweig, Bob Preuss, Hef, and Arnie Morton.

Victor at work and at play—on
promotion trip with playmates in
Miami, discussing the launch of
Show Business Illustrated with
his friend Tony Curtis, and
partying with Hef in the Playboy
Mansion.

The first Playboy Club, Chicago.

"Good evening, sir, welcome to the Playboy Club. . . ." Door Bunnies in Chicago.

The Big Bunny—Hefner flying high.

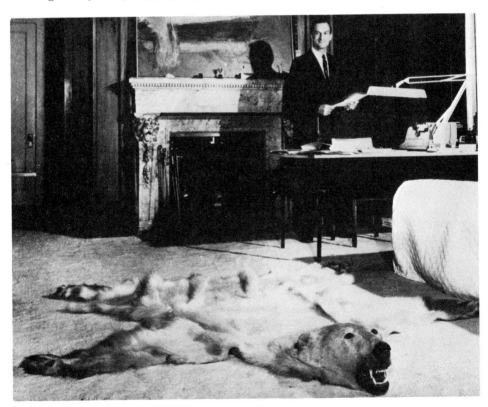

OPPOSITE AND ABOVE: *Hefner, "living the good life."*

A wan, somewhat dispirited bunch of aspiring Bunnies at an "audition" in the London club, in contrast to the triumphant smiles of the first British Bunnies on their return from training in Chicago.

Hefner, Rolls-Royce, and Bunnies as he arrives in London for the opening of the Playboy Club there, 1966.

Hef marshals his legion of British Bunnies for photographers prior to the opening of the London Playboy Club. Later they formed a fluffy-tailed football team as a publicity stunt.

Victor A. Lownes

The Bristol Bunny Belle leaves Paddington Station.

Victor Lownes with colleagues at the Playboy Club.

Hef and Dorothy Stratton. The only Playmate ever to become a star, she didn't live to fulfill her promise.

Hef and Barbi Benton, a regular on "Playboy after Dark."

Shannon Tweed, the first video Playmate of the Month.

Hef and Marilyn Cole.

Hef and Barbi Benton.

Hef in his element—at a Playmate reunion at the Los Angeles Mansion, 1979.

OPPOSITE PAGE:

TOP: *Hef and Sondra Theodore at a Western party.*

BOTTOM: *Hef and Heather Waite.*

*Hef, in crushed velvet, clearly senses
victory in the battle for Marilyn Cole's
affections. He lost. Ms. Cole may now
be found hunting with Victor A.
Lownes in the English countryside.*

ABOVE: *Bob Guccione, principal contender in the Pubic Wars, surrounded by the spoils of victory in his New York mansion.*

CENTER: *Christie Hefner studies the foundering flagship of the faltering empire she will surely inherit.*

BELOW: *Playboy Mansion West at Holmby Hills: Hefner and Barbi Benton dressed up for a "Great Gatsby" party, 1974.*

The beginning of the end? Bobbie Arnstein is arrested outside the Chicago Mansion on a federal drug charge. Hef ended up helping to carry her coffin.

10

A Girl Who Died
for Playboy

At noon on Thursday, March 21, 1974, Bobbie Arnstein emerged from the front door of 1340 North State Street Parkway on her way to another part of the Playboy Mansion. It was sometimes quicker to go out onto the street than up and down the stairs and passageways connecting the two huge houses that comprised the Mansion. She was wearing a tailored trouser suit and sunglasses, as usual, and carried a sheaf of papers and her purse in one hand.

When she stepped onto the sidewalk, a man moved quickly to block her path and asked her if she was Roberta Arnstein. She said she was. He flashed a federal agent's badge and told her she was under arrest. As he produced a pair of handcuffs and snapped them on her wrists, there was a clitter-clatter of camera shutters— newspaper photographers had been tipped off that the arrest was going to take place. Bobbie was speechless for a moment, then wisecracked: "But I haven't had lunch yet!"

She was hustled into an unmarked car and driven downtown to the regional headquarters of the Drug Enforcement Administration on Dearborn Street, where she was formally fingerprinted and photographed and indicted on a charge of conspiracy to distribute eight ounces of cocaine. A gram of cocaine was triumphantly discovered in her purse. Bail was set at $4,500 and she was released later in the afternoon.

The arrest of Hugh Hefner's executive assistant on a drugs charge made the front page of newspapers across America the following day, sharing space with the long-running saga of Watergate. What was not revealed was the real motive for her arraignment: Bobbie Arnstein was a pawn in a massive, covert operation, involving several government agencies, with a single, primary object—to get Hefner.

Hefner's name was prominent on the "enemies list" drawn up by the White House under Nixon. He was a natural target for ambitious prosecutors and politicians, since, in Nixon's law-and-order America, he was very definitely an alien: he flouted conventional morality, mocked the institution of marriage, espoused liberal causes, and flaunted his sexual escapades with an apparently endless stream of young women. Worst of all, it rather appeared as if he was *happy*. The only support Playboy ever received from the Nixon administration before its disgrace was an off-the-cuff remark by Spiro Agnew, who said that the one disadvantage of being vice-president was that "you had to give up *Playboy*."

Bobbie Arnstein offered Hefner's enemies their first opportunity to cut him down to size. By putting sufficient pressure on Bobbie they thought they would be able to persuade her to incriminate her boss. She was known to be emotionally brittle; it was considered she could soon be broken. Later, these tactics would be justified by the Drug Enforcement Administration, the U.S. Attorney General's Office, the Chicago Strike Force, and the Cook County State Attorney's Office on the grounds that they were acting on information received from "reliable sources" (never revealed) that the Playboy organization was drug-riddled, that the Big Bunny was used for trafficking, that drug use in both Mansions was commonplace, and that Hefner and other top Playboy executives were personally involved in the acquisition and distribution of cocaine.

By the time all these allegations were exposed as untrue, it mattered little to Bobbie. She was dead.

Bobbie was nineteen years old when she joined Playboy as a receptionist at 232 East Ohio Street in 1960. *Playboy* was considered a thoroughly risqué magazine in those days and not the kind of place where a nice girl would work, but Bobbie already had a reputation for being daringly "different." At Lake View High School, she had eschewed the pleated skirts and ankle socks worn like a uniform by all the other girls, preferring classic cashmere sweaters, high heels, and *stockings*. She also dyed her hair platinum, the last word in teenage sophistication.

Hefner did not fail to notice the new receptionist, since she bore a resemblance to Anouk Aimée, having the same fine bone structure and big eyes. One day, while he was waiting for the elevator to work its way sluggishly to the top floor, he leaned over her desk and said: "Don't think of me as your boss or the publisher of this magazine, think of me as a guy looking for a date."

Bobbie was happy to comply: she thought Hefner was wonderful. He was so different from a normal boss, with his bounce and boyish charm and capacity to enjoy life. She had no regrets that her name was ritually entered into his book of conquests after a brief affair. Hefner liked Bobbie, too, certainly enough to take her to bed; but she was far too smart, too free-spirited, ever to play the simpering role of his girlfriend. Instead, he asked her to be his personal secretary and offered her an apartment in the Mansion. She accepted, and became closer to him than they had ever been as lovers.

Not long after moving into the Mansion, Bobbie fell in love with Tom Lownes, Victor's younger brother, who had been hired as an editor on *Show Business Illustrated* and transferred to *Playboy* when *SBI* folded. Tom, a Harvard graduate, was quite as personable as his brother and was considered to be an exceptional editor; although he was only in his late twenties, there was talk of his being groomed as Spectorsky's successor. He was as smitten with Bobbie as she was with him and they made a handsome and popular couple at Playboy parties. As soon as Tom's divorce from his first wife came through, they planned to marry.

In the summer of 1963, Tom and Bobbie decided to drive to Florida together for a holiday in the sunshine. Tom was teaching Bobbie to drive and she was at the wheel when their car veered off the highway, bounced across a ditch, and smashed into a tree. Tom was hurled through the windshield and died instantly. Bobbie escaped with a broken arm. She would never forgive herself.

When Bobbie returned to work at the Mansion, she was a changed woman. Everyone tried to help her, but no one could. She began to drink heavily to try to obliterate the terrible memory of the accident. She went in and out of psychoanalysis. For a while, she moved away from the Mansion, hoping that distancing herself from Playboy would help her forget, but she could not stir herself to make a new home and sat night after night drinking alone in a rented apartment virtually devoid of furniture.

Back in the Mansion, she turned to drugs. Hefner was already locked into a cycle of uppers and downers, working on the Philosophy. Bobbie joined him. With amphetamines to get her through the day and barbiturates to bring her down at night, she slowly immersed herself, like Hefner, in the strange, unreal, pampered womb of the Playboy Mansion, rarely leaving the security of its sweet embrace.

As Hefner insulated himself from the day-to-day operations of his business, the pressures on Bobbie increased. Along with Dick Rosenzweig, she controlled access to Hefner and when he did not want to see anyone, which was not at all unusual, it was Bobbie who had to deal with angry editors screaming for some decision that only Hefner could make, or marketing executives insisting that they had to see Hefner immediately on an urgent matter that absolutely could not wait.

Bobbie did not relish her power and became paranoiac that people were using her to try to get to Hefner. It made her suspicious of everyone, friends and strangers alike, and cynical about the motives of anyone who was nice to her. Outwardly, she still appeared to be the beautiful, powerful, superefficient secretary, but behind the hip, wisecracking façade was a painfully insecure young woman with a daunting burden of emotional problems, many of them centered around Hefner and Playboy.

After the death of Tom Lownes, Bobbie had transferred her devotion to the only other man in her life—Hefner. She never hoped for a resurrection of their affair, but it did not stop her loving him. He became her fantasy lover, the man she most wanted to please, and a father figure (her own father died when she was a child). "Bobbie's whole ego," said her friend Shirley Hillman, "was wrapped up in Hefner and Playboy. She was the brightest, funniest person I ever knew, but she didn't seem to be able to handle life outside of Playboy."

In many ways, Hefner needed Bobbie quite as much as she needed him. When he emerged from his bedroom each day, usually around four o'clock in the afternoon, his first question was always: "Where's Bobbie?" She was more than just a secretary; she was his friend, confidante, and fixer. Her priority was always his comfort and happiness, and she did her best to protect him from any kind of unpleasantness; she would shield him from bores at parties, for example, or arrange for girls he fancied to stay behind afterward, making the approach herself to avoid the slight risk he might suffer the embarrassment of a rejection.

Hefner respected Bobbie's intellect and her eagerness to debate anything from morality to philosophy to politics; she was challenging and invigorating and one of the few women with whom he was prepared to discuss serious issues. When he was depressed, she could invariably cheer him up by making him laugh. She had a quick, biting wit from which no one, except Hefner, was immune. When she discovered that Dick Rosenzweig came from Appleton, Wisconsin, she immediately dubbed him the "simpleton from Appleton."

Hefner knew her loyalty and discretion were beyond question and so he liked to tell her about his sexual encounters, describing in uninhibited detail his previous night's adventures. Whenever he fell in love, Bobbie would be the first to know; she would have to sit at her desk trying to look pleased and happy for him while he mooned like a teenager over some new inamorata.

This chore took a particular toll on Bobbie's already fragile ego. "She did not like to hear about his girlfriends," said Shirley Hillman, "because Hefner barely looked at a girl older than twenty-two and it made Bobbie feel old and unwanted. Although she was not yet thirty, she thought she was finished. She developed a fear of becoming an aging coquette in a place where only youth and beauty were appreciated."

For this last reason she became obsessively worried about her looks. Milda Bridgewater, the keeper of Hefner's scrapbook, often found her staring at herself in the mirror in despair. "She hated the way she looked, her bone structure, her hair, everything. She always thought she was too fat, no matter how thin she was. She would look at herself in the mirror and say 'What do I look like?' "

There were many other signs that Bobbie was cracking up. She would go on a ferocious diet for weeks, then eat three huge meals at a single sitting. She would spend hours getting ready for a party, then leave after ten minutes. She had her apartment in the Mansion painted black throughout—walls, ceiling, and floors. She hung strange, troubled kinetic pictures on the walls. Her office was white and as, like Hefner, she rarely left the Mansion, she spent all her time either in a white windowless box or a black one. Milda Bridgewater thought it was "scary."

When Keith Stroup met Bobbie Arnstein in 1970, he attributed her shredded nerves to years of pill-popping. Only when he got to know her better, as her lover and friend, did he begin to realize that her insecurity and deep unhappiness, frequently bordering on despair, were entangled with Playboy. Embowered in the Mansion, she had lost contact with reality. She thought the daffy world of Playboy, where young girls with big breasts were adored, *mattered*.

Stroup was a young Washington lawyer with wire-rimmed granny glasses and a shaggy mop of soft, blond hair, who became involved with Playboy when he was trying to set up the National Organization for the Reform of Marijuana Laws (NORML). Perhaps because it was a symbol, like rock music and long hair, of youthful rebellion, the smoking of marijuana was deemed to be a heinous crime in Nixon's America, and ludicrous jail sentences were being handed out to young people found in possession of this fearful substance.

An enthusiastic proponent of the drug counterculture, Stroup thought it was ridiculous that a society that placidly accepted killer drugs like nicotine and alcohol should outlaw a drug he considered to be utterly harmless and thoroughly enjoyable. But when he tried to do something about getting the law changed, he found it impossible to raise any financial support for a national campaign until someone in Ralph Nader's office suggested he try the Playboy Foundation. He had never heard of it.

Hefner set up the Playboy Foundation in 1965 in response to frequent challenges to "put his money where his mouth was" and provide financial support for the social, political, and legal reforms advocated by the Playboy Philosophy. The first major grants made by the Foundation helped finance campaigns for legalized abortion, sex education in schools, and the reform of a law forbidding contraception in Massachusetts as a "crime against chastity." The Foundation also contributed substantial funds to support the research of William Masters and Virginia Johnson into human sexuality.

It did not take long for Stroup to discover that the Playboy Foundation was likely to be sympathetic to the kind of campaign he had in mind, and he submitted a formal request for a grant of $20,000 to pay for a six-month program. This would include producing a pamphlet explaining the marijuana laws, direct-mail fundraising, a newsletter, and public service television advertising.

In the summer of 1970, he was invited to Chicago to meet Hefner and the other directors of the Foundation at the Playboy Mansion. He was extremely nervous when he arrived, but he was met by Bobbie Arnstein, who put him at his ease and assured him that Hef was very interested in his proposals. She made him laugh when she added that Hef must have considered the meeting important because it had been scheduled for noon, which, for Hefner, was like getting up at *dawn*.

When he was ushered into the conference room to put his case, Stroup spoke with his usual eloquence and passion about kids rotting in jail and the patent injustice of the existing laws. But it soon became clear, in the discussion that followed, that most of the directors were extremely reluctant to become involved in the drug debate and were unsympathetic to Stroup's cause. Perhaps it was not surprising, since most of adult America still thought "reefers" led inevitably to a life of crime and violence.

Stroup did not, at that time, appreciate that the opinions of the directors were of no real consequence: all that mattered was what Hefner thought, and he liked the idea of NORML. Although he did not use marijuana himself and did not like it to be smoked at Mansion parties, he shared Stroup's outrage that some 500,000 young people were being arrested every year for having marijuana in their possession.

A few days later, Stroup received a call from Burton Joseph, chairman of the Playboy Foundation board of directors, to tell him the Foundation had agreed to offer him $5,000 to get NORML off the ground. "Five thousand dollars!" Stroup shouted angrily into the telephone. "Do you think I'm going to quit my job and go out into the cold, cruel world for *five thousand dollars?*"

Joseph assured him it was only a start and he could expect further contributions later if the campaign went well. After discussing it with his friends, Stroup decided to take a chance and use the $5,000 to launch NORML in the hope that a free full-page advertisement offered by *Playboy* would provide sufficient funds to make up the deficit. He had heard that a similar advertisement in *Playboy* on behalf of Vietnam Veterans Against the War had raised around $100,000; Stroup thought NORML might attract twice as much.

He was to be disappointed: the advertisement only drew $6,000. Some readers thought it was phony and had been planted by the government to garner the names of marijuana smokers for FBI files. All the money soon ran out and after being in existence for less than a year, NORML faced collapse. Stroup had worked tirelessly, under constant threat of arrest, but with so little money at his disposal he had been unable to raise sufficient public interest to keep the campaign going.

His last chance was Hefner. He felt if he could get close enough to the man he would be able to spell out the problems and perhaps get sensible funding from Playboy. Bobbie Arnstein liked Stroup, admired his crusading zeal, and promised to help. She said the best place to talk to Hefner was on the Big Bunny and asked him if he had any business in Los Angeles. "Not really," he replied. "Well don't tell Hef that," she said.

A few days later, Stroup was sitting on the Big Bunny with Hefner, Warren Beatty, and Shel Silverstein, talking about NORML's work and the importance of keeping the campaign going. He told them that in Texas long prison sentences were still being handed out for the possession of marijuana and that NORML stood a good chance of getting the law changed if the campaign could be stepped up.

It was a good moment for Stroup to make his pitch, for Hefner had recently, and belatedly, discovered that smoking marijuana increased his enjoyment of sex. Previously he had adopted an unusually puritanical attitude toward drugs: he once sternly rebuked a *Playboy* editor who admitted he had smoked a joint (he considered amphetamines to be a stimulant, like coffee, rather than a drug). But once he realized that marijuana enhanced sexual pleasure, he became a regular and enthusiastic smoker, marveling at its beneficial effect on his love life. Smoking, he would explain to friends, highlighted the difference between fucking and making love.

When the Big Bunny arrived in Los Angeles, Hefner beckoned Stroup into the limousines waiting to transport the entourage up to the Mansion—a sure sign of favor. Stroup had no idea if he was expected to stay, but Bobbie solved the problem by taking him up to her room, where they spent the night smoking and making love. (Bobbie and Stroup were lovers for only a short while, but the best of friends thereafter. And when she became ensnared in the conspiracy to destroy Hefner, she had desperate need of his friendship.)

On November 24, 1971, the Playboy Foundation announced that its grant to NORML was being increased to $100,000 a year.

When she turned thirty, Bobbie began to seek the company of younger men, sometimes picking them up on the street and taking them back to her apartment in the Mansion for sex. Hefner thought it was "groovy" and evidence of the sexual liberation he espoused. Shirley Hillman thought it was a pathetic attempt by Bobbie to emulate Hefner's lifestyle.

One morning, Bobbie showed Shirley a note that had been left in her bedroom after an argument with a boy. He had scrawled across a piece of paper: "Who needs a thirty-two-year-old cunt?" Bobbie pretended to laugh about it. "Ah well," she quipped, "once a butcher's boy, always a butcher's boy." Shirley became increasingly worried about her friend, but Bobbie swore she was okay. She said she had two regular boys: one she kept on call for sex, and the other got her "great drugs."

This last was Ron Scharf, a handsome twenty-four-year-old dealer who regularly slipped in and out the side door in the Mansion that led to Bobbie's apartment. In September 1971, Scharf asked Bobbie to fly with him to Coral Gables, Florida, where he was to score some cocaine from a wholesaler by the name of George Matthews. She agreed. A friend of Scharf's called Ira Sapstein joined them for the trip, which appeared to be uneventful. They returned with half a pound of cocaine.

All this time, Scharf was under surveillance by federal agents. His telephone was tapped and tape recordings were made of his calls to Bobbie; in one of them they discussed a bid for some "dynamite coke."

Early in 1972, Bobbie heard a rumor that she might be indicted on a conspiracy charge because of the trip she had taken to Florida with Scharf. Thoroughly frightened, she called Stroup, who flew immediately to Chicago to see what he could do to help. She told him she had nothing to do with the drug deal; she had not even been present when it took place. Repeatedly called in for questioning, she told the same story over and over again. Agents played tape recordings of her telephone conversations with Scharf, but she steadfastly insisted that she had never been involved in drug dealing.

Scharf, Sapstein, and Matthews were all indicted for conspiracy, but Bobbie was hardly mentioned in the statements they made at the time of their arrest. Stroup thought she was probably in the clear. But she could not shake off the fear and guilt and was tormented by the thought that Hefner would somehow be dragged into the case. She began to talk about suicide and started telephoning Shirley Hillman in the middle of the night to tell her she was going to kill herself. Shirley did her best to comfort her troubled friend.

Meanwhile, Playboy's newly appointed security director, Allen Crawford, was becoming increasingly alarmed about the astonishing quantities of amphetamines being consumed in both the Chicago Mansion and Playboy Mansion West. Hefner claimed he had kicked the amphetamine habit when he decided to end his years of hibernation in the Chicago Mansion. It was not true. Executives turning up for meetings at Playboy Mansion West observed that when the butlers brought him a Pepsi on a silver tray, it was always accompanied by pills.

Crawford discovered that Dexedrine was being supplied to Playboy Mansion West with phony prescriptions written by a local doctor. On April 20, 1972, he sent a memo to Rosenzweig expressing his concern about drug use in the Mansions and warning that staff might be under visual or technical surveillance by law enforcement agencies. "The potential for a PR disaster does not need further elaboration," he added.

This admonition, coming on top of Bobbie's troubles, induced a curious bunker mentality among the staff and guests at both Mansions. There were rumors that the telephones were tapped and that every room was bugged. The microphones in the chandelier hanging over the conference table in the Chicago Mansion were viewed with the deepest suspicion. The Bunnies in the top floor dormitory became convinced they were being watched by secret cameras.

The paranoia reached such a pitch that when a leg of lamb was found hanging on the railings at 1340 North State Street Parkway, Crawford mounted an investigation and reported the results in an unconsciously hilarious memo:

> On Tuesday evening at 6:55 a security officer found a leg of lamb hanging on the front fence. The leg of lamb had a steak knife thrust into the center of it and there was writing on it which could not be made out because it had run on the fat; however, it did appear to be of a foreign nature. A piece of rawhide attached to the lamb appeared to be in the form of a noose. The interior of the lamb was still frozen and after checking the meat thoroughly to see if it contained any articles it was disposed of. A check on Wednesday morning with government sources was unsuccessful in developing any identifying information as to this incident. It was left as a matter of record with the FBI and the U.S. Postal Inspector's Office. They will continue to search their sources and contacts for any possible information. . . .

Further light relief was provided in June, when the Rolling Stones arrived in Chicago to play three concerts at the International Amphitheater during their 1972 tour of America. They stayed at the Playboy Mansion for three wild and debauched nights, gorging, drinking, smoking, sniffing, and rollicking with the Bunnies in heat. No one at the Mansion had ever seen anything like it, and even Hef's smile got a little thin at times as unmannerly members of the touring party helped themselves to his hospitality and his girls. "There were people screwing everywhere," said Milda Bridgewater. "They were running around naked, climbing the draperies. It was an incredible scene." One of the girls in a tangle of bodies under the grand piano was due to be photographed for the centerfold the following day. When she arrived at Alexas Urba's studio, she was covered with bruises and her breasts were scratched and bleeding. "What the hell happened to you?" Urba asked. "The Rolling Stones had a party last night," she replied, as if it explained everything. Urba sent her to the hospital; he was unable to photograph her for ten days.

Bobbie did not join in the revelry, it being a trifle too abandoned for her taste. She retired to her black-walled apartment, telephoned the kitchen, and ordered *three* three-course meals. While riotous whoopee was being made elsewhere in the Mansion, Bobbie sat alone chomping through plate after plate of food. She had just finished a hunk of strong Brie cheese, when the door burst open and Mick Jagger stumbled in, wearing nothing but a pair of skin-tight white leather trousers.

Jagger licked his lips and fell on Bobbie, plastering her with lustful kisses. She was not at all averse to this surprising turn of events but could think of nothing except that her breath must smell from the cheese. Mumbling something about needing to brush her teeth, she pushed him gently away and he reeled back into a chair on which Bobbie had left a chocolate cake. There was a soft squelch. Jagger got up in a daze, grinned at Bobbie, and ambled out, with smeared chocolate cake dripping from the seat of his white leather trousers. Bobbie hardly knew whether to laugh or cry.

Although Bobbie was still not indicted, the drug investigation continued and she lived in constant fear of arrest. Narcotics agents warned her that the case was not closed and she could, at any time, face prosecution. In the fall of 1973, she attempted suicide by taking an overdose of sleeping pills and woke up strapped to a bed in a psychiatric hospital with a fellow patient urinating on the floor beside her bed. Stroup got her out, against the advice of doctors, who warned him she needed further treatment. He accepted responsibility for her and drove her back to the Mansion. "Listen Bobbie," he told her, "if you kill yourself now, I'm really fucked." She laughed.

Early in 1974, George Matthews, the wholesaler who had supplied Bobbie's friend Ron Scharf with cocaine in 1971, was convicted and sentenced to fifteen years in prison for conspiracy. After the trial, he decided to change his story about Bobbie's involvement in the deal. In his first statement, her name was only mentioned in passing. Now, facing a fifteen-year stretch in the penitentiary, he told government agents that not only was Bobbie present when the deal was made, but he had seen her put the half pound of cocaine in her purse. It was enough. Bobbie was indicted.

Hefner was at a backgammon contest in Las Vegas when he heard that Bobbie had been arrested. He immediately telephoned Allen Crawford and ordered him to sweep the Chicago Mansion for drugs. He had no idea what might be found, but since he did not search his guests, he thought it likely that drugs might be around the place and he wanted to get rid of them before narcotics agents showed up on the doorstep with a search warrant. He was also worried that federal agents might try to plant drugs in the Mansion. He spoke to Bobbie, told her to try not to worry, promised he would give her every support, and said that Playboy would pay for the best lawyers in town. Crawford reported back: he had discovered marijuana, cocaine, and some prescription drugs, mainly Dexedrine. He had gathered the lot together and hidden them in an office in the Playboy Building. Hefner told him to destroy the illegal drugs and put the prescription drugs back where he had found them.

Not long after her arrest, Bobbie attempted suicide again. Shirley Hillman began to chafe when she did not put in an appearance in the office one morning and there was no answer from her apartment. A security guard opened the door with a master key and Shirley found Bobbie unconscious on the bed with an empty bottle of pills by her side. It looked as if she had swallowed a cocktail of drugs and Shirley realized that if the news got out, Bobbie would stand little chance of a fair trial. She asked the guard to carry her comatose friend out to a Playboy limousine and told the chauffeur to drive to a hospital in Waukegan, a quiet suburb thirty miles north of town, where doctors managed to bring her around. None of the local newspapers or television channels got wind of what had happened.

In the months leading up to the trial, government prosecutors made little effort to conceal the fact that it was Hefner they were really after. The Drug Enforcement Administration and the Chicago Strike Force, working under the direction of U.S. Attorney James R. Thompson, a Republican with a reputation for cracking down on corruption in high places, mounted a massive investigation into alleged drug use in the Playboy Mansion.

Files on the case of Adrienne Pollack, a Bunny who died of a drug overdose in September 1973, were reopened. Adrienne had lived in the Mansion until a few weeks before her death in an apartment on North Wabash Avenue in Chicago. Her mother told reporters: "I believe my daughter was forced to take those drugs against her will. I believe somebody killed her."

Inquiries were pursued in Canada, where Willy Rey, a former Playmate, had died of a barbiturate overdose just a month before Adrienne Pollack. Willy, Miss November 1971, became a high-priced model after her appearance in *Playboy* but was said to have got involved in hard drugs and black magic: she collapsed and died on the bathroom floor of her parents' house in Vancouver. She was discovered by her father, Johannes, who would afterward be heard to moan: "I wish there had never been a *Playboy*."

During repeated and lengthy interrogations by narcotics agents, Bobbie was constantly advised she could make it easier for herself by telling them the truth about Hefner. What *really* happened at Playboy parties? Bowls of cocaine were openly passed around, weren't they? Who else was involved in drugs, apart from Hefner? Who were his suppliers? He used the Big Bunny to move the stuff around the country, didn't he? In vain did Bobbie try to tell them that they had it all wrong. They would just smile and shake their heads in wonderment that she would not "do herself a favor."

The trial was set for October 27 in the Federal District Court. Bobbie's codefendant, Ron Scharf, refused to testify for fear of further incriminating himself under cross-examination about the drug deals he had discussed with Bobbie in the taped telephone calls. He had told Bobbie's lawyers that he would be prepared to swear she knew nothing about the Florida drug deal if they could get separate trials, but the judge refused an application for them to be tried separately. (Ira Sapstein, who had also been indicted, had disappeared.)

Bobbie wanted to take the stand to say that Matthews was lying, but her lawyers advised against it. They felt she would not be able to handle cross-examination about the tapes, was likely to perjure herself, and could easily suffer a breakdown. Matthews was the prosecution's star witness. Brought to the stand in handcuffs, he swore he had seen Bobbie put the cocaine in her purse. The defense lawyers could not crack his story and could do little but call character witnesses to testify on Bobbie's behalf. They held out little hope of an acquittal.

After three days in court, the jury found both Bobbie and Scharf guilty. On November 26, Federal Judge Bernard M. Decker sentenced Scharf to six years in prison. Bobbie was given a fifteen-year conditional prison term and ordered to undergo ninety days of psychiatric tests, after which she would be resentenced. A psychiatrist who treated Bobbie after her first suicide attempt had warned the judge that if she was sent to prison she would almost certainly kill herself. Stroup thought the prosecutors were taking a cold-blooded gamble that Bobbie would turn against Hefner before resorting to suicide.

Bobbie was devastated by the sentence. Her lawyers lodged an appeal and tried to explain to her that it was no more than a technicality, that the statute required her to be given the maximum sentence so that the psychiatric tests could be carried out. When she came up for resentencing, she was sure to get off much more lightly, probably with nothing more terrible than probation. Bobbie was unconvinced: she was certain she had been given fifteen years because she had refused to incriminate Hefner. It was ironic, really. Even if Hefner had been involved in hard drugs, Bobbie would never, ever have admitted it to outsiders.

The next bombshell was not long in coming. On Sunday, December 8, the *Chicago Tribune* broke the story that had been simmering for months. Under the headline PLAYBOY MANSION GUESTS SUSPECTED, the newspaper reported that Hefner was the "prime target" of a federal narcotics investigation. A "key source" was quoted as saying: "He's in a helluva lot of trouble. There's no doubt about it."

Playboy was thrown into a turmoil by the story, which was immediately picked up by television news channels and other media. Both Mansions were swept for electronic bugs and there was a panic when it was rumored that engineers employed to carry out the sweeps were actually federal agents. Two outside directors, both well-respected Chicago businessmen, resigned, blaming the bad publicity. The First National Bank of Chicago asked Playboy to find another lead bank. "I was in the office when the bank telephoned Preuss," said Bob Gutwillig. "The call only lasted about thirty seconds. When he put the telephone down he was in shock."

By the most unhappy of coincidences, the next issue of *Playboy* magazine carried a major story about cocaine, promoted on the cover. "Cocaine has spilled from the ghetto and the mansion," the story claimed, "to become the illegal drug of choice, second only to marijuana, of many prosperous middle-class Americans." The choice of words could not have been worse: everyone in America knew who lived in a *mansion*.

For Bobbie Arnstein, the fuss only served to deepen her guilt. She blamed herself for dragging Hefner and Playboy into troubles of her own making. Hefner, following events from Los Angeles, was kind and told her not to be silly—she was as much a victim as he was. But he was beginning to recognize the need to put distance between himself and Bobbie. It had been agreed that Bobbie would move to Los Angeles, where Hefner now spent most of his time. After the *Tribune* story, Hefner telephoned her and gently suggested that it might be a good idea if she did not stay in the Mansion but found an apartment elsewhere until the heat was off.

Bobbie took it badly. She could hardly bear to think that she had caused the man she adored so much trouble that she could no longer live under the same roof with him. She began to talk about suicide again, openly discussing it with Stroup and Shirley Hillman as a viable option.

The blow that finally broke Bobbie Arnstein came quite unexpectedly. She was called into U.S. Attorney James Thompson's office in the Federal Building and told that information had been received from two "reliable sources" that a contract was out on her life. Someone, Thompson said, wanted to have her killed and was prepared to pay. He refused to elaborate, but said that if he was in her position, he would trust "neither friend nor foe."

Bobbie was hysterical when she called Stroup. She told him about the contract and said that Thompson had given her the impression that it was Hefner who wanted her killed. She said she didn't believe it, of course, but then she didn't really know what to believe anymore. Stroup flew to Chicago and demanded a meeting with Thompson and the government prosecutors, angrily accusing them of fabricating the "contract" story to put more pressure on Bobbie. She began having nightmares, dreaming about hired killers smashing down the door of her apartment.

On Saturday, January 11, 1975, the day before she was due to fly to Los Angeles, Bobbie had dinner with Shirley Hillman and her husband, Richard, in their apartment on West Diversey Street. She did not appear to be particularly depressed or upset; in fact, Shirley thought, she seemed in a better mood than she had been for some time. She left about eleven that night, saying she was going to a late-night movie with a boyfriend. She got back to the Mansion at about half past one and ordered a drink from the night butler.

Sometime after two o'clock, she packed her vanity case with several bottles of pills and slipped out of the Mansion unobserved. At 2:44 A.M. she checked into the rundown Maryland Hotel on North Rush Street, five blocks from the Mansion. She signed the register as "Roberta Hillman" and told the desk clerk she did not want to be disturbed. Then she took the elevator to room 1716 on the seventeenth floor, hung a Do Not Disturb sign outside, and double-locked the door.

When a maid was unable to get into room 1716 on Sunday afternoon to change the sheets, she called the manager and he summoned the maintenance man to break the locks.

Bobbie was lying on the edge of the bed, dressed in blue denim jeans, a knitted pullover, denim jacket, and boots. Empty pill bottles were scattered on the floor. She had swallowed huge quantities of tranquilizers, barbiturates, and sleeping pills—any one of the drugs would have killed her.

On the bedside table was a letter written on hotel stationery and slipped into an envelope marked "Boring letter of explanation within." In the wastepaper basket were the ashes of other notes she had apparently written but decided to destroy.

Bobbie's brave, defiant suicide note, covering five pages, was addressed to Stroup and Shirley Hillman, "the two persons I know and trust."

It was I alone who acted and conceived of this act. Because of recent developments, it behooves me to specify that it was definitely not the result of any determination or action on the part of my employers—who have been most generous and patient during my recent difficulties. . . .

Despite the (perjured) testimony of the government's "star" witness, I was never part of any conspiracy to transport or distribute the alleged drugs connected with the case. . . . My immediate employer, Hugh Hefner, showed courage, perhaps to his own detriment, though I hope not, and the kind of loyalty for which I hope even as I write this—he is not wrongfully penalized. I don't suppose it matters that I say it, but Hugh M. Hefner is—though few will ever really realize it— a staunchly upright, rigorously moral man—and I know him well and he has never been involved in the criminal activity which is being attributed to him now. That is the irony, but I have come to know that innocence is of small significance when compared to the real purpose and intent of the various government agencies engaged in pursuing him and leveling their harassment against me . . .

Two days later, Hefner arrived in Chicago on the Big Bunny to address a press conference in the ballroom at the Mansion. He looked terrible: he was unshaven, gaunt, and gray, his eyes were red from weeping and glistened dangerously as he stepped up to a lectern to address the assembled reporters and television cameras. "Ah, excuse me if I look a bit harried," he said, "but I'm very upset." He smoothed out crumpled sheets of a yellow legal paper with shaking hands and began to read his prepared statement.

For the last several weeks, I have been the subject of a series of sensational speculations and allegations regarding supposed illicit drug activities at the Playboy Mansion in Chicago and Los Angeles—attempting to associate me with the recent cocaine conspiracy conviction of Playboy secretary Bobbie Arnstein and the death of a Chicago Bunny Adrienne Pollack.

Although I had no personal connection of any kind with

either case, I reluctantly agreed to make no initial public statement on the subject because our legal counsel was convinced that anything I said would only be used to further publicize what—in our view—is not a legitimate narcotics investigation at all, but a politically motivated, anti-Playboy witch hunt.

The suicide of Bobbie Arnstein makes any further silence impossible. Whatever mistakes she may have made in her personal life, she deserved better than this. She deserved—among other things—the same impartial consideration accorded to any other citizens similarly accused.

But because of her association with Playboy and me, she became the central focus in a cocaine conspiracy case in which it appears she was only peripherally involved. There is ample reason to believe that if she had provided the prosecutors with evidence to support any serious drug charge against me, she would never have been indicted. Faced finally with a conditional sentence of fifteen years, the pressure of a lengthy appeal and increasing harassment from Government prosecutors and their agents, an already emotionally troubled woman was pushed beyond endurance—and she killed herself.

It is difficult to describe the inquisitorial atmosphere of the Bobbie Arnstein trial and related Playboy probe. In the infamous witchcraft trials of the Middle Ages, the inquisitors tortured the victims until they not only confessed to being witches, but accused their own families and friends of sorcery as well. In similar fashion, narcotics agents frequently use our severe drug laws in an arbitrary and capricious manner to elicit the desired testimony for a trial.

Testimony thus acquired is, at best, highly suspect, since the witness has good reason to provide whatever the prosecutor wants of him. This is the sort of testimony that was used to convict Bobbie Arnstein; this is the technique that was used in an attempt to force Bobbie Arnstein to falsely incriminate me.

Some of the victims of medieval inquisitional torture died. So did Bobbie.

She was one of the best, brightest, most worthwhile women I have ever known. She will be missed—by me and a great many others as well. . . .

229

Hefner paused and began to weep silently. With his face muscles working, he pulled himself together sufficiently to continue, the tears still streaming down his cheeks.

In supporting her throughout her trial, and in the preparation for her appeal, it was suggested by some that we had secrets to hide. Our secret was simply that we cared very much about this person and felt that she was being unjustly persecuted because of her relationship to me.

What the Chicago prosecutors apparently couldn't or wouldn't accept was the lack of any connection whatsoever between their cocaine case against my secretary and my own rather conservative anti-drug predilections. For the record, I have never used cocaine or any other hard drug or narcotic— I am willing to swear to that fact under oath, and penalty of perjury, if that will put an end to the groundless suspicions and speculations.

The Playboy Mansions are actually corporate guest facilities in which we play host to several hundred friends and associates each month. Since we don't frisk our guests at the door, or spy on them, it is impossible to ascertain or control all of the activities on these premises. But the use of illicit drugs has never been encouraged in either Mansion; and my role as host has never included the distribution of illicit drugs to the guests.

In truth, there is probably more drug use in most of the college dormitories of this country than in either of the Playboy Mansions.

The true motivations for this so-called narcotics investigation are clear enough. As an outspoken critic of all forms of authoritarian repression in our society, and as the major financial backer of the National Organization for the Reform of Marijuana Laws, and for equally obvious other reasons, I'm an all too obvious prime target for such an inquisitional witch hunt.

The zeal with which certain Government agents are pursuing this case says more about the prosecutors, I think, than it does about the accused. It appears that the "enemies list" mentality of Watergate is still with us; and the repressive legacy of puritanism that we challenged in our first years of publication remains as formidable an opponent to a truly free and democratic society as ever.

During questions afterward, Hefner accused Thompson of using the case to further his political ambition for the governorship of Illinois (to which he was elected in November 1976). Thompson refused to be drawn into the controversy. "I'm not sure that what Hefner stands for these days is all that relevant, or that any prosecution of him would mean much," he told the *Chicago Tribune*.

On December 29, 1975, Sam Skinner, the U.S. Attorney in charge of the Playboy investigation, took the unusual step of issuing a public statement exonerating Playboy because he felt that Hefner and Playboy may have suffered adversely as a result of the "widespread negative publicity."

It was brief, but to the point. "No evidence of the unlawful acquisition or distribution of cocaine or other hard drugs by Mr. Hefner, the corporation, or its employees has been adduced. Accordingly, we have concluded our investigation and ended our inquiry."

George Matthews, the drug dealer whose evidence secured Bobbie Arnstein's conviction, had his prison sentence commuted, and was quietly released after serving just four months.

11

This Thing Could Go Sour

While the Drug Enforcement Administration was still investigating Playboy, further serious troubles piled up and plunged the company into crisis. Quite suddenly, it seemed, the magic was gone, the dream soured. Playboy Enterprises, Inc., once hailed as one of America's major business success stories, was on the brink of collapse.

Its flagship, *Playboy* magazine, mauled by the Pubic Wars, was mocked as dull and passé. It was out of step with the permissive society and feminism; its editorial passion for possessions clashed with the antimaterialism then in vogue. Circulation, flagging from the combined effects of inflation and recession, had dropped below six million and was still sliding. *Oui* magazine was in even worse shape, floundering for an identity and notching up substantial losses.

While the big hotel chains like Hilton, Hyatt, and Marriott had been getting out of real estate, preferring to lease new hotels from developers or financial institutions, Playboy went against the trend and invested heavily in building huge resort hotels, none of which turned a profit.

Playboy Productions passed up opportunities to participate in movies like *Deliverance* and *Jaws* and instead bankrolled a series of box-office flops, while Playboy Records had failed to make any money since its inception in 1972, and Playboy Books was heading for its biggest loss ever.

First indication of the clouds gathering on Playboy's previously sunny horizon came in September 1974, with the publication of the 1974 annual report, which revealed an alarming slump in profits, down 48 percent from $11.2 million in 1973 to only $5.9 million. On Wall Street, the price of Playboy stock, which sold at $23.50 per share when the company went public in 1971, tumbled to $2.87.

Preuss and Rosenzweig made soothing noises in the business press about dealing with the problems and the worst being over and the good times ahead. Hefner remained resolutely unavailable for an interview on the subject of his business empire, letting it be known that he found business matters tiresome in the extreme. The first quarterly report of fiscal year 1975 indicated a slight recovery, with net profits of $2.5 million, but by then Playboy was entangled in the drug investigation: nervous advertisers were rushing to cancel space in the magazine, readers renounced their subscriptions, keyholders let their memberships lapse, and convention sponsors retracted reservations at Playboy hotels. There was even speculation that Playboy's liquor licenses might be at risk.

Figures for the second and third quarters showed just how bad the trouble was. For the first time since the cash hemorrhage caused by the *Show Business Illustrated* debacle, Playboy slid into the red. The second quarterly report disclosed a loss of $356,000, with sales down $2.7 million. By the third quarter, sales were down $6 million and the loss was $387,000. In order to pay a 6¢ semiannual dividend to shareholders, Hefner volunteered to give up his own dividend of $398,000 from his personal holding of 6,642,923 shares. "The Board accepted my offer to waive receipt of the dividend on my personal holdings," he announced in a letter to shareholders. "Your dividend check is enclosed."

Rumors that the company was in peril began to circulate widely in September, when publication of the 1975 annual report was inexplicably delayed. When it finally appeared, six weeks late, it was the usual glossy, four-color production, but the best graphic design artistry in the world could not conceal the ominous bottom line: on sales of $197,734,000, Playboy Enterprises, Inc., had only managed to produce a miserable profit of $1,096,000.

On page one there was a color photograph of a smiling Chairman and President in a paisley-patterned shirt open to the waist, posing in front of a stone lion in the garden at Playboy Mansion West. His confident message to shareholders made curious reading alongside the appalling figures, almost as if no one had given him the bad news.

After a brief reference to tightening the corporate belt during the period of transition from a medium-size specialized company to a diversified international corporation, Hefner went on to say how well everything was going, how encouraged and proud and excited he was about the future. "Throughout the first twenty-one years we experienced periods of explosive growth, during which we developed a solid, viable base on which to build for the future. . . .

"While the challenges in fiscal 1975 were great, we were able to meet them—and emerged with a profitable year. As our economy achieves greater stability, we can envision a return to steadily increasing profit levels once again." The message ended with a marvelous example of corporate gobbledygook: "With the promise of future opportunities demonstrated by continuing domestic and international success, our confidence in the years ahead is high."

Hefner clearly did not feel the need to dwell on the state of the company as revealed a few pages further on, in the Financial Section. The fact was that only *Playboy* magazine was making any money, although its profits had dived from $21 million two years previously to $8.5 million. All the other ventures of the "diversified international corporation" Hefner said he was building were losing money in America.

Oui magazine, described in the report as having attracted one of the choicest young audiences in the industry, and "enjoying extraordinary momentum in advertising appeal," lost $2,278,000 in fiscal 1975 as against a $351,000 loss in 1974.

Playboy's Book Division, said to have shown "an improvement in continuing operations," and the Playboy Book Club, "now firmly established," recorded losses of $307,000.

Playboy Clubs were in the black only because of the $3.3 million profit contributed by the Playboy casinos in Britain. Without this injection, the eighteen Playboy Clubs in the United States notched up combined losses of $104,000. Playboy's five hotels lost a staggering $3,779,000. "Excitement, change, and vigorous activity characterize the past year's happenings in Playboy's Club and Hotel group," the report noted. "As expansion in our Club and Hotel Division continues and new policies are instituted, we can look forward to the entire system becoming a renewed source of pride and profit for the corporation."

Renewed profit was not quite the right term to describe the potential of Playboy hotels, since they had hardly ever managed to show a profit at all. The same sorry state applied to the company's Entertainment Group, which had lost money ever since it was launched in 1972. Playboy Productions lost $1,102,000 and Playboy Records lost $1,219,000 in 1975. "In these highly competitive industries," the report boasted, "Playboy is rapidly becoming recognized as both a creative and an artistic force."

Even "Other Operations"—which included product merchandising and licensing, Playboy Limousines and Playboy Models, both "providing excellent service for a growing clientele"—could not achieve a profit. For the fifth consecutive year it was in the red, losing $928,000.

"We weren't building a company with a solid base," executive vice-president Bob Preuss gloomily recalled. "In fact I didn't know what the hell we *were* building."

Only a few years previously, Playboy executives had been talking about taking over the world. "We have our own flag and a Bunny army," Hefner exulted in 1970. "Playboy is a world unto itself, a world within a world."

This is how Preuss foresaw the future early in 1972:

A man gets up in his Playboy townhouse, calls a Playboy limousine to take him to the airport, where he gets a Playboy chartered plane, flies to New York, takes a Playboy limousine to a Playboy hotel in midtown Manhattan, changes into his Playboy suit, takes a Playboy ferry to a Playboy convention center on Randall's Island for his business meeting, that night goes to a Playboy restaurant and then to a Playboy theater where he sees a Playboy movie. That's the Playboy Environment and while we don't have all those things yet, we have many of them and we're exploring the rest.

In those heady days, he explained later, there was a feeling in the Playboy Building that the company was so successful there was nothing it could not do. By 1975, all that was forgotten.

Hefner laid the blame for the distressed plight of the company on the decision to go public in 1971, a decision he had taken with considerable reluctance and one he very soon regretted. He had always considered Playboy to be a "very personal type of company" but by the early seventies there were pressing arguments for a stock offering, primarily to keep pace with the company's explosive growth. Preuss was in favor of it, arguing that it would be easier for Playboy to grow and diversify as a public company. Gutwillig was adamantly set against it, believing that Hefner's idiosyncratic management style was unsuited to a company quoted on Wall Street. Rosenzweig sat on the fence until Hefner had made up his mind.

The attractions of going public for Hefner were few. He liked the idea of Playboy acquiring the respectability of a major public company and he savored the prospect of the people to whom he had given stock making money from a public offering. (He had little interest in increasing his own fortune, since he already had more money than he knew what to do with.) But the notion of being answerable for his actions to stockholders and opening the company to public scrutiny was anathema to him, as was any kind of interference in the way he ran his company, or, more importantly, his life.

In the end, a decision was more or less forced on him by the rapidly escalating construction costs of Great Gorge, a huge, luxury resort-hotel Playboy was building in New Jersey. The original estimates had rocketed from $21 million to $30 million by mid-1971 and were still rising. Preuss finally convinced Hefner of the urgent need to raise more cash, pressing the case for a stock offering as the best option. Hefner, consoled by the knowledge that he would still control the company with more than 70 percent of the stock, acquiesced.

A number of the stuffier Wall Street brokerage houses politely declined to underwrite Playboy stock for reasons that were never explained but were perfectly obvious. Although *Playboy* was lagging modestly behind in the Pubic Wars, it continued to be regarded with hostility in some quarters. The magazine was still unable, for example, to attract advertising from major corporations like Coca-Cola, Gillette, and General Motors. Airlines and insurance companies were also leery of *Playboy* as an "appropriate medium."

Hefner could never comprehend such attitudes and was tickled by a story, widely reported that autumn, about a Mrs. Margaret McClean who had written to *The Houston Chronicle* to complain that her husband, a postman, delivered *Playboy* to a man who was applying for a job as the city's school superintendent. "A man who reads *Playboy* should not have a position in the schools," Mrs. McClean wrote. "To a decent person, *Playboy* magazine is one of the most immoral, obscene, and lewd-type publications and should not be found anyplace in a decent home and never near children."

It was a point of view that would once have attracted a great deal of public support in a town like Houston, but instead the newspaper was inundated with letters supporting *Playboy* and the right of the aspiring school superintendent to read what he liked. The luckless Mr. McClean was suspended from duty for revealing the contents of his mailbag to his wife, and when the new school superintendent showed up for work, he sported a green Playboy tie dotted with little rabbits.

Loeb, Rhoades & Co., an eminent and respected Wall Street broker, finally agreed to underwrite the shares of Playboy Enterprises, Inc., after a small alteration was agreed upon in the design of the stock certificate, which featured a saucy etching of a reclining nude—the Playmate for November 1971, Willy Rey (the girl who was later to die of a drug overdose in Vancouver). To assuage the sensibilities of the financial community, the etching was redrawn so that hanks of Miss Rey's hair curled over each of her nipples.

The prospectus prepared for the stock offering portrayed Playboy as a thrusting, dynamic company with a startling record of success, accelerating earnings, and substantial cash reserves. Pretax profits from the seventeen Playboy Clubs stood at $3,200,000; investment in films, music publishing, and records was presented as logical diversification, and losses shown by the hotels were viewed as a temporary aberration that would soon be reversed.

Playboy Enterprises, Inc., went public on November 3, 1971. A total of 1,158,812 common shares were offered on the New York Stock Exchange and the Pacific Stock Exchange at an opening price of $23.50 and were quickly picked up by investors. Hefner sold 300,000 shares, reducing his ownership of the company from 80 percent to 71.1 percent and adding $7 million to his personal wealth. His 6.7-million-share holding gave him a paper worth of about $157 million and made him one of the richest self-made men in America; the dividend from his holding added about $800,000 to his annual salary of $303,874.

The remainder of the stock was spread between about fifty people, including Hefner's friends, family, Playboy executives, and a writer who had accepted stock instead of a fee in the very early days of the magazine when Hefner had no money to pay contributors. Those who took the opportunity of the offering to cash in all made handsome profits. The company raised around $20 million in exchange for about 10 percent of the ownership. It seemed like a good deal.

Hefner was convinced that the stock would soar above forty dollars and was deeply disillusioned when it soon became clear investors were going to get a jittery ride. In the first days of 1972, the price climbed to $25.50, but then suddenly collapsed to $14. Investors who had been hoping for a quick profit rushed to get out before burning fingers too badly, and Playboy shares began to slide inexorably.

At first it was not easy to pinpoint what was wrong. The corporate balance sheet for fiscal 1972 looked healthy enough—profits up to $10.6 million on revenues of $160 million and per-share earnings up $.09 to $1.16. But the figures did nothing to soothe Wall Street's nerves about Playboy. Part of the problem was that some investors were clearly embarrassed about owning Playboy stock; institutions with highly visible portfolios, like banks and insurance companies, tended to steer clear of Playboy on Wall Street for fear of being accused of investing in smut.

Another problem was Hefner himself, and the high profile he determinedly maintained. Here was a public company run by a man who candidly admitted he was bored by business, did not get out of bed until four o'clock in the afternoon, never went to the office, lived with one girl in Chicago and another in Los Angeles, and spent outrageous sums of money on an apparently endless round of parties.

Fortunately, no outsiders knew just how lightly Hefner viewed his responsibilities. Senior vice-president Bob Gutwillig bitterly complained that Hefner was devoting less and less time to the affairs of the company and that his lack of interest was seriously damaging. "It was a great pity," he said, "because when I joined the company I found him the most perceptive and acute visual editor I have ever encountered."

Executives returning to Chicago from meetings at Playboy Mansion West related depressing anecdotes about how difficult it was becoming to get Hefner's attention, or even to get him up for meetings. No one was ever sure if he had all the material, either verbal or written, on which to make a decision. He often did not bother to read memos addressed to him; at meetings his attention wandered. The consensus in Chicago was that Hefner had more money than he knew what to do with and only wanted to enjoy life. His efforts to keep himself informed by the media meant that he became less and less well informed about what was going on in American life. The richer he got, the more insulated and more irrelevant he became.

None of this would have mattered had Playboy Enterprises, Inc., demonstrated that its multitude of enterprises were capable of making money. It could not. Playboy Productions' first feature film, *Macbeth*, directed by Roman Polanski, ran more than a million dollars over budget and flopped when it arrived at the box office. This was a surprise to no one but Hefner. "I thought we were going into the movies as a business," Preuss griped. "Hefner wanted to go into movies to play around."

Macbeth was the first movie Polanski made after his wife, Sharon Tate, and three friends were murdered. Polanski had been devastated by her death and unable to work until long after the Manson "family" had been arrested and brought to trial. When he was ready to start making films again, he wanted to find a completely new venture rather than pick up any of the projects, with their associated memories, in which he had been involved before Sharon's death.

Polanski met Hefner at a party at Playboy Mansion West and told him he was planning to film *Macbeth*, "the greatest drama of all time," and that Kenneth Tynan, author of *Oh! Calcutta!*, had agreed to adapt Shakespeare's play for the screen. Not long afterward it was announced that Playboy Productions' first oeuvre was to be *Macbeth*, directed by Roman Polanski, with a budget of $1.5 million.

Hefner was *thrilled* at the prospect of becoming a movie producer, particularly in such illustrious company and on such a serious project. Here was Playboy proving it had come a long way from the days of tits-and-ass: bankrolling *Shakespeare*. Perfect!

His enthusiasm was not widely shared at the Playboy Building in Chicago, where no one could see how a movie of *Macbeth* could possibly make any money, which was the very last consideration in Hefner's mind. Preuss and Spectorsky tried to dissuade him from pursuing what both believed to be a disastrous venture. Spectorsky sent Hefner a memo warning of Polanski's reputation for disregarding budgets, adding picturesquely: "He'll lead us down the garden path and leave us there." Hefner was unmoved.

Polanski signed a completion guarantee to bring the movie in on time and within the budget, but it proved to be worthless. Both time and money quickly ran out long before the film was anywhere near completion, and Hefner found himself in a dilemma. He had the right, under the terms of the completion guarantee, to fire Polanski and hire another director to finish the project, but he recognized that without Polanski's name the movie was hardly worth continuing. He paid up and told Polanski he could finish in his own time.

The budget crept up to $2 million, then $2.5 million. There were, however, compensations. Polanski regularly sent the rushes either to the Chicago Mansion or Playboy Mansion West so that Hefner could show them to his friends and they could sit around and discuss the shooting, just like real movie moguls. On April 9, 1971, Hefner's forty-fifth birthday, the rushes arrived in Chicago in time for screening at the party. It was the witches' scene. Polanski used the ugliest old women he could find, stripped to the waist to reveal sagging breasts and made up to look hideous.

They gathered around the bubbling caldron, the essence of evil, then suddenly turned to camera, linked hands and sang "Happy birthday to you, Happy birthday to you, Happy birthday Hugh Hefner, Happy birthday to you." It was the high spot of the party; Hefner thought he would never stop laughing.

The completed film was delivered almost a year late and received a lukewarm welcome from the critics, despite being voted the best motion picture of the year by the national Board of Review of Motion Pictures. Most critics found the film's unbridled violence, blood, and gore too much to stomach, and there were discomforting echoes of the scenes described by detectives after the murders in Benedict Canyon. It was as if Polanski was using the movie to exorcise his memories. In the Playboy Building, it was darkly suggested that the film would have been much improved by leaving in the witches' birthday chorus.

Playboy Productions' next effort, another pet project of Hefner's, was an even greater disaster—a film adaptation of Desmond Morris's book, *The Naked Ape*, starring Johnny Crawford and Victoria Principal. It disappeared without trace, leaving Playboy Productions with losses of more than $2.5 million from its first two films.

Hefner was unrepentant. "The film business is always a crapshoot," he declared. "Only a small percentage of films make money, but it's a calculated risk I'm happy to take, because filmmaking is going to be an increasingly important form of expression as society moves beyond the print era, and I want to be personally involved in Playboy's development of expertise in that field."

Developing Playboy's expertise in the field of hotel management might have proved more fruitful, to judge from the balance sheet. Playboy bought its first hotel, in Ochos Rios, Jamaica, in 1964 for $2.5 million. The 200-room hotel on ten acres of beachfront was profitable from the start and was as dangerous to the company as winning the jackpot at roulette on the first spin of the wheel.

Ochos Rios encouraged Hefner and his aides to believe that the "magic" of the Playboy logo would work wonders in the hotel business, and plans were drawn up to build a 365-room resort-hotel on a 1,350-acre site at Lake Geneva, Wisconsin, only ninety miles from Chicago and thirty-eight miles from Milwaukee. It would offer two golf courses, a lake stocked with fish, a ski area with two chair lifts, horse trails, convention facilities, and a nightclub with seventy-five Bunnies. Lake Geneva cost $18 million and opened for business in May 1968. "More a luxurious country club than a hotel," a brochure boasted, "it is virtually a way of life. The good life. The kind you've read about in the pages of *Playboy* magazine."

Attracting weekenders, tourists, and convention business, Lake Geneva made modest profits for the first couple of years and in fiscal 1970 Playboy Hotels reported pretax earnings of $39,000. But by then the company had embarked on a massive and ill-judged program of hotel and resort investment.

In the summer of 1970, Playboy bought the 456-room Hilton Plaza Hotel in Miami Beach for $13.5 million, apparently unconcerned that the Hilton chain had taken substantial losses on the hotel since it opened in 1967. Playboy spent $1.5 million on renovations, changed the name to the Playboy Plaza, and waited for the customers to arrive. No one came. Miami Beach was a resort favored by middle-aged couples for whom Bunnies held as little attraction as the Playboy lifestyle, and in its first year of operation the Playboy Plaza dropped $2,161,000 and achieved an average room occupancy of only 55 percent at the height of the season.

A few months after clinching the deal in Miami, Playboy bought a lease on the run-down Knickerbocker Hotel, next door to the Playboy Building, intending to incorporate it into the Playboy Center—a "total leisure-time environment" comprising the Chicago Playboy Club, the Playboy Building, and the hotel, renamed Playboy Towers. Sorely needed renovations accounted for $1,750,000. Playboy Towers opened to a fanfare and immediately began losing money—nearly half-a-million dollars in the first six months. "We never really understood the first thing about how to run hotels," Gutwillig confessed.

While it still seemed that Lake Geneva was going to make money, an even more ambitious resort was projected for a 657-acre site at Great Gorge in New Jersey, only fifty miles from downtown Manhattan. Great Gorge was to be the jewel of Playboy resorts—a 674-room luxury hotel evoking the Playboy "look" with slabs of rough textured concrete, stained redwood, and fixtures of walnut and brass. There were indoor and outdoor swimming pools, facilities for golf and tennis, restaurants, bars, and a Playboy Club. Spiraling construction costs were only the first of the problems at Great Gorge: before the resort opened in January 1972, it had swallowed up more than $33 million.

On the day after the opening party, a *New York Times* reporter observed that business was brisk: "Thousands of New Jerseyans poured into the hotel, jamming the dance floor in the futuristic Bunny Hutch Disco, downing beer at the Playmate Bar, shopping for Playboy decals and paperweights in the arcade. They came in families—housewives with blonde beehives piled on their heads, grandmothers in print dresses, swarms of snow-suited children—scarcely noticing the occasional flustered Bunny trying to fight her way through the jammed hallways." It was hardly a description of a Playboy crowd.

Only a few days later, Great Gorge was virtually deserted. "We believed," said Lee Gottlieb, director of public relations, "that because we had 60,000 keyholders in New York we'd be drawing on a vast market. We were wrong. We never did feasibility studies; we were a gut-reacting company." Great Gorge never achieved its break-even occupancy rate of 60 percent. One of the problems was that it had been built in the wrong place—it was in a very isolated position on a winding two-lane road, and was hard to find. It suffered from competition offered by better-established resorts in the Catskill and Pocono Mountains. It was also hampered, in its attempt to drum up vital convention business, by Playboy's image. Hefner, who never laid eyes on the place until the opening party, explained: "On the one hand we were those racy Playboy Clubs, on the other, we needed family and convention business. We never got ourselves a clear focus. I was never really interested in the hotels: they would have done better if I had been, of course."

"Our hotels had a reputation for terrible management throughout the industry," Gottlieb admitted. "The solution was always to fire the manager and bring in a new one—Lake Geneva had fourteen managers in ten years. We didn't even know how to *build* hotels—you couldn't wheel a room-service cart from one end of Lake Geneva to the other because there were steps in the way." In the first four years of operation, Great Gorge lost nearly $6 million.

By then, most of the Playboy Clubs, enveloped by the blight of urban crisis, were losing money. The Los Angeles Club was on Sunset Strip, which had been glamorous in the fifties and sixties, but was now lined by seedy honky-tonk dives patronized by hookers and teenage runaways. In Detroit, Cincinnati, Atlanta, Montreal, Kansas City, and Phoenix, the lights of the Playboy Clubs burned at night in deserted streets in city centers abandoned like ghost towns.

Those few clubs still doing decent business were patronized mainly by blacks and blue-collar workers, a crowd very different from the sophisticated men-about-town who were alleged to populate the world of *Playboy*. "What kind of man reads *Playboy*?" the magazine asked every month. "A robust young guy with a thirst for new adventures . . . a guy with an eye for style . . . a man who plays to win, whether it is a game of chance or the game of romance."

The notion that the clubs were the place where the fantasy promoted by the magazine could be brought to life was no longer taken seriously, least of all by Playboy staffers. "None of the editorial staff would be seen dead in the Chicago Playboy Club," said Gordon Moore, photography editor of *Oui*.

To boost business, all Playboy executives on expense accounts were ordered to entertain in Playboy Clubs wherever possible, an instruction so widely ignored that at one point there were threats that expense accounts including bills from other restaurants or clubs would not be honored. "The attitude," said Gutwillig, "was that any Playboy executive who spent time in a Playboy Club not in the line of duty was too dumb to be a Playboy executive."

Gutwillig wanted Playboy to get out of the nightclub business altogether, but the company was bound by its obligation to nearly a million keyholders, each of whom had paid $25.00 for a key to all the Playboy Clubs. Gutwillig spent weeks with lawyers trying to find a way to get the company off this hook, without success: if the clubs closed, all the keyholders would have to have their membership fees reimbursed.

"I thought while the company was flush with money," said Gutwillig, "it would be better to take the loss, write off twenty million and get out, but I could not sell the idea because I was dealing with three true believers. Hefner, Preuss, and Rosenzweig all believed in the so-called magic of the Playboy name and logo, believed in it as I had never believed, being a latecomer and having worked for other companies. They could not come to grips with the problems because they found it very hard to believe that this thing could go sour."

As none of the clubs could be closed, even though some of them were dropping $500,000 a year, those in the worst slum areas were moved and others were refurbished. The Los Angeles Club on the Strip was shut down and reopened at Century City, a new development close to Beverly Hills; the Phoenix, Montreal, and Detroit clubs were moved out to affluent suburban locations. The New York Club on 59th Street was closed for a $3 million facelift.

But nothing else changed. The Bunnies still tottered about in their cantilevered corsets in the age of feminism; the brush of their perfumed cottontails was still expected to set the pulse racing in the age of the topless bar; the food was still good old American fare in the age of the bistro; the entertainment was still provided by singers and comedians in the age of the disco.

Evidence of Playboy's decline could be most clearly observed on the streets of almost every American city, where rusting jalopies with hanging fenders and smoking exhausts were invariably found plastered with cocksure Bunny decals.

Gutwillig felt that Hefner was becoming a loser.

Hefner did not bother to make an appearance at Playboy Enterprises' annual stockholders' meeting held at Lake Geneva in November 1973. Preuss explained, lamely, that the chairman was sick, but few of the stockholders present believed him. However, it might have appeared they had little to complain about on the basis of the year's results. Profit was up to $11,258,000 on revenue of $190 million. Some $8 million was lost on hotels, films, and music publishing, but what did it matter when *Playboy* magazine made a staggering $22 million profit! Ominously, Wall Street remained unimpressed and Playboy shares languished at around $6.00.

Throughout 1974, Playboy received a drubbing from the business press for its marketing failures, mismanagement, careless squandering of profits, and poorly run hotels. Everything, from Hefner's extravagant lifestyle to the stringy hamburgers served in the clubs, came in for censure. This constant barrage of criticism, added to the problems caused by the Pubic Wars and the drug investigation, undoubtedly sapped confidence in the Playboy Building. Hefner did nothing to help. When he was asked if he thought he should take a closer interest in running the company, perhaps by showing up at the office occasionally, he replied without hesitation: "I've got something more important to do. It's called living."

The only good news of the year was the sale of one of the company's most debilitating profit drains—the Playboy Plaza at Miami Beach, which had been losing more than a million dollars every year. It was sold for book value, $13.5 million. Hefner wanted to sell the Jamaican hotel, which was also losing money, but it was too late. "I had wanted to sell it two years earlier," said Preuss. "It had peaked out and Jamaica was beginning to have serious tourist problems because of the political turmoil on the island. Hefner wouldn't agree. He said he wanted a hotel in the Caribbean. When he finally changed his mind and said okay, let's sell it, I said: 'Who to?' "

After the shock of the loss recorded in the second quarterly report of fiscal 1975, Playboy announced that "broadscale cost-cutting programs" would be instituted to offset any continuing decline in revenue and profits. Hefner and Preuss both took a 25 percent pay cut, and unaccustomed parsimony added to the gloom pervading the Playboy Building. The lobster and cracked crab that had been a feature of editorial meetings were replaced by more mundane sandwiches. The price of soft drinks was doubled and coffee, which had previously been free, now cost a dime a cup. Employees traveling on business found themselves booked on economy seats rather than first class, which was how Playboy had formerly always traveled. Even the Muzak in the elevators was switched off.

After the departure of Karen Christy for Texas, Hefner could rarely be found in Chicago and the fabled Mansion at North Street Parkway was quietly mothballed, Hefner rejecting point-blank any suggestion that it should be sold. The staff of fifty was cut back to twelve, and the Bunnies who lived in the top-floor dormitories were kicked out.

In June, trading in Playboy common stock on the New York Stock Exchange was suspended for seven days while the company considered becoming a privately owned corporation again. Frantic moves were made behind the scenes to raise a bank loan of around $5 million to buy back the 2.6 million publicly owned shares, but none of the leading banks was willing to extend further credit to a company so sorely troubled. In August, Playboy declared it had decided not to "go private," without explaining why.

The economies, which were designed to reduce the company's operating costs by about $6 million annually, at first fell far short of their target. But no one had to look very far to identify the company's most extravagant and pointless expense—the Big Bunny, sitting in the sunshine in Los Angeles and eating up more than a million dollars a year.

Even though Hefner hardly ever left Los Angeles, he could not at first bear the thought of parting with his favorite toy, or the idea of someone else carousing in the skies aboard *his* airliner. It was at such moments that he most bitterly regretted allowing Playboy to become a public company: how could he justify keeping the Big Bunny to shareholders? With the greatest reluctance, he agreed to the DC-9 being put on the market, and it was sold for $4,225,000, nearly $300,000 more than its depreciated book value. The only comfort for Hefner was that the purchaser was the Venezuelan government, which was more interested in the Big Bunny as an aircraft than as "a mind-boggling display of sensual opulence." All the lavish interior fittings were stripped out and replaced by rows of conventional aircraft seats; the fuselage was repainted white, and the flag of Venezuela was painted over the Bunny logo on the tail.

The departure of the lamented Big Bunny, now looking like any other aircraft, for Caracas, unquestionably marked the end of the good times for Playboy. A few months later, when Hefner wanted to attend the opening celebrations of the refurbished Playboy Club in New York, he was obliged to take a scheduled flight from Los Angeles airport. Once a caravan of limousines would have swept up to the Big Bunny and Hef and the gang would have tumbled out and the party would have continued as the Big

Bunny ascended into the Californian skies. Now, Hef and the gang could be found dispiritedly standing in line, clutching their tickets, waiting to board an airliner that would depart at another's behest.

There was, however, some good news that summer: in London something wonderful happened for Playboy. The Arabs arrived.

12

You're Supposed to Call Me Baby!

The surprising appearance, in the fashionable environs of Mayfair and Knightsbridge, of exotic gentlemen swathed in what appeared to be white sheets, wearing tea towels wrapped around their heads and leading posses of mysteriously masked and veiled women, came to be known, in 1976, as the Arab invasion of London. Suddenly, it seemed, the steets were thronged by robed figures with dusky complexions, fulgent eyes, and sandaled feet. They could be observed proceeding wraithlike through the carpeted reaches of Harrods, overflowing the armchairs in the lobby of the Dorchester, and staring uncomprehendingly from the backs of chauffeured Rolls-Royces stuck in West End traffic. As if all this was not enough for the average Londoner, in the same year there rose above the Nash terraces bordering Regents Park the great dome and white minaret of a *mosque*.

For the British, the Arab invasion was a profound culture shock. In the days of the Empire, it was considered perfectly right and proper for Englishmen to travel to foreign lands and disrupt ancient traditions and cultures; what was never envisaged was that it might happen the other way around. Thus it cannot be said that the Arabs, with their strange costumes and stranger ways, were warmly welcomed. The fact that they had money to spend, and they spent it with careless ostentation, made their presence even more offensive to a nation that had previously thought of Arabs as not entirely trustworthy bearers and runners.

Reassuring stories of outrageous Arab behavior were bandied about in clubs and pubs, losing nothing in the telling. It was said that Arabs renting expensive apartments were unaware of the function of the lavatory, that they built cooking fires in the center of priceless Oriental carpets, that they grazed herds of goats in back gardens, that they left hotel suites filthy, with food smeared over the walls. Resentment increased as property prices soared, stimulated by Arab enthusiasm for real estate. When Cubby Broccoli, the James Bond film producer, put his Mayfair home on the market with only twenty-six years of the lease still to run, six Arab buyers stepped forward and offered more than double the £175,000 the lease was expected to fetch. The best London houses, a stately home, and even a couple of castles were snapped up by Arabs willing to pay prices no Englishman could afford.

Under a headline ARABS DOZE ON DOORSTEPS IN CASBAH MAYFAIR, the right-wing *Daily Telegraph* published a long feature in August 1976 that painted a dismal picture of life in the capital under the Arab occupation and did not trouble to conceal its inherent racism. The litany of complaints included "screaming children, all-night parties, lack of Western toilet training, wash hanging in windows, and the Arab taste for life on the street."

In Chesterfield Hill, it was reported, where "one of the prettiest Regency houses is now in Arab hands," passersby were startled by the family's inclination to "squat on the doorstep as late as 2 A.M. rather than live inside." Arabs who were "tired of walking" could also be seen in Curzon Street lying on the pavement against walls and railings and dozing on porches. The reporter claimed to have witnessed pedestrians leaping from the path of recklessly driven Rolls-Royces with "Arab number plates" and to have noted the anger of a clergyman approached by a small Arab boy "emerging from a clutch of yashmakked women in the back seat of a Rolls-Royce, waving a twenty-pound note and asking 'Change, pleeze.' The clergyman replied stiffly 'I don't carry that sort of money.'" Afterward, the worthy cleric was quoted as saying to the *Daily Telegraph*: "Most people seem to think our problems with the Arabs are merely funny. They are in fact most unpleasant."

Unable to stem the Arab invasion, enterprising Londoners did their best to profit from it. Lovable Cockney cabbies plucked fistfuls of notes from purses innocently proffered by Arabs unfamiliar with taxi meters; landlords hastily doubled their rents for clients from the Middle East; hotel porters hustled for £100 tips; Mayfair tarts wheedled Cartier watches and fur coats as presents; nightclubs piled on their charges. No one ripped off the visitors more rapaciously or more successfully than the cream of the British medical profession in Harley Street, an area much patronized by Arabs. Doctors, consultants, and specialists organized themselves into neat little syndicates and passed Arab patients around from one to the other, from consulting room to consulting room, so that everyone in the syndicate had the opportunity of extracting a fee. This cozy arrangement sometimes meant that an Arab who arrived in Harley Street with a pain in his back might easily leave clacking a fine new set of dentures.

Abused, resented, and unwelcome, the Arabs were blithely undeterred in their determination to visit London. The "invasion" could be traced back to the formation of OPEC (Organization of Petroleum Exporting Countries) in the early seventies, which broke the West's stranglehold on oil prices. A barrel of crude oil quadrupled in cost overnight, unleashed a flood of petrodollars throughout the Middle East, and elevated innumerable Arab kings, sheiks, businessmen, and many of Saudi Arabia's four thousand princes to millionaire status. Wealthy Arabs had traditionally journeyed to the fleshpots of Lebanon for recreation: largely drinking, wenching, and gambling, the sensuous pleasures denied to them at home by strict Moslem codes of behavior. But by the time OPEC's price hiking began to be felt along the shores of the Persian Gulf, a bitter civil war had broken out in Lebanon, and Beirut, its decadent, fast-living capital city, lay in ruins.

Disinclined to tangle with Lebanon's fratricidal barbarism, it was natural that the Arabs should choose to seek their pleasures in London. Apart from long-established Anglo-Arab ties dating back to the old colonial days when Britain ruled a large chunk of the Middle East, London offered fine hotels, shops, medical and banking facilities, prime real estate, and investment possibilities.

London also offered night life, girls, and casinos—an unbeatable troika of attractions for an Arab with petrodollars to burn.

Arab gamblers lost breathtaking sums in London casinos during the latter half of the seventies. A princeling from Riyadh disposed of £2 million in three nights at roulette; a businessman from Kuwait frittered away a total of no less than £18 million at the same game. Even a maximum stake of £200 at a roulette table did not defeat determined Arab gamblers—by betting on a number, all the numbers surrounding it, all the sides and corners, they could lay out £8,000 on each spin of the wheel. And the wheels spun, on average, every forty-five seconds.

No casino profited more from the Arab invasion than the Playboy Club in Park Lane, where the Bunnies were a potent attraction. Bunny croupières were obliged by the British Gaming Board to wear "modesty bibs" so that their thrusting cleavages could not be thought to tempt gamblers to the gaming tables, but there was still enough lustrous flesh on display to entice Arab high rollers in their hordes. Between January 1975 and June 1981, an astonishing £660 million was exchanged for chips at Playboy casinos in Britain.

It was a fabulous windfall. Presiding over this glamorous and astonishingly lucrative business, the golden arm of the embattled Playboy empire, was the debonair figure of Victor A. Lownes III.

After being sacked by Playboy in 1962, Lownes kicked his heels in New York as a thoroughly bored "consultant" and then decided it would be nice to live abroad for a while. He had remained on close terms with Hefner and put forward the idea he should investigate the possibility of setting up Playboy Clubs in Europe. Hef was happy to give his blessing, since it would bring Victor back into Playboy but interpose the comforting expanse of the Atlantic Ocean between his mercurial friend and the executives in Chicago, with whom Victor had so frequently clashed.

At the time, no one contemplated running a Playboy Club as a casino. Indeed, when Lownes boarded a plane for London in December 1963, he did not even know that gaming had recently been legalized in Britain. His aircraft was diverted to Manchester because of fog at Heathrow and he completed his journey to London by train. Looking out of the window as the train rattled through the suburbs, he noticed the patchwork acres of allotments with their ramshackle sheds. Things must be bad here, he thought, if people have to live in places like that. He did not realize his mistake until he arrived at Euston and discovered, by happy chance, that London was unquestionably the place to be in the sixties.

Far away from the suburbs, London was, to use the quaint vernacular of the period, where "it" was "at." As *Time* magazine reported in a memorable cover story: "London has burst into bloom. It swings; it is the scene. As never before in modern times, London is switched on. Ancient elegance and new opulence are all tangled up in a dazzling blur of op and pop. The city is alive with birds and beatles, buzzing with minicars and telly stars, pulsing with half a dozen separate veins of excitement."

Victor took to Swinging London in a manner entirely befitting a Playboy emissary. He rented a large house in fashionable Montpelier Square, invited swinging celebrities like the Beatles to his frequent parties, twisted furiously in discotheques, and began enthusiastically seducing every "bird" he could get his hands on. He could be found "making the scene" all over town with dozens of different, always beautiful, girls. One of them, a stunning seventeen-year-old starlet with the unlikely name of Viviane Ventura, deliberately lost her virginity in order to persuade Lownes to make love to her. He claimed he demurred at "making a woman" of her for fear she might become too emotionally involved with him, so she persuaded an actor of her acquaintance to do the deed. "How could I argue with her after that?" Victor asked plaintively. Not long afterward, he was sharing his bed with identical twins, Mary and Madeleine, for what a salacious British newspaper would later describe as "three-in-a-bed sex romps."

In between making women, Victor was making plans to open a Playboy Club in London, just like the one in Chicago. But he was also becoming aware that the real money being made in Swinging London was not in clubs, but in casinos. Gambling spread like a fever in Britain during the sixties, following the passing by Parliament of the 1960 Betting and Gaming Act. This blinkered piece of legislation was designed to legalize the kind of social flutters that vicars liked to feature at church fetes—lotteries, bingo, whist drives, and the like. What it achieved in reality was to launch a gambling bonanza that soon attracted the attention of organized crime.

Within a few years of the passing of the Act, more than 1,500 casinos had opened in Britain, ranging from plush Mayfair establishments like Crockford's, the Clermont, and the Curzon House, where the cream of London society gathered in long dresses and dinner jackets, to seedy backstreet dives where gamblers lucky enough to win were even luckier to get out with their winnings.

They operated via a loophole in the Act that enabled existing clubs to become casinos providing they only offered games of equal chance and that gamblers were given the opportunity of taking the bank if they wished. These measures were intended as safeguards to deter "undesirable elements"; neither worked, because few gamblers were willing to risk taking the bank and supervision was woefully inadequate.

Mafia gambling interests, kicked out of Cuba by Castro's revolution in 1959, could not have asked for more timely legislation by Her Majesty's Government, or a better opportunity to set up offshore gambling operations well away from the scrutiny of U.S. jurisdiction. The Mob first organized junkets, flying gamblers into Britain in chartered aircraft, fleecing them, and flying them home. These proved so successful that the Mafia began taking over clubs, starting with the Colony in Berkeley Square, where actor George Raft was employed as front man.

Vinnie Teresa, an organizer of Mafia junkets to the Colony, reckoned to make a profit of between $50,000 and $80,000 on each one. The Colony, he said, could take in as much as $900,000 on a single junket:

> You know, you bring thirty to forty good high rollers, people who love to gamble and have money to burn, in a casino like that and they'll lose an average of twenty-five to forty grand apiece in a week. That adds up fast.

At the Colony, Raft fronted for Dino Cellini and Meyer Lansky. He was there as an attraction to bring the suckers in. Entertainers would flock to the place because they were his friends. In London, it became the place to be. Raft would come

254

down every night, dressed in a tuxedo. He'd meet all the people, sign autographs, dance with the women—he was in the limelight all the time and loved every minute of it.

Local villains were cut in to provide "protection" and the business was so lucrative that the leaders of London's rival underworld gangs—the Kray brothers and the Richardsons—convened a meeting at the Astor Club to try to agree to a truce. But the discussions were acrimonious and nearly degenerated into a gun battle. The Krays had already reached "an understanding" with Mafia representatives and had no intention of sharing their percentage with the Richardsons. Thereafter, the Krays and the Richardsons were at war and many a casino door was peppered with bullet holes.

Lownes was by no means a gambler, considering it to be a stupid pastime, but he could recognize an opportunity when he saw one and he was unconcerned by the known involvement of organized crime in the London gambling scene, since Playboy had always managed to fend off the Mafia, even in Chicago. During several enjoyable evenings spent, in a spirit of inquiry, seated at Crockford's elegant green baize tables, Lownes accepted the bank whenever he was able to do so and discovered he was able to make a tidy profit. He also witnessed at first hand the frenetic pitch of Britain's gambling fever. From this valuable experience he resolved to include a casino in the new London Playboy Club, a casino that would introduce to the world yet another Playboy innovation—the *Bunny croupière.*

A new seven-story building in Park Lane, designed by Walter Gropius, was about to come on the market and offered a suitably prestigious venue for the club. Lownes thought the building, overlooking Hyde Park, between the Dorchester and Hilton hotels, would be a fine place to run up the Playboy flag and he acquired a sixty-three-year lease at a rental of £80,000 a year, although not without some grumbling from Chicago about the expense.

News of Playboy's impending arrival in Britain inevitably stirred the guardians of public morality into action and when Lownes applied for a liquor license, a vigorous objection was lodged by a gentleman in a clerical collar who claimed that scantily dressed waitresses serving drinks would create terrible temptations and surely lead to other sinful occupations like gambling. He might have saved his breath: the climate of Swinging London was deeply unsympathetic to old-fashioned puritan values and it was hard to believe that the Bunnies' curious cantilevered corset was any more tempting than the mini-skirts every girl was wearing on the street.

As plans progressed, Victor applied himself to the recruitment of British Bunnies, a task he felt he should personally supervise. In the autumn of 1965, the first six British Bunnies, led by former "Miss Bristol Teenager" Dolly Read, were sent to Chicago for "training," an event that made headlines on both sides of the Atlantic. As they stepped from their aircraft at O'Hare airport, clutching bags labeled "Bunnies from Britain," they were greeted by cheering American Bunnies waving "Welcome Bunnies from Britain" banners, a crowd of jostling photographers and, inexplicably, an Irish pipe band. The girls obligingly posed for photographs by a specially made signpost proclaiming it to be "6,433 kilometers to London" and their faint protests that miles were preferred in Britain were brushed aside.

Publicity was one of Lownes's special talents and during the spring and early summer of 1966, Playboy and its Bunnies were rarely out of the British newspapers. Asked by an ingenuous reporter where he found British Bunnies, Lownes cracked: "Oh they just popped up and multiplied." A few weeks before the club was due to open in June, the Archbishop of Canterbury penned a letter to *The Times* expressing his displeasure at being invited to join the Playboy Club and his disinclination to accept, thus generating further publicity around the world. Lownes denied including the good archbishop on the mailing in the hope of just such a response.

Hefner himself flew to London for the opening party, his second visit to Europe. Thirty-two Bunnies assembled at London Airport to welcome him, an occasion described in the newspapers as the arrival of "the King of Bunnies." American citizens in London telephoned the U.S. Embassy to protest that British Bunnies were waving American flags and a spokesman for the embassy expressed his regret at the flag being used in "circumstances not befitting the dignity due to it." Lownes was delighted.

Fifteen hundred guests attended the black-tie revels to mark the opening of the London Playboy Club on the evening of June 28, 1966. Arc lights were set up outside the club for newsreel and television cameras and every arriving celebrity—an eclectic lot, including Jean-Paul Belmondo, Ursula Andress, Ringo Starr, Lee Radziwill, Rex Harrison, the Marquis of Tavistock, Henry Luce III, Dame Margot Fonteyn, and Rudolf Nureyev—was accorded the ritual barrage of popping flashbulbs. Inside, those Bunnies not serving champagne cocktails posed, pouted, and wiggled their little cottontails for the benefit of further perspiring legions from Fleet Street. All the facilities of the club were put at the disposal of the guests and at four o'clock in the morning, when the party was due to end, the roulette wheels were still spinning on the fourth floor and the discotheque still seethed with the pulsating strains of Merseybeat.

By a curious coincidence, the King of the Bunnies was not the only prominent American in town that night. While faces, photographers, VIP keyholders, and gate-crashers were cramming into the London Playboy Club, in a draughty hall at Earls Court, a few miles to the west, Dr. Billy Graham was winding up his month-long evangelical crusade in Britain and inviting people in the audience to step forward and make a decision for Christ.

Although more than twenty thousand keyholders paid a pre-opening subscription of five guineas to avail themselves of the club's discotheque, restaurant, cocktail bars, and twenty-seven gaming tables offering roulette, blackjack, and punto banco, the London Playboy Club—the eighteenth to be opened—was not an immediate success. For the first few months, business was extremely slow and there were gloomy predictions in Chicago that Lownes had "blown it." But once the summer ended, things began to improve, and at the end of its first year, the club reported pretax profits of nearly one million dollars—a handsome return on an investment of only one and a half million dollars.

The club remained open twenty-four hours a day, every day of the year, and no matter what time of the day or night there were always bleary-eyed gamblers to be found sitting at the gaming tables, as if hypnotized by the bouncing ball in the roulette wheel. Some were hopelessly addicted gamblers bent on ruin; the Bunny croupières noted with distaste that it was not unusual for a gambler to wet his trousers rather than tear himself away from the game for a minute or two.

Right from the start, Lownes and his deputy, Bill Gerhauser—

a young accountant sent over from Chicago to "keep an eye on Victor"—set up tight financial controls, rigorous accounting procedures, and a staff regime with the strictest rules and regulations in the business; male employees even had their pockets and the double cuffs on their shirts sewn up to help them avoid temptation. In the handbook issued to all employees was a message from Lownes: "Every employee has a responsibility to report any infractions of the rules to top management or me personally. If you know any rules that are being broken or not being enforced, let us know."

Playboy's determination to run a clean operation was so well known that the mobsters running much of the London gaming scene never attempted to muscle in on Lownes's territory. When the existence of apartments for rent on the top floor of the club led to rumors that they were used by keyholders to entertain Bunnies, Lownes immediately declared the top floors out of bounds to all Bunnies, on pain of instant dismissal. Some girls were terrified of using the lifts in case they were accidentally and inexorably borne up to the forbidden fifth floor and beyond.

The ban on Bunnies dating customers or members of staff was also remorselessly enforced, with one notable exception. When Paulette, the Bunny Training Mother, called in new Bunnies to read out the rules, she added a little rider that never appeared in the Bunny Manual. "All Bunnies are allowed to date Victor Lownes, the chairman and managing director," she said. "Mr. Lownes is not married and there are no restrictions as far as he is concerned." Maureen Nash, a cocktail Bunny working in the London club, recalled an invitation from Victor. "One night he telephoned and asked me to go over to his house. When I got there, he was upstairs in bed with three girls. I said, 'What do you want me for?' He told me he wanted me to *watch*. I walked out."

A year after the London Playboy Club opened, the Labour Government under Harold Wilson addressed itself to the increasingly serious problems posed by the proliferation of gambling and the involvement of organized crime. The first moves were announced by the Home Secretary, Roy Jenkins, who stood up in the Commons to inform the House that eight American citizens concerned in the operation of British casinos, including Mr. George Raft, had been barred from Britain because their presence was not deemed to be "conducive to the public good." Meyer Lansky, alleged finance director of the Mafia's U.S. operations, was identified as the man behind the Colony; Angelo Bruno, of Philadelphia, was said to control the Victoria Sporting Club; and links were established between other London casinos and the New York "family" of Vito Genovese. Soon afterward, a new legislation—the 1968 Gaming Act—was drafted to clean up the business and eliminate the racketeers.

The 1968 Gaming Act was designed to control legalized gambling without encouraging its growth. All casinos would have to be licensed and a newly established Gaming Board would be required to issue "certificates of consent" before anyone could even apply for a license. While Mafia chiefs held a crisis conference in Miami to discuss how to protect their interests in Britain, the new legislation was also causing extreme concern at Playboy, since, under the Act, foreign ownership of casinos was to be prohibited. This provision was aimed specifically at excluding foreign crime syndicates, but it clearly also affected Playboy.

While the Act was being phased in, Lownes began discussions with Sir Stanley Raymond, the first chairman of the Gaming Board, in an attempt to find a way of staying in business. Sir Stanley liked Lownes and knew that the casino in the Playboy Club was operated in an exemplary fashion but was adamant that it could not continue. He was sorry, he said, but there was risk that control could be wrested from Lownes at any time and he was determined not to allow any casinos to be operated on policies dictated by "faceless manipulators" overseas over whom he had no jurisdiction.

To meet Sir Stanley's objections, Lownes and Playboy's solicitor, Arnold Finer, suggested incorporating a new U.K. company, the Playboy Club of London Ltd. (PCL), and transferring 75 percent of the shares to a trust. The directors of the trust would all have to be permanent residents of Great Britain and approved by the Gaming Board, thus ensuring that control of the company would be firmly vested in Britain. To Lownes's relief, the Gaming Board eventually agreed to this arrangement. The trustees named were Lownes, Finer, chartered accountant Lord Desmond Hirshfield, and Clement Freud, a Liberal MP and the grandson of Sigmund Freud.

In 1970, when the new Gaming Act became law, the majority

of casinos and gambling dives in Britain were forced to close their doors for good. Only 131 gaming licenses were issued throughout the country, 25 of them in London. The Playboy Club of London Ltd., with its reputation as pure as driven snow, was one of the successful applicants for a license and the only American-owned company to remain in business. The Gaming Board required only one change in Playboy's operating procedures—the Bunny croupières were required to wear "modesty bibs" in order to conform with that part of the Act that debarred casinos from offering any "inducement to gamble."

Gerhauser, a soft-spoken boyish American as different as it was possible to be from the flamboyant Lownes, took over direct control of the Playboy Club to ensure that the Gaming Act was being scrupulously observed, and to build up the business within the new, tighter regulations. Gerhauser knew about gambling: when he was a young man he lost everything on the horses. At the end of his disastrous career as a gambler, he was forced to sell his house, his business, and his car in order to pay off his debts.

Partly as a result of this experience, Gerhauser's philosophy at the Playboy Club was to try to keep gambling within the realm of entertainment. While table limits were pushed up to attract the really big-time gamblers, individual credit limits were imposed on keyholders by refusing to accept checks beyond a previously determined figure. If checks bounced, Playboy's debt collection procedure was positively gentlemanly, exhibiting both patience and consideration. Bunnies were instructed to be understanding and sympathetic if losers became irritable, and there were always plenty of losers about to get irritable—mathematical probabilities dictated that the casino always won at popular games like roulette and punto banco.

The last days of Swinging London coincided with a property boom; fortunes were made overnight by speculators and asset strippers and the Playboy Club profited handsomely from the patronage of the expanding *nouveau riche*. In 1972, Playboy made an offer for the Clermont Club in Berkeley Square, which Gerhauser had heard was in trouble. Gambler John Aspinall, who owned the Clermont, was accustomed to taking part in the action in his own casino, playing chemin-de-fer with titled friends for high stakes. Under the Gaming Act, directors were forbidden to gamble on their own premises, a restriction Aspinall found intolerable.

The Clermont, with its Palladian interior, marble columns, crystal chandeliers, and grand staircase, was recognized as the most exclusive of all the London casinos and the place where people with *real* money gambled; Annabel's, the nightclub in the basement, was a favorite haunt of Princess Margaret. Aspinall liked to describe it as the kind of casino where English gentlemen could "ruin themselves as elegantly and suicidally as did their ancestors three hundred years ago." Among the regular gamblers was Lord "Lucky" Lucan, later to be sought by Scotland Yard on a murder charge. Aspinall sold to Playboy for £357,000 cash and within nine months, Playboy had recouped its investment across the Clermont's elegant green baize tables.

By this time, Lownes was comfortably resident at 1 Connaught Square, an elegant Georgian townhouse fitted out in a style remarkably similar to that favored by his friend Hefner. The walls were hung with fine paintings (Magritte, Dubuffet, Bacon, and so on) and the obligatory leather, mahogany, walnut, and rich autumnal shades could be found everywhere. Yak fur was selected to line a room leading to the sauna, and in Lownes's bedroom a walnut-veneered console alongside the bed contained a bank of switches to operate various lights, a movie screen, stereo system, and piped music. Even the curtains opened and closed electronically.

Parties at Connaught Square were noisy, glamorous, and frequent, like Playboy parties were intended to be. Lots of Bunnies were always present, along with friends described by Lownes as "some of the world's most adventurous ladykillers and sought-after matinee idols." His habit of disappearing upstairs with two, three, and even four young ladies did not go unnoticed.

Lownes remained a loyal friend to Hef, even though they were not able to see much of each other. After the *Macbeth* debacle, Victor was deeply offended when he read in a newspaper that Polanski was making unpleasant comments about Playboy's money being tainted. Victor knew Polanski well. The diminutive film director met Sharon Tate at one of Victor's parties, and Victor hosted their wedding reception at the London Playboy Club—an act of generosity the happy couple repaid by presenting him with a solid gold phallus.

Lownes thought it treacherous of Polanski to make derogatory remarks about Playboy and returned the present with a note: "In view of recent developments I no longer care to have this full-length life-size portrait of you around the house. I am sure you will have no difficulty finding some 'friend' you can shove it up."

Always anxious to find ways of pleasing Hefner, one Christmas Victor sent him a card with a photograph of Paul McCartney and Ringo Starr holding up a placard painted with the message: "Merry Xmas, Hef." It occupied a place of pride among all the cards at Playboy Mansion West.

Unfortunately the friendship was soon to become somewhat strained when the two most important and powerful men in the Playboy organization fell out . . . over a Playmate!

Marilyn Cole was just twenty-one years old when she arrived in London from her home town of Portsmouth, where she had worked as a clerk in the Co-op supermarket. She was a strikingly pretty girl, tall and slim, with long legs, large, firm breasts, and silky brown hair reaching down to her waist. It was January 1971, and a friend had suggested she should apply for a job as a Bunny. She auditioned in a skimpy bikini and thigh-length snakeskin boots, was accepted immediately, and had barely been issued her Bunny ears before she caught Victor Lownes's notoriously roving eye.

On her first day of training, Marilyn and the other new Bunnies were gathered together at the club to have their photographs taken for the Playboy files. While the official photographer fussed with lights and exposures and getting the poses right, in the background another man was snapping away at the girls, mumbling something about wanting to test a new camera. This was Lownes, checking over the arrivals.

Marilyn was a product of the sixties, disinclined to take life too seriously, cheerfully unsophisticated, relaxed about her body, and always ready for a lark. When, next day, she was asked if she would like to pose for some nude pictures and be considered as a Playmate, she had no qualms about saying yes. It was Victor's idea: he thought his old friend Hef would like to get a look at this stunning new girl. The pictures were dispatched to Chicago and Hefner was clearly interested as he ordered Marilyn to be sent over immediately. Victor inquired if he should perhaps accompany her, but the reply was unequivocal: "No need."

For a girl who only a few weeks previously had been working at the Co-op in Portsmouth, the Playboy Mansion in Chicago was rather more than an eye-opener. As she stepped from the Cadillac that had collected her at the airport, a black butler came out to take her bags and show her up to a room she was to share with a Playmate called Cynthia. On the table was a bowl of roses and a handwritten note: "Welcome to the Mansion—Hefner." Marilyn had time only to remove her false eyelashes before the telephone rang and a woman's voice said that Hefner would be pleased to meet her in the ballroom. She found him dressed from head to foot in crushed velvet, smaller than she expected, charming, and anxious to give her a guided tour.

Marilyn returned to her room to find Cynthia tucking into lobster thermidor and a bottle of vintage French wine. Anything you want, Cynthia explained between mouthfuls, just dial 20 on the internal telephone.

Next day, Marilyn met Bobbie Arnstein and the two hit it off immediately. They recognized in each other a similar sense of humor and an ability to giggle at the cloistered absurdity of day-to-day life within the Mansion. Bobbie liked Marilyn so much she took it upon herself to ensure that Marilyn became one of Hefner's favorites. In the Games Room, while Marilyn was leaning over a pinball machine in a pair of hot pants, Bobbie ran a hand down Marilyn's leg and said to Hefner: "Just look at the length of her legs. Don't you think it's the most graceful thing you've ever seen?" Then she took a handful of Marilyn's hair and commanded: "Feel that. It's more like silk than hair."

Hefner was impressed. That evening, he invited Marilyn to join him for dinner on his round bed, an event she correctly surmised would be a prelude to her seduction. She was, she admits, no blushing virgin and found Hefner attractive. As soon as dinner had been cleared away, Hefner got out his bottle of baby oil and suggested a massage. Later, when he had fallen asleep, Marilyn crept out of the round bed and returned to her own room.

Marilyn, who was no fool, kept out of Hefner's way for the remainder of her stay at the Mansion, reasoning that it would be a wise policy to make herself unavailable. Sensible girl. When the time came for her to leave, after a week of photo sessions, Hefner sought her out to squeeze her hand and say: "Promise you won't forget me."

There was little opportunity to forget. A few weeks after Marilyn arrived back in London, the Big Bunny wafted into town with Hefner and his entourage, including Barbi Benton, on board. Three hundred reporters and photographers waited at Heathrow Airport to record their arrival, although in truth rather more interest was focused on the aircraft than its owner. Victor Lownes naturally threw a welcome party at his house in Connaught Square, and invited Marilyn. It was the first time Marilyn had met Barbi Benton and it was not an occasion noted for its warmth. Marilyn swept laserlike eyes over Barbi's baby-doll outfit of red satin hot pants and a heart-shaped bib and snarled: "So you're Barbi. How very nice."

During the course of the evening, Hefner somehow managed to get rid of Barbi so that he could make love to Marilyn in Victor's bedroom, which Victor obligingly made available. Hef told Marilyn he wanted her to return to Chicago with them in the Big Bunny the following day. Victor also planned to use the opportunity to ditch Connie Kreski, a Playmate of whom he had tired.

The atmosphere on the homeward-bound flight was somewhat fraught. Barbi sat across the aisle from Marilyn, angrily flicking through one magazine after another and not saying a word, while Connie sobbed pathetically and kept up a pretense she would be returning. "I don't know why Victor's butler packed all these bags," she whimpered, "I really don't need all this stuff."

Preparations to welcome the Big Bunny back to Chicago were meticulous—a butler from the Mansion stood waiting at the customs barrier holding a silver tray on which was placed an open bottle of Pepsi to sustain Hefner on the arduous trek through the terminal to the limousines.

Marilyn was to travel back and forth to Chicago several times during the next few months. Hefner justified her travels by constantly rejecting her Playmate pictures. Every time he threw out a new set of pictures, Marilyn would be hauled back to Chicago for more photo sessions during the day and more slippery sex in the round bed at nights. This procedure need not have caused any complications—had not Marilyn fallen for Victor Lownes.

While she was in London, she continued to work as a cocktail Bunny, a situation in which it was likely she would become chummy with Victor, probable that he would ask her out to dinner, and inevitable he would invite her to bed. Marilyn made no secret of the fact that she liked Victor, and when the invitation came it was not surprising that she accepted. After they had made love for the first time, Victor cautioned her not to tell Hefner. "It's not necessary," he explained, perhaps a little gratuitously.

Marilyn and Victor soon became very close, but Hefner remained ignorant of their affair. Shortly before the opening of the new Playboy resort-hotel at Great Gorge, New Jersey, Hefner arranged to meet Victor for dinner at the 21 Club in New York. When Victor turned up with Marilyn, Hefner naturally assumed that his buddy had brought her along for him, as Barbi Benton was not arriving until the following day. Neither Marilyn nor Victor had the courage to disabuse him. Victor sulked all the way through dinner and then, over coffee, raised a glass containing the dregs of his wine. "I know you are spending the night with Marilyn," he announced, glaring at Hefner, "and for this one night you will possess her." He paused, dramatically. "But only for this one night. You see, I'm going to marry her." This was news not only to Hefner but to Marilyn, who was speechless. "I'll believe it when I see it," Hefner chuckled after a moment.

Poor Victor was required to spend the night alone and suffer the knowledge that his girl was in the arms of another. At that moment, Marilyn's body was also being examined by a fair slice of the American male population, for she had at last made her debut on the newsstands as Playmate of the Month in the January 1972 issue of *Playboy* magazine. It was a historic moment, as a Playboy spokesman noted, since it was "the first pose in which a girl displayed all her charms for a full-frontal view."

As the opening day of Great Gorge approached, Victor let it be known that he intended to take Marilyn to the party as his date.

This caused considerable consternation in high quarters at Playboy since it was realized that Hef would not be pleased, even though he was attending the party with Barbi Benton. When Victor and Marilyn arrived at Great Gorge, Marilyn confessed to Bobbie Arnstein that they were in love. Bobbie was appalled. "Are you mad," she said, "what about *Hef*?"

On the morning of the party, Dick Rosenzweig put through an urgent call to Victor. "If you show up at the party with Marilyn," he said, "Hef will be very upset." Lownes at first thought it was a joke, but Rosenzweig was deadly serious. "I can only tell you what I have been told to tell you," he continued. "Let me spell it out. Hef would be gratified if you would kindly both stay in your room while the party is going on."

So it was that while hundreds of guests gathered for cocktails in the ballroom 'round a pyramid of hors d'oeuvres topped by a Playboy Bunny carved in ice, then adjourned to the nightclub for a *filet mignon* dinner and cabaret, Victor and Marilyn stayed in their room, trying halfheartedly to make a joke out of their banishment and ignore the sounds of revelry from below. Meanwhile, Playboy executives excitedly passed a rumor from mouth to mouth that Hef and Victor had actually come to blows and that Victor had a black eye!

Marilyn and Victor left Great Gorge the following day and took off for a short holiday at the Playboy Hotel in Miami Beach, Florida. There, Hefner called Victor to make it up. "He says that if we're enjoying each other's company," said Victor when he put the telephone down, "then we have his blessing."

"Who does he think he is," Marilyn snapped. "The Pope?"

It was not by any means the end of the jealous squabbling over Marilyn. Despite the fact that both her suitors were well into their forties, they continued to act like lovesick preppies. Hefner paid Marilyn back for going off with Victor by selecting her as Playmate of the Year, inviting one thousand guests to the Los Angeles Mansion to witness the presentation ceremony, and then refusing to leave his room. While Marilyn, dolled up on Hefner's instruction in a pink dress to receive a pile of pink prizes, including a pink Volvo sports car and a pink bicycle, waited with increasing embarrassment, Hefner sent word via his social secretary that he was "too tired to make it."

She was furious, but not the kind of girl to bear a grudge. Anyway, as she said, she was busy for the next few months "signing her pussy" on promotion appearances—everyone, it appeared, wanted her autograph on her centerfold picture. When her romance with Victor hit a sticky patch, Marilyn did not hesitate to accept Bobbie Arnstein's invitation to "come over and spend some time" at the Playboy Mansion West. Hefner was delighted, and had her installed in the guest cottage, where she would be available for a "quickie" whenever he could slip away. One afternoon he arrived at the cottage with a bottle of baby oil sticking out of the pocket of his robe and found Marilyn, with her hair in rollers, and another Playmate called Kelly, sitting on their beds watching television. Time was obviously of the essence: he leapt on Marilyn, tore off her clothes, and began squirting her with baby oil. While they were making love, Marilyn was acutely aware of Kelly, disconsolately switching channels on the television.

Marilyn told Bobbie Arnstein about it later and they fell about laughing. Marilyn agreed with Bobbie that Hefner was a virile lover, but confessed that sometimes he went at it for so long it got "borin'."

Victor and Hefner had much more in common than a mutual lust for Miss January 1972; indeed, it rather appeared in England as if Victor A. Lownes III was deliberately trying to overshadow Hefner.

In 1972, Lownes bought Stocks House, a beautiful Georgian mansion outside the Hertfordshire village of Aldbury, in the Chilterns. Once owned by a nineteenth-century prime minister, Earl Grey, Stocks had forty-two rooms and was being used as a girls' school of swiftly fading gentility when it came on the market. Lownes paid £115,000 for the property, spent a million dollars on renovations and improvements, and enthusiastically adopted what he liked to describe as the lifestyle of an English country gentleman, riding to hounds with the Whaddon Chase, stumping the grounds in Wellington boots, and affecting raffish tweeds.

English country gentlemen to the manner born might have had difficulty recognizing some elements of Mr. Lownes's new lifestyle at Stocks, despite his declared passion for hunting. The discotheque he had installed, for example, was not a feature one normally found in English country houses; neither were the pinball machines, which occupied two complete rooms. A large and companionable jacuzzi could be found leading off the conservatory, the bathrooms boasted gold taps and the lavatories monogrammed wallpaper. The private chapel in the grounds was converted, heaven forbid, into a training school for Bunny croupières, thus ensuring that dozens of young and pretty girls could always be found about the place, just like a certain other mansion six thousand miles away in California. In return for using Stocks as a company training facility, Victor got Playboy to pay 90 percent of the running expenses of the house—about $250,000 a year.

Visiting Playboy executives invited out to Stocks could not help but remark on the similarities between Victor's mansion and Hefner's and perhaps speculate on the wisdom of this development. Hefner had a machine to fire tennis balls for solo practice; Victor had a machine to fire tennis balls for solo practice. Hefner had a humorous needlepoint hanging in his mansion; Victor had a humorous needlepoint hanging in his mansion: "The difference between God and me is that I know how to run a class operation—Victor Lownes." Hefner played Pacman all the time; Victor played Pacman all the time. Hefner had a pet monkey; Victor had a pet monkey. Victor also had Marilyn, who had tired of the Los Angeles Mansion and was happily ensconced at Stocks.

Just like Hefner, Victor hosted frequent parties at his mansion. But whereas Hefner's parties were privately getting a reputation for being dull and stereotyped, Victor's parties were getting a reputation for being wild and abandoned, with panties hanging on the chandeliers, much cavorting in the jacuzzi, and all kinds of naughtiness going on. No less than fifteen hundred guests were invited to a lavish frolic in 1976 to celebrate the American bicentennial, Marilyn's twenty-seventh birthday, and the tenth anniversary of the opening of the London Playboy Club, not necessarily in that order. Everyone was given a sweatshirt printed "Stocks, 4 July, 1976. I was there and you weren't."

Sometimes Victor invited only girls to his parties, and he never made any secret of the fact that girls were the overriding interest in his life. In fact, he could get quite tetchy at suggestions that perhaps his playboy image was no more than a public relations gimmick. A friend, Shel Silverstein, cleverly lampooned Victor's anxiety to preserve his swinging image in a cartoon that showed him barking at a secretary: "I don't care if you call me Mr. Lownes when we're alone, but when there are other people around, you're supposed to call me *baby!*"

It was Victor's habit to spend weekends at Stocks in the company of dozens of friends and freeloaders, and the remaining five days of the week in London, where he had a penthouse apartment above the Playboy Club. He was increasingly visible: at the races, at nightclubs, at society parties, and in the gossip columns. Never shy of publicity, he was to enjoy even more of the limelight when the Arabs began arriving in London, as stories of fabulous sums of money lost at roulette at the Playboy and the Clermont casinos inevitably focused attention on the colorful boss of Playboy's gambling interest, particularly as he was always good for a quote. "I've always thought," he said, commenting on the Arab mania for gambling, "that if the Israelis really wanted to get the Arabs to the peace table, it would be best to cover it in green baize."

When the Playboy Club first opened, the highest denomination chip was a £100,000 gold plaque with the figures set in diamond chips. Lownes had it made as a publicity gimmick, never imagining it would ever be used. After 1975, it was bought and cashed so many times that Playboy had to introduce plastic £100,000 chips in order to meet the demand from petrodollar gamblers.

Bill Gerhauser remembered one night at the Clermont when an Arab sheikh came in with £700,000 and rapidly lost it all. He was able to continue gambling since he had a £500,000 credit limit, but he had soon lost that, too, and should not have been allowed to buy any more chips. Gerhauser did not often spend evenings at the Playboy casinos and was only in the Clermont that night because he was entertaining a colleague from Chicago. The Arab recognized Gerhauser and pleaded to be allowed another £100,000. Gerhauser felt sorry for him and relented. The Arab returned to the roulette table with his last £100,000 (at least for that evening) and proceeded to win back everything he had lost. He left the Clermont in the early hours, £300,000 in pocket. Most of the customers were not so lucky.

Many of Playboy's Arab gamblers viewed the Bunnies with lustful, glittering eyes and considered, sometimes correctly, that they could be bought with Cartier watches, diamond bracelets, and fur coats. "Lots of girls had Arab boyfriends," said Maureen Nash. "I know I did. My boyfriend used to telephone from Syria to tell the VIP Room manager to make sure I was serving his table when he arrived."

Enforcing the "nonfraternization" rule became virtually impossible, short of hiring a private detective to shadow every off-duty Bunny. If a girl was discovered to be actively involved in prostitution, or was dating different customers every night, she was sacked instantly; otherwise Playboy executives were obliged to turn a blind eye to the fact that Bunnies were showing up for work dressed like heiresses.

"Arabs gave the girls diamonds and gold," said Bunny Mother Erin Stratton, "the way Englishmen would give flowers and chocolates. One girl got a $12,000 lynx coat just for being *nice*. There was nothing we could do about it—we could not take the presents from the girls and the girls could not give them back without offending the gamblers."

But there were casualties: Bunny Eve Stratford, a beautiful blonde only nineteen years old, was known to date Arab gamblers and was discovered at her home in East London with her throat ritually cut from ear to ear. Her killer was never found.

Petrodollars doubled, then tripled, the gross profits recorded in London. In 1975, the Playboy casinos made £7,500,000 profit. In 1976, it was £13,500,000. In 1977, it was £23,000,000—more than twenty times the profits being brought in by *Playboy* magazine, ostensibly the empire's flagship. Both Lownes and Gerhauser were increasingly bitter at having to pump profits back to America to prop up the other ailing divisions of the business. Lownes made no effort to conceal his contempt for the management in Chicago. "We seem to be making money," he liked to tell his fellow directors, "just so you guys can piss it away."

Relations between London and Chicago cooled rapidly. At the Playboy Building on Michigan Avenue, Lownes and Gerhauser were regarded as overbearing, interfering, and disruptive, arrogantly assuming that the success of their operation gave them the right to rule the roost. At the Playboy Club in Park Lane, the corporate management in Chicago was considered to be hopelessly incompetent, recklessly extravagant, and grossly overmanned.

At meetings of the Finance Committee in Chicago, Gerhauser

constantly complained about the cost of corporate administration. "We are shipping our profit over here," he said, taking a line from Lownes, "and you are pouring it down a hole." When a fourteen-week study was proposed to explore ways of reducing costs, Gerhauser exploded. "What we don't need is a fourteen-week study," he snapped. "I can tell you how to do it. What the publishing division doesn't need and what we don't need, just let it fall away. Get rid of it." After that meeting, the Finance Committee was reconstituted and Gerhauser was no longer a member. Henceforth, he was given the "mushroom treatment." "It means," he explained laconically, "that they keep you in the dark and shit on you."

Although they were not to know it, they were making enemies in Chicago at a time when they would soon need all the friends they could get.

13

You Guys Are Pissing away the Profits

Derick January Daniels, the president and chief operating officer of Playboy Enterprises, Inc., loathed Victor A. Lownes III quite as much as Lownes detested Daniels.

Appointed in October 1976, Daniels was forty-seven years old when he joined Playboy after a high-flying career with Knight-Ridder Newspapers. He was executive editor of the *Detroit Free Press* when it won a Pulitzer for its coverage of the Detroit riots in 1967, and moved into management in 1970, rising swiftly to head the news service that supplied Knight-Ridder's chain of thirty-two newspapers.

His career belied his appearance, for he did not look in the least like a newspaperman or a businessman. He was rather slight and delicate, looking like a pinched cherub with a fluffy mop of tight golden curls. One of his eyes was blue and the other green and he spoke in an affected Southern drawl. But none of these features was as startling as his wardrobe, which might have been purchased complete from the estate of Rudolph Valentino. Even in a company owned by a man who rarely wore anything but silk pajamas, Daniels's attire excited considerable comment.

At a welcoming party held in the Chicago Mansion, the new

president of the company showed up in a white *blouson* top with billowing sleeves, white trousers, white high-heeled boots, and a long white scarf flung around his neck. In the office, he might occasionally sport a business suit, but more often he affected jodhpurs or flying suits with red cowboy boots or tight leather pants and loafers with no socks.

He had not been at Playboy very long before he was featured on the cover of *Miami* magazine wearing a gold lamé jumpsuit unzipped to the navel and staring into the camera with a sultry expression. Behind him knelt his twenty-two-year-old wife in a filmy kimono barely covering her breasts. The picture was taken at a party Daniels hosted at Coconut Grove, a suburb of Miami, and the report inside described how the merrymaking included a great deal of nudity and mentioned that Bunnies from the Playboy Club had been hired to serve drinks.

"Holy mackerel!" Lee Gottlieb bellowed when he saw it. Gottlieb, Playboy's director of public relations, discovered to his horror that Daniels had ordered hundreds of copies of the magazine to distribute to his friends. He hurried into the president's office to ask him to keep the magazine out of Chicago.

"There we were," Gottlieb explained, "trying to affect a posture of being a serious, responsible public company trying to get onto a sound fiscal footing, and there was this magazine cover with the new president in this bizarre get-up at some kind of orgy."

Daniels was brought into Playboy as part of a drastic restructuring of the company instituted in response to the 1975 crisis, an upheaval forced on the reluctant Hefner by the realization that the crisis was caused, in part, by the failure of management to keep pace with the company's explosive growth. Preuss, the executive vice-president, had forty people reporting to him and operated from a corner office of the Playboy Building swamped by manila files stacked on every flat surface.

Both Preuss and Gutwillig were swept aside during the reorganization and a seven-man "office of the president" was set up to manage day-to-day operations while a search was mounted for a new chief operating officer. Preuss, Hefner's former college roommate and a loyal employee for nearly twenty years, was particularly bitter about being deposed and resigned soon afterward. "I was sick of the company by then," he said. "It was no

273

longer a pleasant place to work. Hef brought in a bunch of phony baloneys; the place was riddled with corporate politics."

Before Daniels arrived, Hefner asked Victor to divide his time between London and Chicago so that he could take control of the Hotels and Clubs Division and make whatever economies he thought necessary to try to reduce losses. Victor breezed into town to tackle the job with his customary gusto and high profile. One of the first ideas he was considering, he told reporters, was to move the offices back to East Ohio Street, where there was a lot less space, and then stage a race from the Playboy Building. Everyone who got to a desk at East Ohio Street would keep their jobs, the rest would be out. There were some people who thought he was not joking.

Promised a free rein by Hefner in making cuts, Victor announced he intended to sell the Chicago Mansion, which he described as an "expensive anachronism." Hef almost swallowed his pipe when he heard the news and telephoned Vic to say he did not want the Mansion sold under any circumstances. The following day's newspapers reported Lownes saying it was "all a terrible mistake."

In areas not so close to Hef's heart, Lownes attacked the massive bureaucracy that had mushroomed in the Playboy Building so ferociously he became known as "Jaws." He closed down entire departments and eliminated fifty jobs. There was a "Bunny Department," he discovered, which did nothing but keep track of every woman who had ever been a Bunny because Hef thought it was a nice idea; it was one of the first to go. This "preliminary surgery" trimmed overhead by nearly $3 million a year.

When he was warned he could not close any of the clubs without risking lawsuits by keyholders, his response was typical: "Let's close them first and worry about it afterward." Playboy Clubs in Kansas City, Atlanta, Boston, Baltimore, Detroit, San Francisco, and Montreal were shut. To attract more family and convention business to the hotels, Lownes experimented with removing the Playboy name. "What we did," he told the *Wall Street Journal*, "was admit that the Playboy name and rabbit-head emblem were a detriment to business. That's quite an admission for an outfit that a few years ago was sure it was going to conquer the world."

One day, Victor looked out of the window in his office in the Playboy Building and saw half a dozen television crews hanging around outside the Drake Hotel on the other side of the street. They were waiting, he learned, for the arrival of the West German chancellor. Victor rushed down to the Playboy Club and announced to the Bunnies on duty that he wanted them to go on strike and parade up and down the street with banners demanding "Bunny Lib." Banners were hurriedly put together with slogans like "Wake up Hef, it's 1975."

The moment the Bunnies hit the street, the television crews, hardly able to believe their luck, deserted the Drake Hotel and rushed over to film the "demonstration," a far better story than the boring visit of some European politician no one had ever heard of. That evening, "Bunny Lib" made the television news coast to coast and was on many front pages the following day.

A "protest letter" dispatched to Hef was widely quoted: "Because of the archaic rules you have decreed for Bunny behavior we are made to feel like strange objects out of step with our time. Our private lives should be our own. You have created a caste system through which we Bunnies have become America's 'Untouchables.' We expect to hear from you in a positive way. We have nothing to lose but our tails and ears." Lownes had quite a way with words. Hef responded magnanimously by declaring that henceforth Bunnies *would* be able to date customers, prompting a surge of business in the clubs. Lownes did not confess his role in the affair and confined himself to a single enigmatic quote: "It's too bad everybody is not like me," he said with a wry smile, "perfect."

Lownes's new responsibilities in Chicago led many of his colleagues to believe he was angling for the top job. He dismissed the notion, saying that he wanted to continue living in England, but there was no denying his anger when Derick Daniels was named as president. Lownes had met Daniels only once, over lunch at the University Club in Chicago, but he had disliked him on sight and reported to Hefner that he did not think Daniels would be an asset to Playboy. After Daniels's appointment was announced, Lownes telephoned Hef in Los Angeles and threatened to resign. Hef thought Vic was just upset because he had been passed over in favor of an outsider and persuaded him to stay by doubling his salary and offering him a new contract, which included a right to equity participation in any future ventures Playboy undertook in the gaming business. Lownes calculated he would be earning at least as much as Daniels, whose salary was to be $250,000 a year, and his ruffled feathers were temporarily soothed. Nonetheless, it did not make him like Daniels any better.

During his first weeks at Playboy, Daniels made some depressing discoveries about the company he was expected to rescue. Playboy was bleeding profusely from its losses and was still grossly overstaffed, despite the cuts made by Lownes. Many of its accounting systems were primitive, the SEC filings were always late, and the yearly audit took three months instead of the customary six weeks. Morale, not surprisingly, was low.

Hefner's instructions to Daniels were to "professionalize" the company and groom the young lady Hefner had already decided would eventually take over Daniels's job. She was twenty-three years old, a Phi Beta Kappa and summa cum laude graduate of Brandeis University. Her name was Christie Hefner.

Christie had only recently rediscovered her father. As a child, she had been hurt by how little time he had had for her and she did not get on with her stepfather, Ed Gunn, a lawyer Millie married after her divorce from Hefner. Both Millie's children took the name of Gunn and, to Christie, her father was just the man who occasionally sent a limousine to pick her up so she could play ten-pin bowling in the basement of the Chicago Mansion.

At Brandeis, Christie was a brilliant student. She tried, at first, to conceal the fact that she was Hugh Hefner's daughter and she was furious when a friend blurted it out. It was not, in any case, something she would have been able to hide for very long because, after the kidnapping of Patty Hearst, Christie turned up for classes with an armed bodyguard in tow, who sat outside her classroom fingering the gun lodged in his holster.

During her junior year, Christie began to see a little more of her father and when she was elected Phi Beta Kappa she made a decision that was to mark a turning point in their relationship. As she would have her Phi Beta Kappa certificate for the rest of her life, she decided the name on it ought to be Christie Hefner. When she told her father, over dinner at the Mansion, tears of pleasure welled up in his eyes. From that moment on, the rapprochement flourished.

Hefner enjoyed his unaccustomed new role as proud father and made an appearance on Christie's graduation day, which the Brandeis class of 1974 are unlikely to forget: he arrived in a white suit, with Barbi Benton on his arm, and was trailed by cameramen all over the campus. Almost no one noticed the arrival of the commencement speaker, Saul Bellow.

Christie had been out of college a year, living in Boston and writing for an alternative newspaper, the *Boston Phoenix*, when she decided there was no need to avoid working for her father's company and joined Playboy as "special assistant to the chairman." Her first task was to oversee the opening of a boutique that would sell records and sportswear on the ground floor of the Playboy Building. It was a disaster. Her next project, providing backing for entrepreneurs who wanted to start their own magazines, was no more successful.

Daniels made Christie a vice-president and put her in charge of organizing celebrations for the company's upcoming twenty-fifth anniversary (an event the chairman considered to be of great importance), while he tackled the immediate problems, beginning with a fundamental overhaul of Playboy's reporting and budgeting controls. All department heads were warned that they would be required to justify the continued existence of their departments; every job that could not be justified would be eliminated. Firing began in the summer of 1977 and fearful rumors swept the building about who was going and who was staying. On a single day in September, sixty-seven employees, ranging from senior executives to secretaries, were told they no longer had jobs.

Lee Gottlieb heard from the elevator starter that he was being fired. As he was leaving the Playboy Building on the evening of Thursday, September 8, the elevator starter, an old friend, said: "Gee, Lee, I hear I'm losing a golfing buddy." Gottlieb thought he was referring to another employee with whom they had both played golf. "No, I don't mean him," said the elevator starter, "I heard you were going. I'm sorry." Gottlieb could not believe it— he had worked for Playboy for sixteen years—until he got into the office next morning and received a telephone call from Daniels, who was in Los Angeles: "Lee, this is Derick. I'm sorry to tell you that there is no longer a job for you in this company." It was not that he had been doing a bad job, Daniels explained, it was just that the company was spending too much on administrative functions and the whole corporate public relations department that Gottlieb headed was being eliminated.

Figures for fiscal 1977 appeared to indicate that Daniels's draconian measures were, to some extent, succeeding. Pruning the payroll by ten percent, taking the company out of the record business, and closing the movie theaters, the hotel in Ochos Rios, Jamaica, and eight clubs enabled Playboy to report doubled profits of $4,100,000. But the circulation of the magazine had slipped below 5 million and mounting production costs had slashed its profits to only $2.5 million—down from $8.5 million two years earlier.

Without the $10-million profit contributed by the London casinos, the picture would have looked a lot less rosy, as Victor Lownes never tired of pointing out.

Daniels made his first attempt to get rid of Victor early in 1977. He told Hefner that Victor's personal style was so different from his own and that of the new management he had brought into the company that he thought Victor should go. Hefner would not hear of it. Vic's "bottom-line results" were too important, he said, and the company could not afford to lose him simply because of a "personality clash."

By March, the conflict between the two men had come into the open. Playboy announced it intended to build a huge hotel-casino on the boardwalk at Atlantic City, where a referendum had recently given the green light to legalized gambling. Lownes, as head of the Hotels and Clubs Division and an acknowledged authority on gaming, was naturally determined to take charge of this project. Daniels was equally determined to keep him at arm's length, and tried to thwart Victor by sacking his deputy, Dan Stone. It was a tactical error. Stone had been spending a great deal of time preparing the ground in Atlantic City and remarks he had made about Playboy's prospects at a reception were quoted in a local newspaper several weeks after Daniels had issued a written memo forbidding Playboy executives to talk to the press about the Atlantic City plans.

When Stone arrived back in Chicago, he was summoned to Daniels's office. On the president's desk were just two pieces of paper—the cutting from the Atlantic City newspaper and the memo. Daniels, who was wearing high boots, jodhpurs, and an aviator's shirt, began striding back and forth across the office and firing questions at Stone. Why had he talked to reporters? Had he seen the memo? Was he aware this was a violation of company policy?

Stone explained that he had talked to a great number of people at the reception and he did not know who was a reporter and who was not. But he apologized and pledged he would make no further comments. "You will make no more comments, period," Daniels drawled. "You are no longer associated with this company. Is there anything else you want to talk about?" Stone was mystified by this question. He did not feel much like a chat, he said, as being fired was rather in the forefront of his mind.

When Lownes heard that his deputy had been sacked, he was incensed and fumed at Daniels: "He works for *me*, not for *you!*" Victor immediately complained to Hefner, as did Christie, who was dating Stone at the time. Hef hated any kind of confrontation or unpleasantness and certainly did not want to upset his beloved daughter, so he appealed to Daniels to consider "handling the situation some other way."

A message was dispatched to Stone saying that perhaps something could be worked out, "but not with Victor." Daniels offered him his job back, at a reduced salary. Lownes told Stone to accept the offer and a month later raised his pay to its former level.

Thereafter, no one could fail to notice the open hostility between Daniels and Lownes. When Daniels was trying to conduct executive meetings, Lownes would mutter derogatory comments or crack jokes to make Christie laugh. He mocked Daniels's outlandish appearance behind his back, referring to him as "the bizarro"; the members of Daniels's management team he routinely described as "yo-yos." He took to carrying the profit-and-loss statements around with him, so he could whip the figures out of his pocket and show everyone how much money he was making for the company and how much everyone else was losing. "Almost the first words Victor ever said to me," Marvin Huston, who was appointed chief financial officer in 1977, recalled, "were that I was pissing away the profits."

There was some justification for the barrage of criticism leveled at the management in Chicago by both Lownes and Gerhauser, for while Playboy was issuing confident press releases describing how the company was being turned around and how operating costs were being reduced, corporate overheads under Daniels's management were, in reality, steadily increasing—in fiscal 1978, they were up by more than $2 million to $13.3 million.

After publication of the 1978 annual report, Gerhauser complained that the figures were being "dressed" to conceal the contribution being made by the London operation. For the first time, the revenue from the casinos was grouped with the hotels and clubs, so that the annual report was able to boast a $20-million profit from "Casinos, Clubs, and Hotels," neatly covering up the $3.5 million lost by the clubs and hotels.

Gerhauser made no secret of the fact that he thought the company was badly managed. "There were times when you couldn't get any financial statements that made any sense. Things got so bad that at one point I said, 'I don't know how you can operate this company—you have no information.' The Finance Committee, for example, had discussed the cost of operating the West Coast Mansion and had got agreement that no further capital expenditure would be undertaken at the Mansion without authorization from the Finance Committee. Then we discovered that 'improvements' to Hefner's office and living quarters were still going on and were going to cost $2.6 million. We were aghast."

To add to Daniels's problems, in 1978 the company was subjected to unwelcome scrutiny from outside. First, the Internal Revenue Service challenged the tax deductions claimed for the operating expenses of the Chicago and Los Angeles Mansions and submitted a demand for $13.4 million in additional taxes and penalties for fiscal years 1970 through 1976. Then a shareholder began a derivative action against the company, alleging in an Illinois state court that the rent paid by Hefner for Playboy Mansion West was inadequate and that his occupancy of the Mansion at Playboy's expense constituted a "waste, gift, and embezzlement of the company's assets" and did not serve Playboy's "legitimate business interests." Two months later, the Securities and Exchange Commission announced it was commencing an inquiry into "the possible receipt of undisclosed remuneration by officers of the company and its subsidiaries."

In response to these alarming events, Playboy set up an Audit Committee to mount its own investigation into the extent of any corporate claims the company might have against members of management, Although no evidence of fraud was uncovered, the committee found that Hefner and a number of other senior executives had received unauthorized benefits, over an eight-year period, worth more than $2 million.

Hefner, by far the worst offender, was asked to repay the company $796,413 for perks provided by Playboy for his personal use, or that of his friends and family. It included $150,000 for food and drink served at the Mansions, $74,000 for his valet, $32,000 for limousines, $21,000 for trips taken by friends on the Big Bunny, $74,000 for his laundry and dry-cleaning, and $6,000 for the use by his family of "complimentary keys" at Playboy Clubs. Hefner paid up with barely a murmur, except to mention that he had waived a total of $1,190,000 in dividends in 1975 and 1976 so that the company could continue to pay a dividend to all the other shareholders.

Daniels was presented with a bill for $24,278, for the use of an apartment in the Chicago Mansion and a two-bedroom suite in the Playboy Towers Hotel. Lownes had to repay $50,452 for expenses at Stocks, and Gerhauser $45,425 for his family's use of a three-bedroom apartment owned by Playboy in Belgravia. Christie came out with the smallest bill—just $769 for limousines and entertainment at Playboy Clubs.

The Audit Committee was careful to explain that none of the individuals concerned had made any attempt to conceal the benefits they had received. "This is not a case of surreptitious misappropriation by management. Rather, it is a case of Playboy's failure to adjust practices that began when it was a private company to the standards expected of a company with a 30 percent public ownership."

The SEC largely accepted the findings of the Audit Committee, although it chided the company for failing "in significant respects" to make disclosures about the use of corporate assets for the benefit of directors. It pointed out that up until 1975, Hefner was only paying $650 a month for each of the Mansions—a figure determined as a "fair rent" in 1964 by an IRS agent who had no idea of the extent of the services that were being provided to Hefner. Between 1971 and 1978, the operating cost of the Chicago Mansion was $9,150,000 and the Los Angeles Mansion, $11,500,000.

"Substantial sums," the SEC noted, were spent on parties at Playboy Mansion West. "Playboy has taken and continues to take the position that such expenditures are 'promotional' in nature and thus benefit the company's business activities. The Audit Committee did not take issue with this position. The company has been unable to demonstrate the precise corporate benefits derived from such expenditures. Whatever the promotional motivation, it seems clear that an essential objective of such expenditure was, and continues to be, to provide Hefner with a particular lifestyle."

That lifestyle was well in evidence in January 1979, when Playboy celebrated its twenty-fifth anniversary with a round of parties, dinners, and frolics in New York, Chicago, and Los Angeles that cost more than a million dollars. The anniversary issue of *Playboy* magazine bulged with 410 pages and dwelt, at length, on the subject of how wonderful it was (*Playboy* never made any secret of the fact that it found itself, and its editor-publisher, infinitely absorbing). A nationwide search for the "Anniversary Playmate" produced a girl whose name, Hefner swore, really was Candy Loving.

"When I conceived this magazine a quarter of a century ago," Hefner wrote in a paean to himself, "I had no notion that it would become one of the most important, imitated, influential and yet controversial publishing ventures of our times."

The glossy Silver Anniversary Press Kit distributed to the media contained fulsome details of the many contributions Hefner and his magazine had made to American culture and society. Hef was coyly described as "editor, reformer, philosopher, philanthropist and a great entrepreneur."

Although *Playboy*'s circulation base had dropped to 4.8 million, only marginally ahead of *Penthouse*, the anniversary issue sold 6.4 million copies and augured well for the year. The company's net profits in fiscal 1979 increased to $9.1 million from $6.2 million the previous year. Losses in the Hotels and Clubs Division were drastically reduced to less than half a million. Ominously, corporate overheads increased *again*, up to $16 million, but the casinos brought in their biggest ever profit of $34 million.

In March 1979, work began on the construction of a $135-million hotel-casino in Atlantic City, an impressive glass and steel structure destined to make the convention center next door look even shabbier than it really was. The plans envisaged 60,000 square feet of gaming tables and slot machines, with a projected take of $1 million *a day*. Playboy had been involved in a desperate search to raise finance for the project within the tight time limits set by the New Jersey authorities. A tentative deal with a West German consortium fell through after Frank DiPrima, Playboy's counsel, examined a draft prospectus and announced that it would not pass muster, "even under pre-1933 Fraud Act standards." Eventually a partnership agreement was reached with the Pritzker family, which controlled the Hyatt hotel chain and the Elsinore Corporation. Playboy-Elsinore Associates filed an application for a New Jersey casino license—a ten-thousand-page submission detailing its qualifications and including a $100,000 fee—in September.

Daniels and Lownes remained at knifepoint over Atlantic City, with neither missing any opportunity to score off the other. When Lownes refused to follow Daniels's instructions to take a company lawyer with him to a housing authority meeting in Atlantic City, Daniels told Lownes he would no longer be leading the project. Lownes ignored him. In the summer of 1979, Daniels tried reason and suggested to Lownes that he should voluntarily relinquish overall control of the Hotels and Clubs Division in the United States. "Only when we have satisfactorily won," Victor haughtily replied, "the right to gaming in Atlantic City."

When Daniels tried to recruit Hefner's support to prize power from Lownes, corporate politics degenerated into farce. At a meeting at Playboy Mansion West, Daniels *thought* he had obtained Hef's agreement to relieve Victor of his authority over club and hotel operations outside Britain. Lownes was summoned to Los Angeles to be advised of the decision and the three men sat down to business. During the course of the discussion, Daniels became convinced that Hefner was not supporting him. Hef thought he *was* supporting Daniels and could not understand why Daniels did not tell Vic what they agreed. So neither of them said anything and a slightly perplexed Lownes flew back to London, still boss of the Hotels and Clubs Division.

On August 14, 1980, Playboy suffered another casualty; another name was added to those of Constance Petrie, Willy Rey, Adrienne Pollack, Bobbie Arnstein, and Eve Stratford. In the back room of a two-story Spanish-style stucco house near the Santa Monica Freeway in west Los Angeles, the naked body of a beautiful blonde girl was found lying across the corner of a bed with her face blasted away by buckshot. She was Dorothy Stratten, age twenty, the reigning Playmate of the Year.

Dorothy had been sodomized after her death by the man whose body was lying face down on the floor at the foot of the bed in a pool of blood. Under his chest was the twelve gauge Mossberg pump shotgun with which he had blown out his brains. He was Paul Snyder, age twenty-nine, Dorothy's husband and self-styled business partner.

Hefner was playing pinball in the Games House when the news was telephoned to Playboy Mansion West. He thought at first it might be some terrible, sick joke until he asked the police officer at the other end of the line to give his name and badge number. When Hefner put the telephone down his hands were shaking. He told his secretary to get Peter Bogdanovich, the film director, on the line. Bogdanovich was Dorothy's lover; Hefner knew that they were planning to marry when her divorce was through. "Something terrible has happened, Peter," he said. "Dorothy is dead."

Next day, at the Playboy Building in Chicago, there was a scurry to get Dorothy's pictures out of the October issue of *Playboy* magazine, but it was too late. There was time, however, to lift her photograph from the front cover of the 1981 Playmate Calendar, and a Christmas promotion in which she posed nude with Hef was abandoned.

Dorothy Ruth Hoogstraten was working behind the counter at a Dairy Queen in Vancouver, British Columbia, when she first met Snyder. He looked exactly like what he was: a pimp and small-time hustler. He had thick, black hair with sideburns and a moustache, and wore a mink coat and a jeweled Star of David around his neck. Lately, the pimping business had not been going well and he had gotten into trouble with loan sharks, who had hung him by the ankles out of the window of a room on the thirtieth floor of a hotel to persuade him of the need to repay his debts. When Snyder swaggered into the Dairy Queen and saw Dorothy, he turned to his friend and said: "That girl could make me a lot of money."

There was no doubt that Dorothy was stunning, all the more so since she was entirely unaware of her attractions. She was naïve and impressed by Snyder—his sharp suits, his black Corvette and street-wise manner. They began dating, much to the disgust of Dorothy's mother, who did not need more than a single glance at Snyder to know what kind of man he was.

During the course of his questionable career, Snyder had several times attempted to promote girls as Playmates, always without success. Not long after he met Dorothy, the ballyhoo surrounding Playboy's nationwide hunt for an "Anniversary Playmate" reached Snyder's ears, and he took Dorothy along to a photographer he knew had previously taken pictures for Playboy. Dorothy's test shots were sent to Los Angeles and she was immediately invited to Playboy Mansion West for a further photo session. She left Vancouver in August 1978, her first trip in an airplane.

Although she was not chosen as the Anniversary Playmate (she was a runner-up to Candy Loving), Dorothy was named as Playmate of the Month for August 1979. In the meantime, she was given a job as Bunny at the Los Angeles Playboy Club. Snyder soon followed his protegee to California, more than ever convinced that she would be able to make money for him, and they set up house together in a small apartment.

As Dorothy was drawn into the Playboy orbit, Snyder increasingly fretted that she was slipping out of his grasp. She was frequently invited to parties at the Mansion; he was not. She began picking up bit parts in films, while he was hustling for bucks with tacky promotions like wet T-shirt contests. He began to put pressure on her to marry him, reminding her that they had struck a "lifetime bargain." Dorothy felt obligated to Snyder and believed she owed much of her success to him; they married at the Silver Bell Wedding Chapel in Las Vegas in June 1979.

A few months later, Dorothy was selected as Playmate of the

Year and Peter Bogdanovich, whom she had met at a roller disco party at the Mansion, offered her a role in his new film *They All Laughed*. Shooting began in New York in March 1980. Snyder wanted to accompany Dorothy but she persuaded him to stay behind as the set would be closed to outsiders. Insisting that she should leave Los Angeles like a star, Snyder hired a Rolls-Royce to take her to the airport.

During the filming, Dorothy and Bogdanovich quietly fell in love. She wrote to Snyder, asking him to "Let the bird fly." He was distraught, ravaged by jealousy, and terrified by the prospect of his meal ticket disappearing. He tried several times to talk Dorothy into a reconciliation and had her followed by private detectives. He even tried to replace her by promoting another girl as a potential Playmate, but Playboy did not want anything to do with him. In the end, he seemed to accept that a divorce was inevitable and Dorothy agreed to meet him at their former home in west Los Angeles to discuss a "financial settlement." They fixed the date: August 14.

In the June 1980 issue of *Playboy*, Dorothy had been described as "one of the few emerging film goddesses of the new decade." Her death was a cruel blow to Playboy, since she was the first Playmate, of all the many Playmates, who looked as if she might become a Hollywood star. Hef had always promoted the notion that being chosen as a Playmate was the first step to stardom, but it had never happened. One after another, the Playmates disappeared into obscurity—until Dorothy came along.

14

The Casino Wars

On May 12, 1978, *Private Eye*, a British satirical magazine with a penchant for malicious tittle-tattle of doubtful accuracy and an occasional reputation for brilliant investigative journalism, published a curious story alleging that Ladbroke, owners of four fashionable London casinos, had been indulging in an astonishing range of dirty tricks to steal gamblers from other casinos. The author was a man called Jack Lundin.

For a journalist, Lundin was a deceptively mild-mannered man, prematurely gray-haired, who gave the impression of being somewhat unsure of himself, laughing nervously and rather too frequently in conversation. Yet he was also an investigative reporter of rare skill—fearless, and doggedly determined on the trail of a story. His career had had its ups and downs and it was during a notable down, when he was chasing gossip paragraphs at £25 apiece for the diary of the London *Evening News*, that he got his first whiff of the story that was to spark off the casino wars.

On the morning of Saturday, March 11, 1978, the diary editor called Lundin over to his desk in the newsroom and showed him a note that had arrived in the mail. It was a typewritten sheet of paper headed "Scandals in the Casino World," followed by a star-

tling list of allegations about prostitution, bribery, and corruption
and a demand familiar to all newspapers: WANT MONEY. A name
and telephone number was included in a covering letter and Lundin
was told to look into it and "knock out a couple of paragraphs,"
but not to mention the names of any casinos for fear of a libel
action.

The contact was a man named Andreas Christensen. He was
extremely cagey when Lundin telephoned him in Dorset at the
number that had been jotted down with his name on the covering
letter. At first he refused to answer any questions over the telephone, but Lundin kept him talking and wheedled out the bones
of the story. Christensen had recently been employed as marketing
controller of Ladup Limited, the gambling division of the Ladbroke Group. He had information, he said, that Ladup had mounted
a secret undercover operation to poach gamblers from other casinos, involving teams of private detectives maintaining surveillance on rival casinos and the bribery of policemen to obtain
information from the Police National Computer. Lundin realized
within a few minutes that he was onto a story worth a lot more
than a couple of paragraphs and arranged to meet Christensen for
a drink at the Gloucester Hotel in Kensington.

Christensen did not show up. When Lundin telephoned him,
he made a lame excuse and they fixed another date. This time, he
appeared. He turned out to be a tall, well-built man in his early
thirties, wearing, to Lundin's astonishment, a check suit with baggy
plus-four trousers. Before they began to talk, Christensen said he
wanted money for his story. Like all good investigative reporters,
Lundin disliked paying for information and told Christensen bluntly
that he could "count money out"; it did not take him long to
discover that Christensen had been sacked by Ladup and was looking for revenge as much as for money. The two men eventually
struck a deal: in return for Christensen's help, Lundin pledged that
he would never reveal the source of his information, no matter
what happened. Christensen casually promised to break Lundin's
arms and legs if he went back on his word.

The story Christensen unfolded was sensational. On the top
floor of the Ladbroke Club in Hill Street, Mayfair, was a suite of
luxuriously furnished rooms, known as the *salon privé*, where the
biggest gamblers in the world sat around a roulette wheel and

played the biggest game in the world, with stakes of between £200,000 and £300,000. Among the regular players was Adnan Khashoggi, a Saudi businessman with an international network of companies worth more than $500 million, and Crown Prince Fahad Ben Abdulaziz, brother of King Faisal of Saudi Arabia. Their presence attracted the few high rollers in the world, mostly from the Middle East, who could afford to sit in on a game where a million pounds might change hands in a night.

Khashoggi was the biggest player, staking £1,000 a number on French roulette and betting as much as £40,000 on a single spin of the wheel. When he won, he shouted *mabruk* (an Arab expression of joy) and scattered £1,000 chips among his entourage. The game continued for as long as Khashoggi wanted to play, and at the end of the evening he had sometimes won or lost as much as £600,000. He usually lost, and by the beginning of 1977 it was estimated he had frittered away about £7 million on roulette at the Ladbroke Club. Worried about his reputation as a gambler, he either stopped playing or moved to a different casino in another part of the world. With Khashoggi no longer at the table, the other high rollers began to drift away.

Determined not to lose such lucrative business, Ladbroke attempted to lure the biggest gamblers away from other London casinos, concealing its activities with a baffling smokescreen of accommodation addresses, bogus companies, laundered money, and code names. This cloak-and-dagger deception was necessary, since its activities undoubtedly contravened the Gaming Act and a great deal was at stake: gambling provided about half the Ladbroke Group's profits, then standing at about £24 million a year.

Christensen told Lundin that the dirty tricks began in the early summer of 1977, when Ladup's marketing department surreptitiously hired a firm of private detectives to "isolate and identify" high rollers in London casinos. An elaborate cover story was devised to protect Ladbroke's identity. The client was said to be a Swiss bank—the Indian Ocean Commercial and Development Bank (IOCAD)—interested in investing in the casino industry. Its head office address was a P.O. box number in Lausanne, and mail and Telex facilities were provided through Adfone Services Ltd., a company offering its clients a "prestige address" in Regent Street. Ladup established another phony company—Xeno (Overseas) Ltd., a "non-U.K. trading company"—to launder the costs of the operation. Ladup would write a check to Xeno Ltd. for something like "overseas marketing" and Xeno would issue a check to the detective agency.

Six casinos were kept under surveillance, each of them referred to by a code number—the Playboy Club was "Unit 1," the Knightsbridge Sporting was "Unit 2"—and the whole murky undertaking was known as "Operation Unit Six."

Initial results were promising. Among the names fed by Telex to IOCAD's "offices" in Regent Street were Sheikh Yamani, the Saudi Arabian oil minister, who was said to have unlimited credit facilities at Les Ambassadeurs; Prince Abdul Rachman, who also had unlimited credit at the Knightsbridge Sporting Club; Gunter Sachs, reported to be a dice player at the Playboy Club averaging about £20,000 per visit; and well-known businessmen like Sir Hugh Fraser and publisher Robert Maxwell.

It was not long, however, before a serious drawback presented itself. The detective agency could not be warned to steer clear of Ladbroke casinos without making it obvious that the real client was Ladup and the inevitable happened. A triumphantly detailed report arrived, revealing the details of Khashoggi's gambling at the Ladbroke Club. One of the detectives had "nobbled" a Ladbroke croupier and Ladup found itself in the unenviable position of siphoning money to a treacherous employee for information readily available in its own files.

Further Keystone Kops antics ensued. A detective maintaining surveillance outside "Unit 5"—the Curzon House Club—in the early hours took it upon himself to follow a man seen leaving the club in a dark-brown Rolls-Royce, number BC 999. He shadowed the limousine through the deserted streets of Mayfair, up the Finchley Road, and into Marlborough Place, an expensive residential road in St. John's Wood. The Rolls-Royce pulled into 15 Marlborough Place—the home of Bernard Coral, owner of the Curzon House Club.

After these farcical incidents, Ladup decided on a change of policy. Henceforth, the detectives were only required to note the registration numbers of expensive cars parked outside London casinos. Lundin raised his eyebrows quizzically and Christensen explained that an "arrangement" had been made with a policeman in Nottingham who would supply the names and addresses of car owners for fifty pence a time, using the Police National Computer. Lundin knew that concern had recently been voiced in Parliament about the security of the Police National Computer, which stored a great deal of highly confidential information, as well as details of all cars registered in Britain. The fact that a policeman was selling information from the computer to a casino operator was likely to cause a fine old fuss, he mused with some relish.

Over the next few weeks, Christensen said, thousands of car numbers were passed by Telex to IOCAD. When the numbers had been converted into names and addresses, stage two of the operation went into action. Pretty girls employed in Ladup's public relations department were given the job of making approaches to these likely gamblers, sending out gold-embossed invitations to dinner at one of the Ladbroke casinos, along with huge bouquets of flowers and offers of complimentary membership. Sometimes they were successful, sometimes they were rebuffed.

Lundin scribbled notes as Christensen talked, then he began asking questions. He knew that as he could not reveal Christensen as a source, he would need solid corroboration of the facts if he was ever to get the story published. Christensen hedged at first when Lundin asked him for the name of the detective agency, mumbling something about it being an international company, based in Switzerland and specializing in industrial espionage. Lundin pressed for a name and the other man hesitantly said he thought it was called International Corporate Services. The representative, "Mr. Douglas," could only be contacted by leaving a message at a London telephone number: 262-7448. By the time the interview ended, Lundin had decided his first task was to track down the detective agency.

There was no record of the existence of International Corporate Services, either in Britain or Switzerland, but Mr. Douglas obligingly called back every time Lundin left a message for him, although he always firmly declined a meeting for reasons of "security." During the course of several telephone conversations, Mr. Douglas let slip that he knew the real identity of his client and had actually sued Ladup at one point for payment of outstanding fees.

This was a possible lead to the real identity of "International Corporate Services," as the company's correct name must have appeared on the writ. Lundin asked the *Evening News* reporter at the High Court to check through the writs issued in 1977 to find one issued against Ladup Limited. The reporter said it was impossible, since writs were filed in alphabetical order under the plaintiff's name. If the plaintiff's name was unknown, it would mean going through every single writ.

Next day, Lundin could be found sitting in the dusty writ room at the Queen's Bench Division of the High Court, slowly thumbing through one writ book after another. He kept at it for hours, not even knowing if he was in the right court, but his patience was rewarded. When he reached the letter W, he found a writ issued on behalf of one Ian Douglas Withers against Ladup Ltd. for "£2,281.66, being the balance of the Plaintiff's account for work done as a private investigator on behalf of the Defendant at its request."

Lundin hurried back to his office, found a telephone number for Withers from the yellow pages, and checked him out in the *Evening News* cuttings library: he turned out to be a rather seedy private eye who operated, to judge from frequent court appearances, at the edge of the law. Lundin put a call through to "Mr. Douglas" and left a message for him to telephone the *Evening News*. He rang back within half an hour and Lundin pretended he had a couple more questions to ask. As soon as they had finished talking, Lundin put down the telephone, picked it up immediately and dialed Withers's number. "It's Jack Lundin here," he said to the familiar voice that answered. "We were just speaking. You're Douglas, aren't you?" Withers confessed and reluctantly agreed to be interviewed at his office in Brighton.

Bit by bit, Lundin pieced the story together. From Withers he obtained photostat copies of long lists of car numbers supplied to IOCAD, plus copies of earlier reports on individual gamblers. He tracked down businessmen who had been approached by Ladup's public relations girls. One of them allowed Lundin to use his invitation to dinner at the Ladbroke Park Tower casino in Knightsbridge. At another casino, Lundin identified himself as a journalist and was promptly slipped a Mickey Finn—a gin and tonic of a peculiar brown hue that sent him reeling to the lavatory where he vomited several times. He even obtained copies of the building society account used by "Xeno Ltd." to launder payments to Withers.

After he had been working on the story for a couple of weeks, he began receiving threatening telephone calls in the middle of the night on his ex-directory number at his apartment in London. The message was always the same—a gruff, foreign-sounding voice grunted: "Lay off the car numbers story."

By the beginning of April, Lundin was ready to confront Ladup Ltd. and he arranged an appointment to see Alex Alexander, the managing director, at Ladup's white-painted offices in Woods Mews, off Park Lane. The interview was not a success. Alexander began by snapping: "I am not interested in any of your questions. You are here to answer some of mine." He at first denied all knowledge of the car numbers scheme and said he took a "very dim view" of Lundin's investigations. "Vere Harmsworth [proprietor of the *Evening News*] is a very good friend of mine," Alexander warned Lundin, "and if you step out of line with this article, I promise you I'll come down on you like a ton of bricks."

Lundin worked through the following weekend to finish writing the story and warned the *Evening News* that Ladbroke might take legal action to prevent publication. On Monday, he pleaded with the news editor to publish the story immediately, but was told there was "no hurry." On Tuesday, April 11, 1978, Ladup Ltd. obtained a High Court injunction forbidding the *Evening News* from publishing any report about its activities.

Furious at being thwarted, Lundin took his story to *Private Eye*, which he guessed, correctly, would have no compunction about publishing such deliciously juicy scandal.

Private Eye appeared on the streets with the Ladbroke story on Wednesday, May 10, 1978. It was a remarkably detailed report, naming the names and describing in detail exactly how Operation Unit Six worked. Typically, the magazine added insult to injury by publishing a photograph of Ladbroke's chairman, Cyril Stein, taken in 1966, with an editor's note under the caption: "It is understood that Mr. Stein may look even worse twelve years later."

Reaction to the story was immediate and widespread. At Ladbroke, those executives who did not know what was going on were appalled, realizing that if the allegations were proved, Ladup would almost certainly lose its gaming licenses and be forced to close its casinos. Those executives who did know what was going on began shredding documents in anticipation of a visit from Gaming Board inspectors or the police.

On the Stock Exchange, the Ladbroke Group took a hammering and nearly £6 million was wiped from the value of the company's ordinary shares. At the offices of the Gaming Board, on the top floor of a nondescript office building in Holborn, there was a general feeling of astonishment and anger that a leading casino operator would apparently dare to disregard, so blatantly, the careful provisions of the Gaming Act. At West End Central Police Station, the chief superintendent of the Club Squad authorized an immediate investigation. In Nottingham, the Deputy Chief Constable ordered an inquiry into the alleged breach of the Police National Computer's security. In Fleet Street, to its shame, the story was ignored by every national newspaper.

Curiously, at Playboy there was more amusement than outrage at Ladup's clumsy attempts to steal Playboy gamblers. Gerhauser thought the scheme was ridiculous and exhibited a deep lack of understanding of the psychology of the high roller, who tended to move from table to table, or casino to casino, in his tireless quest for luck and therefore could never be effectively "poached." As far as records were able to show, Playboy did not lose a single gambler to Ladbroke casinos during the clandestine shenanigans of Operation Unit Six.

Lownes, too, at first affected an air of disdainful indifference. He had little love for *Private Eye*, having once sued the magazine for libel; subsequently he was always described in its columns as Victor "Disgusting" Lownes, a hurtful appellation for a man of noted charm and hospitality. He respected, however, the magazine's reputation for investigative reporting and had no doubt that its report about Ladup was essentially accurate. But why should he, Mr. Clean, concern himself if a competitor wished to indulge in questionable activities?

Irritation only began to set in when he became aware that people outside the casino industry assumed Ladbroke's dirty tricks were symptomatic of the way all rival casinos behaved. When he protested that this was not the case, that the industry was highly respectable and tightly controlled, as often as not he received a nudge and a knowing wink and a "tell us another one" smile of disbelief. It was as a result of this treatment, bruising to the ego as well as the ribs, that Victor became fatally enamored of the idea of being seen as the man in the white hat, protecting the good name of the casino industry and reserving for it an image of Fauntleroylike purity.

Thus was the stage set for a bitter, and strangely personal, battle between two rich and powerful men who could hardly have been more different. Lownes loved the limelight quite as much as Cyril Stein hated it. Whereas Lownes was a roistering, girl-chasing, cigar-smoking American, Stein was a quiet family man with no recorded interests outside his business. Then fifty-two years old, he had joined forces with his uncle, a racetrack book-maker who traded under the name of Maxie Parker, in the mid-fifties and built the small family business into a major public company with interests in hotels, catering, property, and betting shops as well as casinos. Over the next couple of years, the two men were to develop a fierce antagonism toward each other.

All through the summer of 1978, *Private Eye* continued printing stories about Ladbroke, elaborating on its dubious practices and its frantic attempts to cover them up. It was said that officers of the Club Squad, investigating the allegations in cooperation with Gaming Board inspectors, were met by a "wall of silence." The police eventually raided Ladbroke's four London casinos and carried away large numbers of files, despite the wholesale shredding of documents.

Toward the end of the year, there were signs that the police and the Gaming Board were planning a blitz on the casino industry. In the early hours of December 8, about two hundred officers from the Serious Crimes Squad, briefed in total secrecy, raided the Victoria Sporting Club, a casino in Knightsbridge. Five directors were arrested on criminal charges of fraud and theft.

Lownes was entirely unconcerned by rumors of an impending crackdown as he believed, with some justification, that the Play-boy casinos were beyond reproach. When representatives of foreign governments visited Britain to study the gaming industry, both the police and the Gaming Board often recommended that they visit the Playboy Club, as a model of how a good casino should be run. Clive Winston, a solicitor who represented the police at gaming license hearings, was on record as saying that the "running of the Playboy casino was characterized by such a high standard of integrity that the police would be reluctant to object to any reasonable proposal envisaged by the Playboy organization."

Occasionally, Victor was called upon to testify before various agencies in the United States investigating the ramifications of state-controlled gambling and he always liked to begin his testimony in the same way: "As the only American operating a casino in the United Kingdom, I believe that I have a unique overview of what is considered to be the most well-conceived and best-regulated casino industry in the world. . . ." Modesty was not one of Victor's more obvious attributes.

On April 5, 1979, the Ladbroke Group issued an angry denial of newspaper reports that the police were planning to object to the renewal of Ladup's gaming licenses. Next day, the police did precisely that, claiming that Ladup was not "fit and proper" to run casinos. A week later, to the amazement of the gaming industry at large, Playboy also lodged a formal objection to the renewal of Ladbroke's licenses.

Lownes consulted no one, not even Gerhauser, about the wisdom of this move. His motive, he said, was to show that the industry was concerned about its own standards. Only a slight adjustment to his white hat was needed for it to accommodate a halo.

An angry Cyril Stein turned up for a meeting of the British Casino Association at the Curzon House Club on May 30. It was very rare for him to attend Association meetings, but this time he had plenty to say. Victor was present, wearing a saintly expression. During the course of a lengthy statement, Stein warned the Association there would be trouble unless Playboy withdrew its objections to the Ladbroke licenses. "The mud is really going to fly," he promised, "and it's not just going to be at Playboy."

While Stein was talking, Victor scribbled a note: "He's trying to use you guys to get me to withdraw my objections," and passed it to his neighbor, who read it and nodded. "Fuck him!" Victor wrote on a second note. The response was another nod.

When Stein pointed out that Ladbroke was the biggest company in the gaming industry, Victor muttered audibly: "At the moment!" and was rewarded with a poisonous glare from Stein. Lownes was obliged to leave the meeting early, claiming pressing business elsewhere, but before he departed, Stein repeated his warning that the mud was going to fly. Victor shrugged, unconcerned. However, a couple of days later he did take the precaution of checking with Gerhauser and other senior executives that there was nothing going on in any of the Playboy casinos that would give Stein ammunition to hit back. He was assured the Playboy operation was "one hundred percent clean."

No one in the gaming business thought that Stein would take Playboy's attack lying down, but Victor was not in the least troubled. "I am *inviting* them to hit back at me," he told *The Financial Times*, "because I know my house is clean."

Stein needed no invitation; he was already bent on revenge and made it known he would be prepared to pay between £5,000 and £10,000 for any information regarding misdemeanors at Playboy casinos. Ladbroke's personnel files were combed to identify employees who had previously worked for Playboy and each of them was interviewed at length. Problems of conscience were assuaged by simply pointing out that if Playboy's objections succeeded, all Ladbroke casino employees would be out of work. Every scrap of information—fact, rumor, or gossip—was filed in a special dossier opened by Michael Surridge, Ladbroke's security chief. Some of it was wild stuff: among general accusations of widespread prostitution and drug-taking was a specific allegation that Lownes had had three Bunnies murdered.

Of more interest to Ladbroke was hard evidence that Playboy had violated the Gaming Act. It was provided by Tom Ambrose, formerly a receptionist at the Playboy Club, and Roy Hodges, who was the gaming administration manager with special responsibility for looking after the high rollers. Both had applied for jobs with Ladbroke after being fired by Playboy and they knew a great deal—so much, in fact, that Ladbroke paid each of them £5,000.

By the time Hodges and Ambrose stopped talking, the dossier contained plenty of information to shoot the Man in the White

Hat. Playboy, it appeared, had offered free membership to the head porters of leading London hotels so that they could take hotel guests into the casino and circumvent the rule that prevented gamblers from gambling until forty-eight hours after becoming a member. Sometimes a hotel porter would show up at the Playboy Club with a group of people, sign them in as his "guests," and then return to the hotel. This was not strictly against the letter of the law, but it certainly contravened the spirit of the forty-eight-hour rule, which was designed to prevent "impulse" gambling.

Another serious accusation was that Playboy frequently accepted "no-account" checks as a means of extending credit to high rollers, a facility forbidden by the Gaming Act to protect gamblers from running up massive debts. When a high roller ran out of money at the Playboy Club or the Clermont, he was apparently allowed more chips by writing a check drawn on Playboy's own bank, Lloyds of Park Lane, which was then held as an I.O.U.

Credit restrictions were very tightly controlled by the Gaming Act, to prevent a return to the "frontier" days when gamblers stayed at the gaming tables until they were ruined and strong-arm tactics were used to recover debts, welding links between the casino industry and the underworld.

The dossier also included some interesting names. Clement Freud, a director of Playboy, was said to have gambled in Playboy casinos—in contravention of the Gaming Act, which debars directors from gaming in their own casinos. Freud was a well-known broadcaster and television personality, with a lugubrious face familiar to the British from a successful series of commercials advertising dog food. An even more unlikely figure frequenting the Playboy Club was a mysterious Lebanese by the name of Abdul Khawaja. A close friend of Lownes, to whom he lost a great deal of money playing backgammon in Lownes's office, Khawaja was said to be a pimp who procured Bunnies for his rich Arab friends. He was banned from a number of other casinos in London for misbehavior, but enjoyed Lownes's protection at the Playboy Club.

Lownes knew nothing of these inquiries or the existence of the dossier. For most of 1979, the Playboy dossier, lodged with other confidential files in the office of Ladbroke's security chief, sat ticking like a time bomb under the pedestal upon which Lownes had placed himself.

That summer, it might have appeared to Victor that he could do no wrong. *Chicago* magazine said he was "perhaps the most valuable man in the Bunny empire." The *Guinness Book of Records* named him as "Britain's Highest Paid Executive," with a salary of £243,700 a year. (It was a debut he shared, to his delight, with a Monsieur Mangetout, said to have eaten a bicycle in fifteen days.) The weather that summer was wretched: one cold, wet gray day followed another until Victor decided to throw a twenty-five-hour party at Stocks to celebrate Playboy's twenty-fifth anniversary. On the morning of the party, the skies miraculously cleared and the sun shone down on the funfair and the marquees and the bands and the roller disco and the hot air balloons assembled for the pleasure of Victor's three thousand guests.

The party started at eleven o'clock on a balmy Saturday night with a firework display and ended at midnight on Sunday with another firework display. There were fireworks, too, from Victor's current girlfriend, Silvana Suarez, the reigning Miss World. She had an argument with Victor shortly before the festivities were due to begin and packed her bags. By the luckiest of coincidences, a Miss Debbie Chenoweth, a charming blonde, was on hand to step in as Victor's date; indeed, it was rumored that her proximity might have had something to do with Miss Suarez's sudden departure. Auberon Waugh, who was among the bevy of journalists invited to the party, noted that Debbie had recently flown in from Los Angeles, "possibly in a box of orchids." To those few journalists sober enough to ask questions at the end of the celebrations, Victor cheerfully confessed the party cost £75,000.

A few days later, the South Westminster Justices—five lay magistrates sitting behind a table appropriately covered in green baize in a meeting room in Central Hall, Westminster—began hearing the case of the police and Playboy *v.* Ladbroke. By an unfortunate administrative oversight, the Gaming Board had neglected to lodge its own objection to the Ladbroke licenses within the time stipulated by the Gaming Act. This meant that Playboy solicitors had to play a far more prominent role in the proceedings, supporting the police in the absence of the Gaming Board, than Lownes would have preferred.

The case went badly for Ladbroke. During the hearing, every

word of Jack Lundin's story in *Private Eye* was read out and the police complained bitterly about the lack of cooperation they had received from Ladup. Ladbroke's counsel mounted a savage attack on Lownes, accusing him of being motivated by the lucrative pickings that would be available from the "carcass" of the company if the licenses were not renewed. The justices were unimpressed and favored the police counsel's view that Ladup's behavior had been totally unacceptable. They ordered the cancellation of the licenses at the Ladbroke Club, the Hertford Club, and the Park Lane Casino, all in Mayfair. After the hearing, Ladbroke shares dropped from 200p to 174p on the Stock Exchange, cutting £15 million from the market value of the company. The three casinos remained open, pending an appeal.

Playboy emerged unscathed from this encounter and smelling sweeter than ever in the twitching nostrils of the Gaming Board. At a meeting in Lownes's office at the Playboy Club, Gerhauser pleaded with Victor to rest on his laurels. "We've registered our objection," he said. "Let's leave it at that. There is no point in continuing." Victor at first agreed, but after a weekend closeted with his cronies at Stocks he changed his mind. He was thoroughly enjoying his new prominence as the "white knight" of British gaming and he announced that Playboy would support the police and the Gaming Board in opposing Ladbroke's appeal. "I suppose," he confessed later, a trifle glumly, "I got carried away with my image as Mr. Clean."

When a message arrived at Playboy from the solicitors acting for Ladbroke inquiring if there was any way Lownes could be persuaded to withdraw his objections, he loftily suggested a donation of £100,000 to a charity of his choice. There was no reply. After this, Victor described his determination to pursue the case as a "matter of honor."

Some of the friends Lownes made in July he lost in August when Playboy bought the Victoria Sporting Club for £6 million. At the time, the Victoria was fighting a losing battle to retain its license after the police raid in December. Lownes believed that the challenge to the Victoria's license would probably be dropped if the casino was taken over by a company with the record and reputation enjoyed by Playboy.

He was wrong. The police and the Gaming Board badly wanted

the Victoria Sporting Club to be closed down. During earlier license hearings, the police gave evidence that the owners of the Victoria were "driving a coach and horses" through the Gaming Act; the raid had uncovered so much evidence of fraud, theft, and illegal gaming that the Gaming Board described it as the worst example of casino crime in Britain.

Lownes was surprised when the objections to the Victoria's license were not dropped after the casino had been acquired by Playboy, but he was not discouraged: he still believed Playboy would win a license when the case came up before the justices.

While Victor was charging here and there in his White Hat, a subtle, though perceptible, change was taking place in the climate in which casinos operated. The police raids, the evident hardening of the new Thatcher government's attitude toward gaming, and rumors of renewed criminal infiltration fueled public disaffection with the whole business. The news that gaming was Britain's fastest growing business, yielding a 432 percent return on capital in the London casinos—far more profitable than oil exploration in the North Sea—did not lead to dancing in the streets.

A debate in Parliament on the findings of the Royal Commission on Gambling was notably hostile. Home Secretary William Whitelaw warned of the continuing involvement of criminal elements and the need for greater powers to exclude "undesirables." Right-wing MP Sir Timothy Kitson called for an eightfold increase in taxation levied on casinos and left-wing MP Robert Mellish described the sums of money squandered on gaming tables as "nauseating, immoral, and disgusting," adding that it would probably benefit the country if every casino was shut.

It appeared, in some quarters, that the Gaming Board was trying to achieve that objective. During the early hours of Friday, November 2, 1979, four hundred uniformed policemen from the Serious Crimes Squad and Special Patrol Group staged simultaneous raids on four Mayfair casinos owned by the Coral Leisure Group—Crockfords in Carlton House Terrace (where, 150 years earlier, the Duke of Wellington headed the membership list), the Curzon House Club, the International Sporting Club, and the Palm Beach Casino. Twenty-six men were arrested on various charges of conspiracy and theft.

Four days later, Ladbroke's appeal against the cancellation of its licenses opened at Knightsbridge Crown Court. The four-week hearing was a disaster for Ladbroke. Damning evidence about the company, its chairman, and its attempts at a Watergate-style cover-up mounted up day after day. Playboy's counsel, Brian Leary, played a leading role in the attack, alleging that Cyril Stein had almost certainly lied at the hearing, that Ladbroke had been party to organized prostitution, and that attempts had been made to seduce information from Playboy employees. Playboy subpoenaed the general secretary of the British Casino Association to repeat Stein's warning that the "mud would fly."

Ladbroke's defense was that everyone involved in illegal activities had left the company or been fired and that the company had been restructured in such a way that the casinos were now operated by a new, entirely blame-free subsidiary. It did not wash with the judge and the four presiding magistrates. The only word to describe the past conduct of Ladbroke casinos, said Judge Gordon Friend, was "disgraceful." The appeal was dismissed, and Ladbroke's three Mayfair casinos were closed immediately.

During the hearing, the clock on Playboy's time bomb advanced substantially. Not long after the case opened, Playboy's counsel stood up and complained to the court, with an air of injured righteousness, that Ladbroke had not produced all the documents relating to their casino activities. In response, John Matthew, counsel for Ladbroke, politely offered the police free run of the ten thousand files in Ladbroke's security office.

Among those files was the dossier on Playboy. One of the first people to read it was Detective Chief Superintendent Brian Sparks of the Club Squad. He thought it was *fascinating*.

There were warnings that trouble was brewing for Playboy, but they were not heeded. While preparations were being made to defend the gaming licenses at the Victoria Sporting Club, Playboy's solicitor, Arnold Finer, asked the secretary of the Gaming Board, William Stephens, if he would write a letter saying that Playboy was running the Victoria well and that the company had "always striven to ensure punctilious observance of the law." Stephens refused.

Later, during a preliminary hearing in the Divisional Court, Richard Du Cann, counsel for Playboy, met Simon Tuckey, counsel for the Gaming Board, in a corridor outside the court and asked Tuckey if he would agree in court that Playboy's record was unblemished. Tuckey replied that Playboy "might not like the answers" he would give. Du Cann urged Lownes to write to the Gaming Board and request a meeting to discover "what was going on." Lownes's first letter was ignored. He wrote again, six weeks later, and this time received a reply that the board was "not disposed" to arrange a meeting.

Around this time, Lord Allen of Abbeydale, who had succeeded Sir Stanley Raymond as chairman of the Gaming Board, received a vicious poison-pen letter accusing Lownes of entertaining his friends by providing them with "samples of Playboy Bunnies." It was common knowledge, the letter alleged, that drug-taking of all forms was rampant at Lownes's weekend parties, and that his "special treat" was group sex. Young girls of eighteen and nineteen were being lured into Playboy, "the best finishing school in the country for prostitution."

In March 1980, Playboy's application for a license at the Victoria Sporting Club was opposed by both the police and the Gaming Board and was turned down because of evidence of "massive criminality" by the previous owners. The Gaming Board wanted to have the premises disqualified to establish the principle that a casino operator who grossly misbehaved would cast a blight on his property that would make it impossible for him to profit by simply selling out to another casino. Playboy immediately lodged notice of appeal.

Three weeks later, a television documentary, "The Casino Wars," investigated the battle between Playboy and Ladbroke and revealed that Ladbroke had paid Hodges and Ambrose for information with which to wreak revenge on Playboy. The most serious accusations against Playboy centered around violations of the forty-eight-hour rule with the "hotel porter scheme." Lownes was interviewed on the program and admitted that such a scheme had been in operation briefly but pointed out that he had stopped it as soon as he had become aware of it.

He did not feel Playboy had come out too badly in the documentary, an opinion confirmed by the fact that both the Playboy Club and the Clermont were relicensed without difficulty the following month.

Ladbroke, on the other hand, received a mauling in "The Casino Wars" and in May, Cyril Stein announced that the Ladbroke Group was pulling out of the casino business altogether. The Gaming Board was poised to lodge objections to the renewal of its eleven provincial casino licenses and an appeal to the High Court to overturn the Crown Court ruling had failed. Its only remaining London casino, the Park Tower, closed its doors for the last time and all the provincial casinos were put up for sale. Ironically, only a few weeks before, Stein had announced record profits for the group—£49 million, half of which was contributed by gaming.

Lownes disdained to crow over Ladbroke's capitulation in the Casino Wars, not out of a sense of munificence but more because he was preoccupied with the struggle to regain a license for the Victoria Sporting Club, on which he had staked Playboy's reputation. The appeal came up before Knightsbridge Crown Court in October, and Playboy introduced considerable evidence to prove that since acquiring the Victoria Sporting Club it had been operated in an exemplary manner.

Gavin Lightman, counsel for Playboy, attacked the philosophy of disqualifying premises for gaming, arguing that previous misdemeanors could not have arisen from the "degeneracy of the establishment itself, as an incurable cancer that could not be excised." Playboy, he said, as "unblemished operators" would cleanse the casino of all its ills.

It was an argument that carried the day: Playboy's appeal was allowed. Lownes composed an exultant telegram for his friend Hef, sitting in Los Angeles far from the cut and thrust of the Casino Wars. It was clearly designed to occupy a prominent position in the company history: VICTORIA VICTORIOUS, VISION VINDICATED, VALUE VERIFIED, VERILY VICTOR.

In a magnanimous message to the staff, Victor pointed out that the Victoria triumph was doubly sweet, for not only had the court underscored Playboy's reputation for the "highest standards of integrity," more important, the livelihood of casino employees need not be put at risk by the "greed and dishonesty of a few men at the top."

Gavin Lightman joined Victor for a celebration dinner after the hearing and cast a faint shadow over the proceedings by warning Victor that the police and the Gaming Board would be gunning for him. Lightman was acutely aware that the authorities wanted the Victoria closed down and that the Crown Court ruling had angered the Gaming Board. "You must make sure," he told Victor, "that your own house is in order." Victor smiled confidently and said there was "no problem."

With the licensing of the Victoria, Playboy became the biggest gaming operator in Britain, with three London casinos, two fully owned provincial casinos, two partly owned, seventy-two off-track betting shops, and six bingo parlors, these last acquired with the Victoria purchase.

For a time, Lownes was content to rest on his substantial laurels. He knew that the police and the Gaming Board were investigating Playboy, but then they were always investigating casinos. It was a carefree Victor who returned to his favorite pursuits of parties, girls, backgammon, Pacman, and hunting.

On Thursday, February 5, 1981, Victor was out with the Bicester Hunt on his bay gelding, Prairie. It was a clear, crisp, cold afternoon and the chase was hectic. Victor was about to change mounts to give Prairie a rest when he suddenly felt the horse slipping sideways on an icy patch in the road. He hurled himself in the opposite direction to avoid being crushed under the horse, and woke up in a hospital three days later with a fractured skull.

Among the many get-well cards he received was one from Hef. It showed a horse sitting up in bed with a thermometer in its mouth and the caption: "Once upon a time there was a horse that had what you have . . ." Inside it said: "They shot him! So hurry up and get well." Hef had scrawled underneath: "And stay away from those crazy horses—love, Hef." Victor asked his secretary to have the card framed so he could hang it on the wall at Stocks.

While he was still recuperating in the hospital, the police raided Playboy. On February 20, officers from the Club Squad assisted by Gaming Board inspectors, armed with search warrants, staged simultaneous raids on the Playboy Club, the Clermont, and Playboy's administrative offices in north London. Staff were interrogated and a large number of files were confiscated.

Victor was astounded when he heard about it. Was he not the *white knight* of gaming? He could only assume that the raids were nothing more than a token gesture by the police to show that all

casino operators were being equally treated and that Playboy was
not getting any preferential treatment, despite its untainted reputation.

A few weeks later, the Ladbroke time bomb exploded. The
police and the Gaming Board announced they intended to object
to the renewal of all Playboy's gaming licenses.

15

You've Just Blown
the Licenses

In the executive suites of the Playboy Building in Chicago, the news that the police had raided the Playboy casinos in London was greeted with shock and dismay. No one needed Victor Lownes to tell them (although he did so, constantly) that the casinos were propping up the company and the sybaritic lifestyles of its employees. In fiscal 1980, gaming contributed $31 million to the corporate profits of $32 million.

A glance at the balance sheet showed just how bad things would be if the raid led to the casinos being closed. Playboy made $14.7 million from magazine publishing and another $2.7 million from other businesses. But the clubs and hotels lost $5 million and corporate overhead, which had almost doubled in five years, was eating up an astonishing $18.5 million. Without the profits from gaming, Playboy Enterprises, Inc., was a hollow shell, a corporation without substance.

Until Arnold Finer telephoned Chicago to break the news of the raid, no one had been aware of any problems in London, although the casino wars, which had been widely reported in American newspapers, had provoked some unease. Most of the directors believed Lownes made a mistake in challenging Ladbroke and openly inviting trouble, certainly they believed they should have been consulted before Playboy jumped in. But then Lownes did not like to consult anyone about anything. As Hef often said: "That's part of the mixed bag you get with Vic."

There was further irritation when Victor did not bother to inform Chicago about his appearance on "The Casino Wars" television documentary. On April 25, 1980, Daniels sent a peevish memo to Huston, saying that he had only learned of the existence of the program from the Elsinore Corporation. "It is a bit appalling," he noted, "that we had to hear about this for the first time through our partners. . . . As a corporation and as a management team, we have far too much at stake to permit this sort of thing to continue."

The most favored rumor in the Playboy Building at that time was that Daniels was waiting for the outcome of the Victoria case before making a move against Victor. Lownes had bragged that Playboy's purchase of the Victoria Sporting Club would persuade the police and the Gaming Board to drop their objections to its license. He was wrong. He then said the licensing justices would approve Playboy's application for a license at the Victoria. He was wrong again. If the Crown Court turned down Playboy's appeal, Lownes would have effectively gambled £6 million of corporate funds—and lost.

But not only did the Crown Court allow Playboy's appeal, they did it with a great deal of trumpeting about the excellence of Playboy's reputation and management. How could Daniels shove Victor off his pedestal after that? As Christie said, the outcome of the Victoria case was "great for our company's image."

Gerhauser was gloomily convinced that Daniels and his cohorts were plotting to take over the London operation, a foreboding confirmed by a curious incident at the end of the Victoria hearing. Gerry Goldberg and Jim Radtke, from Playboy's internal audit department, had been sent over from Chicago to sit in at the hearings as observers. When judgment was announced in Playboy's favor, both looked strangely downcast. "Cheer up, fellas," Lownes quipped breezily as he left the court, "we did *win*, you know."

The delighted Victor could not understand why they looked so miserable. Gerhauser knew. "They're looking for any opportunity to get rid of us," he warned. "They're unhappy because they thought we'd lose and that would have been an opportunity to get us out." Victor didn't believe it.

Gerhauser had begun to fret about a conspiracy when Daniels indicated that he wanted to exert some supervision over the U.K. operation. The trust deed, which laid down that control of the casinos must remain in the hands of U.K. resident directors, had allowed Lownes and Gerhauser to run their business as a fiefdom far beyond the reach of corporate headquarters. But management in Chicago was increasingly unhappy that the bulk of Playboy's profits was being contributed by a foreign subsidiary about which they knew very little and over which they apparently had no control. Daniels actually discussed with Hefner, perhaps somewhat hopefully, what might happen if Lownes was "run over by a truck."

To strengthen legal and financial controls and to improve the information flow between Playboy (U.K.) and the parent company, Huston suggested hiring an inside counsel based in London who would report directly to Chicago. In addition, he proposed replacing the separate outside auditors of the U.K. operation with Price, Waterhouse, who already handled the outside audit for Playboy.

Lownes grudgingly agreed to these proposals, although Gerhauser, by then suffering the "mushroom treatment," viewed them with the gravest suspicion. Not long afterward, Gerhauser acquired handwritten notes of a meeting held at the Playboy Building, during which a reorganization of the company was discussed— and neither he nor Lownes was included in the new structure. Then one of the accountants working for Playboy in London returned from a business trip to Chicago and told him: "Gee, Bill, I had no idea those guys over there hated you so much."

Victor dismissed his deputy's fears with the assertion that although the "yo-yos" in Chicago were unquestionably stupid, none of them could be stupid enough to contemplate getting rid of the two men who were keeping the company afloat. But then the police raided Playboy's casinos.

By February 20, 1981, the Division of Gaming Enforcement in New Jersey was winding up its investigation into Playboy's "suitability" to be granted a casino license in Atlantic City and a report was ready to be filed indicating there were no objections to Playboy-Elsinore's application. But when Michael Brown, the director of the division, read the newspapers on the morning of February 21, he immediately issued instructions to hold up the report while he made contact with London to find out what was going on.

Daniels, Huston, and DiPrima were similarly occupied, once they had recovered from the shock. Over an echoing transatlantic telephone line, both Lownes and Gerhauser told them there was nothing to worry about: the raid was politically motivated, probably because a couple of cops in the Club Squad had a "hard-on" for Playboy, and even if infringements of the Gaming Act were uncovered they would only be of a minor, technical nature, certainly nothing serious enough to threaten Playboy's licenses.

The Chicago troika were slightly reassured, but not for long. David Swede, the counsel they had hired to oversee the London operation and report directly to Chicago, seemed to display a lot less confidence. After the raid, Swede was in frequent contact with lawyers acting for the police and the Gaming Board and what he was hearing was not good. He was told that the files removed from the Playboy Club indicated that there might have been breaches of Section 16 of the Gaming Act—a section dealing with restrictions on extending credit for gaming. Violations of Section 16 would be deemed particularly serious, Swede explained, because the Gaming Board considered control of credit was fundamental to the control of gaming as it protected gamblers against themselves. "We were increasingly worried," said Huston, "by the conflicting reports. Swede was telling us what documents and records were being held by police and said he was more and more concerned about the seriousness of the situation while Victor and Bill were telling us there was nothing to worry about."

In his office in Trenton, Brown was discovering, to his considerable frustration, that British officials intensely disliked talking on the telephone, particularly long distance. He came to the conclusion that he would have to go to London if he wanted to get any information, and he left on March 22, having arranged appointments with the Club Squad, the police solicitor, and Lord Allen, Chairman of the Gaming Board.

Two days later, Hefner chaired a crisis board meeting at Playboy Mansion West. Lownes, still nursing a sore head from his hunting accident, flew to Los Angeles to report on the situation in London. Although it was clear to those present that he had not completely recovered from the accident—he slurred his words and kept repeating himself—he was even more bombastic than usual, airily dismissing the fears of his fellow directors. He was completely unaware of any wrongdoing, he said, and thoroughly confident that the impeccable character of the company would be upheld.

The raid was all to do with "internal politics" in the police department, he declared, cracking a joke about the two officers involved being named Marks and Sparks. One of the reasons why so many files had been taken away, he added with a smirk, was that some policemen wanted to get the home telephone numbers of the Bunnies. "Mr. Lownes summarized," the minutes noted, "by stating that he felt strongly no threat existed to the continued operation of the Company's British casinos."

Victor had plenty to say about other items on the agenda, too—one of them was a proposal to buy a $300,000 armor-plated limousine for Hefner. (After the shooting of John Lennon, Hefner's name had appeared high on a psychologist's survey of other likely targets of psychopaths.) Lownes thought it was a ridiculous idea, not least because Hefner hardly ever left the grounds of the Mansion. Perhaps, he sneered, as corporate overhead had been maintained at *only* $18.5 million, his colleagues felt free to spend shareholders' money at will? The purchase was agreed, with only Lownes dissenting and loudly wondering why he wasted his time traveling six thousand miles just to oppose decisions everyone else "nodded through."

After the meeting, Victor wandered off to the Games House, while Hefner, Daniels, Huston, and DiPrima, with much nudging and winking, secretly gathered upstairs to discuss Victor's analysis of events. All of them admitted to varying degrees of unease. Hefner and Huston both believed it was probably true the raid had been politically motivated, possibly because Playboy had exposed police corruption during the casino wars, but Huston felt that Victor had played down its significance and had not answered their questions very convincingly. Daniels tartly considered Lownes's explanation to be "frivolous." They decided that DiPrima should go to London as soon as possible, without informing Lownes, to conduct his own investigation.

DiPrima returned to Chicago to make arrangements for the trip but, before he could pack his bags, he was summoned to New Jersey for a meeting at the Division of Gaming Enforcement with Director Brown, who had just come back from London. Accompanied by Playboy's New Jersey counsel, Marilu Marshall, DiPrima met Brown in Trenton on Friday, March 27. Brown obliquely confirmed that the trouble in London was serious and announced that as a precondition of Playboy-Elsinore receiving a temporary casino license, Lownes, Gerhauser, and two other executives of the Playboy Club of London would be required to formally disassociate themselves from the Atlantic City project. Up until this moment, there had been no hint of any problems with the New Jersey gaming license.

When this development was relayed to Hefner and Daniels, there was no longer any doubt that Playboy was up to its Bunny ears in trouble. "That was the turning point," said Hefner. "When we discovered the New Jersey investigators had been to London and seen evidence we did not have and demanded that Victor step aside, it indicated to me that things were much more serious than I had thought."

DiPrima was able to negotiate formal "step-aside" agreements with the Division of Gaming Enforcement and, on April 3, Playboy-Elsinore Associates were granted a temporary casino license on condition that the agreements were promptly signed by the parties involved. Lownes and Gerhauser were in Nassau, in the Bahamas, where Playboy was having a few problems with a small casino it operated in the Ambassador Beach Hotel, the most significant of which was that the casino was losing money. DiPrima, accompanied by Huston, caught a flight to Nassau, intending to meet Lownes and Gerhauser and get their signatures on the "step-aside" agreements.

The meeting was long, and sometimes acrimonious, but in the end both Lownes and Gerhauser signed. After dinner, Lownes went to bed and Gerhauser stayed up chatting with Huston and DiPrima. They fell to talking about the casino wars and Gerhauser expressed the view that the trouble all began when Victor became involved in a personal struggle with Cyril Stein. "He who lives by the sword," said DiPrima in a strangely conspiratorial tone, "shall die by the sword."

Next day, Huston returned to Chicago and Lownes and Gerhauser both caught a flight to Florida, Lownes to visit his mother, and Gerhauser to join his family for a holiday. DiPrima announced, to the undisguised surprise of Lownes and Gerhauser, that he had decided to go to London "for an update." When Lownes got back to London a couple of days later, he discovered that DiPrima had virtually disappeared. It was known he was in town, but no one at Playboy knew where he was. Lownes made a joke of it and began referring to the missing lawyer as "DeSchema."

In fact DiPrima was closeted with David Swede in a suite at the Hilton, carefully sifting through what was then known about the Playboy investigation. On April 9, he telephoned Huston in Chicago to tell him the picture looked bleak.

Not bleak enough, of course, to mar the celebrations that evening at Playboy Mansion West, for April 9, 1981, was a very important date—Hef's fifty-fifth birthday. Gathered in a huge marquee on the back lawn were his closest friends—all the fading football stars and failed movie producers and fawning bootlickers who so regularly enjoyed the Mansion's legendary hospitality—and a sprinkling of celebrities like Lance Rentzel and Dick Van Patten. In their open shirts and designer jeans and gold bracelets and expensive toupees, who would have guessed that almost every man present was old enough to have fathered every girl present? And what girls they were—Playmate clones, California blondes with huge, wobbling breasts, tiny waists, and tight little bottoms, just how Hef liked 'em, flashing their white teeth in the lights of the television cameras on hand to record the occasion for posterity.

The highlight of the evening was a special show laid on by some of the gang and announced as: "The Fifty-fifth Annual Calamity Awards, an event that will live in the anus of show business." Hef sat in the front row, clutching his pipe and Playmate Sondra Theodore, his mistress of the moment, as his friend Lee Wolfberg stepped up onto the rostrum and introduced "an actor and a young lady with a French name who some people say was responsible for the *erection* (loud groans from the audience) of the Eiffel Tower—Miss Monique St. Pierre and Jimmy Caan!"

Miss St. Pierre was a Playmate with a décolletage quite as unlikely as her name, but Caan concentrated on the job in hand and, in the manner of the Oscar awards, proclaimed the first category of the evening was for "outstanding achievement in producing box office disasters." "Oddly enough," he added with a grin, "all the nominees bear the proud banner of our fearless leader, Mr. Hugh Hefner." He then read out a list of all the Playboy-financed movies: *The Fiendish Plot of Dr. Fu Manchu*, "Now this was the last picture that Peter Sellers ever made. Some say he died of shame"; *And Now for Something Completely Different*, "the story of Hef's first attempt at copulation with a woman over twenty-one."

Macbeth was declared to be the winner, and Caan's ten-year-old daughter, a pretty little girl with bouncing blonde curls, stepped up to accept the award on behalf of Roman Polanski. "My husband couldn't make it tonight," she lisped into the microphone, "but thank you." The audience went wild.

Next Wolfberg introduced "someone close to Hef's heart—and other vital organs! She's a lady we all loved—till Hef found out—but we are all still crazy about. Sondra Theodore!" Sondra was a ravishing twenty-two-year-old blonde whose residency at the Playboy Mansion was soon to be terminated.

She, of course, was not to know this and played her part like a real trouper. "Thanks, Lee. How can you say everyone loved me? *You* never did [hoots from the crowd]. The next category is for the best picture made by a producer who doesn't own a magazine. The first is *Key Largo*. I remember Hef showed me this one about a week after I was here at the Mansion. I really loved it. It was the first chance I got to sit up [more immoderate laughter]. The next film is *Citizen Kane*—is this the one where you pulled out the Cool Whip? Wrong picture! Sorry! Next is *Lawrence of Arabia*. I always liked this one. You know when Lawrence yells 'Charge'? So does Hef! The last time, he missed the bed and pole-vaulted right over my oasis. Memories. . . . The fourth nominee is *It's a Wonderful Life*. Hef told me it was a biography of Barbi Benton! The night he showed it to me he said the greatest experience in life is having sex with the one you love. And to prove it, he continued to play with himself and *I* watched the film."

Harry Reems accepted the award on behalf of the "winner," Orson Welles, saying: "After all, he's one of the biggest guys in his field, too, right?" He left the stage to the orchestral accompaniment of "You're the Cream in my Coffee."

Yes, it certainly was a wonderful party. Next afternoon, when Hef woke up, he was told there was further news from London: the police and the Gaming Board had lodged objections to the renewal of the licenses at the Playboy Club and the Clermont, citing numerous violations of the Gaming Act to show that Playboy was not "fit and proper" to run casinos.

If there was any comfort to be derived from this development, it was that objecting to the renewal of gaming licenses was the least serious course of action open to the authorities in Britain; after raids on other casinos, they had applied for cancellation of the licenses or even "disqualification" of the premises. But there was a long list of objections, some of them damaging. The grounds were varied:

That between 1975 and 1979 a credit scheme was operated by which at least 30 heavy gamblers were permitted with the full knowledge of the casino to draw checks "on a massive scale" on banks where the patron had no account, ultimately leaving the casino with a credit debt;

That bets were allowed to be "called," that is, placed without any money having been staked;

That patrons were permitted to continue gambling although they already owed the casino considerable unpaid debts;

That debts were unlawfully discounted and settled;

That porters at six London hotels were made honorary members of the Club for the purposes of introducing guests to game therein;

That a director of the Club took part in gaming on the premises;

That the Club had withheld information requested by the Gaming Board;

That the Club had failed to bar or control the activities of a member, Abdul Khawaja.

When Lownes had read through the list, he was not overly concerned, except about the allegations of "no-account checks" and the settlements, of which he knew nothing. All the other police raids on casinos had led to criminal charges; in Playboy's case there was not a hint of dishonesty or criminal misdemeanors. He was surprised that accepting checks from gamblers who already owed money had been included as an objection, as it was common practice in London casinos—it was known in the business as "check on check"—and one that he had discussed with the Gaming Board to ask for a ruling on its legality. Lord Allen had admitted it was a "gray area." As to all the other points raised, he either considered them unimportant, or felt able to answer them satisfactorily.

His confidence was not, in truth, widely shared, and in particular it was not shared by the man who was to occupy center stage that busy weekend—Gavin Lightman, the barrister who had won the Victoria case for Playboy. Lightman was the very last man anyone would have expected to get involved in the faintly picaresque world of Playboy. Carefully spoken and an eminently respectable barrister with chambers in Lincoln's Inn, he wore thick horn-rimmed spectacles and had a fuzz of unruly black hair, most of which had deserted the top of his head. After the Victoria case, Lownes hailed Lightman as Britain's foremost legal expert on gaming law, although in fact the Victoria case had been his first gaming brief.

Before the Nassau meeting, Lightman advised both Lownes and Gerhauser that in his view they should not "lose any sleep" over the police investigation: any objections to the renewal of Playboy's licenses would probably revolve around technical breaches of Section 16, which he did not think would pose any problems. But that was before the objections had actually been lodged. By the time DiPrima made contact with him on Saturday, April 11, to ask his advice about what to do, Lightman had had a fundamental change of heart. He told DiPrima that he believed Lownes and Gerhauser had lost the confidence of the British gaming authorities and the only chance Playboy had of retaining its licenses was to replace the management immediately.

Although Lightman was fond of Victor, he felt he had no

alternative but to advise his dismissal. He viewed some of the objections—particularly the acceptance of "no-account checks"—as serious breaches of the Gaming Act and was worried that further misdemeanors might come to light. Whether or not Victor knew what was going on was immaterial, he said. If he knew, he should be sacked for allowing it to happen. If he did not know, he should be sacked for incompetence. Finally, Lightman said that Victor's flamboyant lifestyle—the parties at Stocks, the Bunny croupières resident there, Victor's enthusiasm for playing backgammon at the Playboy Club for large stakes—had created a moral atmosphere that made him an unsuitable steward of the company's activities. He warned DiPrima that the police might start making allegations about Bunnies being involved in prostitution.

Lightman was to preach to the converted for the entire weekend; none of Playboy's senior executives needed much convincing that it would be a good idea to sack Victor Lownes. DiPrima asked him if he would repeat his advice later that evening on a "conference call" to the United States. Lightman agreed, if he could take the call from the weekend cottage in Oxfordshire. DiPrima told him to stand by for "a call from Marvin Huston." The English barrister did not bother to inquire why the call should come from Huston, forbearing to become involved in the unfathomable ways of Playboy.

At eleven o'clock on the evening of April 11, the participants who were to seal Lownes's fate were linked by transatlantic telephone lines. Lightman was in Oxfordshire; DiPrima and David Swede were in London; Huston and Daniels were in Chicago; Hefner, Christie, and Don Parker, a Hefner aide, were listening in on separate telephones at Playboy Mansion West. Significantly, no one thought to ask Victor Lownes to take part in the discussion.

When it was established that everyone could hear everyone else, Lightman put his case. In his view, he said, the objections were far more wide-ranging and potentially serious than originally anticipated and there was an urgent need for the company to "clean its house." His advice was, first, to sack Lownes and Gerhauser. Second, set up an independent board of inquiry to look into the operation of Playboy casinos in Britain and rectify procedures where they did not absolutely comply with the letter of the law.

Third, put responsible interim management in place. Fourth, appoint a new board, new trustees, and new management, all of whom must meet criteria laid down by the Gaming Board.

The conference continued long past midnight. Lightman was asked about the trust's restrictions on foreign control. Who could immediately replace Lownes? The trust, he said, was a nonsense, a device without teeth. Better put in Americans, than do nothing. The risks entailed in leaving Lownes and Gerhauser in charge were heavier than risks relating to foreign control prohibitions.

Hefner asked if there was a way other than sacking his friend. Perhaps a suspension? Lightman again went over the reasons why he thought Lownes must go and added that as a result of the casino wars it could well be that Lownes, not the company at all, was the "target" of the police raid. By removing the likely target, they would reduce the risk of nonrenewal.

By the time the conference call ended in the early hours of the morning, Lightman believed his advice would be followed. There were further long transatlantic calls during the course of Sunday, and by the evening Hefner had given his assent to his friend's dismissal. Neither Hefner nor Daniels consulted Lownes to ask him if he had satisfactory answers to the police objections; neither even considered it necessary to seek a second opinion. "I had started to think anyway," said Hefner, "that Victor had become uncontrollable and was beginning to believe his own press clippings. While I never questioned his honesty, I certainly questioned his judgment."

On Monday, Daniels and Huston prepared to fly to London to carry out the sackings and DiPrima surfaced long enough to ask Lownes to be available for a meeting to "discuss strategy" at four o'clock on Wednesday afternoon. While he was talking to DiPrima, Lownes admitted he knew nothing of the "no-account checks" or of any debts being settled and, in DiPrima's presence, he telephoned Gerhauser in Florida to ask if it was true. Gerhauser said it was nonsense that "no-account checks" had been accepted "on a massive scale," as the police were alleging. Only a handful of gamblers were involved, mainly wealthy Arabs who used "no-account checks" to continue gambling and later redeemed them with valid checks, often drawn on a foreign bank. Gerhauser admitted he had made four or five settlements but said he did not think it was illegal because the remaining unpaid debt had not been released. Lownes was angry that he had not been told of this earlier, but he was still convinced, as he told DiPrima, that the licenses were safe.

On Tuesday, the plush Playboy Hotel and Casino in Atlantic City, with its 1,300 slot machines, huge casino, and cozy cabaret lounge seating 1,000 guests, opened for business on its temporary license. In London, Huston and Daniels met Lightman to review the dismissal decision "in the light of any new information." They asked Lightman if the Gaming Board should be consulted, but he advised against it, saying Playboy Enterprises had "no standing" to approach the Board, and expressing concern that the Board might "tip off" Lownes. There was no knowing what Victor might do, Lightman warned, if he had advance warning of his impending dismissal.

On Wednesday, Victor turned up for the "strategy meeting" at the offices of Clifford Turner, a firm of solicitors in London. He found quite a gathering of people around the long polished table in Clifford Turner's fifth-floor conference room. Daniels was there, in a natty white suit, along with DiPrima, Huston, Lightman, and various other executives. The meeting opened with a great deal of nervous fidgeting and some rambling discussion of the nature of the objections to Playboy's licenses. Daniels said he appreciated Victor's agreeing to step aside from the Atlantic City project but asked him if he would be kind enough not to attend the opening party. The press would be paying him too much attention, he said, and that would "annoy Hef." This was familiar territory to Lownes, and he pointed out that if he did not show up it would be assumed that he had something to be ashamed of, which he did not.

After a while, Daniels came to the point. "As a matter of fact, Victor," he said, "the feeling is that these objections the police have put in against your clubs are going to cause us a lot of unwanted trouble. We know Bill Gerhauser has been handling all that side for you and we think he should resign."

Victor was astonished and protested that Gerhauser had done no wrong and that he had complete confidence in him. Daniels interrupted. "As a matter of fact, Victor," he drawled, "the feeling is that you should step out."

Lownes could not believe his ears. "You've got to be joking!" he snapped. "You really want me and Bill to step out. Who's going to run the gaming—*you*? You must have started believing in your own press notices. Does Hefner know about this?"

Daniels nodded, pointed to a telephone on the sideboard and said: "Call him."

"I'm not going to call that pinball wizard," Victor blustered. "You obviously brainwashed him before you came out here, didn't you?"

Daniels did not answer, but pushed a sheet of paper in front of Lownes and told him it was his resignation; he had half an hour to sign it. "You've got to be kidding," Lownes shouted. "You're firing me. And I want the public to know you're firing me. Take your paper away and don't get your nose so close to my left fist— I'm left-handed."

Lightman, blinking behind his horn-rimmed glasses, thought for a moment that Lownes was going to take a swing at Daniels, but Daniels stalked out of the room without another word. A previously prepared press release was immediately issued, announcing that Mr. Marvin Huston would be replacing Mr. Lownes as chairman of Playboy (U.K.) and Mr. Frank DiPrima would be taking over from Mr. Gerhauser as managing director.

By the time Victor, looking very disheveled, arrived back at the Playboy Club, a crowd of photographers and reporters was waiting for him. "They're acting like idiots," was all he could manage to say. Up in his penthouse, he tried to put a call through to Hefner, but was brusquely informed that "Mr. Hefner is off the property." Later in the evening, Victor and his girlfriend, Debbie Chenoweth, went over to the Clermont Club, where he knew he would find Huston and DiPrima. His intention was to discuss the terms of his departure, but he lost his temper after a few minutes and stormed out, bellowing: "You're a load of assholes."

"Who could blame me?" he plaintively inquired later. "That morning I was the Bunny King of Britain, one of the highest paid executives in Britain. I had a fleet of Rolls-Royces to take me wherever I wanted to go. I had the use of a penthouse in Park Lane and over a half a million dollars coming in. That night, when

I took a sleeping pill and went to bed, I was just another one of Britain's growing army of unemployed."

Gerhauser was playing golf in Florida when he got the news. His wife came out to him in a golf buggy and said: "Your secretary telephoned. You and Victor just got fired." Gerhauser did not care—by then he was sick to death of Playboy.

That night, Daniels telephoned to say how sorry he was it had happened. "It's the worst decision you have ever made, Derick," Gerhauser said. "You've just blown the gaming licenses."

16

Rien ne va plus

Lord Allen of Abbeydale, chairman of the Gaming Board, first learned that Victor Lownes had been sacked when he switched on the television to watch the evening news. He was, in his upper-crust way, somewhat "ruffled" that he had not been consulted. But he was furious when he later discovered that Lightman had advised against notifying the board for fear that he would "blab."

As a peer of the realm, a former undersecretary of state at the Home Office, and a member of Britain's Security Commission, Lord Allen did not take kindly to the imputation that he could not be trusted with a confidence. Neither did he look kindly on the biggest gaming operation in Britain being secretly taken over by Americans with no experience or knowledge of British gaming laws. Playboy had entered into a trust deed arrangement with the Gaming Board designed specifically to *prevent* this eventuality. The company had not only breached the trust but had also con-travened the 1968 Gaming Act, which required applicants for gaming licenses to be resident in Britain.

Ever since the police raid, Lord Allen had imagined that Hugh Hefner would get in touch with him to discuss the best way of resolving Playboy's difficulties. Like many similar watchdog agencies under the umbrella of the British government, the Gaming Board was structured to allow informal consultation with casino operators, to offer advice and thrash out regulatory problems. It did not seem unreasonable to Lord Allen to expect a call from the head of Playboy when Playboy casinos ran into trouble. How was he to know that he stood a better chance of a visit from the man on the moon? Hefner was firmly resident in Los Angeles and about to fall in love again (with Miss November 1981, one Shannon Tweed), a distraction he found infinitely more beguiling than the prospect of tangling with complex British gaming laws.

After Lownes's dismissal, Allen summoned Daniels, DiPrima, and Huston to a meeting at the Gaming Board on April 27. The atmosphere was not exactly cordial. The Americans sat meekly side by side on a sofa in the conference room, while Allen, normally a soft-spoken and mild-mannered individual, angrily read the riot act and announced that they were "unacceptable" as operators of a British casino.

Shamefaced and eager to apologize, they explained that they were acting on advice that they had "no standing" to make contact with the board. In any case, they emphasized, their tenure was strictly temporary; as soon as an acceptable candidate was found to take over as chairman of Playboy (U.K.), they would step aside. Allen remained patently displeased. It was clear, he said, that board meetings in London simply "rubber-stamped" decisions made in Chicago and that effective control of the company would in the future be "vested in Chicago." The visitors left the Gaming Board much chastened.

Allen privately believed that Playboy would have the greatest difficulty finding a man of sufficient reputation and experience to assume control of its casinos, but in any case so far as he was concerned, the damage was already done. On the first occasion the trust deed had been put to the test, it had proved worthless as a guarantee that control of Playboy's casinos would remain in the hands of U.K. residents approved by the Gaming Board.

Not long after Daniels, DiPrima, and Huston had signally failed to impress, the Gaming Board lodged three further objections to the renewal of Playboy's licenses, charging that the applicant was effectively controlled by its United States parent company, contrary to the spirit and intent of the Gaming Act; that control had been acquired in breach of the trust deed; and that Daniels, Huston, and DiPrima were not British residents and were without knowledge or experience of British gaming, contrary to the spirit and intent of the Gaming Act.

Gavin Lightman had not warned Playboy that installing Huston and DiPrima in London, even temporarily, might lead to further objections to Playboy licenses, because he had not anticipated this eventuality. Lightman believed the issue of foreign control was a "red herring."

But in the gaming business, the view was rather different. The issue of foreign control raised all the old fears about allowing the Mafia to muscle in, bullet holes in doors, bodies in cement overcoats, crooked games, and loaded dice. When the Gaming Board objected to the Playboy casinos in London being controlled from Chicago, of all places, there were many who believed that Playboy had been delivered the coup de grace.

A wide variety of aberrant behaviors were often ascribed to Victor Lownes, but no one had ever accused him of dabbling in black magic. It was just as well, because it rather appeared as if someone had put a curse on the company after Lownes's dismissal: simply nothing went right for Playboy after April 15, 1981.

Early in May, Huston and DiPrima set up the Board of Inquiry that Lightman had recommended was necessary to "clean house." A leading Queen's Counsel and a senior accountant were appointed to the board and instructed to conduct a searching investigation into the management of Playboy casinos. They were to "pull no punches" and "let the chips fall where they may." Thirteen weeks later, the board produced an extraordinary final report that contrived to further blacken Playboy's reputation.

Lownes's regime, said the report, "would not be ill-described as Byzantine. Top management was self-indulgent and complacent. There were cliques. There was favoritism. There were spies. There was corruption. There was even nepotism."

According to the report, any casino that managed to keep its doors open in London during the seventies would have made money because of the influx of Arabs into the capital; Playboy's profits were "inevitable" and could have been even higher had the management been better.

Lownes's management was characterized by his "habit of screaming at people" and Gerhauser, probably undone by Lownes's despotic style, also screamed. Sometimes Lownes and Gerhauser screamed at each other, although most of the time, the report claimed, they did not communicate at all.

Many of the witnesses interviewed by the Board of Inquiry were happy to twist the knife in Lownes's back. He was "vicious," "frightening," "difficult to cope with," and "only interested in publicity." Everyone knew that Playboy paid the bulk of the expenses at Stocks and that the guests Lownes entertained every weekend were friends, not clients. One witness said that every Friday night, cars would be loaded with food and drink from the Playboy Club to be delivered to Stocks.

Business meetings were not properly recorded and would often take place while Lownes was holding court in the office with his show business friends. Meetings of the trustees were irregular, called at a few hours' notice, and usually conducted in Lownes's office with the television on and telephones ringing incessantly.

As for Gerhauser, he was lazy, bored, abusive, stridently rude, a very bad judge of people, and more interested in horse racing than business—"appointments at the casino for management business would be cancelled because of Goodwood or Ascot."

Also contained in the Board of Inquiry's report was some fascinating detail about the gambling habits and adventures of Playboy's most profligate clientele, almost all of whom came from the Middle East. There was Prince Fahad Bin Sultan Aziz, a member of the Saudi royal family and just twenty-one years old, who lost £200,000 in a single evening at the Clermont. There was a Mr. Beh-Behani, an Arab merchant who had put his name to checks worth more than £18 million at the Playboy Club. There was a Mr. Essa Khalifa, who was said to have had a "notorious relationship with a Bunny." There was Sheikh Al Thani, who appears to have displayed a lot more ingenuity than many of his countrymen—having run up a huge debt with "no-account checks," he somehow tricked the casino staff into letting him look at them, and promptly tore the lot up.

Finally, there was Abdul Khawaja, Victor's friend and backgammon partner, who was described as a pest, a pimp, a degenerate, and a buffoon. Mr. Khawaja apparently led his Arab friends to believe that he could fix them up with the Bunnies of their choice and regularly disturbed the gaming by picking up other gamblers' chips, trying to kiss the Bunnies, and screaming complaints about the fall of the cards.

Gerhauser knew them all, of course. Many of them had sat in his office, weeping and bewailing their misfortunes. Mr. Beh-Behani begged not to be allowed to write any more checks, lest he bring ruin on his family. A Mr. Halwadi pleaded to be released from his debts, sobbing that he would otherwise have to return to Iran, where his life under the Ayatollahs would be worthless. On very rare occasions, when he felt that genuine hardship was involved, Gerhauser accepted settlement of a debt for less than the full amount. "I never interpreted the Gaming Act," he said, "as requiring us to recover every last penny and perhaps break a gambler. Our policy was that debts had to be collected, but some of the losers were very pathetic. We had one old boy who had lost all his money, but used to come into the casino every day for a free meal. He couldn't play anymore, but we never stopped him coming in."

"In our judgment," the Board of Inquiry concluded, "Mr. Lownes and Mr. Gerhauser were able to wield in Playboy something approaching absolute power. That power has been the cause of all the Company's troubles. . . . With compliant directors, inactive trustees, and picked managers, it was possible to suspend the corporate conscience." Had there been independent directors and regular, recorded meetings, "Mr. Lownes could not have made the gratuitous and, it may prove, fatal challenge to Ladbroke which, in our judgment, has been the origin of the Company's present predicament."

Daniels and his colleagues were pleased that the findings of the Board of Inquiry amply justified the sacking of the London management, but were dismayed at the merciless destruction of the good name Playboy had previously enjoyed as a model casino operation. They were also faintly mystified. If the management was "a right shambles," as one witness had put it, how had it escaped the scrutiny of the frequent visits by Gaming Board inspectors and the accountants and auditors who constantly monitored the business?

The accusations of "crass incompetence" contained in the report were also strangely at odds with the evidence given in the recent Victoria Sporting Club license hearings, at which it was agreed by everyone that Playboy's operating procedures were exemplary. Only a few weeks before the Board of Inquiry's revelations, Daniels sent a letter to all Playboy's two thousand employees in Britain reiterating his determination to retain the licenses and "maintain our high standard of integrity and efficiency in managing casinos."

Neither Lownes nor Gerhauser gave evidence to the Board of Inquiry. As it was set up and financed by the company from which they had just been dismissed, they were both suspicious of its "independence." At his elegant Georgian manor house in the Surrey hills, Gerhauser brooded over the injustice of it all, and dismissed the report as a "pack of lies." He had had a very good working relationship with Victor from the moment he arrived in Britain, he said. The suggestion that they never communicated except to scream at each other was "bullshit."

Lownes agreed. "It was lies," he said. "All lies. It was terrible what was happening. Like a Greek tragedy playing itself out." Victor was shattered, emotionally, by his sacking from Playboy. He could think about nothing else, talk about nothing else. He was obsessed by the belief that he could have saved the licenses. The objections were all technical, he said, and most could have been satisfactorily answered. But by sacking the management, Playboy had tacitly and stupidly admitted guilt. "It was suicidal, crazy. Playboy laid its head on the chopping block. They wrecked my career and they wrecked their business."

On May 6, Lownes wrote to Hefner in Los Angeles:

I am sorry that after I spent twenty-six years in the company you've let these chaps carry out their plan to destroy my reputation in order to realize their inordinate ambition to take over the gaming operations and thereby justify their existence. . . .

There is a problem here, a serious one, but I had it under control and would have resolved it. I'm known here, trusted here, and respected by the authorities. By sacking me, these incompetents, who have no experience in casino administration, no knowledge of British gaming law, and no proven record of integrity over here, have jeopardized the whole company. . . . A terrible injustice has been done to both myself and Bill, but, worst of all, to the company itself.

Hefner replied, six weeks later, and said he was convinced the "most prudent and appropriate" action had been taken. The letter looked, Lownes huffed, as if it "had been written by a team of forty lawyers." Lownes wrote again on July 11, complaining about allegations made to the Board of Inquiry reflecting on his conduct.

No one has had the decency to advise me as to the "substance" which has been "discovered" but I know that I have a totally clear conscience and I have never at any stage breached the Gaming Act, nor allowed the company to do so, nor encouraged any illegality on any premises with which Playboy is in any way associated (including my own home, Stocks). If I could be given a sensible opportunity of proving this assertion I genuinely believe that the company's prospects would be considerably enhanced. I want to do everything to assist the company in defense of the licenses.

This time, Hefner did not reply. If Lownes had any doubt about how he was viewed by his old friend and his former colleagues, that doubt was removed by a spiteful little slap administered from Los Angeles. A few years earlier, Hef had presented his friend with a lifetime subscription to *Playboy* magazine in gratitude for his achievements in the company. The framed certificate, with Hefner's signature and the corporate seal, hung in the entrance hall at Stocks. In the summer of 1981, the magazine suddenly stopped arriving.

Lord Allen had emphasized to Daniels, Huston, and DiPrima, at a second meeting at the Gaming Board, the vital importance of hiring someone with experience in gaming to run the company. The trouble was, they could not find anybody. The Gaming Board and the police had mounted so many raids on London casinos that businessmen with gaming experience and unblemished reputations were in rather short supply. Even finding a suitably prestigious executive *without* gaming experience was not easy because the company was Playboy (girlie magazine), the business was gambling (questionable), and the future of the company was in the balance.

In July, Playboy announced, with a certain sense of triumph, that the problem had at last been solved and the new managing director of Playboy (U.K.) would be Admiral Sir John Devereaux Trencher, former Second Lord of the Admiralty and Commander-in-Chief of NATO's Northeast Atlantic Forces and recently chief executive of National Car Parks. At a press conference he admitted that he had no experience in gaming, but, as he said, thirty-five years in the Navy wasn't all just "wind and spray and yo-heave-ho."

Fleet Street columnists and cartoonists had a great deal of fun at the prospect of an admiral "taking over the helm" at Playboy and being put in charge of all those Bunnies and roulette wheels. When Lownes's view was sought, he snarled: "Terrific! Maybe Playboy thinks that now an Admiral of the Queen's Na-vee is in charge, the British are going to stand up and salute instead of taking away their licenses. Well, if he loses, he can always turn the Park Lane casino into a car park."

A number of Fleet Street's more salacious newspapers had been digging for sex-and-scandal stories about Playboy ever since it was rumored that the police had uncovered evidence of Bunnies working as prostitutes. (DiPrima had warned a Playboy board meeting in June that he believed further objections relating to prostitution were being prepared.) In August, a flurry of headlines promised some nasty headaches for the admiral. BUNNIES LURED INTO VICE RING shrieked *The Sun*. "A vice madam and a millionaire gambler lured beautiful Playboy Club bunnies into a call-girl service for wealthy Arabs, The Sun can reveal today. . . ."

SCANDALS AT THE BUNNY HUTCH countered the *News of the World*, known in Fleet Street as "The News of the Screws." "Today we lift the lid on the Playboy Club and the scandals surrounding London's plush Bunny casino. . . ."

There was not much substance in any of it. Lots of smut, innuendo, unsubstantiated allegations, and unnamed Bunnies talking about sleeping with gamblers and going to orgies. "Once I had a Mercedes given to me," a Bunny supposedly called Mira told the *News of the World*, "but I had to give it back when I refused to sleep with the guy."

No prostitution charges were brought by the police because they could not garner sufficient evidence, but it was the kind of publicity Playboy absolutely did not need on the eve of the license hearings. Underlining the importance of the licenses to Playboy, the annual report for fiscal 1981 showed that the company would have taken a loss of more than $14 million without the income from the casinos. Gaming brought in a record profit of $39 million on revenues of $110 million, whereas magazine publishing could only manage a profit of $6 million on revenues of $136 million.

Caxton Hall, where the fate of Playboy's multimillion-pound gambling business was to be decided, was a red brick Victorian building in Westminster best known to the British as the preferred venue for those show business and society weddings that, for usually unmentionable reasons, could not be conducted in church. Why it should be so favored is a mystery, for it is a particularly dreary pile of municipal meeting rooms.

In the second largest of these rooms, the case of the Metropolitan Police and the Gaming Board *v.* Playboy opened on September 14 before the South Westminster Gaming Licensing Committee, five lay magistrates, four of them women. Playboy's leading Queen's Counsel, Robert Alexander, was optimistic, despite the fact that the police had filed an additional objection alleging that unlawful use of the Playboy Club had been "habitual." This was an important semantic development, since it meant that a finding against Playboy would mean mandatory refusal of a license. Nevertheless, Alexander's assessment of the alleged violations was that they were "minor" or "technical" in nature.

The police and the Gaming Board gave evidence for the whole of the first week, producing figures that drew gasps of surprise from many of those present. Between January 1976 and June 1981, the "drop" in Playboy casinos was more than £660 million. The police said that Playboy had accepted "no-account checks" on a scale that constituted a deliberate scheme to advance credit to gamblers. The most favored gamblers were allowed to run up huge debts by writing checks drawn on a Park Lane branch of

Lloyds Bank, where Playboy held its account. Playboy also accepted so many checks from gamblers who already owed the casino money that checks worth more than £22 million bounced. The luckless Mr. Beh-Behani's gambling career was explained in particular detail, no doubt to his shame; he was said to owe Playboy around £2 million.

During the second week of the hearing, Playboy sought to put the objections "into perspective," pointing out that only twenty-one members out of 34,500 were involved in writing "no-account checks" and all of them were extremely wealthy men, perfectly capable of meeting their debts. The "hall-porter" scheme had been stopped as soon as it had been brought to the notice of the management, and "check-on-check" gambling was a "gray area" of the Gaming Act on which Playboy had striven to get a ruling. The Khawaja objection was a "damp squib," Alexander claimed, since he had done nothing worse than make a nuisance of himself.

Unfortunately for Playboy's case, the two men best qualified to answer the objections were not invited to give evidence. Both Lownes and Gerhauser had offered to testify on Playboy's behalf, but both were turned down. Even so, most observers thought the case was going well: only when it came to the issue of foreign control was the company shown to be dangerously vulnerable.

"Who wields the real power in this organization?" asked Simon Tuckey, counsel for the Gaming Board. "There is a continuing doubt as to the extent of the control likely to be applied by Chicago, since this is a subsidiary that provides most of the money for its parent company. I have no doubt that people will be saying how could they be so silly as to interfere, when by doing so they risk killing the goose that is laying their golden eggs."

The hearings lasted eleven days and on October 5, the licensing justices reconvened to announce their decision. In an adjoining room at Caxton Hall, Playboy had made preparations for a champagne celebration. It was not needed: the justices ruled that Playboy was not "fit and proper" and denied the renewal of its gaming licenses. On the New York Stock Exchange, Playboy shares dropped 2.73 points to a new low of $5.75.

Both casinos remained open, pending appeal, but after a hurried series of melancholy conferences in London and Chicago, Playboy decided to cut its losses and clear out, rather than risk going to appeal at the Crown Court. "If we lose in the Crown Court," Daniels told Hefner, "we'll have nothing to sell." On November 3, 1981, Playboy Enterprises issued a press release announcing the sale of all its United Kingdom gaming operations to Trident Television for $24.8 million, rather less than two-thirds of the profit the casinos had earned during fiscal 1981.

Gavin Lightman, the barrister who had advised the overthrow of Lownes, later said he thought the issue of foreign control had a significant impact on the adverse decision of the licensing justices.

Hefner and his fellow directors, desperately seeking a reason for their failure, decided it was some sinister plot aimed at Playboy. Huston spoke for them all when he said: "The objections were chickenshit objections and everyone knew they were chickenshit. They amounted to nothing."

Which left Victor Lownes and Bill Gerhauser perplexed. Why had they been fired if the objections were "chickenshit"?

The loss of the casinos in London was an unmitigated disaster for Playboy and led to a rash of pessimistic headlines, on both sides of the Atlantic, predicting the fall of the Playboy empire. Without the income from gaming, the *Wall Street Journal* noted, earnings from the other operations would cover only "fractions" of Playboy's considerable administrative and promotional costs. "Its domestic clubs and resort hotels have been unprofitable for years. Its books and entertainment divisions don't earn enough to cover overheads. The circulation and advertising pages of its flagship publication, *Playboy* magazine, have been dropping steadily." Playboy Enterprises, Inc., the *Wall Street Journal* concluded, was a "weak and troubled company."

On November 10, Hefner made a special statement at the 1981 stockholders' meeting to try to bolster morale. "Rumors about our demise," he said, "are somewhat an exaggeration." With or without gaming, Playboy was an uncommonly strong company with a "very, very real and bright future."

The challenge arising from the London situation was "simply one more part of an ongoing saga with which I have grown very accustomed. Controversy, I guess, is the Playboy kind of name of the game. One of the motivations for the sale in England was to put an end to the speculation in terms of the future of the company because we really have been . . ." Hefner hesitated, fumbling for words, "and this, again, is part of the controversy, I think, that goes with Playboy—we really have been—I wouldn't—perhaps victim is an overstatement, but we certainly have been the focus for an uncommon amount of press attention, particularly in England, starting with the notion that perhaps this was the beginning of the end for the Playboy empire."

Figures had been quoted out of context, Hefner claimed, to give a completely inaccurate picture of the company, its potential to show profit, its focus, and its strength. "While the profits for the coming year will obviously be down, there *will* be profits and we expect them to be significant."

Four days later, Playboy received another unexpected and wounding body blow. On November 16, the Division of Gaming Enforcement in New Jersey announced it would be opposing Playboy's application for a license in Atlantic City, and published the result of its two-year investigation into the company. Instead of the clean bill of health Playboy had been led to expect, the hundred-page report raked up a great deal of dirt, ranging from alleged links between the Playboy Clubs and organized crime, to the New York State Liquor Authority scandal twenty years earlier, when money had been extorted from Playboy in return for a liquor license at the New York Playboy Club. The drugs investigation at the time of Bobbie Arnstein's suicide was held up as another question mark over the company, as was the loss of the license in London. DGE investigators had even discovered that Hefner once employed Sidney Korshak, a lawyer publicly named as "the most important link between organized crime and legitimate business."

Daniels, Huston, and DiPrima were stunned when they read the report. Until that moment they had all thought that Playboy's application for a permanent license was proceeding smoothly. DiPrima had been in close contact with Michael Brown, director of the Division of Gaming Enforcement, during the unfolding of events in London, and Brown had assured him that the "elimination of Lownes" greatly enhanced Playboy's credibility in New Jersey. In August, DiPrima had dispatched a confident memo to his colleagues after a meeting with Brown: "The New Jersey regulatory authorities would welcome the opportunity to rule in our favor without undue controversy—we are welcome in New Jersey."

Very early on, DiPrima had been assured by the DGE that the New York State Liquor Authority business, "a million years ago," would not be a problem. Now, out of the blue, it had come back to haunt them. Hefner, already paranoid about the *real* reasons why Playboy had lost its licenses in London, could not help but ponder the *real* reasons why the New Jersey authorities had dragged up this old, unhappy, and half-forgotten incident. Was New Jersey out to get him, because he and his magazine had always been on the cutting edge of social change? Viewed from his gilded cloister, that was certainly the way it looked to Hugh M. Hefner, publisher, philosopher, reformer, and so on.

The DGE Investigative Report was filed with New Jersey's Casino Control Commission, a body set up to decide gaming license applications, and a date was set in early January for the case to be heard. To be awarded a permanent license, Playboy's qualifications would have to be approved by at least four of the five commissioners.

Playboy desperately needed to retain its stake in the $150 million Atlantic City venture. Although the huge 500-room Playboy Hotel-Casino on the Boardwalk, the seventh to be opened in the resort, had started slowly, business was picking up and Atlantic City showed every sign of being a gold mine for casino operators. While Las Vegas was suffering from the effects of the recession and its isolated position in the Nevada desert, three hundred miles from the nearest major population center, Atlantic City, only one hundred miles from New York, was booming. More than fifty million people lived within driving distance of Atlantic City, a market potential five times bigger than that of Vegas, and the casinos were proving such a draw with day-trippers that, in 1981, Atlantic City pulled ahead of Florida's Walt Disney World to become the single most popular travel resort in the United States. Every night, crowds six- to eight-deep could be found pressed around the gaming tables in the Boardwalk casinos, and gamblers with fistfuls of quarters lined up to feed the slot machines.

Hearings before the Casino Control Commission began on Monday, January 11, in a special room at the commission's offices in Lawrence Township, an uninspiring suburban development on the outskirts of Trenton, New Jersey. It was cold and snowing hard when Hefner, the first witness, arrived in a black and gray Cadillac, accompanied by Miss Shannon Tweed and two bodyguards. He had forsaken his silk pajamas for this occasion and wore a dark three-piece business suit, with a white shirt and a tie. Miss Tweed sported a figure-hugging sweater that was to cause much eyeball swiveling.

Hefner's testimony occupied the first three days and was generally agreed to be calamitous. As a witness, he was pitiful. Assistant Attorney General James Flanagan, a deceptively genial, pudgy little man, with his hair combed across the top of his head to conceal its shining baldness, began his cross-examination with the amiable pronouncement: "Hugh Hefner, this is your life." He then proceeded to make a devastating case that it was a far from blameless life, and Hefner appeared powerless to defend himself, largely because he could remember very little about the events Flanagan raised. Apart from what he described as "islands of recollection," the chairman of Playboy Enterprises, Inc., demonstrated a regrettable lack of awareness about what was going on in his own company. Sitting with his chin in his hand, grinning boyishly, he often rambled when he was able to answer a question and frankly admitted he had made no attempt to prepare himself for the hearing.

"Were there any documents *at all* that you looked at," Flanagan asked at one point, his voice heavy with sarcasm, "notwithstanding the fact that you indicate you didn't prepare very much for your testimony?"

HMH: What documents do you have in mind?

JF: Let me rephrase the question. Are you aware of the fact that the Division of Gaming Enforcement submitted a report on Playboy and on Elsinore, your partner?

HMH: Yes.

JF: And are you aware that at approximately the same time, a statement of so-called issues was also put forth by the Division of Gaming Enforcement?

HMH: Yes.

JF: And did you have an opportunity to look at both of these documents, that is, the report as well as the statement of issues?

HMH: No. I went over a synopsis of same, but not the actual report.

JF: So you have never read the report to this very moment?

HMH: That's correct.

JF: Did you have an opportunity to read the statement of issues that the Division put forth?

HMH: I think—how long is that?

JF: It's about three pages.

HMH: Yes.

JF: You read that?

HMH: Yes.

Dealing with the loss of the gaming licenses in London, Hefner blamed Lownes, "a flamboyant and overly self-assured executive," for not warning Playboy executives in Chicago what was happening. "He, in a very real sense, misled us," said Hefner, "as to the seriousness of the situation."

On the subject of the drugs investigation and the suicide of Bobbie Arnstein, Hefner said Bobbie was frightened into killing herself by narcotics agents working for James Thompson, the governor of Illinois. Thompson wanted to damage *Playboy* because the magazine was "a very easy mark, much like voting against sin." After Bobbie's arrest, he ordered the Mansions in Chicago and Los Angeles to be swept for drugs because he feared that Drug Enforcement Administration agents would try to plant drugs in one of them. (Thompson, who was seeking a third term as governor, issued an immediate statement describing Hefner's accusations as "absolutely untrue.")

Flanagan questioned Hefner at length about his friends and associates and contrived to leave an impression that they were a somewhat unsavory group. Two and a half hours were devoted to Hefner's relationship with Joe DeCarlo, an alleged associate of underworld figure Mickey Cohen, and one-time manager of Sonny and Cher. Hefner agreed that he had helped DeCarlo finance Pips, a restaurant and disco in Los Angeles. He also admitted that he had lent his best friend John Dante $2 million to set up a club called Touch, but he could not remember if he owned the land on which the club was built. He had made loans to Dante to help him repay his gambling debts, but he could not remember how much or when.

He did remember paying Sidney Korshak $50,000 to act as intermediary when Universal Studios filed a suit claiming that films in Hefner's private collection infringed their copyright. He had gone to Korshak, he explained, because he was a friend of Lew Wasserman, chairman of MCA, which owned Universal. He knew there was some question about Korshak's reputation and his involvement with criminals, but assumed it was the nature of a lawyer's business to deal with criminals.

The pivotal testimony of the hearing concerned the New York State Liquor Authority shakedown, and Hefner's surprising inability to recall details of an incident that, even though it had occurred twenty years earlier, must have been a traumatic experience: bribery and corruption involving state officials with connections in high places, a Grand Jury investigation, and criminal charges. Hefner's "islands of recollection" only revealed that he thought of himself more as a victim of extortion than the offerer of a bribe, and although he admitted that "some other way" should have been found to handle the problem, Playboy had cooperated fully with the authorities as soon as the Grand Jury investigation began.

"Mr. Hefner," the resolutely polite Flanagan asked, "do you know whether or not you got immunity before the County Grand Jury in New York County?"

HMH: I don't know.

JF: Have you ever, to your knowledge, received immunity from any Grand Jury or prosecuting agency?

HMH: I don't know. I'm not aware of any. I don't know. It's possible in this particular case. I don't know.

JF: So that this would not be another island of recollection? Is that correct? It would not be another island of recollection?

HMH: What?

JF: My question to you as to whether or not you testified before a County Grand Jury in New York County. You are unable to remember, so you just don't have any recollection?

HMH: I did appear before them.

JF: And the question was, do you know whether or not you received immunity?

HMH: And I indicated that I don't know whether I did or not.

JF: And I asked you whether or not you had gotten immunity on any other occasions.

HMH: I don't think so. I can't think of any other instance.

Flanagan wanted to prove that far from courageously stepping forward and blowing the whistle on corruption, Hefner and his friends had only agreed to testify after lawyers negotiated an immunity deal. Unfortunately, the transcript of the Grand Jury hearing, which would have shown if they had been granted immunity, had completely disappeared from the files in New York, and no copies could be traced.

Hefner was rattled by the hostility of the grilling he received before the Casino Control Commission and fell back, for an explanation, on the old story: "I think the unique nature of Playboy's success makes it a particularly appropriate target," he told the *Philadelphia Inquirer* after his testimony. "There is also a great tendency to idolize our heroes and tear them down. There was a great deal of satisfaction in tearing Kennedy down a few years ago, and look what they did to Charlie Chaplin. It's fascinating. If something can bring a person down, it sort of reaffirms and reassures the people who are not on top."

As the hearings progressed, it became clear that the New York State Liquor Authority incident was the central issue. Playboy called Jeremiah McKenna, an attorney formerly with the Manhattan District Attorney's office, who had prosecuted one of the SLA offenders. He testified that in his view Playboy had been a "victim of moral extortion." The Division of Gaming Enforcement called David Goldstein, an Assistant District Attorney in Manhattan at the same time. He asserted that as Playboy made payments to SLA officials voluntarily, in his view it amounted to bribery, rather than extortion.

The involvement of these two expert witnesses resulted in another stroke of bad luck for Playboy. Goldstein and McKenna were old friends and before they were called to testify, Goldstein had asked his friend if he could refresh his memory by looking through McKenna's old case diaries—McKenna was notorious for meticulously filing every scrap of paper. While looking through McKenna's files, Goldstein found a dog-eared and yellowing copy of the Grand Jury transcript.

With a flourish, Flanagan produced the transcript after Hefner had made a second trip to the witness stand. It showed that the

books and records of the New York Playboy Club had been subpoenaed on December 12, 1962, and that on the following day,
Playboy had sent an emissary to the district attorney's office to
negotiate an immunity deal in return for cooperation.

Flanagan read out a telling passage in Hefner's evidence before
the Grand Jury:

> Q: You knew at the time that paying off a public officer is not
> a right and proper thing?
> A: Yes.
> Q: What persuaded you to go through with this arrangement?
> A: Because it was obvious that to take the matter through the
> courts would cost us, even without any special legal harass-
> ment, probably a like amount.

After thirty trial days and formal submissions by both sides, the
hearing was adjourned on March 8 and the commissioners retired
to study the 6,000 pages of transcribed testimony and the 568
exhibits admitted into evidence, including the entire transcript of
the Playboy hearing in London before the South Westminster
justices.

By a curious coincidence, while Playboy was in court in New
Jersey defending its Atlantic City investment, the man who had
indirectly kindled the casino wars was in court in London defending his rights. Investigative journalist Jack Lundin, whose
story in *Private Eye* first exposed Ladbroke's dirty tricks, had agreed
to cooperate with the subsequent police investigation providing
they agreed not to call him as a witness. He explained he did not
want to be put into a position of being asked in court to identify
the source of his story.

A detective chief superintendent gave Lundin such a pledge
and then ignored it. To his fury, Lundin was called as a witness
in the trial of a police sergeant charged with selling information obtained from the Police National Computer. Ordered
to identify his informant, he refused and was charged with contempt. Without his evidence, the trial could not proceed and the
sergeant was acquitted. In the High Court, the Attorney General
sought an order for Lundin's committal to prison, but on February

20, 1982, two judges ruled that Lundin was not obliged to reveal his source since his answer was "not necessary to the interests of justice."

Lundin was allowed to go free, to his great relief, and rue the irony of events: for exposing crime and corruption and honoring a promise, he had very nearly been sent to prison.

On April 7, the Casino Control Commission rendered its decision in the case of Playboy-Elsinore's application for a permanent license. All five commissioners found Elsinore qualified. Three commissioners found Playboy and Hefner qualified, noting that the shadow cast by the SLA incident had "given way to the light shed by a career of social commitment, honest business dealings, and an otherwise unblemished personal record of integrity." Commissioner Carl Zeitz found Playboy was qualified, but Hefner was not. Commissioner Martin Danziger, who was an assistant D.A. in New York at the time of the SLA scandal, found both Playboy *and* Hefner were unqualified.

It was a finding that left Playboy in the unhappiest of dilemmas: Playboy Enterprises, Inc., was *in*, Hugh Hefner was *out*. With four votes of approval from the commissioners, the company was qualified for a permanent gaming license in Atlantic City, but not under the leadership of Hefner, who had only received three votes.

Commissioner Zeitz cited bribery of public officials in New York as his reason for disallowing Hefner. He found Hefner's testimony "lacked candor," and considered it to be inherently incredible that he could forget the "searing experience" of invoking the Fifth Amendment to receive immunity from prosecution before testifying in front of a Grand Jury. Zeitz said that in his view Playboy's actions could only be considered bribery. "That Hefner clings to the fiction that at all times he and his company were victims of extortion, without the free will to release themselves from the squalid demands of corrupt officials in the State of New York, is not acceptable and without justification."

The fifth commissioner, Danziger, could find nothing good to say about either Hefner or Playboy. He quoted bribery of public officials, regulatory offenses in the United Kingdom, the SEC investigation, and "organized crime ties" as the reasons why licensing Hefner and Playboy would "make a mockery of New Jersey's casino regulatory system." He found Hefner's testimony "untrue and unsincere" and an "attempt to mislead the Commission." Danziger rejected the argument that Hefner was contrite and should be forgiven for events that took place more than twenty years ago.

"Licensing Playboy," Danziger declared, "would be tantamount to encouraging corporate leaders to believe this Commission has ruled that time will cure even the most reprehensible conduct . . . and would signal the abandonment of virtually all licensing criteria requiring ethical restraint. If the unethical practices and illegal acts of corporations are not checked, the future of a crime-free casino industry in Atlantic City would be in jeopardy."

At the offices of the Division of Gaming Enforcement in Trenton, the attorneys who had opposed Playboy at the hearings before the commission all agreed that Hefner's three days on the stand were fatal for Playboy. As Flanagan said,

Hefner was a terrible witness. He couldn't seem to focus on anything, he was not as candid as he should have been and did not seem to appreciate the significance of why he was there. He turned off the Commissioners when he said he had not bothered to read the investigative report into his own company and it was all downhill from there. Even showing up with Shannon Tweed was a mistake. One day she wore a leather suit so tight that if it had rained she would certainly have been strangled.

He definitely downplayed his role in the SLA affair. He could have saved the day if he'd come along, eaten a little crow and said "I'm sorry, I made a big mistake." But no, he had to say that he was the victim of extortion and then, whenever something detrimental was raised, he couldn't remember. If Hefner stepped aside, the company could get a license tomorrow.

This last, outrageous, suggestion was briefly and half-heartedly discussed at a Playboy board meeting on April 21, but all those present concurred, according to the minutes, that "Mr. Hefner's *persona* was essential to the continued value of the Playboy trade and service marks, and his personal influence was similarly essen-

tial to the continued profitability of *Playboy* magazine." Rosenzweig, the "simpleton from Appleton," made no secret of his
belief that severing Hefner from Playboy would result in the collapse of the company. A press release was issued stating that Hefner's close identification with Playboy made it "inconceivable that
he would choose to disassociate himself from the future of the
company he founded twenty-eight years ago."

Playboy notified the Casino Control Commission that it would
rather pull out of Atlantic City than sever ties with its beloved
founder and chairman. Pending appeal, lawyers negotiated a deal
with the commission under which Playboy's interests in the casino
were placed in escrow. The company was given sixty days in
which to submit detailed divestiture plans.

As far as Hefner was concerned, it was a lost cause:

I was probably as honest a guy as ever applied for a license in
Atlantic City, but there was so much personal animosity, jealousy, and disapproval involved, that I did not think it was
possible for Playboy or me to get what one might call an
unbiased, or objective, evaluation.

Over the years we questioned through the magazine some
of the traditional values that people take very seriously and we
exposed ourselves because of that. There was no more logic
to the decision in Atlantic City than there was to London. Why
did they do what they did to me in London? It all comes down
to human beings and prejudice. That isn't justice.

Unquestionably, Playboy had arrived at its darkest hour. The
sequence of misfortunes that began with the casino wars ended
with the announcement of the company's results for fiscal 1982.
Instead of the "significant profits" promised by Hefner in November, Playboy Enterprises, Inc., reported a loss of $51,681,000.

Playboy staffers, stoic in adversity, took to cracking a cynical
little joke as they left the Playboy Building each night: "Last one
out, turn off the Bunny Beacon."

17

Christie's Coup d'Etat

While the anticipated rich pickings from Atlantic City were slipping through Playboy's fingers, Derick Daniels was supervising what he described as "corporate restructuring" in Chicago. What he was really trying to do was amputate the bleeding limbs of the Playboy empire to try and compensate for the loss of gambling revenue from Britain. *Oui* magazine was unloaded in 1981 for an undisclosed sum, and the resort hotels at Lake Geneva and Great Gorge, which had cost more than $50 million to build and lost millions more in operation, were sold for $42 million. In March 1982, Playboy announced that its book publishing operation was up for sale. Playboy would be putting renewed emphasis, Daniels explained, on its "profitable magazine publishing, licensing, and franchising activities, as well as its new venture in pay cable television."

Christie Hefner, who was by then a forceful and dynamic member of the board, had some ideas of her own about corporate restructuring, which she raised in early April with her father. In what she portrayed as a "nuts and bolts" conversation about the future of the company, she pointed out that without the income from gaming, Playboy Enterprises, Inc., would have lost money every year during Daniels's tenure. There were still too many layers of management, morale was in a rut, and there was an urgent need to streamline operations and focus on fewer businesses. The company needed to take on a new face to recover from the setbacks in England and New Jersey. She had a face in mind. "*I* want to run the business," she declared with nary a blush. Hef, already a committed admirer of his daughter, could think of no one better.

On April 28, 1982, it was announced that Christie Hefner, aged twenty-nine, would be taking over from Derick Daniels as president of Playboy Enterprises, Inc. Daniels graciously admitted to no surprise at being replaced rather sooner than he had expected. In a Playboy press release, he was quoted as saying: "For many reasons, this is an extremely logical time for Christie to move into the presidency." He left the Playboy Building for the last time displaying the same sartorial flamboyance that had been so much in evidence when he arrived six years earlier. Sauntering out in a white leather jumpsuit, he drove off in a white chauffeured Mercedes, sipping champagne from a bottle wrapped in a white towel, en route to the opera. It was an exit considerably sweetened by a pay-off of nearly half a million dollars.

As the pretty new president of Playboy, Christie became an instant media celebrity, photographed and interviewed everywhere. There was, of course, no shortage of critics. "It's difficult to imagine," wrote syndicated columnist Joan Beck, "any intelligent, well-educated woman with a smidgen of self-respect who would be willing to preside over the kind of lecherous exploitation of women that built the Playboy empire and now sustains what is left of it in its declining years."

Christie was perfectly accustomed to dealing with criticism on that score. *Playboy*, she said, was a "fundamentally liberal and humanistic magazine," and in its attitude toward hiring and promoting women and its editorial and financial support of issues like abortion and the Equal Rights Amendment, the company was more supportive than most of feminist politics and philosophies. "I'm living in a country where the president wants to make abortion a crime," she told several interviewers, "and some segment of the women's movement is suggesting that Playboy is a major enemy in society. I think that's crazy."

In the hothouse of warring fiefdoms that comprised the Playboy Building, Christie's appointment was generally welcomed.
She was popular, widely respected for her formidable intellect,
ability, and energy, and had a reputation for being a good manager,
if somewhat brusque. Many an executive had been silenced by
Christie snapping "Bullshit!" The fact that she was the boss's
daughter was not, curiously, held against her in any way since she
was the only executive in the company who was not overawed
by Hefner, not interested in second-guessing his wishes, and not
afraid to tell him exactly what she thought.

Christie moved swiftly to assert her authority. Nearly one
hundred executives were ejected from the comfort of their Playboy
offices and deposited on the sidewalk on North Michigan Avenue
with a farewell, a severance check, and the memory of Christie's
sweet, regretful smile. During her first few months in office, she
slashed corporate overhead by nearly $8 million and demanded
stringent economies in every department. "In contrast to Hef,"
an awed *Fortune* magazine reported, "she has an affinity for balance
sheets, a tolerance for daylight hours, and a gregarious personality.
She also shows an admirable willingness to control people and to
fire and promote without years of soul-searching."

The one economy Christie assiduously avoided was to curb
the chairman's risible lifestyle at Playboy Mansion West. By 1983,
it was costing more than *three and a half million dollars* a year to
run the Los Angeles Mansion in a manner pleasing to Mr. Hefner.
While the company was losing millions of dollars, the parties
continued just as they had when the company was making millions
of dollars. Indeed, the turmoil that had afflicted Playboy Enterprises, Inc., caused barely a ripple in the tenor of life at the Mansion, although Hef made his own little contribution to the economy
drive by sending a memo to the kitchen asking the chef to give
him smaller portions of his favorite dishes. He was often not able
to clear his plate and it was, he said, an unnecessary waste. Some
of the butlers, one of them confessed, had a hard time keeping a
straight face for a few days afterward. They would start thinking
about the memo and smirk and stifle a giggle and then rush back
to the kitchen to get it over with.

Christie's first few months as president were characterized in the Playboy Building as a "reign of terror," but at the Mansion the major topic of conversation was the sudden departure of Shannon Tweed. One minute she was Playmate of the Year, Hef's girl, and violins were playing. Next minute she was gone, having confessed to the butlers that she felt the Mansion was becoming like a prison. "Hefner was heartbroken," a butler admitted. "He used to leave her little cutesie-pie notes all over the place."

The new president turned out to be recklessly overoptimistic about how quickly she would be able to solve the daunting problems she had inherited. In the summer of 1982, she was coolly predicting a profit of at least $10 million for fiscal 1983. It never materialized. Playboy Enterprises posted a $17,500,000 loss in fiscal 1983. All its operations, except the magazine and Playboy products, lost money.

In the summer of 1982, Christie predicted the magazine would hold its circulation guarantee at 5 million and increase its advertising revenue. In 1983, the circulation guarantee dropped first to 4.4 million, then to 4.1 million. Revenue from advertising and circulation fell by $18 million.

As the flagship of the company, *Playboy* magazine effectively foundered years ago. It might be the biggest-selling men's magazine in the world, but with rising production costs, falling circulation, and an increasing reliance on subscriptions (the death knell of many fine magazines), *Playboy* will never in the future be able to sustain a corporation the size of Playboy Enterprises.

Neither is it likely that Playboy Clubs will ever again make money, despite frantic juggling with dozens of new ideas to try to bring the customers back. Even Hefner himself admits the days of the Bunny are numbered. "It is clear that having been around since 1960," he says, sucking on his pipe, "there is something kinda antiquated and almost camp about the notion of the Bunny. I'm not planning on chucking out Bunnies, because you're talking about a world-famous symbol and a fascination with that symbol that continues today. But we are looking for ways of contemporarizing the clubs *conceptually*."

The future of the company is now vested in a multimillion-dollar gamble on pay television and video cassettes. The Playboy Channel, a video version of the magazine launched on cable television in November 1982, aims to offer adult entertainment reflecting the "wit, style, and taste" of *Playboy*'s printed pages. Hef loves it: he often sits watching it all night, with only occasional breaks to play his favorite video game, Donkey Kong.

If the Playboy Channel is a success, then Playboy Enterprises can survive. If it flops, there will be nothing left but the magazine, which was the way it was in the beginning.

Tailpiece

Hugh Hefner, prominent champion of the First Amendment, only put one condition on cooperating with me when I was researching this book—he asked me to be "straight." There was no mention of wanting to see, or approve, the manuscript; no hint of the troubles to come until I asked if Playboy would be willing to supply photographs for the book.

"Hef thinks," said an aide in Los Angeles, "that if we give you pictures, he should get a look at the manuscript. He doesn't want to censor it, of course, he just wants to check it for factual accuracy." I refused on principle, explaining that I did not want the book to be considered an "approved" or an "official" version of events. This message was relayed to Hef. The response was childish, but not unexpected: "Hef says if you won't let him see your book, he won't let you have any pictures."

Not long afterward, Playboy lawyers weighed in. Playboy's general counsel, Howard Shapiro, fired off a threatening letter containing every conceivable warning. "Even though Mr. Miller has met with Hugh M. Hefner and other employees of Playboy to gather material for his book, we believe the book may contain information that is heresay [*sic*], inaccurate, libelous, false, misleading, damaging to Playboy's and Mr. Hefner's reputation, and/ or which may interfere with or damage other rights and interests of both Playboy and Mr. Hefner. . . . It is suggested that extreme caution be taken by you in this matter. . . . Of course, the best source to determine whether the material contained in the manuscript is false, misleading, or otherwise invades the rights of Playboy or Mr. Hefner, is Playboy. Be advised that we are prepared to review the manuscript. . . ."

When this letter was ignored, an English solicitor acting for Playboy tried his luck. "Our Clients are willing to review the manuscript prior to publication and invite you to submit it to them for that purpose. Should you decline to give them the opportunity so to do, we are instructed formally to inform you that our Clients will pursue their legal remedies . . . and if necessary would seek an injunction restraining publication." No reply was sent to this kind invitation.

In the light of the above, it was perhaps not surprising that soon after the first finished copies of the book were delivered to the publisher in London, a Playboy emissary somehow got hold of one and dispatched it posthaste to Chicago, addressed to Ms. Christie Hefner, president and chief operating officer of Playboy Enterprises, Inc.

Nearly three weeks before first publication, Christie Hefner wrote to me, making it clear she had read the book and expressing regret that my "interesting, sometimes fanciful" view of Playboy's thirty-year history did not take into account the "major strides" made by the company under her stewardship during the last eighteen months. Playboy Enterprises, Inc., returned to profitability in fiscal 1984, she said. The Playboy Channel boasted nearly 720,000 subscribers on 450 cable systems nationwide; Playboy home video cassettes and disc sales also generated profits, as did the products division, which capitalizes on the popularity of the Rabbit Head symbol.

"Playboy has indeed had an exciting Thirtieth Anniversary year," Ms. Hefner enthused. "As evidenced by successive quarterly profits and a solid balance sheet, Playboy has established a secure place in the communications and entertainment field. We look forward to a second successful 30 years."

Ms. Hefner is an extremely confident young woman. Her slim

hand has been on the tiller through the worst crisis in Playboy's history and she has certainly confounded the critics who sourly prophesied that she was too young and too inexperienced to rescue the company. Yet while her achievements are considerable, the Bunny is not quite as bright-eyed and bushy-tailed as she would like the world to believe.

In the annual report for fiscal 1984, Playboy Enterprises proudly boasted a profit for the year of $27.3 million, compared with losses of $17 million and $51 million in fiscal 1983 and 1982. It appeared to be a remarkable recovery, except that the profit was almost entirely attributable to divestitures and tax benefits. Playboy's four operating divisions only managed to produce a profit of $1.6 million on revenues of $187 million, a far from glittering performance.

The best hope for generating more substantial profits in the future is the Playboy Channel, which signed 500,000 subscribers in its first six months and was hailed as one of America's fastest-growing cable television services. Early offerings included "Sex-cetera, The News According to Playboy," a television newscast with oleaginous co-anchors linking ribald news items; "The Great American Strip-Off," a nationwide competition for amateur strippers; and "Playboy on the Scene," in which the centerfold is brought woodenly to life by filming the photo session. It was not the kind of material to place an undue strain on the intellect, but this did not inhibit Playboy, with its characteristic corporate restraint, from making extravagant claims on behalf of the new enterprise. "Focus group research noted," said the company, "that couples frequently watch The Playboy Channel's erotic offerings . . . during moments of intimacy. In fact, many couples surveyed indicated that Playboy's programming has helped them improve their relationships by providing guidance and information about the delicate balance between the sexes, and that our programs have made their mates 'more loving.' "

Although the video division posted an overall loss of $300,000 in fiscal 1984, video operations turned a profit for the first time in the last two quarters, boosted by a lucrative spin-off from the Playboy Channel—sales of home video cassettes and discs. "The young and rapidly growing pay-television industry continues to offer great promise for Playboy Enterprises," says the 1984 annual report.

But the climate, in Reagan's America, looks distinctly uncongenial. Although the Playboy Channel is very far from hard-core pornography, it does concentrate on sex and nudity at a time when much of America, following the lead set by the White House, is embracing conservatism and a return to "religious values." Even in this age of permissiveness, many Americans remain ambivalent about sex and pornography and a major obstacle to the growth of the Playboy Channel is the increasing reluctance of cable operators to risk offending local communities, particularly since a Supreme Court ruling in 1978 gave local communities the right to decide what was, or was not, obscene. Cable television franchises are granted by local city councils or mayors and are thus highly susceptible to political pressure. If, by taking the Playboy Channel, a cable operator upsets the local community, he jeopardizes his license. Already a number of operators have dropped Playboy rather than take that risk. When a cable operator in Washington County, Tennessee, refused to withdraw the Playboy Channel after protests from the community, local businessmen taped Playboy programs and showed them in churches throughout the county, where they provoked predictable outrage. Within a few months, the Playboy Channel was no longer available in the area.

It is readily admitted in the Playboy Building that while the success of the Playboy Channel is essential for the future growth of the company, much more important, in real terms, is the continuing success of *Playboy* magazine. "Everything still stems from the magazine," says a senior executive. "Any threat to the magazine is a threat to the whole organization." Indeed, it was the magazine that pushed the balance sheet into the black at the end of 1983, for the first time in two years, when an aging actress came to the aid of the beleaguered company. The December 1983 *Playboy* featured the charms of Joan Collins, soap-opera star of "Dynasty," in a variety of saucy disrobed poses that made it difficult to believe she was fifty years old. The issue was so hot that more than a million extra copies were sold on the newsstands and as a result Playboy Enterprises, Inc., was able to report a $1.2 million profit for the December quarter.

The magazine is still solidly profitable—in fiscal 1984 it reported earnings up from $6.4 million to $17.8 million, but advertising was down 10 percent and the revenue produced by Playboy has been falling relentlessly since 1979. Increased profits were only achieved last year by production economies and freak sales of the Joan Collins issue, which carried through to the following Thirtieth Anniversary issue.

Playboy's circulation appears to have bottomed out at 4.2 million, a far cry from the early 1970s when it peaked above 7 million, but nevertheless a respectable figure that still enables it to proclaim itself the most popular men's magazine in the world. The trouble is that the majority of its circulation is sold at a heavy discount by subscription and the real profit from magazine publishing in the United States comes from newsstand sales, where *Playboy* only sells 1.9 million copies. Current circulation of *Playboy*'s main rival, *Penthouse*, is only 3.2 million—but no less than 3 million copies are sold on the newsstands. Worse, *Penthouse* is now indisputably the "hot book," since publishing controversial nude pictures of Vanessa Williams, the first black Miss America.

Playboy editors recognize the need to attract more newsstand readers by updating the magazine's image, but they are frankly terrified of tampering with the format that has proved successful for so many years. Lately, there has been much talk about "editorial refocusing" to attract someone called the "new male," an exercise that *Playboy* claims has been well received by readers, although in truth readers could be forgiven for not realizing that anything had changed, so subtle was this "refocusing."

While Hugh Hefner is happy to let his daughter run the company day by day, he still calls the shots. Christie, for example, would like to pull out of the nightclub business altogether, but her father won't hear of it: probably because closing the clubs would mean the demise of the Bunny and the loss of such a potent corporate symbol would provide powerful ammunition for the gloomy legions constantly predicting the fall of the Playboy empire. So the remaining Playboy Clubs must remain open, regardless of increasing losses ($2.9 million in fiscal 1984). Most Playboy Clubs are now operated as franchises in small towns like Des Moines and Omaha, but the company still owns the three biggest clubs, in Chicago, Los Angeles, and New York.

Vacillation at the executive level has considerably delayed the opening of a promised "new look" Playboy Club in New York. When the building occupied by the New York club was sold in

1982 to raise assets, plans were made to open a new club with a "redefined concept" in space rented in a hotel on Lexington Avenue and 48th Street. Intended to provide a future direction for all the clubs, the aim was to attract younger keyholders by the extensive use of electronic entertainment and the latest video technology. "We've been living with a thirty-year idea that has done everybody proud," said a Playboy spokesman. "But it's time to step into the eighties."

High time, indeed. But the targeted opening date, February 1984, passed without a murmur. Now it is said the club will open in early 1985.

Drastically slimmed, Playboy is now a company with a realistic management structure, defined strategies, and profit objectives. But despite Christie's confidence in the future, the company still faces formidable problems. One of them, unquestionably, is a recluse in silk pajamas who believes he can stay in touch with the real world without emerging from the pampered womb of the Playboy Mansion in Los Angeles.

Index

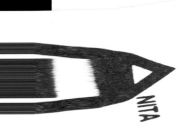

Index

355